OVERCOMING CHILD ABUSE: A WINDOW ON A WORLD PROBLEM

Issues in Law and Society
General Editor: Michael Freeman

Titles in the Series:

Children's Rights: A Comparative Perspective
Edited by Michael Freeman

Divorce: Where Next?
Edited by Michael Freeman

Exploring the Boundaries of Contract
Edited by Roger Halson

Law as Communication
Edited by David Nelken

Iraqgate: The Constitutional Implications of the Matrix-Churchill Affair
Edited by Rodney Austin

Positivism Today
Edited by Stephen Guest

Governing Childhood
Edited by Anne McGillivray

Legislation and the Courts
Edited by Michael Freeman

Overcoming Child Abuse: A Window on a World Problem
Edited by Michael Freeman

Law and Religion
Edited by Rex Ahdar

Law, Culture, Tradition and Children's Rights in Eastern and Southern Africa
Edited by Welshman Ncube

Locality and Identity: Environmental Issues in Law and Society
Edited by Jane Holder and Donald McGillivray

Science in Court
Edited by Michael Freeman and Helen Reece

Overcoming Child Abuse: A Window on a World Problem

Edited by
MICHAEL FREEMAN
University College London

LONDON AND NEW YORK

First published 2000 by Dartmouth and Ashgate Publishing

Reissued 2018 by Routledge
2 Park Square, Milton Park, Abingdon, Oxon OX14 4RN
711 Third Avenue, New York, NY 10017, USA

Routledge is an imprint of the Taylor & Francis Group, an informa business

Copyright © Michale freeman 2000

All rights reserved. No part of this book may be reprinted or reproduced or utilised in any form or by any electronic, mechanical, or other means, now known or hereafter invented, including photocopying and recording, or in any information storage or retrieval system, without permission in writing from the publishers.

Notice:
Product or corporate names may be trademarks or registered trademarks, and are used only for identification and explanation without intent to infringe.

Publisher's Note
The publisher has gone to great lengths to ensure the quality of this reprint but points out that some imperfections in the original copies may be apparent.

Disclaimer
The publisher has made every effort to trace copyright holders and welcomes correspondence from those they have been unable to contact.

A Library of Congress record exists under LC control number: 99030102

Typeset by Manton Typesetters, Louth, Lincolnshire, UK.

ISBN 13: 978-1-138-32378-0 (hbk)
ISBN 13: 978-1-138-32381-0 (pbk)
ISBN 13: 978-0-429-45121-8 (ebk)

Contents

Notes on Contributors		vii
1	Child Abuse: The Search for a Solution *Michael Freeman*	1
2	Child Protection Law in Australia *Patrick Parkinson*	15
3	Child Abuse: The Bulgarian Case *Velina Todorova*	39
4	Maltreatment of Children in Chile *Ines Pardo de Carvallo*	63
5	Abused and Neglected Children in the Republic of Croatia *Dijana Jakovac-Lozic*	77
6	The Definition of, and Legal and Management Responses to, the Problem of Child Abuse in England and Wales *Christina Lyon*	95
7	Dealing with the Problems of Sexual Abuse of Children in Finland *Sirpa Taskinen*	155
8	Child Abuse and the Law in the Federal Republic of Germany: Current Situation and Prospects *Stefan Heilmann and Ludwig Salgo*	167
9	Child Abuse in Hungary *Klára Kerezsi*	189

vi   *Overcoming Child Abuse: A Window on a World Problem*

10 Taking Stock of a Revolution: Child Abuse and the Law in
    Israel, 1989–97   205
    Tamar Morag

11 Child Abuse in Japan: The Current Situation and Proposed Legal
    Changes   231
    Yukiko Matsushima

12 Child Abuse and Neglect: A Malaysian Perspective   257
    Zaleha Kamaruddin

13 Protecting, Reporting and Supporting: Child Abuse and the
    Assessment of Risks in the Netherlands   281
    H.E.M. Baartman and L. de Mey

14 Child Abuse in New Zealand   305
    Bill Atkin

15 Child Abuse: The Nigerian Perspective   329
    Eunice Uzodike

16 'Let Him Take His Wife': Marriage, Protection and Exploitation
    of Girls in Zimbabwe   353
    Alice Armstrong

Index   371

Notes on Contributors

Alice Armstrong is a Freelance Consultant on Gender and Children's Issues in Harare. She was formerly a lecturer in law at the University of Zimbabwe. She has also acted as co-ordinator for Children and Law in Eastern and Southern Africa.

Bill Atkin is Reader in Law, Victoria University of Wellington.

H.E.M. Baartman is Professor of Psychology at the Free University of Amsterdam.

Ines Pardo de Carvallo is Professor of Family Law and Private Law at Universidad Católica of Valparaiso and a Consultant to the Senate Commission on Family law.

Langha de Mey is in the Department of Psychology at the Free University of Amsterdam.

Michael Freeman is a Professor of English Law, University College London, the Editor of the International Journal of Children's Rights and General Editor of this series. He is also Vice President of the International Society of Family Law.

Stefan Heilmann is Assistant at the Constitutional Court of the Federal Republic of Germany. He has taught at the Johann Wolfgang Goethe University in Frankfurt am Main.

Dijana Jakovac-Lozic is a Professor of Law at the University of Split.

Zaleha Kamaruddin is Deputy Dean Student Affairs and Development and Associate Professor at the International Islamic University, Kuala Lumpur.

Klára Kerezsi is Senior Researcher, National Institute of Criminology, Budapest.

Christina Lyon is Professor of Law, University of Liverpool. She is a solicitor, sits as an Assistant Recorder and is Joint Editor of the Journal of Social Welfare and Family Law.

Yukiko Matsushima is Professor of Law at Dokkyo University, Tokyo, an attorney and mediator of the Tokyo Family Court, an executive member of the Ass – Japan Family Law Association, and Vice-President of the International Society of Family Law.

Tamar Morag is Legal Director, National Council for the Child, Jerusalem. She also teaches law at the Hebrew University, Jerusalem.

Patrick Parkinson is Associate Professor of Law, University of Sydney.

Ludwig Salgo is Professor of Law at Johann Wolfgang Goethe University of Frankfurt am Main.

Sirpa Taskinen is a researcher at the National Research and Development Centre for Health and Welfare in Helsinki.

Velina Todorova is at the Institute for Legal Studies in Sofia and is a leading member of a group involved with the reform of child law in Bulgaria.

Eunice Uzodike is Associate Professor of Law, University of Lagos.

1 Child Abuse: The Search for a Solution

Michael Freeman

Child abuse is endemic. It comes in many forms and its categories are not closed. There is physical abuse, the first to be 'discovered'; emotional abuse,[1] still underestimated; and sexual abuse, the 'new' cancer eating into the family. Neglect too may be considered a form of abuse, though it is curiously neglected in the literature. New examples constantly emerge, such as Munchausen's syndrome by proxy.[2] Behaviour, not previously considered, is labelled as child abuse: domestic violence,[3] parental smoking,[4] the consumption of drugs while pregnant.[5] Greater concerns are now being voiced about the abuse of children with physical or learning disabilities.

Different countries have different views as to what is abuse: ten countries now consider hitting a child, even mildly, and for educational purposes, a form of abuse.[6] There are cultural differences, too: female circumcision,[7] culturally approved in much of Africa and the Islamic world (though not mandated by the Koran), is regarded as genital mutilation in others and is designated a criminal offence in several countries.[8] Abandonment, a clear instance of abuse, is rare in most countries today, but is common, for example, in the countries formerly within the communist bloc of Eastern Europe.[9]

Child abuse is found within the family and within institutions, often in those established to protect and nurture children at risk. Parents commit it: it is perpetrated also by step-parents, live-in boyfriends, older siblings, relatives, care workers and teachers. There is organized abuse, too, though it is now thought not to be the case that it is sometimes associated with Satanic ritualism (the moral panic associated with Satanic abuse has now all but died).[10]

Child abuse is rarely out of the news, and when a particularly gross scandal occurs, a Maria Colwell, a Cleveland, the Dutroux affair in Belgium, it dominates headlines across the globe. Breasts are beaten and souls are searched. But we are no nearer finding a solution than we were when we were first sensitized to the problem and it first hit the public agenda.

Although there were earlier historical instances,[11] this happened less than 40 years ago. It was at a symposium organized by Dr Henry Kempe at the American Academy of Pediatrics in 1961 that the phenomenon of the abused child first attracted major attention. A year later Kempe (and colleagues) published his now classic article on the clinical, radiological and psychiatric manifestations of serious injuries to children inflicted by parents and other caretakers. He coined the phrase 'battered baby syndrome' to refer to the phenomenon: this term remained in common usage for a decade. It is interesting to recall that Kempe explained abuse largely in psychopathological terms. Having hypothesized that 'psychiatric factors are probably of prime importance in the pathogenesis of the disorder', he noted that parents were often of 'low intelligence ... Alcoholism, sexual promiscuity, unstable marriages and minor criminal activities are reportedly common amongst them. They are immature, impulsive, self-centred, hypersensitive and quick to react, with poorly controlled aggression'.[12] In Britain, the first paper on the subject was published in 1963,[13] and three years later the British Paediatric Association published a memorandum. This drew attention also to neglect.[14]

In the 1960s, interest in the problem of child abuse spread also to the social work profession. Young's *Wednesday's Children*[15] was a particularly influential book. She noted that abuse crossed socioeconomic lines (it had been assumed to exist only within a working class sub-culture) and she also drew attention to the problem of the 'other' parent who behaved, she suggested, 'as if [a] prisoner of the other marriage partner, hopelessly condemned to a life sentence'.[16] She also noted an interrelationship between child and spouse abuse. Now we have come to see domestic violence as a form of child abuse as well: then (in 1964) violence against women had yet to have the whistle blown on it (Erin Pizzey's *Scream Quietly or the Neighbours Will Hear*[17] was not published for another decade).

By the end of the 1960s, child abuse had emerged as a social problem in other parts of the world too, and case histories were flooding the periodical literature. Gil, in the USA, had attempted to discover the true incidence rates.[18] Helfer and Kempe had published their first collection of essays.[19] All the states of the USA had passed, often as panic measures in reaction to Kempe's revelations, reporting laws,[20] and questions were being raised about whether Britain needed a reporting law too.[21] In the Netherlands, the response was to construct a system of confidential doctors (or medical referees):[22] this model was subsequently followed elsewhere.[23] In Britain, the first NSPCC study was published[24] (in 1969) and, within a year, the government had issued its first memorandum designed to increase awareness of, what was then still called, 'battering', amongst the social work and medical professions.[25] In 1970, also, Hugh Bevan gave his inaugural lecture at the University of Hull – surely the first time a law professor used such a prestigious occasion to discuss child protection.[26]

It was at this time, too, that attempts to understand child abuse emerged. Essentially, there were two explanatory models: the psychopathological 'Anyone who would abuse or kill his child is sick',[27] and the socio-environmental, in which a major cause of child abuse was situated within stress and frustration resulting from 'multifaceted deprivations of poverty and its correlates'.[28] Remarkably, neither of the two dominant understandings made any attempt to explain the phenomenon in terms of the status of the child in culture. Yet, as I have argued for some 20 years,[29] it becomes so much easier to understand the wrongs perpetrated against children in terms of a denial of their personality and integrity and in terms of the power which others exercise over them. Children's rights – or their absence – are very much a key to the understanding of abuse and neglect. Children without rights are by that very fact vulnerable.[30]

An example of this is the practice of corporal chastisement.[31] The link between abuse and physical punishment was not forged in the early literature on abuse, but few now writing on abuse do not acknowledge a connection. Sweden (in 1979) became the first country to make it unlawful for parents to hit children.[32] They realized the connection, and they also acknowledged that parents needed education rather than stigmatization through criminal sanctions. Other countries have followed Sweden's lead, and not just its Nordic neighbours.[33] In Italy, the Supreme Court ruled in 1996 that the use of violence by parents for (allegedly) educational purposes was no longer lawful. It found the principle for this within its own constitution, and within international law.[34] In Belgium, part of the response to its child sex murders scandal is the introduction of legislation (in 1998) guaranteeing children the right to 'respect for [their] person ... and individuality, and stressing that they shall not be subjected to degrading treatment, nor to any other form of physical or psychological violence'.[35] In 1998, too, the European Court on Human Rights ruled that the law in the United Kingdom had failed adequately to protect a child from inhuman or degrading punishment because its laws allowed reasonable corporal chastisement.[36] The United Kingdom will respond by outlawing inhuman or degrading punishment of children by their parents, but the so-called 'safe smack' will survive, despite the well-founded assumption that child abuse is not infrequently corporal punishment which has gone badly wrong. And today's abuse is all too frequently yesterday's punishment.

As this collection illustrates, child abuse has been variously defined, and there is no universally accepted definition.[37] There is found in the literature both narrow definitions (which emphasize serious physical or sexual abuse), broader ones which focus on maltreatment more generally, and broader ones yet (such as David Gil's) which include any interference with the optimal development of children.[38] Arguments surrounding definitions of child abuse reflect ideological differences, and may prove intractable. Much depends on who is doing the defining, and for what purpose(s).[39] A definition for a reporting law, or for management guidance, has very different functions from one developed for operational research. The definition selected may have important implications for civil liberties, since it may be used for deciding where and with whom children should live, how rights and resources are to be distributed, or is who is to be entitled to particular services.

Approaches to and discourses about child abuse differ and may change over time within a particular country. In England, the strategy of tackling abuse has changed only recently in line with a shift in ideology from child protection to family support.[40] The dominant approach until the mid-1990s, which emphasized child protection, was thought to focus attention on securing the safety of a small number of children at risk of 'serious' abuse, while at the same time drawing into the bureaucratic net many more cases for which it was not appropriate.

In 1995, the Department of Health published *Child Protection: Messages from Research* and, noting the foregoing, commented:

> Protection issues are best viewed in the context of children's wider needs. It is important to ensure that inappropriate cases do not get caught up in the child protection process, for this could have several undesirable consequences. Of particular concern is the unnecessary distress caused to family members who may then be unwilling to co-operate with subsequent plans. Professionals ... may have to rebuild a sense of trust with family members to enable them to participate. Ultimately, it will be necessary to decide when and how to permit a case to leave the child protection arena.[41]

The premise is that serious abuse is rare, and perhaps this is so as far as physical abuse is concerned. But this not only begs the question as to what is 'serious' and what constitutes 'abuse', it ignores the fact that child sexual abuse is all too common. Perhaps 20 per cent of girls are sexually abused (there are suggestions that it may be as many as one in three) and, though fewer boys are abused in this way, it is by no means uncommon.[42]

By adopting the family support model, the English approach to child abuse moves closer to the dominant strategy found in other parts of Europe (though there is no hint, in *Messages from Research* for example, that this assimilation is deliberate). The Dutch may have been the first to see intervention in terms of support as well as protection.[43] The confidential doctor system grew up in the 1970s and has since spread to Belgium. Hetherington *et al.*, describing the Belgian system, say that confidential doctor centres 'accept and follow up referrals from other agencies and from individuals, while preserving their anonymity, but will only intervene with the agreement of the parents and children. It is not impossible for referral to be made to the legal system but it is very unusual'.[44] Germany (when the Federal Republic) was influenced by Dutch developments too. Their child protection centres are there to help the affected family and work with it to solve its problems. The affected family is free to decide whether it accepts offers of assistance.[45] As with the Dutch system, there is strict confidentiality: 'the intervention of a third party only takes place with the agreement of the family and as a rule with the family itself present'.[46] Austria, too, has come under this influence. So, as Planicka describes it, 'child protection centres operate without the threat of punishment'.[47]

The family support model is found also in the Nordic world.[48] Harder and Pringle emphasize that, in Finland and Denmark, 'there is relatively little tendency to separate child abuse as a wholly distinct and different phenomenon from the wider context of childcare generally'. And they note, correctly I believe, that 'this approach contrasts with the highly differentiated one in England and Wales where child abuse has almost been reified into a separate entity with virtually no connection to wider concerns about promoting positive childcare'.[49] The structure in France is different, but the philosophy is not far removed from this one.[50] On the other side of the world, New Zealand's family group conference,[51] increasingly influential in other countries,[52] including England, espouses a similar family-oriented model, making it pivotal to decision making.

A number of commentators have made it clear that they believe the switch from child protection to family support is right.[53] But it will be noted that an emphasis on family support conflates the interests of the parents (and they may not be identical) with that of the child (whose interests may well conflict with those of her parents or, at least, one of them). There is a danger that a system of family support can serve to reaffirm and perpetuate power differentials within the family, those of age and, in the context of sexual abuse especially, those of gender. There is a danger also that the child's voice will be suppressed. Article 12 of the United Nations Convention on the Rights of the Child emphasizes the importance of a child's participation in the decision-making process,[54] a value re-emphasized in the European Convention on the Exercise of Children's Rights.[55] But what space does the family support system afford the child victim? Not surprisingly, the system is being questioned. There is concern now in France that the child's perspective is often unheard by the *juge des enfants*.[56] In the Netherlands, Van Montfoort has commented that the welfare approach risks 'overlooking power relationships within the family'.[57]

Strategies and solutions presuppose an understanding of the problem. The psychopathological model endows – as it was probably intended to[58] – the medical profession with the answer. The socioenvironmental stress model requires us to find ways of reducing the stress which follows, inter alia, from poverty.[59] The cultural model looks forward to, in effect, a cultural revolution.[60] The different approaches adopted in different countries at different times reflect different interpretations of abuse, its aetiology and its implications. If abuse is interpreted as a system of family dysfunction, then solutions will be looked to which work to rehabilitate the family as a functioning unit.[61] Thus, Cooper et al., writing of child protection work in France, can describe it as 'first and foremost a family affair'. They add: 'It is not the individual child who is the primary focus of concern and intervention but the child-as-part-of-the-family and the whole thrust of the French system is towards maintaining children as part of their families of origin'.[62] Of Finland, Tuomisto and Vuori-Karvia write that 'Traditional, individual-oriented forms of care have been criticised for being expert-dominated, time-consuming and apparently ineffective. These traditional forms of care have been widely replaced by approaches based on systems theory.'[63]

But does a family systems explanation satisfactorily account for child abuse? Even conceding that there is no one explanation and that the causes of child abuse are multilayered, the family systems model woefully underplays the agency and responsibility of the abuser, disempowers the non-abusing parent and, in the case of sexual abuse, glosses over the power issues related to masculinity which are now generally agreed to be so central to our understanding of this.[64] Since sexual abuse dominates thinking about abuse today, I will examine the recent shift in English thinking and the policies this engenders in the context of sexual abuse.

As with other abuse, the tendency has been to locate the causes within sick individuals[65] (and now dysfunctioning families)[66] or within socioenvironmental factors[67] (it was once thought that incest behaviour was inversely related to socioeconomic status).[68] One factor in child sexual abuse does, however, stand out and separate such abuse from other forms of it. Most perpetrators of child sexual abuse are men, and most victims are female.[69] Abuse is 'an expression of a patriarchal sexual culture';[70] its source is located in masculine sexuality. Until recently, discussion of sexual abuse rarely made the gender of the perpetrator explicit. For example, discussion about the Cleveland affair was invariably about 'parents'.[71] A major study of the prevalence of sexual abuse in Great Britain distinguished 'intra-familial', 'extra-familial' and 'stranger' abuse, but singularly failed to mention the gender of the abuser.[72] It is common to find mother blaming in the orthodox literature on child sexual abuse.[73] Nelson notes that 'professionals cling to the collusive wife theory like drowning men grasping at flotsam'. 'Could it be,' she asks, 'because it is such a powerful defence against admitting the male abuse of power?'[74] Of course, without this assumption of the role of the wife/mother, the family therapist begins to look like the emperor without clothes.

Feminism offers a different and more penetrating insight into child sexual abuse because it makes us ask questions about culture and about power (which are equally relevant to an understanding of other forms of abuse).[75] Feminism not only offers a different interpretation of child sexual abuse, but also challenges the responses of orthodoxy (which new English 'official' thinking and practices now encode). Family systems theory asks what is wrong with the functioning of the family, and how its fragmented pieces can be successfully reconstructed. But it refuses to indict, to blame: instead, it prefers to share responsibility. But, as one feminist critic puts it: 'The father rapes, abuses, brutalizes and assaults the children and the mother, but somehow it is the mother's or child's fault.'[76] Men have been taught that they have the right to have their sexual urges satisfied: belief that there was open access to wives led to the marital rape immunity surviving in England until 1991.[77] The extension to that other chattel – the daughter – seems quite logical.

An understanding of abuse requires an understanding of power. We have come to accept that rape is not so much a crime of sex, but a power trip.[78] In part at least, sexual abuse has to be similarly understood. Herman[79] documents the way in which fathers of incest victims appear to those victims, when they are interviewed as adults, to have been dominating and authoritarian. These men, she found (as others have done) exercise rigid and authoritarian control over wives and daughters, if necessary, using force to impose their domination. And Jackson notes that 'child molesters and child rapists are almost invariably men who have learnt to express their sexuality through aggression, to seek power over others and to be attracted to the vulnerable'.[80] Sex, dominance and abuse do not have to be linked: there is no biological inevitability.[81] But in our culture they are, and they produce the conditions in which sexual abuse of children is perpetrated and in which excuses are offered.

If the family support model presupposes a family systems theory, there is legitimate concern that its endorsement will lead more to the protection of adults than to securing the safety or promoting the welfare of children. One of the ironies of the English move towards tackling the problem in the way adopted in so many continental countries is that understanding of the causes of abuse seems more advanced in the English-speaking world. Certainly, also, we in England were aware of the problem and of its prevalence before our continental counterparts. This is in part why the Dutroux case in Belgium, the Roum affair in Denmark and the scandals in Ireland,[82] all recent, provoked such concern and media attention in those countries. Harder and Pringle have pointed to the 'real tragedy of the situation in England and Wales' that 'the enormity of the problem has been more fully realised there than elsewhere in Western Europe but the system designed to deal with it is wholly inadequate'.[83] That abuse, particularly sexual abuse and not just the sexual abuse of children but sexual violence against women generally, is better known about in Britain is in large part because the problem has been politicized by feminists[84] and others (anti-racists, for example)[85] who have challenged the very cosy arrangements which (unintentionally) family systems theorists and practitioners endorse.

The attempt to embrace a more continental approach may be wrong for another reason too. It presupposes that solutions can be isolated from ideologies and from structures. But we have a different context, a different view of society and the individual (perhaps more individualistic), a different vision of the role of the state and of community.[86] Hetherington *et al.* address this: 'When services for children are enshrined by the principles of social solidarity, subsidiarity and citizenship, one consequence is that the institutions which organise, deliver, and shape local responses to child protection are structured into, and derive their authority from, a total conception of society.'[87] These principles, they argue, are absent from a Britain where 18 years of Conservatism 'witnessed a consolidation of ideologies of individual rights ... and a general decline in ideas of collective responsibility'.[88] And, as they agree, the roots of this are deeper, grounded as they are in a set of assumptions about the relationship of the individual to society and government.

The child protection model did not work, but that is only part of the reason why England recently rejected it. The family systems model does not work either. There is evidence of that from countries where, given their assumptions about society, it was more likely to work. Given the enormity of the problem, it cannot be expected to work in Britain any more than elsewhere. And it is not just a question of resources. Both models rely, I would suggest over-rely, on professionals to solve the problem. I would not wish to underplay the pivotal role of professional expertise: the emergence of the family group conference is alarming because it vests the family (and potentially the abuser) with too much decision-making power.[89] We must find a role for the family. It must be a role in prevention, not one assigned to decision making. We must find ways of empowering non-abusing family members. But a role in prevention must be found for non-family members too. James Bulger would not have died had one of the 38 (or more) adults who witnessed his fateful walk intervened.[90] The community has a role to play in preventing child abuse. What Gerrilyn Smith has called 'a protected environment'[91] needs investigation. She argues that 'Our prevention programmes should be aimed first at the adults who surround children in their day-to-day lives: parents, extended family members, childminders, nursery workers, and teachers among others.'[92] The Bulger case, she observes, shows that 'we, as a community of adults, are reluctant to take responsibility for protecting other people's children. Hence protectiveness has become increasingly professionalised and more removed from the natural networks that surround children where it would be most effective'.[93] Of course, whether such networks are effective depends on a number of variables. It depends on children 'telling' – but it is more likely they will tell persons known to them than statutory agencies[94] – and it depends on how such persons perceive abuse: they are more likely to respond to sexual abuse, which generally appals, than to physical abuse, which is commonly interpreted as punishment and therefore acceptable. And it depends on education: of adults, and also of children.

This book looks at responses to aspects of abuse in all five continents. The definitions are different, though not all that different, the legal emphases vary and so do management techniques. The essays reveal the importance of culture and structure, as also of commitment to eradicate the problem. We can, I believe, learn to think critically about our own system by studying those of others.[95] Kempe and Kempe, 20 years ago, wrote that 'before [child abuse] could be acknowledged as a social ill, changes had to occur in the sensibilities and outlook in [in their case, American] culture'.[96] If we are to solve the problem, many changes in sensibilities and outlook are needed. We must ask why children's bodies are still exploited, sexually molested and subjected to physical and psychological violence, and we will find that answer in the way childhood has come to be constructed. The key to unlocking child abuse lies in the way societies have regarded children. If we are to conquer the abuse of children, we must learn to take children's rights seriously, we must acknowledge their entitlement to 'equal concern and equal respect',[97] we must accept that children are not property or pretty playthings or (literally) whipping boys, but individuals whose physical, sexual and psychological integrity is as important as – indeed, more important than – that of the adult population.

NOTES

1 J. Garbarino and G. Gilliam, *Understanding Abusive Families* (Cambridge, Mass.: Lexington Books, 1980). And see C. Doyle, 'Current Issues In Child Protection: An Overview of the Debates in Contemporary Journals', *British Journal of Social Work*, **26**: 565–76, 1996. Doyle's unpublished PhD thesis, referred to in her article, found 29 per cent of respondents reporting emotional abuse (more than twice those who claimed they had been physically abused and more than three times the figure for sexual abuse).

2. R. Meadow, 'Munchausen Syndrome By Proxy', *Archives of Disease in Childhood*, **57**: 92, 1982; J.A. Libow, 'Munchausen by Proxy Victims In Childhood', *Child Abuse and Neglect*, **19**: 1131–42, 1995.
3. See A. Mullender and R. Morley, *Children Living With Domestic Violence* (London: Whiting and Birch, 1994). See also H. Astor, *Position Paper on Mediation* (Sydney: National Committee on Violence against Women, 1991).
4. See D. Ezra, 'Sticks and Stones Can Break My Bones, but Tobacco Smoke Can Kill Me', *Saint Louis University Public Law Review*, **13**: 347, 1993.
5. D. Johnsen, 'The Creation of Fetal Rights: Conflicts with Women's Constitutional Rights to Liberty, Privacy and Equal Protection', *Yale Law Review*, **95**: 599, 1986.
6. M. Freeman, 'Children Are Unbeatable', *Children and Society*, **13**: 130, 1999.
7. E. Dorkenoo, *Cutting the Rose: Female Genital Mutilation, The Practice and its Prevention* (London: Minority Rights Group, 1995).
8. In the United Kingdom, see Prohibition of Female Circumcision Act 1985. For evidence that it has not worked, see J.A. Black and G.D. Debelle, 'Female Genital Mutilation in Britain', *British Medical Journal*, 310, 17 June 1995, 1590–92. In the United States, see Female Genital Mutilation Act 1996, discussed by Erika Sussman, 'Contending with Culture: An Analysis of the Female Genital Mutilation Act of 1996', *Cornell International Law Journal*, **31**: 194–250, 1998.
9. It was reported widely in November 1998 that there are as many as 1.5 million abandoned children in those countries.
10. Organized abuse is defined by the Department of Health as 'a generic term which covers abuse which may involve a number of abusers, a number of abused children and young people and often encompasses different forms of abuse. It involves to a greater or lesser extent, an element of organisation' (Dept of Health, *Working Together*, London: HMSO, 1991). See, further, B. Featherstone and E. Harlow, 'Organised Abuse: Themes and Issues', in B. Fawcett *et al.* (eds), *Gender Relations and Violence Theories and Interventions* (London: Sage, 1996).
11. See G. Behlmer, *Child Abuse and Moral Reform in England 1870–1908* (Stanford: Stanford University Press, 1982).
12. C. Kempe *et al.*, 'The Battered Child Syndrome', *Journal of the American Medical Association*, **181**: 17–24 at p.18, 1962. On concerns of the use of this model even today, see G. Jack, 'Discourses of Child Protection and Child Welfare', *British Journal of Social Work*, **27**: 659–78, 1997.
13. See D.L. Griffiths and F.J. Moynihan, *British Medical Journal*, No. 5372, 1558, 1963.
14. British Paediatric Association, 'The Battered Baby', *British Medical Journal*, 5 March 1966, 601.
15. L. Young, *Wednesday's Children* (New York: McGraw-Hill, 1964).
16. Ibid., pp.49–50.
17. Harmondsworth: Penguin, 1974.
18. D. Gil, 'Incidence of Child Abuse and Demographic Characteristics', in R. Helfer and C.H. Kempe (eds), *The Battered Child* (Chicago: University of Chicago Press, 1968).
19. R. Helfer and C.H. Kempe (eds), *The Battered Child* (Chicago: University of Chicago Press, 1968).
20. See M. Paulsen, G. Parker and L. Adelman, 'Child Abuse Reporting Laws: Some Legislative History', *George Washington Law Review*, **34**: 482, 1966.
21. See S. Maidment, 'Some Legal Problems Arising Out of the Reporting of Child Abuse', *Current Legal Problems*, **31**: 149–75, 1978.
22. See M.D.A. Freeman, 'The Dutch Confidential Doctor System', *Family Law*, **7**: 53, 1977; see also the contribution of Baartman and de Mey in the present volume.

23 For example, in Belgium: see C. Marneffe, E. Boemans and A. Lampoo, in M. Davies and A. Sale (eds), *Child Protection Policies and Practice in Europe* (London: NSPCC, 1990).
24 A. Skinner and R. Castle, *78 Battered Children: A Retrospective Study* (London: NSPCC, 1969).
25 DHSS, *The Battered Baby* (London: DHSS, 1970).
26 H.K. Bevan, *Child Protection and the Law* (Hull: University of Hull Press, 1970).
27 As summarized in a critique by Richard Gelles, 'Child Abuse as Psychopathology: A Sociological Critique and Reformulation', *American Journal of Orthopsychiatry*, **43**: 611, 1973.
28 Per D. Gil, 'Unraveling Child Abuse', *American Journal of Orthopsychiatry*, **45**: 346 at 352, 1975.
29 M.D.A. Freeman, *Violence in the Home: A Socio-Legal Study* (Aldershot: Saxon House, 1979), pp.31–2, 117–20; and M.D.A. Freeman, *The Rights and Wrongs of Children* (London: Frances Pinter, 1983) ch. 4.
30 See Michael Freeman, *The Moral Status of Children* (The Hague: Martinus Nijhoff, 1997).
31 See Peter Newell, *Children Are People Too* (London: Bedford Square Press, 1989). A number of studies on the relationship between punishment and physical abuse has been published, including C. O'Brian and L.S.W. Lau, 'Defining Child Abuse in Hong Kong', *Child Abuse Review*, **4**: 38–46, 1995; V. Corral-Verdugo *et al.*, 'Validity of a Scale Measuring Beliefs Regarding The "Positive" Effects of Punishing Children: A Study of Mexican Mothers', *Child Abuse and Neglect*, **19**: 669–707, 1995; N.A. Vargas *et al.*, 'Parental Attitude and Practice Regarding Physical Punishment of School Children in Santiago de Chile', *Child Abuse and Neglect*, **19**: 1077–82, 1995; U.A. Segal, 'Child Abuse by the Middle Class? A Study of Professionals In India', *Child Abuse and Neglect*, **19**: 217–32, 1995; and F.B. Berrien *et al.*, 'Child Abuse Prevalence in the Russian Urban Population: A Preliminary Report', *Child Abuse and Neglect*, **19**: 261–4, 1995.
32 For the context, see J. Durrant and G. Olsen, 'Parenting and Public Policy: Contextualising The Swedish Corporal Punishment Ban', *Journal of Social Welfare and Family Law*, **19**: 443–61, 1997.
33 It has been made unlawful in Austria, Cyprus, Croatia and Latvia as well.
34 See the *Cambria* case, reported at *Foro It*, II, 1996, 407.
35 See Belgian Senate 1997–1998 Session: Proposal For a Law Inserting an Article 371 bis into the *Code Civil*, tabled by Mme de Béthune.
36 *A v. United Kingdom*, 23 September 1998.
37 And see Jill E. Korbin, *Child Abuse and Neglect: Cross-Cultural Perspectives* (Berkeley: University of California Press, 1981). But see D. Finkelhor and J. Korbin, 'Child Abuse as an International Issue', *Child Abuse and Neglect*, **12**: 3–23, 1988. See also Michael King, *A Better World For Children* (London: Routledge, 1997) ch. 2.
38 See *The Rights and Wrongs of Children*, op. cit., note 29, 108–14.
39 It may also depend upon discourses about the child, about children's rights and about child protection.
40 See N. Parton, 'Child Protection, Family Support and Social Work', *Child and Family Social Work*, **1** (1): 3–11, 1996.
41 Department of Health, *Child Protection: Messages from Research* (London: HMSO, 1995) p.32.
42 D. Finkelhor *et al.*, 'Sexual Abuse In a National Survey of Adult Men and Women', *Child Abuse and Neglect*, **14**: 19–28, 1990.

43 H. Armstrong and A. Hollows, 'Responses to Child Abuse in the EC', in M. Hill (ed.), *Social Work and the European Community* (London: Jessica Kingsley, 1991).
44 R. Hetherington et al., *Protecting Children: Messages from Europe* (Lyme Regis: Russell House Publishing, 1997) p.59.
45 See P. Hutz, 'West Germany', in M. Davies and A. Sale, op. cit., note 23.
46 See W. Wustendorfer, 'Violence Against Children in Germany', in C. Birks (ed.), *Child Abuse in Europe*, vol. 1 (Nuremberg: Emwe-Verlag, 1995).
47 See H. Planicka, 'Child Abuse in Austria' in op. cit., note 46, p.68.
48 See, in relation to Finland, R. Tuomisto and E. Vuori-Karvia, 'Child Protection in Finland' in M. Harder and K. Pringle (eds), *Protecting Children In Europe: towards a New Millennium* (Aalborg: Aalborg University Press, 1997). See also Taskinen, Chapter 7 of the present volume.
49 'Conclusion: Transnational Comparisons and Future Trajectories', in Harder and Pringle, op. cit., note 48, p.153.
50 See Michael King and Judith Trowell, *Children's Welfare and the Law: The Limits of Legal Intervention* (London: Sage, 1992).
51 On which see J. Hudson, A. Morris, G. Maxwell and B. Galaway, *Family Group Conferences* (Annandale, NSW: Federation Press, 1996) and Atkin, Chapter 14 of the present volume.
52 For example, South Australia: see Michael Freeman, 'Protecting Children on Both Sides of the Globe', *Adelaide Law Review*, **16**: 79–98, 1994. And for its influence in Australia, see P. Ban and P. Swain, 'Participation and Partnership – Family Group Conferencing in the Australian Context', *Journal of Social Welfare and Family Law*, **19**: 35–52, 1997. In England, see P. Marsh in op. cit., note 51.
53 For example, David Thorpe, *Evaluating Child Protection* (Buckingham: Open University Press, 1994).
54 See Michael Freeman, 'The Right To Be Heard', *Adoption and Fostering*, **22**: 50–59, 1999.
55 This is discussed by Margaret Killerby, 'The Draft European Convention on the Exercise of Children's Rights', *International Journal of Children's Rights*, **3**: 127–33, 1995.
56 See Armstrong and Hollows, op. cit., note 43.
57 A. Van Montfoort, 'The Protection of Children in the Netherlands: Between Justice and Welfare', in H. Ferguson, R. Gilligan and R. Torode (eds), *Surviving Childhood Adversity* (Dublin: Social Studies Press, 1993) p.62.
58 It is first developed within paediatric literature; and see S. Pfohl, 'The Discovery of Child Abuse', *Social Problems*, **24**: 310–23, 1977.
59 See N. Parton, *The Politics of Child Abuse* (Basingstoke: Macmillan, 1985) pp.175–6.
60 On which see Freeman, op. cit., note 30, ch. 17.
61 Examples are R. Porter, *Child Sexual Abuse Within the Family* (London: Tavistock, 1984) and P. Mrazek and A. Bentovim, 'Incest and Dysfunctional Family Systems', in P. Mrazek and C.H. Kempe, *Sexually Abused Families and Their Children* (Oxford: Pergamon Press, 1981). But valuable insights can be found in C-A. Hooper and C. Humphreys, 'Women Whose Children Have Been Sexually Abused: Reflections on a Debate', *British Journal of Social Work*, **28**: 565–80, 1998.
62 A. Cooper, R. Hetherington, K. Bristow, J. Pitts and A. Spriggs, *Positive Child Protection: A View From Abroad* (Lyme Regis: Russell House Publishing, 1995) p.6.
63 Harder and Pringle, op. cit., note 48, p.89.
64 See K. Pringle, 'Current Profeminist Debates Regarding Men and Social Welfare: Some National and Transnational Perspectives', *British Journal of Social Work*, **28**:

623–33, 1998. But cf. M. King, *A Better World for Children* (London: Routledge, 1997) pp.36–42. On sexual abuse by women, see J. Forbes, 'Female Sexual Abusers: The Contemporary Search for Equivalence', *Practice*, **6**: 102–11, 1992–3.
65 For example, S.K. Weinberg, *Incest Behavior* (New York: Citadel Press, 1955).
66 And see D. Finkelhor, *Child Sexual Abuse: New Theory and Research* (New York: Free Press, 1984).
67 But D.E.H. Russell, *The Secret Trauma* (New York: Basic Books, 1986) found no association between sexual abuse and measures of father's occupation or education.
68 See early work by J.C. Flugel, *The Psychoanalytic Study of the Family* (London: Wolff, 1926) and M.S. Guttmacher, *Sex Offenses* (New York: Norton, 1951).
69 But see P. Hodgson, 'Women Abusers: The Last Taboo?', *The Observer*, 8 April 1992, and O. Wolfers, 'Same Abuse, Different Parent', *Social Work Today*, 12 March 1992. And on non-believing mothers, see J. Roberts, 'Non-Believing Mothers of Sexually Abused Children', *Practice*, **6**: 268–70, 1992–3, and E.A. Sirles and P.J. Franke, 'Factors Influencing Mothers' Reactions to Intrafamily Sexual Abuse', *Child Abuse and Neglect*, **13**, 1989.
70 Per B. Campbell, *Unofficial Secrets* (London: Virago, 1988) p.62.
71 Typified by the Report itself (*Report of the Inquiry into Child Abuse in Cleveland 1987*, London: HMSO, 1988, Cmnd 412).
72 A. Baker and S. Duncan, 'Child Sexual Abuse: A Study of its Prevalence In Great Britain', *Child Abuse and Neglect*, **9**: 457–67, 1985.
73 For example, B. Justice and R. Justice, *The Broken Taboo – Sex in the Family* (London: Peter Owen, 1980).
74 S. Nelson, *Incest: Fact and Myth* (Edinburgh: Stathmullion, 1987) p.108.
75 See M. MacLeod and E. Saraga, 'Challenging The Orthodoxy: Towards A Feminist Theory', *Feminist Review*, **28**: 16–55, 1988.
76 E. Wattenberg, 'In a Different Light: A Feminist Perspective on the Role of Mothers in Father–Daughter Incest', *Child Welfare*, **64**: 203–11, 1985, at p.206.
77 See *R. v. R.* [1992] 1 AC 599.
78 See H. Schwendinger and J. Schwendinger, 'Rape Myths', *Crime and Social Justice*, **1**: 18, 1974.
79 J. Herman, *Father–Daughter Incest* (Cambridge, Mass.: Harvard University Press, 1981) ch. 5.
80 S. Jackson, *Childhood and Sexuality* (Oxford: Blackwell, 1982) p.173.
81 See S. Frosh, 'Issues for Men Working with Sexually Abused Children', *British Journal of Psychotherapy*, **3**: 332–9, 1987.
82 See H. Buckley, 'Child Protection in Ireland', in Harder and Pringle, op. cit., note 48.
83 Ibid., p.168.
84 For example, S. Nelson, *Incest: Fact and Myth* (Edinburgh: Strathmullion, 1987); R.E. Dobash and R.P. Dobash, *Women, Violence and Social Change* (London: Routledge, 1992); L. Dominelli, 'Betrayal of Trust: A Feminist Analysis of Power Relationships in Incest Abuse', *British Journal of Social Work*, **19**: 291–307, 1989.
85 For example, L. Dominelli, *Anti-Racist Social Work* (London: Macmillan, 1988).
86 See K. Pringle, 'Protecting Children in England and Wales', in Harder and Pringle, op. cit., note 48.
87 Hetherington *et al.*, op. cit., note 44, p.34.
88 Ibid., p.85.
89 More generally, see B. Corby, M. Millar and L. Young, 'Parental Participation In Child Protection Work: Rethinking The Rhetoric', *British Journal of Social Work*, **26**: 475–92, 1996.

90 See Blake Morrison's description in *As If* (London: Granta Books, 1997) ch. 4.
91 G. Smith, 'Reassessing Protectiveness', in D. Batty and D. Cullen (eds), *Child Protection: The Therapeutic Option* (London: British Agencies for Adoption and Fostering, 1996) p.77.
92 Ibid.
93 Ibid., p.79.
94 In a study by L. Kelly, L. Regan and S. Burton (*An Exploratory Study of the Prevalence of Sexual Abuse in a Sample of 16–21 Year Olds*, Polytechnic of North London Child Abuse Studies Unit, 1991), 50 per cent of the sample who had experienced sexual abuse had told someone, and of those, only 5 per cent told a statutory agency.
95 A good discussion of some of the problems of so doing is R. Hetherington, 'Issues in European Child Protection Research', *European Journal of Social Work*, 1: 71–82, 1998.
96 R. Kempe and C.H. Kempe, *Child Abuse* (London: Fontana, 1978) p.17.
97 See R. Dworkin, *Taking Rights Seriously* (London: Duckworth, 1977) pp.272–8.

2 Child Protection Law in Australia

Patrick Parkinson

THE GOVERNMENT'S RESPONSIBILITY FOR CHILD PROTECTION IN A FEDERAL SYSTEM

Child protection is a fundamental responsibility of government. There are many aspects of social life which could function well (and perhaps better) without government involvement. The extent to which the state should be involved in managing the economy, running industries, and even in providing a safety net for old age are issues on which political parties divide. Yet there is really no debate about the government's role in child protection. Where an act of child abuse constitutes a criminal offence, the state may be involved as prosecuting authority. When parental care places the safety and well-being of a child in serious jeopardy, the state has a power and duty to intervene in its civil jurisdiction. The state, and only the state, through the courts, has the power to remove children from the parents and to deprive the parents, temporarily or permanently, of parental responsibility. That fundamental responsibility of government is given support in international law by the United Nations Convention on the Rights of the Child which places responsibility on state parties to protect children from all forms of abuse and neglect.[1]

If the responsibility of government for the protection of children is not in doubt, there is nonetheless a question to be asked in Australia about which government should have responsibility. Australia has a federal structure. There are six states[2] and two territories[3] which have their own parliaments and law-making powers. There is also a federal government which has law-making authority within the confines of the Federal Constitution.[4]

Child protection is a responsibility of the states and territories. Each state and territory has its own government department with responsibility for child protection, and each has its own legislation. The private law concerning the parental responsibility of children following the breakdown of a relationship is a matter for the federal government under the Family Law Act 1975. Family law matters are dealt with in the federal family court, but child protection matters are determined in the children's courts or youth courts of the various states and territories. Adoption is generally a matter for the Supreme Court in each state and territory. The criminal law is also a matter for state courts. While there are some criminal laws in the federal sphere, most criminal offences against children are prosecuted under state law and in state courts. While there have been calls for the federal government to take a greater role in child protection work,[5] and theoretically the constitution might allow it to legislate in this area,[6] there are practical difficulties in the way of greater federal involvement. In particular, it is difficult to ensure a national approach to child protection when there are not only eight different laws but eight different government departments which have statutory responsibility for child protection, each with distinctive legal and administrative structures.

It is impossible to generalize about child protection law in Australia. Not only are there different definitions of child abuse between the states and territories, and different legal responses, but these differences reflect, to some extent, different understandings of child abuse as a matter of social policy, and different characterizations of the problem. The definitions and characterizations of the problem as a matter of law, therefore, say much about the way child abuse is perceived in Australia.

THE NATURE AND EXTENT OF CHILD ABUSE IN AUSTRALIA

The differences between the states and territories in terms of definitions of child abuse, and the different operating definitions used by welfare departments for the purposes of their own record keeping,[7] have made it very difficult to gain a national picture concerning the known incidence of child abuse in Australia. In recent years, the states and territories have been able to agree on common definitions for statistical purposes. Physical abuse is defined as any non-accidental physical injury inflicted upon a child. Emotional abuse is any act which results in a child suffering any kind of significant emotional deprivation or trauma. Sexual abuse is any act which exposes a child to, or involves a child in, sexual processes beyond his or her understanding or contrary to accepted community standards. Neglect involves any serious omissions or commissions which, within the bounds of cultural tradition, constitute a failure to provide conditions which are essential for the healthy physical and emotional development of a child.[8]

Using these definitions, there were 29 833 substantiated cases of child abuse in Australia in 1995–6, involving 25 558 children.[9] This represents

5.8 children per 1000 of the population of children aged 0–16 years. The breakdown of these substantiated cases of abuse and neglect by the most serious type of abuse found in each case was as follows:[10]

Physical abuse	28%
Emotional abuse	31%
Sexual abuse	16%
Neglect	25%

These overall national figures, however, disguise significant variations between states in the levels of different kinds of abuse as proportions of the total in each jurisdiction. In New South Wales (NSW), which accounts for nearly half of all the substantiated cases of child abuse and neglect in Australia,[11] 38 per cent of the cases in 1995-6 were assessed as emotional abuse. In contrast, in Western Australia the figure is 4 per cent and, in the Northern Territory, 7 per cent. Just as there are variations in the proportions of different kinds of abuse, so there are variations in the numbers of cases per 1000 children in the population. Thus, in 1995–6, NSW recorded 1.7 cases of sexual abuse per 1000 children and South Australia had 1.6 cases. In contrast, Queensland had just 0.3 cases per 1000 and Victoria 0.6.[12]

It is doubtful that there are such significant differences in incidence of child abuse between states and territories. Explanations for these variations are therefore more likely to be found in differences in policy and practice between states. Thus NSW and South Australia, which have a strong emphasis on mandatory reporting of sexual abuse,[13] may receive more notifications than in other jurisdictions which do not have such a strong emphasis on reporting. Other factors may also be at work. The extent to which definitional and practice factors enter into the construction of child abuse may be seen particularly in the variations in levels of emotional abuse between jurisdictions.

Emotional abuse: definitional issues and social work practice

Not only do the Australian jurisdictions vary enormously in the proportions of cases which are classified as emotional abuse, but the variations are significant in terms of the numbers per 1000 children. In NSW, the rate is 3.0 per 1000, and in Victoria, 2.2 per 1000, compared to a national average of 1.8. In Tasmania and Western Australia, the figures are 0.1 per 1000 and in the Northern Territory it is 0.3.[14] What is the explanation for such significant variations? The answer is likely to lie in three factors. First, there are variations in the legal definition of emotional abuse. In NSW, to abuse a child emotionally is to 'expose or subject the child to behaviour which psychologically harms the child'.[15] In the Northern Territory, the relevant definition, of emotional maltreatment in s.4 of the Community Welfare Act 1983, is as follows:

> Serious emotional or intellectual impairment evidenced by severe psychological or social malfunctioning measured by the commonly accepted standards of the community to which he belongs, because of the ... emotional or social environment in which he is living or where there is a substantial risk that such ... environment will cause such emotional or intellectual impairment.

If this test must be satisfied before a child can be classified as subject to emotional abuse then it is no wonder that few children in the Northern Territory are classified as emotionally abused. Only those cases in which serious emotional damage has already been caused or is likely fit within this definition and, by the time such a serious situation becomes evident, it may be too late to prevent lasting damage to the child. Thus the definition works against strategies of early intervention.

A second reason why there are such significant variations between the states in levels of emotional abuse is the use to which definitions of this kind are put. Research in NSW in the late 1980s demonstrated that the category of emotional abuse was being used as a generic category for all cases where the child was deemed to be 'at risk' in a non-coping family and there were no grounds for stating that the child had been either neglected or physically or sexually abused.[16] In a significant percentage of these cases, there was no information on the files which would indicate behaviours by the parent which could psychologically harm the child, nor were there reports of discernible harm to the child. Drug dependency, psychiatric illness and other such signs that the children may be at risk were all common reasons for listing a child as being 'emotionally abused'. Until February 1997, the Department of Community Services had no way of classifying, on its information system, those children about whom there were serious concerns, but who had not yet been abused. If a child could not be classified as abused, or a parent as abusive, there was much less likelihood that they would receive any services. It was only in 1997 that the Department significantly changed its practice, and it is anticipated that there will be a significant fall in cases where emotional abuse is recorded. By contrast to NSW, in Western Australia, a report of emotional abuse will not be substantiated unless there is evident harm to the child.[17]

A third reason for differences between the states concerns the way in which domestic violence is viewed. There is a growing awareness in Australia that domestic violence is a child protection issue. Children living in violent households may well suffer serious adverse effects as a result. Numerous research studies conducted in various parts of the world have demonstrated that children whose mothers have been victims of domestic violence display greater behavioural problems than children from non-violent homes, and show signs of anxiety and low self-esteem.[18] The worst effects are experienced by those children who have both been abused and have observed interparental violence, but the findings generally show significant harm to children who were exposed to violence without being directly victimized.[19] In NSW, the guidelines on domestic violence issued by the Department of Community Services state that 'children living in violent relationships are always at some risk physically, psychologically and emotionally' and that 'even if some children do not experience physical violence they may be harmed emotionally or neglected'.[20] If there is no evidence of physical violence, it is most likely therefore that the case will be classified as one of emotional abuse.

Aboriginal and Torres Strait Islander children

Throughout Australia, Aboriginal and Torres Strait Islander children are over-represented in child abuse and neglect statistics. The rate of substantiated child abuse and neglect was 18.0 per 1000 Aboriginal children in 1995–6, compared to 5.4 per 1000 non-Aboriginal children. Aboriginal children represented about 3 per cent of the population of children aged 0–17 in 1995, but about 10 per cent of all substantiated cases of child abuse and neglect.[21] The greatest difference lies in the statistics for substantiated neglect (see Table 2.1).

The over-representation of Aboriginal and Torres Strait Islander children in the child abuse and neglect statistics is especially a cause for concern because of the history of child welfare intervention in Aboriginal communities which resulted in the large-scale removal of children from Aboriginal families. For much of the twentieth century, there was a systematic policy in Australia of removing Aboriginal children from their families in order to promote their assimilation into white Australian society. In the early part of the century, this was achieved through special legislation governing the 'protection' of Aborigines. Each state, and the Northern Territory, had either an Aboriginal Protection Board or a Chief Protector of Aboriginal People, who had sweeping powers to control the lives of indigenous Australians. In some states, and the Northern Territory, for example, the Chief Protector was made the guardian of all Aboriginal children, displacing the rights of the parents.[22] These powers were used to remove many Aboriginal children from their families. The basis for this removal was not proven abuse or neglect, but colour. The assumption

Table 2.1 Substantiated child abuse and neglect: Aboriginal and non-Aboriginal children

	Aboriginal children	Non-Aboriginal children
Physical abuse	4.5	1.6
Emotional abuse	4.7	1.7
Sexual abuse	1.9	1.0
Neglect	6.9	1.1
Total	18.0	5.4

Note: Rates per 1000 children.

Source: A. Broadbent and R. Bentley, *Child Abuse and Neglect, Australia, 1995–96* (Canberra: Australian Institute of Health and Welfare, 1997) p.30.

was that lighter-skinned children ('half castes') would be more likely to be accepted into non-indigenous society. Removal, usually to large, dormitory-style children's homes away from their families, was intended as a means of acculturating these children to white Australian society.

From the 1940s onwards, the policy changed. Removals still took place, and in large numbers, but on the basis of general child welfare laws rather than specific legislation directed at Aboriginal people. The Human Rights and Equal Opportunities Commission report on these 'stolen children' comments about the use of these laws:[23]

> Under the general child welfare law, Indigenous children had to be found to be 'neglected', 'destitute' or 'uncontrollable'. These terms were applied by courts much more readily to Indigenous children than non-indigenous children as the definitions and interpretations of those terms assumed a non-indigenous model of child-rearing and regarded poverty as synonymous with neglect.

It was not until 1966 that all eligibility restrictions on indigenous people's entitlements to social security were lifted, and so the safety net funding which was available to non-indigenous Australians was not necessarily available to keep Aboriginal families together.[24] No-one knows how many Aboriginal children were removed from their families under these policies. Estimates vary between one in three and one in 10 between 1910 and 1970. Even if one in 10 is taken as the lowest estimate, it is certain that, in certain regions and at certain periods, the figures were very much higher. Few Aboriginal families have been left unaffected.[25]

With this history, it is not surprising that in aboriginal communities there is often a deep distrust of state welfare organizations and great concern about the numbers of indigenous children still being removed from their families on the basis of abuse and neglect. It is doubtful now that the serious over-representation of indigenous children in the welfare system can be attributed to racism or insensitivity to different cultural norms and child-rearing practices, although this may still be a problem.[26] More likely causes are chronic alcohol and substance abuse, domestic violence and the consequences which flow from poor health and nutrition within Aboriginal communities. Indigenous children are also much more likely than non-indigenous children to live in a one-parent household.[27] A key contributing factor in parenting problems in these communities is the lack of appropriate parenting role models for Aboriginal people who were removed from their families and brought up in children's homes.

Although there is almost certainly a significant over-representation of Aboriginal children in the welfare system, the raw statistics also require cautious analysis. They do not point only to the existence of a greater problem of child abuse and neglect in Aboriginal communities. They may also represent a greater involvement of child welfare services with the Aboriginal community than with the general population. The designation of a child as 'neglected' in governmental statistics may not necessarily mean that the child's most basic needs are not being met. It may also be a label used to legitimize government expenditure to support the child and family or to give financial assistance to relatives who take over the primary care of the child. It is, after all, only in comparatively few cases in Australia that substantiated child abuse and neglect cases lead to coercive intervention through the children's court.[28] In far more cases, the labels operate as an administrative categorization to trigger a welfare response and to justify the allocation of resources.

Some evidence for this comes from the substitute care figures in NSW. In 1995–6, 61.43 per 1000 Aboriginal children were included in a substitute care programme, a total of 1940 children. This compares with 6.15 per 1000 children from an English-speaking background and 4.18 per 1000 children from a non-English-speaking background. These statistics would at first sight indicate that Aboriginal children are about 10 times as likely to be taken into substitute care as non-Aboriginal children. However, the placement statistics provide a different picture. Only 38.7 per cent of these children (750) were placed by substitute care services. The remainder received support services: 39.6 per cent (768) were placed with their family while a further 21.8 per cent (422) received support in a placement outside the family (usually with relatives). In total, 83 per cent of Aboriginal children were placed with carers from the same cultural background, while 9 per cent were not. In the remainder of the cases, the children or young people were placed in youth refuges, hostels or family group homes with a range of workers from a variety of cultural backgrounds.[29]

The pattern of placement in NSW reflects a deliberate policy, which exists in all states and territories, to adopt distinctive approaches to the needs of Aboriginal children which are culturally sensitive. Two main strategies have been adopted. The first is the implementation of the Aboriginal placement principle, which provides that, as far as possible, an Aboriginal child who cannot live with his or her parents should be placed within the Aboriginal community. Some states and territories have adopted this in legislation. For example, NSW has given legislative effect to this principle in s.87 of the Children (Care and Protection) Act 1987. This provides that, when a court is making orders about an Aboriginal child, it must consider the following placement options, in descending order.

1 Placement in the care of a member of the child's extended family, as recognized by the Aboriginal community to which the child belongs.
2 Placement in the care of a member of the Aboriginal community to which the child belongs.
3 Placement in the care of some other Aboriginal family residing in the vicinity of the child's usual place of residence.
4 Placement in the care of a suitable person approved by the Director-General after consultation with members of the child's extended family and Aboriginal welfare organizations.

In the law of NSW, each placement option can only be rejected if it can be shown to be 'not practicable' or detrimental to the child. A weakness of this section is that the provisions of s.87 are activated only after a child has formally come into care by way of a court order. One law reform option being considered in NSW is that the Aboriginal placement principle should apply, in a modified form, to the placement of all Aboriginal children, whether or not they come into care by means of a court order.[30]

A second strategy, related to the Aboriginal placement principle, is to involve Aboriginal child welfare organizations officially in the process of placement and support of Aboriginal children in substitute care. This is given statutory effect in South Australia. Section 5 of the Children's Protection Act 1993 provides that:

> No decision or order may be made under this Act as to where or with whom an Aboriginal or Torres Strait Islander child will reside unless consultation has first been had with a recognised Aboriginal organisation, or a recognised Torres Strait Islander organisation, as the case may require.

Furthermore, one of the duties of the relevant minister in South Australia is to 'assist the Aboriginal community to establish its own programmes for preventing or reducing the incidence of abuse and neglect of children within the Aboriginal community'.[31]

Similar provisions exist in Victoria. A court cannot make a permanent care order for an Aboriginal child until it has received a report from an Aboriginal agency.[32] Furthermore, no placement of an Aboriginal child may be made with a non-Aboriginal carer without the approval of an Aboriginal agency.[33]

While these provisions go a long way towards ensuring the preservation of cultural ties for Aboriginal children who are unable to remain with their families, these arrangements have been criticized for not going far enough. The Human Rights and Equal Opportunities Commission report on the 'stolen children' comments:[34]

> 'Partnerships' between Indigenous children's agencies and government departments, where they exist, are unequal partnerships. Departments retain full executive decision-making power and the power to allocate resources affecting Indigenous children's welfare. Judicial decision making occurs within non-Indigenous courts. In no jurisdiction are Indigenous child care agencies permitted to be involved in the investigation of an allegation of neglect or abuse. The difference between being allowed to participate and having the right to make decisions is evident in Indigenous communities' experiences of child welfare systems.

The report recommends that indigenous communities should be given a greater degree of self-determination in relation to the well-being of indigenous children and young people. This may include the transfer of legal jurisdiction where an indigenous community or organization so desires it.

LEGAL RESPONSES AND THE CONSTRUCTION OF CHILD ABUSE

The way in which the law responds to child abuse depends in part on how the problem is perceived and constructed. In Australia, there are three different possible responses to child abuse within the traditional court system. The first is to respond to child abuse by invoking the criminal jurisdiction. The second is to bring proceedings under the child welfare jurisdiction which allows children to be taken into the care of the state. The third approach is to deal with the matter in the family law jurisdiction, treating it as an issue of private law. This is most likely to occur in those cases where the welfare of the child may be sufficiently protected through orders made in the family court concerning residence and contact following the breakdown of the parental relationship.

Not all these legal responses are available in all cases. In particular, child welfare law jurisdiction and family law jurisdiction only arise where either the perpetrator of abuse is a parent, or the parent has failed to protect that child from harm and may fail to protect the child in the future. Where child abuse occurs outside the home, and is not indicative of any parental failure, the only legal response is to prosecute the alleged offender for breaches of the criminal law.

Intrafamilial child abuse: criminal or civil jurisdiction?

Where there is a choice, the way in which that choice is exercised says much about the society's characterization of the problem. Typically, child sexual abuse has been perceived as a problem demanding a criminal law response. Since the early 1980s, when child sexual abuse first became a major public issue, there has been a strong emphasis on prosecuting child sex offences in all states and territories. In all these jurisdictions, changes have been made to the laws of evidence to make it easier for children's evidence to be admitted. As in other countries, closed-circuit television has also been introduced for child witnesses and some states have also allowed videotaped evidence from the child to be admitted.[35]

The punitive response to child sexual assault contrasts sharply with the response to physical abuse of children, which is not often prosecuted in Australia. For example, a study in Western Australia found that prosecution occurred in 28 per cent of cases where a report of sexual abuse was substantiated by the relevant welfare department, while in physical abuse cases, the figure was only 8 per cent.[36] This is in spite of the fact that physical assault is often easier to prove. In some cases of sexual abuse there are physical indicators which may best be explained by penile or digital penetration of the vagina or anus, or other indicators such as the presence of a sexually transmitted disease, which provide corroboration for a child's accounts of sexual assault. There are other cases in which there is evidence which may identify the perpetrator, such as the presence of semen or pubic hairs. However, much sexual abuse occurs without vaginal or anal penetration and without leaving any other physical indicators (or indeed any other form of corroboration of the child's story). This is particularly the case with younger children. In contrast, there are very likely to be signs of physical abuse, if it is sufficiently serious to attract the attention of the child welfare authorities. While sometimes it is not possible to say with any degree of certainty whether an injury was accidental, at other times there is such a discordance between the nature of the injuries and a parent's explanation for their causation that the diagnosis of non-accidental injury is almost inevitable.

Why, then, is there such a disparity between the rates of prosecution for physical assault and the rates of prosecution for sexual assault? The characterization of physical abuse as a matter for the children's court rather than the criminal courts perhaps reflects an attitude that a parent's physical abuse of a child is not a matter for state intervention unless there is serious danger to the life or physical safety of the child. The confinement of physical abuse to the private sphere contrasts with changes in societal attitudes to domestic violence which have brought it out of the private sphere and into the public arena, with an emphasis on the unlawfulness of violence against women in the home. In cases of domestic violence, restraining orders have played a useful role in emphasizing to the perpetrators the criminality of their conduct, while putting them on notice that further incidents of violence or intimidation could lead to criminal charges. In contrast, there has been little use made of restraining orders to protect children from physical abuse. A consequence of this is that, unless the violence is so serious that the child cannot be allowed to remain in the family home, it is likely that nothing will be done about the physical abuse of a child.

The criminal law response to child sexual abuse is, of course, justifiable. Prosecution emphasizes firmly the unlawfulness of sexually exploiting children. The voice of the criminal law thus counteracts other voices in the community which explicitly or implicitly condone the sexualization of children. Despite the clear public condemnation of child sexual abuse as reflected in the demands for criminal prosecution, Australian society still demonstrates a certain ambivalence about the sexualization of children. This ambivalence may be seen, for example, in the use by the fashion industry of very young adolescent girls as models, posing in sexually suggestive ways. It may also be seen in the widespread acceptance of sexually explicit themes in television programmes and magazines aimed at young adolescents. To the extent that these media images portray children and young adolescents not only as sexual beings but as sexually available, they support offenders' own rationalizations of sexual exploitation as consensual and beneficial to children. The unequivocal support for treating sexual exploitation of children and young adolescents as criminal in nature thus sends clear messages about the limits of sexual freedom, the age at which the law will regard a young person as mature enough to consent and the constraints upon sexual exploitation.[37]

Nonetheless, the characterization of child sexual abuse as criminal may displace other characterizations of the problem which are also of significance in understanding and responding to child sexual abuse. In particular, there has been comparatively little emphasis on paedophilic orientation as a psychosexual problem. While there are some treatment programmes for sex offenders in prisons, New South Wales is the only state in Australia to pass legislation combining a criminal law response with a therapeutic response. The Pre-trial Diversion of Offenders programme in NSW was established by statute in 1985[38] to provide a means of diverting incest offenders from the courts and offering them a therapeutic alternative to prison. The programme is available, after rigorous assessment, to those who plead guilty to intrafamilial sexual abuse, and are deemed suitable for the programme. It involves intensive work on an 'outpatient' basis, not only with the offender but also with the non-offending spouse and the children. Although a conviction is recorded, the offender is not sentenced for the offence as long as he successfully completes the programme. This normally takes two years. If an offender fails to adhere to any of the conditions of the programme, he may be returned to the court and sentenced for the original offence.

The emphasis on criminal prosecution for sexual offences against children has met also with mixed success. In New South Wales for example, prosecutions for child sexual assault increased markedly between 1982 and 1992, but despite this increase in prosecutions, there has not been a proportionate increase in the rate of convictions. Indeed, both the guilty plea rate and the rate of convictions after trial has declined dramatically over that period, as Table 2.2 shows.[39]

Table 2.2 Convictions for child sexual abuse (New South Wales)

Year	Plea rate (%)	Guilty at trial (%)	Conviction rate (%)
1982	83.6	58.8	92.3
1984	79.0	47.8	87.3
1988	55.0	33.8	70.0
1989	55.0	39.9	75.0
1990	50.6	38.6	70.3
1991	55.5	41.3	74.1
1992	58.0	43.4	76.5

This evidence suggests that changes to the rules and the courtroom furniture which make it easier for children to testify are only one of the issues which need to be resolved if these cases are to be successfully prosecuted. A more fundamental issue which has not been addressed is the way in which child abuse is constructed by the criminal law. Whereas child abuse and, in particular, child sexual abuse, is often a continuously occurring experience in the life of a child, for the criminal justice system, each separate act of abuse is a separate criminal act, just as each robbery or car theft is a separate criminal act. The victim does not have to give exact dates, but he or she must describe each abusive act with sufficient specificity for each incident to be proved beyond reasonable doubt. Indeed, not only must each offence be proved beyond reasonable doubt, but the elements of each offence must be proved specifically.[40]

For many victims of child abuse, however, it may be very difficult to remember each specific event. They may be able to describe with painful detail the story of how they were abused over a period of time, but what exactly happened when, what he did on one occasion or another, may be quite difficult to describe in a way which does not appear suspect under cross-examination. Where a child has been abused over a long period of time, one incident of abuse may blur with another. Details may become confused, and descriptions vague. This is particularly so if the child dissociates during the abuse.

In a criminal trial, the evidence which is allowed to be heard by a jury is also very narrow.[41] Any evidence which is more prejudicial to the defendant than probative of the offence is excluded, and in this way the incident may be shorn of some of its context. The focus is only on the incidents charged, and evidence will be excluded about any incidents which did not form the basis of criminal charges.

A recent decision of the High Court of Australia illustrates the problem.[42] A girl alleged sexual abuse by a man with whom she had stayed on numerous occasions, and who had stayed with her family on other occasions. She said it had begun when she was 13 and lasted until she was 16. She asserted to her mother and to the police that she had been the victim of many sexual acts committed by this man over an extended period of time. The prosecutor chose to charge the defendant only with 13 offences relating to seven specific occasions. In the course of her evidence, the young woman made reference to being sexually abused on other occasions which were clearly outside the domain of the offences charged. The judge warned the jury in summing up that they should put out of their minds any evidence of hers which did not relate to the offences charged, but the High Court held that was insufficient: the jury should have been discharged and a new trial ordered. The High Court said that the references to other times when sexual penetration occurred outside of the offences charged was 'highly prejudicial and inflammatory'.[43] From a legal point of view, this was a sufficient ground to say that the trial miscarried.

The non-legal observer might well be left wondering, however, that the legal system could be so perverse, first, to charge the defendant with only some of the offences which she alleged and, second, to regard the trial as miscarrying when she makes reference to the totality of her experience. No doubt, as she stepped into the witness box, she promised to tell the truth, the whole truth and nothing but the truth. The law did not allow her to tell the whole truth and, when she tried, regarded her testimony as prejudicial and inflammatory.[44]

This perhaps illustrates the problem that health professionals, social workers and lawyers tend to look at the issue of child abuse from such different perspectives within their professional discourses. The health professional looks at the whole history as related by the child and known from means such as a medical examination. Some details will be very clear, and others more vague. Individual events matter less than the cumulative experience of the abuse and its cumulative effects, both physical and psychological. The lawyer, on the other hand, dissects the cumulative picture into tiny pieces, and selects only some of those pieces as being legally relevant.[45] In this way, the courts examine each individual tree minutely (or at least those trees considered to be relevant to the charges) without necessarily seeing, or being allowed to see, the wood.

Intrafamilial child sexual abuse: public or private law?

A further issue of characterization is whether child sexual abuse within the family should be seen as a matter of public law, requiring state intervention to ensure the protection of the child, or merely private law, being significant in deciding the issue of whether access (or now, 'contact') should be allowed following the breakdown of the parents' relationship.

Even where there is not sufficient evidence to launch a criminal prosecution, or where for other reasons criminal prosecution is contraindicated, it remains open to the state authorities to take protective action through its child welfare jurisdiction in the children's court. Whether or not child welfare proceedings are taken in Australia is in large measure dependent on the attitude of the non-offending parent. If the parents have separated, and the alleged offender has no contact with the child, the child welfare authorities may decline to take further action. A variation on this scenario is that the determination of whether the case of sexual abuse is substantiated is left to the Family Court of Australia in determining an application for access, or contact, from the alleged offender.

Many such cases are resolved in the family court without the participation of the relevant child protection authority, other than perhaps in giving evidence of its investigations. In some cases, this is because the child protection authority does not believe the case is strong enough to take to the children's court; in others, it is suspicious of the veracity of the claims of sexual abuse precisely because the allegations have been made in the context of a custody or access dispute. Too often, however, the decision not to get involved is a matter of cost shifting. With the paucity of resources at state and territory level for child protection, and the workload of the children's court in handling these cases, it is all too easy to leave the litigative burden on the non-offending parent, and the cost of adjudication on the federal government which funds the family court. Since few people can afford the cost of protracted litigation in the family court, many such cases are settled, perhaps with privately supervised access arrangements, in a way which may be contrary to the best interests of the children concerned.

The family court's approach to dealing with child abuse allegations deserves comment, for in Australian law an unusual position has been taken to the issue of sexual abuse allegations in family law proceedings. If a child protection case is brought in the children's court or a youth court of a state or territory, usually the case has to be proved on the balance of probabilities. The exception is in New South Wales where, under the current law, it must be proved to be 'very highly probable' that the child is in need of care.[46] In the family court under the Family Law Act 1975 (Cth), a lower burden of proof is required. The High Court of Australia held in *M* v. *M*.[47] that 'a court will not grant custody or access to a parent if that custody or access would expose the child to an unacceptable risk of sexual abuse'.[48]

In *M* v. *M*, and a companion case, *B* v. *B*,[49] the High Court affirmed the decisions of trial judges to deny access entirely even though they had not been satisfied on the balance of probabilities that the father was guilty of sexual abuse of the child. Neither judge could say that the father had *not* sexually abused the child. Both said they were left with lingering doubts about the child's safety if access were to be allowed. The test of 'unacceptable risk' therefore did not require affirmative findings either that the child had been abused or that, if she had, the father was responsible.

The notion that a court may determine the result of a case adverse to one of the parties even where the crucial factor is not proven on the balance of probabilities may at first sight appear a strange one. The High Court's decision clearly runs in a contrary direction to the decision of the House of Lords in *Re H and others (minors) (sexual abuse: standard of proof)*.[50] The justification for this decision was that the role of the family court was not to decide whether one of the parties was guilty of a criminal offence. It was to determine the best interests of the child. The issue of sexual abuse was only one of the factors which might affect this determination. Indeed, the High Court discouraged the family court from making positive findings on the question of sexual abuse unless compelled by the evidence to do so.[51]

An unacceptable risk is a risk that the court considers is unacceptable. Little more can be said about the meaning of the test, for ultimately it is a subjective test based on the judge's impression of the available evidence. There is no definition of what an acceptable risk might be, nor have any cases been reported in which judges have held that, despite some evidence pointing to sexual abuse, the risk is acceptable and access should be permitted. Instead, the battleground shifted after *M* v. *M* to the question of whether, in such cases, access should be supervised or denied entirely. This was a matter left open by the High Court in *M* v. *M*. In *Bieganski and Bieganski*[52] the full court of the family court held unanimously that, where there is an unacceptable risk of abuse, access should be denied entirely. They emphasized the psychological harm which might be caused by continuing contact with the perpetrator even if supervision ensured the physical safety of the child.[53] In this case, however, the trial judge had made affirmative findings of sexual abuse against the father. In a later case, *K* v. *B*,[54] no such affirmative findings were made, and the decision of the majority of the full court to follow *Bieganski*, in denying access provoked a vigorous dissent. The debate continues.

Child protection: saving children or supporting families?

A third issue in terms of the characterization of child abuse and neglect in Australian law is the role of welfare departments. Is it primarily one of saving children or supporting families? In mature social work practice, such a dichotomy is unrealistically stark. It is axiomatic that the best way to promote children's long-term interests is to find the means, if it is possible, for them to be maintained safely within their families of origin. Removal is a last resort, and cannot occur without the risk of harm which arises from the severing of important emotional ties and the dangers of insecure placements within the substitute care system. Thus the work of child protection frequently involves supporting families in order to promote the safety of the children.

While the dichotomy is too stark as a description of the dilemmas of social work practice, it is a more accurate characterization of the differences in approach which may be seen in child welfare laws across Australia. Underlying these laws, it is possible to discern a variety of different philosophies.[55] New South Wales perhaps provides the clearest example of a focus on the notification and investigation of child abuse rather than on support of families, and the government's role, as defined in the legislation, is one of policing families in order to protect children from abuse. The legislation in South Australia, by contrast, not only recognizes that the family may be the source of the problem, but places a great responsibility on the family to offer solutions, supported and facilitated by the government.

In NSW, the Children (Care and Protection) Act 1987 is characterized by an emphasis upon state intervention to protect children. The grounds on which a child may be said to be 'in need of care' are quite broad. For example, one of the grounds is that 'adequate provision is not being made, or is likely not to be made, for the child's care'. Another is that the child is being, or is likely to be, abused. There is no legal requirement to show that the child has suffered harm as a consequence of the abuse or inadequate provision, or is likely to do so. This contrasts with the position in Victoria, where, as under the Children Act 1989 in England,[56] there is a threshold requirement of 'significant harm'.[57]

There is also a strong emphasis on notification of abuse. As in almost all states and territories in Australia,[58] some professional groups are mandated to notify. Once a notification has been made, the Director-General of the Department of Community Services in NSW has a duty[59] to

(a) promptly cause an investigation to be made into the matters notified to the Director General; and
(b) if the Director General is satisfied that the child in respect of whom the Director General was notified may have been, or is in danger of being, abused or is a child in need of care, take such action as the Director General considers appropriate, which may include reporting those matters to a member of the police force.

The system in NSW, as reflected in its legislation, is thus driven by responding to child abuse notifications rather than prevention and early intervention. The duty to investigate is backed up by a range of powers to remove children in an emergency and to seek care orders through the children's court. New South Wales is, of course, not unique in these respects. Emergency powers and removal powers pursuant to court orders are features of all child welfare laws. What is absent from the NSW legislation is very much indication that the government should be involved in supporting families or helping parents as a means of reducing the incidence of abuse and neglect. While the Act allows the minister to 'provide assistance and support for non-government organisations and persons concerned in the establishment or development of welfare services for children and their families', it does not *require* the minister to do so.[60] Nor does the legislation require the government itself to do much to support parents and families.[61] Thus the government has many powers to protect children, but few obligations.

In part because of the statutory priority given to the investigation of abuse notifications, supportive work with families, which may reduce the incidence of abuse and neglect, has been given low priority. Indeed, child protection work has been so driven by the system of notification and investigation that, even when parents ask for help, this has been classified as a 'notification' in order to justify the provision of services.[62]

By way of contrast, the South Australian legislation gives to the minister a range of obligations, including the following:[63]

> The Minister must seek to further the objects of this Act and, to that end, should endeavour:
>
> (a) to promote a partnership approach between the Government, local government, non-government agencies and families in taking responsibility for and dealing with the problem of child abuse and neglect;
> (b) to promote and assist in the development of co-ordinated strategies for dealing with the problem of child abuse and neglect;
> (c) to provide, or assist in the provision of, services for dealing with the problem of child abuse and neglect and for the care and protection of children;
> (d) to provide, or assist in the provision of, preventative and support services directed towards strengthening and supporting families, reducing the incidence of child abuse and neglect and maximising the well-being of children generally;
> (e) to assist the Aboriginal community to establish its own programmes for preventing or reducing the incidence of abuse or neglect of children within the Aboriginal community;
> (f) to provide, or assist in the provision of, information or education services for parents, prospective parents and other members of the community in relation to the developmental, social and safety requirements of children.

The South Australian Act thus reflects a different philosophy of child protection in which one of the significant roles of government is to support parents, family members and community organizations with the goal of reducing the incidence of child abuse and promoting the well-being of children. In the long term, this may be a more positive and effective approach to the work of child protection in which the symptoms of family dysfunction are not isolated from their context. The Human Rights and Equal Opportunities Commission report on the 'stolen children' called for this kind of approach with respect to indigenous communities:[64]

> Evidence to the Inquiry repeatedly indicated a community perception that the problems which result in removals need to be addressed in terms of community development. However, welfare departments continue to pathologise and individualise protection needs of Indigenous children. At the same time, recognition of past failures, under-resourcing and, in some instances, racist attitudes frequently result in a failure to intervene until the family crisis is of such proportions that separation is the most likely or even the only possible course.

The philosophy of family involvement in resolving child protection issues is reflected in the statutory role given in South Australia to 'family care meetings' which are based upon the family group conferences found in New Zealand's Children, Young Persons and Their Families Act 1989. Section 27 of the Children's Protection Act 1993 in South Australia, as originally enacted, provided: 'If the Minister is of the opinion that a child is at risk and that arrangements should be made to secure the child's care and protection, the Minister must cause a family care meeting to be convened in respect of the child.' The purpose of such meetings is to 'provide a proper opportunity for a child's family, in conjunction with a Care and Protection Co-ordinator, to make informed decisions as to the arrangements for best securing the care and protection of the child; and to review those arrangements from time to time' (Children's Protection Act 1993 s.28). Participants in such meetings may include the child, parents, relatives, support people for the parents and 'any other person who has a close association with the child' (s.30). The invitations are made by the care and protection coordinator, attached to the youth court, and a child or other person may not be invited if it would be contrary to the child's best interests (s.30(2)).

The South Australian legislation thus followed the New Zealand model of mandating a meeting in all cases before a court application was made. The experience of practitioners in the first two years of the operation of the legislation indicated that, in some instances, these meetings were unproductive. In some cases, this was because extensive work had already been done informally with the extended family and nothing could be added through a formal meeting. In other situations they were unproductive because of the entrenched positions which were held on either side and on which no compromise was possible.[65] Consequently, an amendment was passed in 1995. The requirement that the minister 'must' cause a family care meeting to be convened was replaced by an instruction that he or she 'should' do so. The amendments also provided that a family care meeting need not be convened in certain circumstances, including that where it has not been possible to hold a meeting despite reasonable endeavours, where an order needs to be made without delay, or where the guardians of the child consent to the matter going straight to court.[66]

Family group conferences have also been introduced in Victoria (without a legislative base) following a successful pilot programme in that state.[67] A pilot programme is also being conducted in NSW.[68] The legislative adoption of family care meetings in South Australia has been criticized because it imported a structure which was developed in the specific cultural context of New Zealand without significant parallels in South Australia, because it fails to understand family dynamics and because it risks making the welfare of the child less important than the unity of the family.[69] Even if these criticisms are accepted, it does not mean that family group conferences have no role. The issue is how they should be used. The success of such meetings must depend in part on whether there are matters about which the parties are able to negotiate. There can be little room to negotiate if the fact of abuse is denied. Here it is better for there to be an adjudication on the evidence in accordance with due legal process. Experience in the pilot programme in Victoria also suggested that such conferences could be useful as long as the ground rules were clear.[70] If it was accepted that the children could remain in the parental household with appropriate supports, a Family Group Conference could be useful in generating options for appropriate supports to be provided. Similarly, if there was an acceptance that the children should be removed from home, the Conference might be useful in resolving issues about where the child should live and how contact arrangements should be organized. It is doubtful, however, that family group conferences will fulfil a useful role in every case or that they ought to be a mandatory process. They may have the effect only of delaying permanency planning for the child.

CONCLUSIONS

It is difficult to generalize about child protection in Australia. At different periods, quite different philosophies of social work intervention have prevailed. The relevant legislation is undergoing major reform in four states. A new Bill has been introduced in Tasmania,[71] Bills are expected to be introduced in 1997 into the Queensland and Western Australian Parliaments, and the Review of the Children (Care and Protection) Act 1987 in NSW is nearing completion. The amount of reform activity suggests that child protection work in Australia is in a state of flux. States are looking not only at new approaches and systems but new philosophies of child protection. It remains to be seen whether any one approach or philosophy will come to dominate.

NOTES

1   Arts 19, 34.
2   New South Wales, Queensland, South Australia, Tasmania, Victoria, Western Australia.
3   The Australian Capital Territory and the Northern Territory.
4   The Commonwealth of Australia (Constitution) Act 1900 (Imp.).
5   Human Rights and Equal Opportunity Commission, Australian Law Reform Commission, *A Matter of Priority: Children and the Legal Process*, Draft Recommendations Paper, (Sydney: AGPS, May 1997), ch. 9; M. Rayner, *The Commonwealth's Role in Preventing Child Abuse* (Melbourne: Australian Institute of Family Studies, 1994).

6   The Commonwealth has legislative authority in relation to 'external affairs' and this gives it authority to enact legislation to implement conventions and treaties. Consequently, Australia's ratification of the UN Convention on the Rights of the Child would probably give the Commonwealth the power to enact national child protection laws to implement the Convention.
7   The legal definition of child abuse and neglect, and the definitions used by departments responsible for child protection, are not necessarily the same. In NSW, for example, abuse and neglect are quite broadly defined in the legislation. Thus the Children (Care and Protection) Act 1987, s.10 defines a child as being in need of care if 'adequate provision is not being made, or is not likely to be made, for the child's care'. To abuse a child physically is to 'assault or ill-treat' the child (s.3). These definitions are operationalized in the Department of Community Services by the provision, in staff procedural manuals, of a range of specific examples of different kinds of abuse and neglect. See S. Parker, P. Parkinson and J. Behrens, *Australian Family Law in Context* (Sydney: LBC, 1994) p.904.
8   A. Broadbent and R. Bentley, *Child Abuse and Neglect, Australia, 1995–96* (Canberra: Australian Institute of Health and Welfare, 1997) p.15.
9   Some children were the subject of a substantiated report of child abuse more than once in that year.
10 Broadbent and Bentley, op. cit., note 8, p.20.
11 14 063 out of 29 833.
12 Broadbent and Bentley, op. cit., note 8, p.27.
13 New South Wales only mandates doctors, school principals, teachers and school counsellors to report sexual abuse, but other professionals in the employment of the government are also required to report by departmental directive. South Australia mandates a large number of professional groups to report child abuse.
14 Broadbent and Bentley, op. cit., note 8, p.27.
15 Children (Care and Protection) Act 1987, s.3.
16 T. Monnone, E. Craig, D. Barry and L. Young, 'An Investigation into the Nature of Registered Emotional Abuse', in NSW Department of Family and Community Services, *Child Abuse and Neglect* (Sydney: for the Australian Child Protection Conference, 1990) p.138.
17 Broadbent and Bentley, op. cit., note 8, p.11.
18 P. Jaffe, D. Wolfe and S. Wilson, *Children of Battered Women* (Beverly Hills, CA: Sage, 1990); J. Fantuzzo and C. Lindquist, 'The Effects of Observing Conjugal Violence on Children: A Review and Analysis of Research Methodology', *Journal of Family Violence*, 4(1): 77, 1989; G. Goodman and M. Rosenberg, 'The Child Witness to Family Violence: Clinical and Legal Considerations', in D. Sonkin (ed.), *Domestic Violence on Trial: Psychological and Legal Dimensions of Family Violence*, (Springer, 1987), p.97; A. Blanchard, 'Violence in families: the effects on children', *Family Matters*, 34: 31, 1993.
19 H. Hughes, 'Psychological and Behavioral Correlates of Family Violence in Child Witnesses and Victims', *American Journal of Orthopsychiatry*, 58(1): 77, 1988.
20 NSW Department of Community Services, 'Domestic Violence Guidelines' September 1993, p.10.
21 Broadbent and Bentley, op. cit., note 8, p.25.
22 Human Rights and Equal Opportunities Commission, *Bringing Them Home: National Inquiry into the Separation of Aboriginal and Torres Strait Islander Children from their Families* (Sydney: AGPS, 1997) p.28. This is also known as the 'stolen children' report.

23 Ibid., p.33.
24 Ibid.
25 Ibid., p.37.
26 See the examples of cultural insensitivity and misunderstanding in recent years recorded in the stolen children report: *Bringing Them Home*, pp.451–3.
27 The 1991 census showed that 37 per cent of indigenous children aged 10–15 were living in single-parent families, compared to 13 per cent of non-indigenous children in the same age group. (*Bringing Them Home*, op. cit., p.545).
28 In New South Wales, about 5 per cent of all notifications result in a determination by the children's court, whereas about 45 per cent of notifications of abuse and neglect are substantiated by departmental officers: Review of the Children (Care and Protection) Act 1987, Discussion Paper 1, *Law and Policy in Child Protection* (Sydney: Department of Community Services, 1996) p.22.
29 Figures provided by the Department of Community Services, 1997.
30 Review of the Children (Care and Protection) Act 1987, Discussion Paper 1, op. cit., note 28, pp.131–4.
31 Children's Protection Act 1993 (S.A.) s.8.
32 Children and Young Persons Act 1989 (Vic.) s.112.
33 Children and Young Persons Act 1989 (Vic.) s.119(2).
34 *Bringing Them Home*, op. cit., note 22, at 449.
35 For an important research study on the use of closed-circuit television, see Australian Law Reform Commission, Children's Evidence, RP 1, *The Use of Closed Circuit Television for Child Witnesses in the ACT* (1993). Western Australia has been the most innovative Australian jurisdiction in the use of video-technology. See M. Dixon, '"Out of the Mouths of Babes..." – A Review of the Operation of the Act Amendment (Evidence of Children) Act 1992', *Western Australian Law Review*, **25**: 301, 1995. For a review of developments in Britain and Australia, see G. Davies, 'Children in the Witness Box: Bridging the Credibility Gap', *Sydney Law Review*, **15**: 283, 1993.
36 R. Cant and R. Downey, *A Study of Western Australian Child Protection Data 1989–1994* (Perth: Department for Community Development, WA, 1994).
37 I have discussed this issue of consensual sexual activity between adults and young adolescents in P. Parkinson, *Child Sexual Abuse and the Churches* (London: Hodder & Stoughton, 1997) pp.72–83.
38 Pre-Trial Diversion of Offenders Act 1985 (NSW).
39 J. Cashmore, *The Evidence of Children* (Sydney: Judicial Commission of NSW, 1995) p.55.
40 *S v. The Queen* (1989) 168 CLR 266.
41 See, further, J. Spencer and R. Flin, *The Evidence of Children*, 2nd edn, London: Blackstone Press, 1993) pp.220–29.
42 *Crofts v. R* (1996) 139 ALR 455.
43 Ibid., at 465, per Toohey, Gaudron, Gummow and Kirby JJ.
44 For a similar situation where the rules of evidence limited the child's capacity to tell her story, see Alice's story in P. Parkinson, *Child Sexual Abuse and the Churches* (London: Hodder & Stoughton, 1997) pp.249–52.
45 M. King and C. Piper, *How the Law Thinks About Children* (London: Gower, 1990). See also M. King and J. Trowell, *Children's Welfare and the Law: The Limits of Legal Intervention* (London: Sage, 1992). King and Piper apply Luhmann's theory of autopoiesis. According to autopoietic theory, law is a system which, like other social systems, is normatively closed but cognitively open. It is normatively closed because its functioning is self-referential, and it is not directly influenced by environmental

conditions around it. However, it is cognitively open in that it draws selectively from its environment. In doing so, law interprets the world according to its particular construction of reality, and reconstructs the information gained from its external environment according to its own coding of legality and illegality. See N. Luhmann, *A Sociological Theory of Law*, 2nd edn (London: Routledge & Kegan Paul, 1985) pp.281–8; G. Teubner, *Law as an Autopoietic System* (Oxford: Blackwell 1993); M. King, 'The Truth About Autopoiesis', *Journal of Law and Society*, **20**: 218, 1993.

46 Children (Care and Protection) Act 1987 (NSW) s.70(2). The Act is currently under review, and this test, which is unique to this jurisdiction, has been widely criticized. See Review of the Children (Care and Protection) Act 1987, Discussion Paper 1, op. cit., note 28, p.74.
47 (1988) 166 CLR 69.
48 Ibid., at 78.
49 (1988) 166 CLR 182.
50 [1996] 1 All ER 1.
51 This may have reflected a concern that the adjudication of guilt in serious cases of this kind ought to be the exclusive province of the criminal courts, applying the strict rules of evidence.
52 (1993) 16 Fam. L.R. 353.
53 For the therapeutic arguments which might be made in favour of this, see E. Jones and P. Parkinson, 'Child Sexual Abuse, Access and the Wishes of Children', *International Journal of Law and the Family*, **9**: 54–85, 1995.
54 (1994) FLC 92–478. See also *C and J* (1996) FLC 92–697.
55 For a discussion of the philosophy which underlies Victoria's Children and Young Persons Act 1989, see T. Carney, 'A Fresh Approach to Child Protection Practice and Legislation in Victoria', *Child Abuse and Neglect*, **13**: 29, 1989.
56 Children Act 1989, s.31. For discussion of the significant harm test in the Children Act, see M. Freeman, 'Legislating for Child Abuse', in A. Levy (ed.), *Refocus on Child Abuse*, (London: Hawkesmere, 1994); J. Fortin, 'Significant Harm Revisited', *Journal of Child Law*, 151, 1993.
57 Among the grounds of finding a child to be in need of protection in s.63 of the Children and Young Persons Act 1989 (Vic.) are the following:

(c) The child has suffered, or is likely to suffer, significant harm as a result of physical injury and the child's parents have not protected, or are unlikely to protect, the child from harm of that type;

(d) The child has suffered, or is likely to suffer, significant harm as a result of sexual abuse and the child's parents have not protected, or are unlikely to protect, the child from harm of that type;

(e) The child has suffered, or is likely to suffer, emotional or psychological harm of such a kind that the child's emotional or intellectual development is, or is likely to be, significantly damaged and the child's parents have not protected, or are unlikely to protect, the child from harm of that type;

(f) The child's physical development or health has been, or is likely to be, significantly harmed and the child's parents have not provided, arranged or allowed the provision of, or are unlikely to provide, arrange or allow the provision of, basic care or effective medical, surgical or other remedial care.

58 Western Australia is the exception.
59 Children (Care and Protection) Act 1987, s.22(7).
60 Children (Care and Protection) Act 1987, s.12.

61 Children (Care and Protection) Act 1987, s.57(3) provides that a care application shall not be made unless the Department is satisfied that 'no adequate alternative means are available to provide for the welfare of the child'. This requires the Department to explore all the alternatives to a court order, although there is no requirement for the Department to document the reasons why it considers there are no adequate alternatives as part of the application.
62 Review of the Children (Care and Protection) Act 1987, Discussion Paper 1, op. cit., note 28, p.40.
63 Children's Protection Act 1993 (S.A.) s.8. Other functions are also listed in this section.
64 *Bringing Them Home*, op. cit., note 22, pp.453–4.
65 Meeting with Children's Solicitor, Legal Aid, Adelaide, November 1995.
66 Statutes Amendment (Female Genital Mutilation and Child Protection) Act 1995 (SA) s.6.
67 P. Swain, 'Letting the Family Decide? Family Group Conferences and Pre-Hearing Conferences in Victoria's child protection system', *Alternative Dispute Resolution Journal*, 7: 233, 1996.
68 The pilot programme is being conducted by Burnside, a non-government child welfare agency.
69 M. Freeman, 'Protecting Children on Both Sides of the Globe', *Adelaide LR*, **16**: 92–3, 1994.
70 Meeting with Paul Ban, project coordinator, Melbourne, 1995.
71 Children, Young Persons and Their Families Bill, 1997.

3 Child Abuse: The Bulgarian Case

Velina Todorova

INTRODUCTION

The most obvious question likely to be posed by the reader of this chapter is: in what way is the Bulgarian response to child abuse novel, interesting or offering an insight or perspective which might be useful to those concerned with the problem elsewhere in there world? Bulgaria is not famous for cases of abuse, as, for example, Belgium was recently, or England, with its institutionalization of corporal punishment, has been in the recent past. There are scandalous cases but these are limited, isolated examples. The phenomenon, of course, does exist. Cases of child abuse are often commented upon by the press. The most shocking examples in recent years were the cases of sexual and physical abuse and murder by the mothers of infants born outside state hospitals.[1]

The problem, however, persists, for the above-mentioned cases have stirred neither public opinion nor the politicians' commitment to the initiation of changes in the relevant legislative and social practices. For instance, the April and May issues of two of the Bulgarian central dailies (one of them the daily with the largest circulation[2]) described a case which is extreme in terms of both the violence committed and the inadequate reaction of the judiciary.

The abuser was the father of three daughters from two marriages. From 1993 to 1997 he raped repeatedly two of his daughters and molested the third. His stepdaughter was the first victim and he abused her for the first time when she was 11. At the age of 14, the girl gave birth to a child begotten by her stepfather. Later on, the father raped his own daughter from the first marriage who was then 14. Criminal proceedings were initiated against him in the regional court of V. His native daughter of the second marriage was molested by him at the age of five and then in May of the current year (when she was nine). After the latest act the abuser was arrested and taken into custody, whereupon new criminal proceedings were taken against him which have not yet been brought before the court.

There are at least three reasons for seeing the case as emblematic for Bulgaria. First, it reveals a typical situation: neither the child nor the other parent was able to use the family or anyone else to seek and receive help in the face of extreme, persistent violence. There are no social structures providing services for children and parents who are exposed to risk or against whom violence was committed. Secondly, it reveals a refusal of the judicial system, verging on absurdity, to exercise its functions in protection of children (as the law stipulates) who had become the victims of violence. The legal prosecution of the abuser took four years, in which time he continued to live with his children (his victims) and take advantage of the opportunity to rape them. It turned out, moreover, that the only accessible protective institutions, such as the police and the court, were habitually ineffective. Thirdly (and this is probably the most alarming fact in this case), the case itself did not arouse any social reaction, nor did it provoke the reaction of the legal system.

In short, neither society nor the court is prepared to react adequately to cases of child abuse, especially if it is committed within the family. Street violence and crime in general occupy the attention of the judicial system and the public to a much greater extent than a case such as the above, which is considered mainly a private matter. The fact is that, in the recent past there has been no actual identification or recognition of 'child abuse' in Bulgaria. There has been no intellectual or cultural understanding of the problem or any conceptualization of the phenomenon. However, some increase in social awareness can be noted, which is due to the media attention.

This chapter is intended to find answers to some alarming and challenging questions, while drawing a critical parallel with relevant Bulgarian legislation and practice in reaction to cases of child abuse. What are the reasons for refusing to admit this social problem into the public and especially into the political debate? What are the limits within which the lawmaker and society can recognize the phenomenon? How soon will actual measures be taken for the provision of competent professionals and structures prepared to respond to and treat the consequences of child abuse?

THE BULGARIAN CONCEPT OF CHILD ABUSE

In search of the reasons for the missing concept

The understanding and the articulation of the child abuse phenomenon is something new in Bulgaria. There have been no attempts to define it within the national context. Therefore it will be difficult to determine when Bulgaria became aware of the phenomenon. Unlike other countries, where the exact year and even the date can be indicated (1962 for the USA, 1963 for Great Britain, the late 1960s for the Netherlands, and so on),[3] no such periodization can be indicated for Bulgaria. Should we specify any formal beginning, however, as the practices of western tradition suggest, it must be the late 1980s. It happened within the narrow circle of the medical profession and, more specifically, among *children's psychiatrists*, who had made the diagnosis of *child abuse* in cases where the psychiatric certification of children was required for the divorce application of their parents. It is of significant importance that the doctors did not begin to talk about the problem within Bulgaria, but abroad, at international conferences.[4] For the time being, the problem was not discussed inside the country; the first brief note appeared in 1995.[5] Until now, however, there have been no further scientific publications on the issue.

The main reason for this is that the phenomenon *has not yet been problematized*. The absence of the social problem prevents the emergence of a theoretical one. The more expressive verbalization of the phenomenon (especially by the media) is inspired by the western tradition and the opening of society after 1989. Looking for the reasons, we may say that the definition proper of the social problem of child abuse depends on the degree of social or even economic developments, the historical traditions and the established cultural norms and attitudes towards violence. Therefore, for a clearer understanding of the Bulgarian case, an outline will be presented of the social, historical and cultural context.

The macro problems exhaust public attention and interest

The basic feature of Bulgarian society at present is that it is a transitional society. It is undergoing a fundamental change of its sociopolitical and economic structure. Currently, it is engaged predominantly with macro-level problems and the processes. What happens at the micro level (in interpersonal relations, in close groups such as the family) seems too far from the focus of public debate. This is why private problems are not made public. People tend to be much more occupied with the prospect of global change and the reality of street violence. Violence in the family is sensationalized by the media from time to time, without any attempt to analyse the problem or to promote its normative comprehension. *Domestic* cases of child abuse seem far less scandalous when compared to their *foreign* counterparts, which are reported and debated on a much wider scale (as with the Belgian paedophilia case).

Thus violence against children in Bulgaria remains mainly a private problem in terms of its comprehension and discussion, as well as in terms of the opportunities for reaction against it. Probably, when certain levels of stability and security are attained within society, closer attention will be given to the smaller world of the family and the child. Unfortunately, the situation in the field of theory and scientific research is much the same. The family, the child, violence against children, and against women as well, do not receive the necessary attention, understanding and serious theoretical analysis.

As the latest social survey on children and families in Bulgaria shows, the 'big' problems of the adults and society push the problems of children and 'the infantile problems' of society to the periphery of social space. This adds to the extent and the acuteness of the problems and consigns children to a marginal position in society, blurring their status. Being the most helpless and vulnerable part of society, children are the first to bear the consequences of social crisis: higher death and morbidity rates, violence and exploitation.[6]

The paradox – the child is a superordinate value but his/her dependence on the parents is prevailing value. Society pushes the problems of children inside the family

Bulgarian society since 1989 has been trying to adopt the democratic values which incorporate human rights. It is these values, together with the ideas of freedom and autonomy of the person, human dignity and inviolability, which are replacing the former prevailing values of the guarantee of collective rights and of social security provided by the state. This process is not supposed to end within a short time. It is evident that the subject of violence is a part of the broader issue of *human rights* and their protection. Unlike the rights of adults, which have been treated recently with much more respect (so that there is a chance for them to develop into a social and personal value), the rights of children are far from enjoying the same status. To a great extent children are viewed as the object of protection and not as the subject of rights.

In the Bulgarian cultural milieu we may identify quite controversial attitudes towards children. First of all, the child is still considered as one of the supreme but *family* values. He or she is mostly thought of as a part of the family, or even as the property of his or her parents, whose authority is based both on the historical tradition and on the economic dependence of the child upon them. Parental care and support for the children will often last a lifetime. The 'victim–parent' is a typical Bulgarian phenomenon. This is partly due to the poverty of the society as a whole. On the other hand, the closed structure of society and the absence of significant personal perspectives for most Bulgarians turn the child into the basic value and the main reason for the existence of the family. The voluntary 'childlessness' which is so popular in modern societies is much less common in Bulgaria. This is why cultural norms and traditions still give more support to the dependency of the child on the parents than to respect for the personality of the child.

As a consequence, Bulgarian law sets forth the important position of the family in the structure of society, as well as the fundamental assumption that the child is a part of the family, and conceives of children as a collective, a group, which is in special demand for protection. According to the constitution, 'the family, motherhood and childhood shall enjoy *the protection* of the state and society' (Article 14 of the Constitution, Articles 3 and 5 of the Family Code). In the same vein, the Family Code states that 'the full protection of the children' and 'their upbringing' is its major goal (Article 2) and principle (Article 3). This approach to the child is still considered to be *exhaustive* in terms of theory: the *protection of children* is the 'the basic meaning of all regulations referring to the position of children within the family'.[7]

Being approached in this way, the problem of violence remains outside the context of the protection of the rights of children and becomes largely dependent on subjective judgements and the situation as a whole. The protection of children from violence presupposes the recognition of their human dignity and right to inviolability in the manner in which these rights are recognized for every human being. This is why Bulgarian doctors, who are the first to encounter the individual cases, could not be expected to demonstrate sensitivity to child abuse either in the past or today. It required the adoption of a personal position: children ought to have been considered as independent persons, separate from their parents with their relevant rights and entitlement to protection.

On the other hand, the traditional attitude of Bulgarians to the child lacks the aspect of cruel, purposeful violence which is present in so many other cultures. The combination of this with the firm view of a child's dependency on parents creates the thinking that the upbringing of children must be left to the parents and that they must be free to choose the methods of such upbringing. This may be one of the reasons that explains the tolerant attitude to corporal punishment and the reluctance of Bulgarians to admit that anyone might interfere with the upbringing of their children. Bulgarian parents are not apt to communicate facts about family violence. It is well known that in other societies the parents or the members of a kinship community would readily report facts about violence. The specific thing about Bulgaria is that, if a parent or a relative ventured to do so, he or she would come upon two obstacles: social mistrust and the absence of accessible social mechanisms for support and protection. Things get even more complicated when the parent in question is the mother, who is usually the psychologically and economically weaker party. This explains why, in spite of its existence, violence in the family is concealed, pushed back, locked up within the family.

The institutionalization of children: one Bulgarian response to child abuse

In the context of the refusal to recognize the problem of child abuse, a series of myths[8] were reproduced in the area of family relations. It was inadmissible, for instance, to consider the existence of serious conflicts of social significance within the family, except for divorce, which was accepted rather as a private problem. On the contrary, where the attitude towards the child was concerned, well-being, agreement and mutuality of interests reigned. The ideologically imposed myth of agreement led to the total neglect of the necessity of setting up services addressed to the parents and their children for the solution of possible contradictions between them and resulted in the absence of professionals who would be expected to identify the fact and respond to it. Within the tradition of the patriarchal culture and philosophy prevailing over the last 50 years, the social policy of the Bulgarian state regarding services for families and children offered only services aimed at *the collective needs of children as a group*. A comparatively good system of nurseries and kindergartens was set up, taking children aged six months to six years. This situation came to support another myth about the happy childhood of Bulgarian children and their complete satisfaction as they were cared for by the 'mother-state'.

This was intended to fulfil several objectives. In the first place, the family model was preserved with both parents working outside the home. (It was impossible for a family to live on the income of one parent.) In the second place, the care establishments exercised control on behalf of the state over the upbringing of children. The public care of children, for its part, provided for the development of irresponsible parental attitudes. The generously offered service of infant care led to an almost unrestricted opportunity for the parent to leave his or her child entirely to the custody of the state. This is how a specific form of violence emerged, the institutionalization of Bulgarian children, which will be examined in more detail later. Collective upbringing led to other types of violence, such as emotional abandonment, neglect and insufficiency of individual attention and personal contact.

THE LEGAL CONCEPT OF CHILD ABUSE

In Bulgaria there is no contact between the specialists in various areas who are competent to deal with the problem. This presents an obstacle to its multidisciplinary study. Medical doctors and lawyers use different language in reference to the phenomenon. Doctors show an inclination to term it 'abuse', or 'violence', and they also use the established medical term 'battered child syndrome'. Their language, therefore, is more universal. Sociological writings speak of children 'exposed to risk', but within the context of the negative factors which influence the child and childhood in general.

The phenomenon is conceptualized mainly in the field of criminal and family law. Regardless of the absence of an explicit concept of child abuse, the thinking of the legislator may be traced by the forms of violence against which protection is provided for the child. Family law and criminal law share the concept of the *child in danger*. Any action of the parent which endangers the basic values of the child – health, physical, moral or emotional development – may be used as a reason to seek protection. The danger justifies the intervention of the state in the parent–child relationship with a view to the protection of the child. Therefore the interference with the private relations of parents and children is admissible *only through a legal procedure* which would determine whether the child is endangered by the behaviour of the parent. Where this is proved, the court is to take measures to protect the child. The general provisions in the field state:

> Where the behaviour of the parent jeopardizes the personality, upbringing, health or property of the child, the regional court ex officio or at the request of the other parent, or by the public prosecutor, decrees appropriate measures in the interest of the child, and where necessary settles the latter in a suitable place ... A parent or guardian who leaves a person, who is under parental care or guardianship, without supervision and sufficient care and thereby creates a danger for his physical, spiritual or moral development, shall be punished by deprivation of liberty for up to one year or by corrective labour, as well as by public censure. (Article 74, para. 1 of the Family Code, 1985; Article 182, para. 1 of the Penal Code, 1968)

The law does not define the term *danger*. By 'danger' the law implies either the overall absence of care or the exercise of parental rights in prejudice to the interest of the child. The specific status of being endangered is left to the definition of the judge and therefore it depends on the values and standards held by the judge in this respect. Of course, the judge's decision will be based on the opinion of the experts if they are appointed. According to the case law,[9] average criteria have to be applied for the identification of the normal conditions, or their absence, accepted by society, under which the upbringing of a child should be carried out. There is no discussion of what are the criteria and standards shared by parents as regards the normal practice of child upbringing.

The notion of 'danger' could be interpreted also as a situation of the child at risk, prior to the occurrence of an actual injury. This means that it would be admissible for the court to take measures if there was a well-founded suspicion that the child might be harmed. According to the judicial practice, however, the threshold of legal intervention has been placed much higher. The court will not provide for the protection of the child if there is only a suspicion (even a grounded one) of the future possibility of harm. Under the regulations of the Family Code, legal procedures are usually initiated after the child has been seriously harmed as a result of the incorrect exercise of parental rights and obligations. Examples are the leaving of the child without support for a long time, neglect of the emotional needs of the child, and the child being involved by the parents in illegal or immoral activities, such as prostitution. It is considered necessary for the danger to have occurred and to have brought about the harmful consequence.

According to the Penal Code, the actions of the parent must have been intended. There are provisions, however, which treat the accidental neglect by the parent as an indictable offence (for example, when the child swallows a poisonous substance left within reach by the parent or hurts himself in a manner predictable and preventable by the parent). The Family Code provides protection in the cases of both deliberate, that is, intentional action and in situations in which the parent objectively is not at fault. As Article 74, para. 2 of the Family Code reads: 'Similar measures are undertaken where the parent, due to long physical or mental illness or to prolonged absence or other objective reasons, is unable to discharge his or her parental rights.' This means that the subjective estimation of the parent of his own actions will not determine whether these actions will be deemed dangerous and whether they will serve as a reason for the public and legal protection of the child. The law is intended to give protection against any danger and not only against intentional actions. If the child is mistreated, the intentions of the parent will not be taken into consideration.

The Penal Code criminalizes various forms of child abuse, the mildest being the neglect of the child, increasing through emotional violence and physical maltreatment to sexual abuse. The law provides for reinforced protection where the parent of the child is the perpetrator of the abuse. We can say that the concept implied by the relevant Bulgarian legislation approximates to the widest definition of the phenomenon, according to which each action injuring the optimal development of the child is abuse.[10]

FORMS OF CHILD ABUSE

As mentioned earlier, without being based on any common concept of child abuse, Bulgarian laws implicitly cover a wide range of violent action against the child. The UN Convention on the Rights of the Child may also be referred to in this respect. Bulgaria ratified the Convention in 1991 without any reservations. Under the Bulgarian Constitution, the Convention is incorporated into domestic law, which means that, where there is a contradiction with any domestic legal act, the Convention must be applied by the court.[11] As a result of this the child may directly enjoy the protection stipulated in Article 19 of the Convention against 'all forms of physical or mental violence, injury or abuse, neglect or negligent treatment, maltreatment or exploitation, including sexual abuse, while in the care of the parent(s), legal guardian(s) or any other person who has the care of the child'.

Neglect of the child by the parents

The two texts cited above refer to the minor forms of mistreatment of the child, such as *abandonment or neglect*. To be left without supervision or sufficient care is treated as a criminal omission of the parent in the cases where his care is deemed necessary. The type of supervision and care is determined with respect to the age of the child. The lower the age, the greater care is due by the parent. The unprovided care may be considered to have effect on the physical survival and development of the child as well as on his emotional and moral progress. In all cases, the insufficiency of care is considered to have created 'danger' or threat to harm significantly the fundamental values of the child.

The Family Code deals with both the omission of the parent (creating danger to the child) and *active treatment*. Various types of abuse may be included within this range: inappropriate upbringing, abandonment, emotional and mental violence and even physical maltreatment. In parallel with the 'dangerous actions' in general, the law sets forth some *concrete forms* of parental action which constitute an especially harmful manner of neglecting the child. According to the Public Education Law, 'not providing for school attendance by the child' constitutes an action of the foregoing type (Art. 47). The parent is subject to administrative penalty if he ignores the right of the child to education.[12] The Family Code also specifies two definite forms: 'Where, without a valid reason, the parent continuously fails to care for the child and does not support him/her' or 'Where the parent has left the child to be brought up at a social institution and has not contacted the authorities within a year from the day on which he/she had to take the child back'

(Article 75, para. 1). Where a persistent (durable according to practical criteria) 'self-exemption' of the parent from his duties is detected, the court will order their deprivation of parental rights. In this case it is not deemed necessary for a danger to have been created for the child. On the contrary, he/she may be receiving the necessary care from his/her grandparents. The same applies to the abandonment of the child into a children's care institution. The assumption behind these two propositions is that the parent on his/her own volition exempted him(her)self from his/her parental functions. The law treats this as an especially severe harm to the interests of the child and stipulates that the parent should be deprived of his/her parental rights.

The institutionalization of children: a special type of abuse

The abandonment of a child into a children's residential home and its neglect by the parent is a form of violence common in Bulgaria. The statistics are alarming:

- There are 177 residential homes in Bulgaria, with 30 000 children, (or about 0.02 per cent of Bulgarian children). *Only 4 per cent of these children are orphans; the parents (one or both) of all other children are living and known.* Most of the children are of ethnic minority origin, mainly Roma, and they stay longer in care than the ethnic Bulgarian children.
- About 40 per cent of the children in the residential homes are put up for adoption, with 20 per cent of them being adopted annually by Bulgarian citizens and about 300–350 children being adopted by foreign nationals (mainly from France, Italy and the USA).

These institutions have developed the major function of taking care of parentless children or of children abandoned by their parents. The alternative opportunity is for the child to live with a guardian. The parents can fairly easily leave their child to the care of a home. The main reasons for doing this are of a social character; 67 per cent of the children are placed in care because of economic hardships, single parenthood, large families and so on. The remainder are so placed because they are disabled in some way. In these cases the parent usually leaves the child under a contract for temporary care and simply 'forgets' to come and fetch him/her afterwards. Such parents normally have no fixed residence and the staff of residential homes find it difficult to contact them. This dooms the children to being brought up in various homes until they become of age. They cannot be adopted because the parents have not given their consent in advance. The fate of such children is unpredictable. It is scientifically proven that the upbringing of children by institutions can be intensely traumatic. The deficiencies which children experience in their emotional, social and moral formation are reproduced in serious public problems: they often develop antisocial behavioural stereotypes and their social adaptation and realization also presents difficulties.

A number of reasons can be indicated for the emergence of this problem which is being very widely debated by the public at the present time. First, as has already been mentioned, the institutions provide for controlled public upbringing and education of the children. Presumably, this was the reason they became preferable to the family-based alternatives for bringing up abandoned children. Secondly, there was a deliberate attempt to conceal the fact that Bulgaria had such children: abandoned, nobodies, unwanted. If there were no children, the problem of their abandonment and abuse would not exist. Therefore it was not deemed necessary to establish special structures for proper solution inside the family. The establishments were located in small isolated villages on the border of administrative counties; the public access to them was limited and so were the possibilities for control over the conditions for the admission of children.

Physical and emotional abuse

The Penal Code criminalizes violence against children, sexual abuse and actions which undermine the emotional and mental development of the child. The young age of the victim is an aggravating circumstance which leads to a heavier penalty for the abuse. By the amendments of the law in 1995 and 1997, new forms of abuse were introduced as criminal offences and the former terms of penalty for crimes against children were extended.

A heavier punishment is stipulated for the *murder* of a 'biological son or a biological daughter' or of 'a person who is in a helpless situation' (Article 116, paras 3 and 4). Any person who *endangers the life* of a child (Article 137) and consciously refuses to assist him/her (Article 138) shall be deemed criminally responsible.

Any person (a parent included) shall be criminally responsible for causing *physical traumas* to a child, 'severe, medium or minor bodily injury', depending on the seriousness of the injury (Articles 128, 129 and 130). For all cases where the victim of violence is a child, heavier penalties are stipulated (Article 131, para. 1, item 4 and the amendments of the Penal Code from 1997). A special regulation criminalizes the *torture of a child* by any person in whose care the child may be (Article 187). The *use of children for begging* (Article 189) is also subject to criminal prosecution. (This phenomenon has spread very widely in recent years, especially in the larger towns and cities. It is practised most by the Roma ethnic group. The legal texts, however, seem ineffective since neither the police nor the prosecution authorities take advantage of them to provide assistance to the children.)

Sexual abuse

Sexual abuse is divided into the following forms in the Penal Code. First: *any sexual intercourse with a person below the age of 14* is a crime (Article 151). Second: *rape*. If the victim is a child below the age of 16 or a younger blood relative the penalty is heavier (from three to 10 years' imprisonment: Article 152, para.2). Third: *incest*. All sexual relations between parents and children or between adopters and adopted are considered illegal (Article 154). Fourth: *molestation defined as any sexual assault without intercourse* against a child below the age of 14 (Article 149). The penalty is heavier where the act is accompanied by violence and is threatening. Acts of molestation committed against a child above the age of 14 are subject to penalty if they are accompanied by violence and threat (Article 150). Fifth: *acts of homosexual assault against a child below the age of 16* (Article 157, para. 2). Sixth: *the sexual exploitation of children – their luring or involving in prostitution or for acts of debauchery, where the victims are under age* is a crime subject to a heavy penalty (Article 188, para. 2). The abduction of female under-age persons for the purpose of debauchery is subject to a heavier penalty (Article 156, para. 2). This is a common form of violence which has been growing in Bulgaria in the recent past. Prostitution of children has become part of the structures of organized crime.[13] The most widespread mechanism of the crime is luring into prostitution by loosely organized groups (taxi drivers, bartenders and waiters) of girls of 12–13 coming from problem families or of runaways from the residential homes. Others are forcibly abducted and compelled to prostitute themselves by procurers (predominantly Roma). There are many cases of girls who are transported abroad by special channels for the performance of sexual services. This activity has recently been criminalized by amendments to the Penal Code made in August 1997. Seventh: the distribution of *pornographic material* (Article 159). There is no special text, however, which criminalizes the use of children for pornography. There are other violations against children, although these are common only in the Roma ethnic group: for example, *the forcible persuasion* of a child below the age of 16 *by a parent to enter into marital cohabitation*, and this too is a crime (Article 190).

THE PROBLEM OF CORPORAL PUNISHMENT

The question of where the margin lies between physical abuse and the corporal punishment of children has not been publicly discussed. Bulgarian society does not consider the physical punishment of children by their parents as maltreatment, but as a type of disciplinary measure. *There has never been a time, however, when the physical punishment of a child in Bulgarian society would be conceived of as a ritual* (as perhaps was the case in England) *nor was it ever charged with any special social functions.*

This attitude is historically and culturally predetermined. In the patriarchal Bulgarian family, the authority of the father was indisputable. For possible disobedience, the father had the right to punish the child physically, or even to kill him/her. This was characteristic of the time when the Bulgarians did not have their own state and law, but were subjugated to the Ottoman Empire. This made them confine themselves within smaller social communities, where obedience to the head of the family was a matter of the survival not only of the family but of the nation as a whole. The modern Bulgarian family is subject to a profound change of values in parent–child relations. The extended family based on the authority of the father has been replaced by the nuclear family, nurtured by the emotional attachment between the spouses and the children. Parental authority can no longer be enforced and children refuse to accept it if they cannot trust it. These changes in values have not yet affected the paternalistic attitude towards the children. This is why modern Bulgarian society has not abolished corporal punishment as a disciplinary measure. The margin of tolerance to physical disciplining is the extent of severity of the punishment. And, though there are no criteria for its measurement, if the 'disciplining' results in physical injury, it may attract criminal liability. Penal sanctions against parents are rare and tend to be founded on the strong paternalist ideology of the legislation.

In parent–child relations respect for the parents and the prohibition of physical violence against parents are important. According to the Family Code, 'children are *obliged* to respect their parents and help them. They have the same *obligation* to their stepmother and stepfather' (Article 69). The Penal Code is neutral as to bodily injuries caused by the parent to the child. It deems the injury caused to the mother or the father as a qualifying circumstance (Article 131, para. 3), but not the bodily injuries inflicted upon the child by the mother or the father. It was only in *1997* that a qualified text was introduced for bodily injuries inflicted to under-age persons, but the legislator again overlooked the hypothesis of *infliction by a parent*. This means that the parent will be treated on a par with any third person who causes injuries to the child. This is why it cannot be anticipated that corporal punishment within the family will be prohibited by the law in Bulgaria in the foreseeable future.

Physical violence against children in institutions

In children's institutions, regardless of whether they are public or private, corporal punishment is strictly and expressly prohibited. According to the Regulations for the Application of Public Education Law (1992) the school authorities are held responsible for 'allowing any behviour or actions which humiliate the dignity of the student or infringe upon his/her rights' (Article 21, para. 4). 'Committing physical or mental violence against the student is prohibited' (Article 95). The student is entitled to protection by the school and other institutions if his/her personal dignity is hurt or his/her human rights is infringed (Article 102). Accordingly, the penalties which may be applied in Bulgarian schools are reprimands, reprobation or expulsion from school (Article 104). This prohibition on corporal punishment is sometimes broken in practice, but this happens rarely. Public awareness of this as well as parental sensitivity to corporal punishment applied by teachers is exceptionally high. This shows the somewhat 'dual morality' nature of Bulgarian parents. The usual reaction is to claim legal and disciplinary redress against a teacher who punishes a child improperly. Such cases are normally made public through the media. Therefore a 'dual standard' is applied: society is taught not to accept beating at school, but at home taboos and secrecy prevail.

In practice, however, corporal punishment is applied at educational boarding schools.[14] They admit children above the age of eight who have committed antisocial acts. They also serve as an alternative corrective institution for juvenile delinquents above the age of 14. Their objective is to exercise corrective and resocializing influence over the children.[15] Violence in such schools is frequent, but they are far from public attention and the problems of the children there do not evoke public sympathy and interest. According to the Report of the Central Commission on Combating Juvenile Delinquency (Central Commission):[16] 'non-pedagogic measures are applied, such as beating, mental torture, ill-treatment by the teaching and support staff'. The secretary of the same Commission states that 'there are educational boarding schools where the human dignity of the children is harmed systematically by battering, maltreatment and acts of homosexuality. ... In the form in which they exist, they cannot perform their corrective functions. We merely isolate the children there, society gets rid of them. In addition, we place them under conditions which violate their rights in a drastic way'.[17]

In fact these establishments were created in the past, not to assist the children, but to solve the problems of society generated by them. This is why they embody the idea of repression against the children. The measures taken in the recent past include closing down the most unsuitable schools (five of them), more regular control over the staff, attributing legal responsibility for any acts of violence, the dismissal of older personnel and the appointment of younger and qualified teachers.

After the changes of 1989, a new phenomenon emerged and grew in Bulgaria: the growth of *street children*. Their numbers vary between 800 and 1000. They inhabit the stations and the streets of larger cities, where they live on begging and stealing. According to the observations of Bulgarian and international human rights organizations,[18] violence is committed against these children by the police. They are also subjected to sexual molestation and forced by adults into committing crimes. The measures taken in their defence (as a rule, insufficiently effective) are temporary confinement to asylums or permanent confinement in child care homes, or returning them to their parents.

STATISTICS

In the crisis situation, which affects all spheres of Bulgarian society, child abuse is only a part of the environment of risk which faces children. They are exposed to many risks. In the first place there is a *low standard of living*, predetermined by the macro processes of impoverishment of the greater part of Bulgarian families, followed by the deteriorating quality of health care, education and recreation. In response to these processes the following negative demographic tendencies can be observed:

- Bulgaria has the lowest birth rate in Europe. It has been decreasing continuously since the end of the 1950s and reached its lowest level in 1996 with 8.6 infants born per 1000 capita;
- the population of Bulgaria is 8 400 000 people. The percentage of the children in it is falling constantly: from 2 417 000 in 1960 to 1 000 844 in 1990; the decrease since 1992 is the most serious: 294 000 or 16 per cent. Now children comprise only 22 per cent of the total population (20.4 per cent of the Bulgarian population is aged 60 and above).

The structure of the family is undergoing a change:

- the single-child family has became the typical family model in Bulgaria: more than half of the families have only one child and the number of families with two and more children is falling.

- every tenth child is reared by a one parent family: 84 000 families consist of a divorced mother and children, and 15 000 families consist of a divorced father and children;
- one in four of children are born out of wedlock.

It is difficult to measure the specific risk of child abuse. The reason is that there is no system for reporting cases of violence, and especially ones within the family. There are no specialized institutions to respond to violence against children. The *Police Statistics on Violent Crimes Committed Against Children* and the reports of the Central Commission may be used as a source of data, but, as there is no system for the tracing of the phenomenon and its developments, the figures are often contradictory and may give only an approximate picture of the situation. According to the Central Commission, for example, there is a tendency towards increase in physical and mental maltreatment of children within the family, in the street and at school. The children's psychiatrists, however, claim otherwise: it is not, they say, violence that is growing, but the rates of reported and uncovered cases. The head physician of a children's psychiatric consulting surgery states that therapeutic measures are taken for an average of eight children per month who were victims of violence within the family. According to the *Police Statistics*, statistics are as shown in Table 3.1. Further data from the police show that, in 1994, 120 children below the age of 13 and 217 children below 17 were admitted to the Emergency Medical Aid Institute in Sofia with the diagnosis of *battered child syndrome*.

Table 3.1 Violent crimes committed against children (1994–7)

Crimes	1994	1995	1996	Jan–June 1997
Total number	2 356	2 040	2 119	1 203
Murders (attempted murders)	18 (9)	16 (12)		6 (5)
Rape	283			92
Molestation	153	242	422	169
Bodily injuries		27		

According to judicial statistics, the numbers of parents sentenced under Article 182 of the Penal Code for leaving a child without sufficient care and supervision are as follows:

1992	1993	1994	1995
13	22	13	29

According to the Central Commission, 337 children, from a total of 7141, who were registered with the Children's Education Offices in 1994, reported systematic maltreatment within the family. An indirect indicator of the violence committed is the number of parents against whom sanctioning administrative measures were taken under the provisions of the Juvenile Delinquency Act. In 1994, 1000 parents were sanctioned; in 1995 their number was 1524, and in 1996 there were 1060.

THE LEGAL RESPONSE TO THE PHENOMENON

Child abuse: a type of criminal behaviour

In Bulgaria child abuse is conceptualized as a *crime* rather than as a malfunction of the family, or as a conflict in terms of the family law. Therefore it is articulated mainly in terms of criminal law. It is treated as a *socially dangerous* action which disturbs social order and violates the rights of the citizens. This means that the abusers are predominantly conceived of as criminals against whom the *repression of the state* needs to be applied. The social reaction is also expressed by the requirement to punish the criminal. Less attention is paid to the study of the reasons and the consequences of the abusive behaviour and thus no measures are taken to counsel or treat the victim or the violator. This categorization has a number of drawbacks:

1 the absence of specialized structures within the police, the prosecution authorities and the court, as well as an absence of competent professionals and, consequently, lack of heightened awareness of the problem;
2 an underestimation of the problem because of the absences as well as the overburdening of the criminal justice system. As a result, *most of the crimes against children remain unpunished* and the respective texts of the Penal Code are treated by prosecutors themselves as 'dead letters'. For instance, the use of children for begging and theft, the involvement of children into organized prostitution, the sale of under-age girls for the purpose of marital cohabitation and so on are all crimes committed in public. Abusers know they will get away with it and treat society's rules with disdain;
3 it is difficult to produce the necessary evidence to convict the abuser; there are problems also with collecting and using evidence from the child concerned;

4 there are cases where it is difficult to initiate a criminal trial at all. According to the Penal Code of Procedure, where the injuries are not of the most serious type, the victim is required to lodge a complaint. The child victim would have to do so through his or her legal representative who would be the other parent, and this is clearly not easy.

The most serious problem remains *the degree to which the emphasis on criminal prosecution shifts the focus from the necessity to protect the child to the necessity to protect society from the abuser*. This pushes resources in the wrong direction. If violence remains a problem of the criminal law, then the problem is supposedly solved by the punishment of the criminal, and society can finally breathe freely. But this ignores the child. Criminal law takes an insufficient interest in caring for the victims of crime.

Violence as an issue of family law

Bulgarian law on the relations of parents and children is based on the notion that the parents are the primary caretakers of the child: they have all the *rights and obligations* for bringing up the child (Article 47 of the Constitution and Article 68 of the Family Code).[19]

The relations between parents and children are private and state intervention is admissible only in specific cases in the order provided for by the law (Article 47, para. 4 of the Constitution). The only reason for a public institution to intervene in the parent–children relationship without asking the consent of the parent is that the child is 'at risk'. Where the behaviour of the parent (either act or omission), endangers the life or health or mental and moral development of the child, the court is to take measures for his/her protection. The danger for the child constitutes the reason for public intervention in parent–children relations. It is unclear, however, what type of harm or potential harm would motivate legal intervention. This issue is settled by the judge, usually when the interests of the child are seriously harmed. The court examines the situation in the family and where necessary orders measures for the protection of the child. The measures take the form of restriction or termination of the parental rights. For instance, the parent may be barred from dealing with the property of the child or from visiting him/her if they live separately. Should the court decide, the child may be taken from his/her home and sent to a 'suitable place'. The 'place' may be at his/her grandparents, some other relatives or in a public residential home.[20]

The court may order the termination of the parental rights of one or both parents. This extinguishes the legal relations between the parent and the child. In such cases the parental rights may be assigned to the other parent. Where both parents have been deprived of their parental rights, a guardian is appointed. The application of these regulations, however, is obstructed by the following obstacles that make the protection of the child rather ineffective.

1. Legal protection takes the form of sanctioning the parent rather than protecting the child. The court assumes the role of a parent without being able to provide a complementary or substitute care for the child. The law does not set forth the exact measures which the court might take in protection of the child, nor does it have sufficient alternative options. In Bulgaria, there are still no social services of a therapeutic or preventive character. The court usually finds it hard to order the separation of the child from the family (even where this is a last resort) for there are few, if any, housing and child-rearing alternatives. In order to examine a case, the court relies on expert evidence and not on the entire history of the case traced by a social worker. There are no social workers to attend to children and families affected by violence.
2. It is difficult to obtain legal protection and this is all that there is available to the child at present. The court may be approached by the other parent or the prosecutor,[21] or initiate legal procedures ex officio. The parent, however, is not always interested in claiming legal procedures. Warnings may be given by relatives, friends or neighbours, but the courts and the prosecutors are not very keen to act since they would by charged with the responsibility of collecting evidence on the case. There have been cases where, even after being warned of a serious neglect or maltreatment of a child by the parents, the prosecutor or the court would refuse to initiate legal procedures. This type of case is handled by the ordinary civil courts and there is little time for the prosecutor to get involved in such cases.
3. The procedure is not aimed at the protection of rights but at the protection of interests. It is almost as if the judiciary is there to protect the parents. The court is obliged to examine the relations between the parents and the child; the interests of the child are not independently represented. The parties in the lawsuit are only the parents or the state in the person of the prosecutor. The child is not a part of the proceedings and is not even entitled to be present. The law does not provide for a representative for the child, or for a social worker to be party to the proceedings. The philosophy of the law is that the interests of the child will be well enough protected by the parent (a presumption which is easily disproved in practice) or by the state in the person of the court.
4. The Family Code does not provide for the emergency protection of the child or for his/her urgent rescue from the home of the parents if necessary.

THE ADMINISTRATIVE RESPONSE TO CHILD ABUSE

As already mentioned, there is no institutional system for the discovery and regulation of child abuse in Bulgaria. There is accordingly no mandatory reporting of child abuse. The possible reasons for this may include the following.

- There is no tradition to offer *personally* oriented social services, as is normal in western societies. The conflict within the family (where child abuse is classified) is an entirely private problem. The refusal of the state to establish mechanisms for responding to it is in fact a refusal to recognize it.
- Bearing in mind that repression is the prevailing reaction promoted by the concept of the phenomenon, little attention is paid and little effort is made for the development of the philosophy of conflict in the family and the development of the institutions and the professionals needed for their treatment and prevention.

The *police* are charged with no special authority or obligations for the protection of children. The general text of the National Police Act (1993) obliges the police authorities to take measures as follows: 'The police are obliged to provide assistance to the persons who are the victims of crimes or of other antisocial acts ... as well as to the persons rendered helpless' (Article 23). In fact, however, the police will seldom respond to signals for help in cases of domestic violence. They are also believed to be responsible for violence against street children.

Doctors and children's psychiatrists, as well as *nurses*, are the group expected to react most adequately to the cases of abuse. Their involvement with the problem, however, is to a great extent a matter of personal enthusiasm and competence. Although the problem of the 'battered child syndrome' is being studied in the general curriculum of medicine, interviews with children's physicians reveal that awareness of the problem varies from specialist to specialist. The Children's Psychiatric Clinic in Sofia has already established a separate unit dealing with the therapy of children who are victims of violence. The children's paediatricians, however, are reluctant to communicate cases of child abuse. They regard it as an unresolvable conflict between the supposed necessity to report a case of child abuse and the obligation to preserve patient confidentiality. (As indicated, following the European tradition, Bulgarian law does not provide for obligatory reporting of child abuse cases.) They also fear getting involved in court procedures or becoming victims of the violence of the parents. They report that they are often forced by the parents to terminate the clinical treatment of the child, although such treatment is necessary.

The only decentralized administrative system for dealing with children in Bulgaria is addressed to the children at risk of delinquency or who have demonstrated criminal behaviour. This category of children gives the state its greatest trouble and they are the only ones on whom its attention has been 'bestowed'. The Juvenile Delinquency Act was passed as long ago as 1958 and has been modified and amended. According to this Act, a Central Commission and Local Commissions were established (the local ones are attached to the municipalities). They are vested with special authority to apply administrative measures to, and exercise influence over parents who show neglect in the upbringing of their children. They may condemn the parents, force them to attend special courses and undertake counselling on issues of child rearing, and impose fines. The commissions may report the parent to the prosecutor or to the court when they find that violence has been committed against the child by the parents. The Children's Education Offices are also institutions attached to the municipal authorities. They have the special functions of 'identifying and registering children who are the victims of criminal assault, maltreatment or neglect'. The law introduces a concept of the 'public tutor' and the 'social worker', but they are overburdened (in terms of their functions as well as of their public image) with the problem of dealing with juvenile delinquency. Accordingly, they cannot be expected to perform an effective managerial function on child abuse. They lack further the knowledge and sensitivity required to deal properly with the phenomenon.

A significant role in discovering child abuse could be given to *teachers and school psychologists* but they lack competence. They too are affected by the absence of a social network providing adequate assistance to the victim child. As with the doctors, the activity of the teachers at present is a matter of personal enthusiasm, motivation and personal compassion regarding the problem.

CONCLUSION

The foregoing outline does not merely explain the delay in recognizing the phenomenon of child abuse in Bulgaria, but reveals the type of obstacles to its problematization at present: cultural and ideological inertia and its influence on social policy. One of the major reasons for the current situation is also the lack of economic resources which could be allotted for the establishment of a system of organs and specialists to deal with the identification and management of child abuse and for the development of treatment and consulting services. *This explains the absence of political interest in the problematization of the phenomenon.* The state seems uninterested in initiating a public debate on the issue. Violence against children is both a personal problem and the problem of society. Society, however, is incapable of solving it now. The systems which exist to protect the children from violence fully, such as are found in modern societies, are too expensive and would be regarded as a luxury in present-day Bulgarian society. For instance, according to the chief secretary of the Central Commission: 'there is violence in reform schools for juveniles with deviant behaviour, *but we cannot afford to close these schools down*. We have to make efforts to eradicate violence from them.'

It is difficult, therefore, to answer the question, posed at the beginning of this chapter, as to how soon actual steps will be taken to introduce a system of competent professionals and structures prepared to respond to and treat the consequences of violence.

It is good that Bulgaria is not known for child abuse. In time, it may become noted for its efforts to protect children and respect their rights. But this time is some way off.

NOTES

1. See *24 Nours*, 22.2.1994, 24.4.1997, 14.10.1996, 1.2.1997; *Trud*, 10.10.1995, 7.3.1997, 20.3.1997, 17.4.1997; *Duma*, 19.4.1997.
2. *24 Nours*, 26 May 1997, *We, the Women*, 9 April 1997.
3. See M. Freeman, *The Rights and Wrongs of Children* (London: Frances Pinter, 1983), p.106; *Responding to Child Abuse and Neglect: The Dutch Case*, report by Marian A.S. Roelofs, Family Studies, University of Nijmegen, and Herman E.M. Baartman, Dept. of Education, Free University, Amsterdam, 1995, pp.2–3.
4. See reports: 'Forms of Masked Parental Aggression' and 'Children of Early Divorced and Lonely Mothers', First Eu. Conference on Child Abuse and Neglect, Greece, 1987; 'Family Life and Specific Forms of Child Abuse in Bulgaria', 3rd Eu. Conference on Child Abuse and Neglect, Prague, 1991; 'PTSD Parents and Forms of Intrafamilial Child Abuse', 4th Eu. Conference on Child Abuse and Neglect, Italy, 1993; 'Living in School as a Victim', 13th International Congress of International Association for Child and Adolescent Psychiatry and Allied Professions, San Francisco, 1994. Authors of the reports are: N. Polnareva, M. Achkova, and M. Michova. All reports are unpublished.
5. N. Polnareva, 'Child Abuse – problems of identification', *Social Medicine Journal*, 2, 1995.
6. *Children in Bulgaria*, a survey on the status of Bulgarian children, carried out by the Youth and Children Committee at the Ministry Council in 1996.
7. See L. Nenova, *Family Law in Bulgaria* (Sofia: Sophy-R, 1994) p.42.
8. See M. Freeman. The Limits of Children's Rights', in M. Freeman and P. Veerman (eds), *The Ideologies of Children's Rights* (Dordrecht: Kluwer, 1992), pp.30–31.
9. In Bulgaria this refers to the practice of the Supreme Court, which is binding on the lower courts, district and regional.
10. In the language of David Gil. See further, in relation to definitions of child abuse, M. Freeman, *The Rights and Wrongs of Children*, op. cit., note 3, pp.108–11, 115–16.

11 According to Art. 5(4) of the Constitution, 'Any international instruments which have been ratified by the constitutionally established procedure, promulgated and come into force with respect to the Republic of Bulgaria, shall be considered part of the domestic legislation of the country. They shall supersede any domestic legislation stipulating otherwise.'
12 This sanction, however, cannot be applied efficiently where there is premature dismissal of children from school or failure to attend school at all, which is beginning to assume threatening dimensions. The reason lies in the impoverishment of families rather than in the negligent attitude of parents. According to statistical data, 45 000 children did not attend school for the academic year 1994/95 and 67 per cent of them have no primary education.
13 See the Report of the Central Commission on Combating Juvenile Delinquency, at the Chief Prosecutor's Office of the Republic of Bulgaria for 1994.
14 They were established on the basis of the Juvenile Delinquency Act (effected in 1958 and amended for the last time in 1997) and the Public Education Law (1992).
15 There were 11 such schools in Bulgaria in 1996, with 782 children sent there in 1996–7. These schools experience various problems: they are located in isolated and thinly populated areas of the country, the staff are poorly qualified and insufficient, their necessary equipment is of bad quality, no medical services are provided for the children, and so on.
16 This is a central administrative institution dealing with juvenile delinquency and asocial behaviour. It is under the administrative control of the Chief Prosecutor's Office of Bulgaria and its director (the secretary) is at the same time a prosecutor in the Chief Prosecutor's Office.
17 See *Demokratzia*, January 1995.
18 See Human Rights Watch, Children's Rights Project, *Children of Bulgaria, Police Violence and Arbitrary Confinement*, (Helsinki: Human Rights Watch, 1996).
19 Where the parents are deceased, unknown or are deprived of their parental rights, a guardian is appointed for the child (through an administrative procedure), vested with different authorities according to the age of the child. For children of unknown parentage who reside in care establishments, these functions are assigned to the director of the establishment.
20 The parental rights, however, are *not* transferred to the establishments. They may only exercise their content, without being their holders.
21 In this case the prosecutor acts in the capacity of a defender of the social interest and the interest of the child. According to the Juridical Power Law, the prosecutor is a litigant in specific civil trials and acts as a representative of public interest.

4 Maltreatment of Children in Chile

Ines Pardo de Carvallo

Child abuse,[1] by which is understood all conduct by an adult that by his/her action or omission interferes negatively with the physical, mental or sexual development of children, has been studied as an integral social problem in Chile since the end of the 1980s. From then on, there has been a reappraisal of the fact that violence exercised against a minor constitutes a serious problem; given its complexity, it requires careful analysis.

Considering the child as a person whose interests are paramount is now an established modern trend, subject to debate and investigation particularly since the ratification of the United Nations Convention on the Rights of the Child by the Chilean Government, enacted by Supreme Decree and published on 27 September 1990, in the Official Gazette (*Diario Oficial de la República*).

In 1994, UNICEF (United Nations Children's Fund) carried out a survey based on a sample of 1533 children in the eighth grade, with alarming results. Of all the children surveyed, 63 per cent declared that they had been subject to parental maltreatment.[2] Another report published in the social communication media, referring to an examination made of a stratified sample which included 1904 young persons, revealed the existence of physical maltreatment in 13 per cent of the cases and of sexual abuse in 8.3 per cent of the cases.[3] The fact that at the same time several cases of excessive cruelty against minors occurred, some of them with fatal results, contributed to increasing even more the concern on this matter.

Before this, some forms of maltreatment had been considered private family affairs with no legal relevance. The justice system was supposed to be concerned only with major incidents of violence such as those that cause grievous bodily injury to the victim. In this scheme of things, the cataloguing as well as the investigation and legal classification of crimes such as violation, sexual abuse, rape, sodomy, injury or murder – all of which are crimes stipulated in the Penal Code or set out in Article 62, of 8 March 1997, Law of Minors, as a specific crime of maltreatment – belonged in the field of the punitively criminal and were not to be considered as matters deserving interdisciplinary actions.

In the area of private law, many different laws had been promulgated for the protection of the minor, the first one as long ago as 1811. The Chilean Civil Code, in force since 1857, rules that 'It is the responsibility of both parents jointly, or the surviving father or mother, to undertake the personal care of upbringing and educating their legitimate children', and Article 233, Clause 1, of the same code states, 'Parents have the authority to correct and punish their children so long as they do so moderately.' In the case of an illegitimate child the same rights and duties are bestowed on the father and/or mother, whoever has legally recognized that child. There was thus clear proof of the evident concern to give protection to the child, but it was equally obvious that such norms were insufficient to cope with the problem. It is believed that the incidence of maltreatment of children is particularly high in Chile.

Until now, the subject of child abuse/maltreatment of minors/battered children has not been approached in any systematic manner. The legislation is piecemeal and the administrative finding response badly organized. Errors have been committed in a succession of laws to solve particular crises or problems; laws which having totally or partially revoked previous ones have done nothing but complicate the issue and break the system into fragments. Therefore, what follows is an attempt to systematize the subject in order to bring about a better understanding of it.

Within the Chilean legislation, maltreatment of minors (child abuse) activates two kinds of judicial proceedings with two different objectives. On one hand, the courts of first instance, for minors, have the authority to decree the better interest of the minor and to decide about his or her future when his or her life is in physical or moral danger. On the other hand, the law gives different courts jurisdiction to punish those guilty of child abuse, though this does not necessarily lead to the deprivation of freedom of the abuser. Even so, in some of the punitive proceedings protective measures are included, for example, 'the precautionary measures designed to guarantee both the physical or mental safety of the victim and the peaceful living, adequate means of support and patrimonial integrity of the family group'.[4]

JUDICIAL PROCEDURES FOR THE PROTECTION OF CHILDREN

According to the current law for children,[5] jurisdiction is conferred on professionally qualified children's judges to 'resolve questions about the future life of the child when he or she is in physical or moral danger'.[6] The same law (Article 15) orders the welfare department for children, among its functions, to 'take into their care children in unsuitable conditions who need assistance or protection'. Article 16, clause 6, states that 'in the case of a child who has been detained the department must notify the motive for such a detention to the parents or legal guardian and take measures to give the child back to them. If for any reason whatsoever the parents or legal guardians are not available and it be obvious that the child needs assistance and protection, the department are to request the judge to decide what steps should be taken'. The judge can then take one of the following measures[7] (Article 29):

1   return the child to his or her parents, guardians or persons in whose charge he or she has been;
2   entrust the child to special educational establishments for a period of time deemed fit;
3   put the child under the care of a person willing to provide him or her with a family life.

These measures will last for as long as the judge determines, and can be revoked or modified if circumstances change.

In suitable cases the judge can authorize the Technical Board of the corresponding Casa de Menores[8] to apply the suitable measures for a given period of time, not exceeding 20 days. The judge possesses wide powers of control over the procedures adopted. He can determine the facts and consider the child's best interests and request medical and psychological reports and other information about the child. If practicable, he may listen to the adolescent child and, if he deems it necessary, he may listen to a child who has not yet reached puberty. The children do not need to be legally represented: that the judge himself must be a member of the bar is, it seems, sufficient.[9]

Some aspects of this legislation are in conflict with the norms established by the UN Convention on the Rights of the Child which consider the child to be a legal person. According to Articles 12 and 13 of the Convention, the children have the right to express freely their opinions on all matters that concern them, and will have the right, be it directly or through a representative, to be heard in all the legal procedures that affect them. As we have already said, the legislation compels the judge, if it is practicable, to listen to the views of an adolescent and also, if he deems it necessary, to listen to a child who has not yet reached puberty. But the child is not given a fully empowered counsel for the process in which his standing is being discussed. In addition, the measures that the court may adopt will extend for an essentially variable period of time and will depend solely on the discretion of the court. But, when taking measures relating to children at risk, the judges will have to bear in mind the provisions of the Convention because the Convention has been ratified by Chile, and has accordingly become part of the laws of the republic, and so prevails over the provisions of the former law.[10]

It is doubtful whether the power conceded to a judge to delegate his authority to the Technical Board of the children's home for the application of precautionary measures in qualified cases is within the law. However efficient these council members may be, they are not judges and therefore cannot decide about the future life of a child, not even for a short period of time, particularly if it is considered that to do so they are not required to listen to the parents or to the child.

PUNITIVE JUDICIAL PROCEDURES

The law tackles child abuse in three different ways. The application of these laws depends on two different factors: first, the nature of the abuse and, secondly, whether it occurs within the family or outside it. These circumstances thus determine the competence of particular courts and will set in motion one of the following: the Penal Code and the jurisdiction of the Criminal Courts; the Domestic Violence Act No. 19.325; prosecution for domestic maltreatment, as contemplated in the Minors Act 16.618.[11]

The application of the Penal Code

The offences of which children may be victims can be classified according to the following groups: bodily or fatal injuries, abandonment, sexual abuse.

Bodily or fatal injury

The Penal Code sanctions malicious or negligent forms of injuries. Article 391 No. 1 of the Penal Code refers to severe injuries which can be very severe or less severe. Very severe bodily injury can cause the victim madness, impotence, work incapacity, physical disability of a limb or notable deformity. These injuries can be punished by long-term rigorous imprisonment in its maximum degree (five years, one day to 10 years).

The actual bodily harm or serious injuries are those that cause illness or work incapacity for over 30 days and can be punished by a medium-term rigorous imprisonment in its medium degree (541 days to three years).

Concerning Article 399, less severe injuries, not described above, are punished by a medium-term rigorous imprisonment in its minimum degree (61 to 541 days).

Fatal injury

Qualified or simple homicide   Homicide will be considered qualified in cases of extreme cruelty, aggravated brutality, treachery, wilfulness, poison or if it is a contract killing. The corresponding sanctions range from long-term rigorous imprisonment in its minimum degree (five years, one day to 10 years) to death.

Infanticide   This is the killing of a newborn baby during the first 48 hours after birth, where the act is committed by its father, mother or by an ascendant relative. The punishment for this offence is a long-term rigorous imprisonment in its minimum to medium degree (five years, one day to 15 years).

Abortion   The Penal Code in Article 342 makes a distinction in this offence for the purpose of determining the sanctions to be applied. If it is caused by an act of violence, the offender will be condemned to a long-term rigorous imprisonment in a minimum degree (five years, one day to 10 years). If it is caused without an act of violence and without the mother's consent, the corresponding sanction is a medium-term rigorous imprisonment in its maximum degree (three years, 1 day to five years). If the abortion is caused with the mother's consent it is punished with a medium-term rigorous imprisonment in its maximum degree (541 days to three years).

Article 343 establishes that whoever causes an abortion with violence, although there be no intention of doing so, if the pregnancy is notoriously visible, or the person who so acts knows the condition, he/she will be punished by a medium-term rigorous imprisonment in its minimum to medium degree (61 days to three years).

The woman who provokes her own abortion or consents to having it caused by another person will be punished with medium-term rigorous imprisonment in its maximum degree (three years, one day to five years). It will be considered an extenuating circumstance if she does it to hide her dishonour.

Finally, the physician who, abusing his functions, effects an abortion or cooperates in this act can have applied to him the penalties mentioned in Article 342, as aggravated.

Abandonment

Abandonment is distinguished from neglect. Neglect of a child is not a criminal offence. A number of types of abandonment may be distinguished. First, there is abandonment of a child under seven years of age at a place where he or she is likely to be found by others. Article 346 of the Penal Code punishes this conduct with medium-term rigorous imprisonment in its minimum degree (61 to 541 days). Secondly, if the abandonment is effected by the parents or guardians of a minor, and abandonment is effected less than 5km from a town or from an orphanage, the sentence prescribed is medium-term rigorous imprisonment to its maximum degree (three years, one day to five years). If, on the other hand, the abandonment brings about grievous bodily harm or the death of a minor, the penalty increases to a long-term rigorous imprisonment in its medium degree (five years, one day to 10 years).

Where a minor is exposed to the elements by being abandoned where no-one is likely to find him or her, then, if the child is 10 years old or younger, the punishment prescribed by Articles 349 and 350 of the Penal Code is that of long-term rigorous imprisonment in its minimum degree (five years, one day to 10 years).

Sexual abuse

This may be sub-divided into a number of categories.

Abduction Abduction is defined[12] as the removal of a woman from her home for dishonest purposes. Where the woman has a good reputation, the offence is more serious and the offender will be sentenced to a medium-term rigorous imprisonment in its minimum to maximum degree (three years, one day to 10 years). But where her reputation is not deemed to be good, the penalty is medium-term rigorous imprisonment in any of its degrees (61 days to five years). If the victim is a girl under 12 years of age, the punishment is that of a long-term rigorous imprisonment in any of its degrees (five years, one day to 20 years). Depriving a child of his/her freedom for sexual purposes is punished as an abduction, and the penalties are prescribed in Article 341 of the Penal Code.

Ravishment Sexual intercourse with a female induced by force or intimidation, or where the woman is mentally ill or learning disabled, is punished by long-term rigorous imprisonment in its medium to maximum degree (three years, one day to 15 years). If the victim is under 12 years old, even if the above-mentioned circumstances do not obtain, the penalty is increased to long-term rigorous imprisonment in its medium to maximum degree (10 years, one day to 20 years).

Rape Rape is defined as unlawful sexual intercourse induced by fraud with an under-age woman, previously a virgin. It is punished according to Article 363 with medium-term rigorous imprisonment in any of its degrees (61 days to five years). If the girl is under 12 years old, this offence will not be considered rape but ravishment.

Incest Incest is committed when a relative has sexual intercourse with a family member knowing that there exists a family relationship between them. The punishment applicable to this case is that of medium-term rigorous imprisonment in any of its degrees (61 days to five years).

Sodomy If the victim is under age 14, it is irrelevant to the legislator that the offence was carried out with or without the victim's consent. The penalty applicable will be that of a long-term rigorous imprisonment in its medium to maximum degree (10 years, one day to 20 years).

Dishonest abuse There is also a residual offence which consists of the carrying out of sexual acts that offend moral propriety, meaning by this any act which infringes the sexual norms of society. The penalty prescribed is a medium-term rigorous imprisonment in any of its degrees (61 days to five years).

Corruption of minors This is committed by one who, habitually, with abuse of authority or breach of trust contributes to the prostitution or corruption of minors to satisfy the sexual needs of others. The penalty is a long-term rigorous imprisonment in any of its degrees (five years, one day to 20 years) and a fine.

Domestic Violence Act 19.325

On 27 August 1994, Act 19.325 was published in the Official Gazette (*Diario Oficial de la República*), thus becoming the law of the republic. The Act covers the situations of abuse of children by parents, guardians or people who have them in their care. Article 1 of the law does not especially define child abuse. The concept thus needs to be abstracted from the norms generally. An act of violence is

> any maltreatment that puts in jeopardy the physical or mental health of a child who has, in respect to his offender, the quality of a descendant, an adoptive

child, pupil, relationship by collateral consanguinity, up to a fourth degree inclusive, or is under the care or dependency of any member of the family group living under the same roof. Whoever participates in any of these acts, even though he does not live with the family, is to be punished according to Article 4 of the same Law.

Within this concept are included slight injuries and threats with firearms. On the other hand, those matters which come within the Penal Code, where a severe or less severe injury, as well as any sexual assault, is involved must be excluded. The Penal Code does not apply where there are only minor injuries to children. Under the Domestic Violence Act, jurisdiction for such cases is conferred on the civil courts.

Such cases begin with a complaint, either oral or written, or an accusation that can be made by anyone who is in direct possession of the facts. Both Carabineros and Policía de Investigaciones are under the obligation of receiving such allegations, presenting them immediately to the court. But, once the judge receives the accusation or complaint, and assuming that it is an offence, he will declare himself incompetent because his court is without jurisdiction, and will send it immediately to the criminal court judge.

If this maltreatment is not considered as an offence, once the complaint or demand has been received, the parties concerned will be personally summoned to give evidence. The judge, without prejudice, after verifying the facts and if the gravity of the case so merits it, can order any precautionary measure designed to guarantee the physical and mental health of the victim. Among other measures, he can forbid, restrain or limit the presence of the offender at the victim's home; order a return home of the person who has been unjustly forced to leave; authorize the victim to leave his or her home and order the immediate delivery of his or her personal effects; forbid or limit the attendance of the offender at the place where the victim works unless they work in the same place; provisionally settle alimony obligations and provide an allowance for the personal care, upbringing and education of the children or minors who comprise the family nucleus. These measures will be essentially temporary and may not extend beyond 60 working days.

At any time the judge may, using his discretion, or on the request of the parties, postpone, limit, modify, substitute or render the measures without effect. Moreover, for very serious and urgent reasons, he can set an extension of time for a maximum period of 180 working days, in total. In this procedure, it is not necessary to be represented by a lawyer, unless the judge so determines it, or if the other side is so represented. The lawyer who is representing the minor will be his guardian *ad litem*.

By law, the judge has the obligation to request a report from the Civil Registry and Identification Service with the accused's records of convictions for maltreatment. These convictions are recorded in a special register that this service is required to keep at a national level. The judge may also order medical, psychological and social reports. A summons or call for conciliation is obligatory under Act 19.325 and it must be proposed by the judge, at the hearing.

The perpetrator may be punished in any of the following ways: (a) by being compelled to attend therapeutic programmes, (b) by fines, or (c) by imprisonment in any of its degrees (and this may be commuted to a community service order). The judge will control the compliance with the precautionary measures and sanctions, and will have the power to delegate these functions to institutions qualified to perform them.

Act 19.325 on domestic violence constitutes an outstanding improvement in dealing with the problem that acts of maltreatment exercise within the family group. But, as there is no specific set of rules addressed particularly to the case of minors, these rules present some defects in their application which become more visible when it is assumed that the victim of maltreatment is a minor and the said maltreatment is not shared with other adult members of the family. But attention may be drawn to the following problems.

1. Civil court judges have jurisdiction for hearing cases concerning minors. Although the purpose of the legislator was that of depenalizing maltreatment of minors as an offence of a criminal nature, it seems to have been forgotten that there is an organized judicature for minors in Chile, with the capability to take cognizance of matters relating to persons who have not reached their age of majority (which is 18 years in Chile).

   This anomaly has the consequence of producing a structure for the process and a set of rules that has been thought mainly for application in cases of maltreatment among adults and only tangentially applied to minors when they have become involved in acts of violence that mainly concern adults. The legislator should have made a distinction between minors and adults in the suffering of maltreatment. If the victim was a minor, the full knowledge of the facts and its judgment should be handed over to a judge of minors.

2. Although the law demands that the accuser be in full knowledge of the facts and thus excludes mere suspicions and intuitions, in practice the police often put through complaints without verifying the circumstances. On the other hand, many complaints formulated do not contain enough information to initiate the legal process. This has given rise to a procedure not foreseen by the law, that is a decision of the courts that consists in demanding the 'confirmation of the complaint' previous to

proceeding with the case. Evidently this practice slows down the process.[13]

3   The requirements imposed on the accuser to identify himself, describe the facts in detail in his accusation and to appear at a hearing, can discourage many people outside the family group, and make them desist from presenting charges of child abuse. Refraining from getting involved in the problem will, in fact, limit the coverage of the law because there will be no way of knowing the circumstances of maltreatment that are occurring and so these cases will continue to remain concealed.

4   If the maltreatment is suffered by a minor and the perpetrators are his/her parents, guardians or any other adult under whose care the child is, and these people to do not present themselves at the hearing to which they have been summoned, the judge, with the intention of clearing up the facts, after a second summons will have no other option but to order precautionary measures.

5   The obligatory call to conciliation appears pointless, if the victim is a minor and is not represented by a lawyer. This alternative way of ending the proceedings does not guarantee in any way the safety and integrity of the minor who would not, by himself, be in a position to reach a conciliation. Equally valueless is a conciliation reached by a father and a mother where one of them is responsible for the abuse of their child. It is not thought likely that either the violent individual's good intentions or his promises regarding modification of his future conduct, in the absence of therapeutic measures, will truly bring about a change for the better in him.

A study of the application of this law has shown that there is no control mechanism for the conciliation procedure, so it is impossible to evaluate its effectiveness.[14]

6   If abuse is carried out in the privacy of the family, and the child only receives slight injuries, the matter will never be known by the criminal court judge. Concern must focus on when an injury should be considered a slight injury. According to penal literature, the injuries can be classified as mutilations, severe injuries, less severe injuries and slight injuries. If an injury provokes illness or inability to work for a period of up to 30 days, the injury will be considered less severe or slight, depending on the condition of the person and the circumstances of the occurrence, and this will depend on the court's decision. Thus it follows that the judge who receives the accusation should first qualify the severity of the injury and, in accordance with this qualification, keep the matter under his jurisdiction, or refer it to the criminal court. But the medical criterion to qualify the injuries is not congruent with the

legal point of view and so, in practice, it is the police officer in charge at the emergency service where the minor is attended to who makes the decision as to the extent of the injuries, taking as a basis the medical report. It is this which decides if the report is to be sent to the ciminal court judge or to a civil magistrate.

7   The obligation to report the facts that constitute domestic violence is imposed only on the police. It is my belief that this should be extended to the medical profession, health workers, social workers, nurses, schoolteachers and so on – to people who, because of their professions and occupations, may have knowledge of acts that present the characteristics of maltreatment. The medical profession is under an obligation to report all cases where a felony or misdemeanour has been committed but, as we have seen, such matters have been excluded from Act 19.325.

8   As regards the penalties that a judge may apply to the perpetrator of an act of domestic violence, it may be noted that the application of one of these penalties excludes the others, when the possibility of linking the measures should have been allowed. In the majority of cases thus far, the tendency has been to order the offender to attend a therapy programme. Furthermore, civil court judges are reluctant to apply a penalty of imprisonment because they consider that the application of such a sanction is proper only to the penal process.

9   The register of the sentences handed down on domestic violence cases is very useful. It allows the judge to know of previous episodes of violence, and it will indicate to him when the abuser has not modified his conduct. It is also useful for evaluating the impact of the different measures adopted by the judge. However, the information the register contains is incomplete. It only covers those cases of violence which fall within Act 19.325.

10 Even though the civil court judges are not obliged to refer to the reports of other convictions given by a criminal judge for offences committed by an offender, it would be preferable for them to do so because of the undoubted gravity of these offences.

Domestic maltreatment

According to the present Article 62, Clause 2, any action or omission that results in the impairment of the physical or mental health of a child outside the family can constitute abuse. But excluded from this jurisdiction, and consequently not brought to the knowledge of the children's courts, are actions or omissions that have a sexual character, or such that cause severe or less severe injuries and threats with firearms. To come within Article

62(2) the victim must be a minor (under 18 years of age), and the perpetrator of the abuse must not belong to his family or live under the same roof as the child. In my opinion, a judge presented with such a case should initiate proceedings for misdemeanour.[15] Such proceedings are brief and oral, with the first hearing taking place within five days of the accusation or criminal complaint. At the hearing the relevant evidence must be presented.

This procedure allows for the appointment of a public prosecutor, but this is not commonly done in Chile, with the result that this function may be discharged by a police officer who either reported the act or presented the defendant, or by any other person whom the court designates. The evidence must be carefully considered by the judge, who should come to a conclusion as soon as the hearings are over or by the following first working day. He can make one or all of the following orders.

1. That the perpetrator attend a therapeutic programme or a family guidance programme under the control of an institution that the judge may deem suitable for such a purpose, such as the National Service for Women, National Service for Minors, Diagnostic Centres pertaining to the Ministry of Education, or Family Mental Health Community Centres. The chosen institution is, from time to time, to send reports regarding compliance with the rulings of the court.
2. That he carry out certain determined work to the benefit of the community, of the municipality or in municipal companies which exist in the municipality corresponding to the home of the offender. This is ordered if the offender requests it, and the activities assigned to him will be similar to those he performs in his usual occupation or trade. This work will not interfere with his daily activities.
3. That he be fined, to the benefit of the municipality, the equivalent of one to 10 days' wages earned by the offender. The orders in this article apply also when the persons indicated in Clause 1 abandon a minor or corrupt him.

A number of comments are called for. First, the possibility of imprisonment does not exist. The sanctions envisaged differ from those in domestic violence. This distinction cannot be justified and this law's sanctions should be assimilated to those for domestic violence. Secondly, the concept of Non-Domestic Violence in Article 62 is specific to the situation under study, and more limited than that in the Domestic Violence Law. Finally, the sanction of requiring attendance by the perpetrator at a family guidance programme seems to have little value in the case of the violence being discussed here, since the person convicted is not part of the family nucleus.

CONCLUSION

After analysing and criticizing the rules envisaged by the Chilean legislation on maltreatment of minors, a number of conclusions may be made. First, as a general rule, the maltreatment of minors is not penalized as a criminal act if the victim sustains slight injury. It seems that the legislator has preferred to use other sanctioning measures which do not deprive the perpetrator of his freedom, a policy that could be dangerous because it could possibly bring with it a high degree of impunity and abuse of power. Where abuse is repeated, the sentence should bring about other consequences for the violent individual in regard to his own family relationships, as well as to his civil rights. For example, loss of parental authority, visiting privileges and incompetence to act as a tutor, guardian or teacher could be contemplated as sanctions for a person who has not reformed his conduct after a previous sentence.

Secondly, it is necessary to intensify public campaigns and the education of citizens to create consciousness of how harmful it is for a minor to suffer maltreatment.

Thirdly, it needs to be established that it is a binding obligation on physicians, nurses, social workers, schoolteachers and so on, to report acts of violence against children, regardless of the extent of the injuries suffered by the victim.

Finally, although parental autonomy is important, it needs to be established that child-rearing is not purely a private affair. Children have rights too and, when authority is abused, there should be ways of bringing that abuse to an end.

NOTES

1. Not always coincident with the special laws currently established regarding maltreatment are the definitions used by some private organizations, by authors specializing in the subject and by other public health entities. Another difficulty arises among the regulating bodies with reference to maltreatment of minors. Some authors generally emphasize child abuse, which is not synonymous with the above, but it is included in it.
2. Instituto Libertad y Desarrollo, No. 296, 19 July 1996.
3. Florenzano et al., *Instituto Libertad y Desarrollo Gazette*, No. 26, 19 July 1996.
4. Article 3° h of Act 19. 325.
5. No 16.618, 3 February 1967.
6. Article 27, no. 7.
7. See Article 29.
8. Home for Minors.
9. Article 36, final clause.

10 Act 16.618.
11 Article 62.
12 See Article 358.
13 Data reported by SERNAM (*Servicio Nacional de la Mujer*) corresponding to the Woman's Institute Final Report on a Follow-Up Study of the Domestic Violence Law, 1995.
14 See note 13.
15 There are some Chilean authors who think the procedure to follow is a civil summary proceeding. I disagree with this interpretation, as the Law for Minors, Article 63 establishes a special rule that has precedence over the general provisions.

5 Abused and Neglected Children in the Republic of Croatia

Dijana Jakovac-Lozic

INTRODUCTION

'A happy childhood is one of the best gifts that parents have it in their power to bestow,' said English authoress Mary Cholmondeley.[1] It is clear that this statement cannot be questioned.[2] It is hard to say exactly how many children actually enjoy the benefits of 'a happy childhood'.

Childhood traumas in the second half of the twentieth century (according to Ellen Key's 1900 book 'Century of the Child')[3] in which, on one hand, the child is the centre of love and all other permanent and positive relationships and, on the other hand, the centre of all types of abuse and neglect and all other forms of inhumanity, occur every day, not only in the streets and community, but most often within the family circle, since most children live in a familial environment. Potentially, that family has a double role: as protector or as high-risk factor for the child's psychosocial development.

Child abuse and neglect are exceptionally important subjects: first, because they concern the most vulnerable section of humanity, children, who are exposed to many types of abuse and neglect from adults and, second, because this group is not yet aware of its rights and, accordingly, the right to defend and protect these rights.

It can justifiably be said that all the frightening events of World War II forced the international community to introduce a document to protect all human rights and to promote the idea of protecting the rights of children as *sui generis* rights. Not until the twentieth century, the children's century, when there was sufficient interest in children and their rights, were the right questions asked: what are the factors which hindered the recognition of children's rights for so many generations, and what were the events and charges which demonstrated these findings? Understandably, it was asked why, historically, man was ready to offer protection to and legalize the rights of other living creatures[4] before children who, after all, are the future.

Answers to these questions can probably be found in the fight against male domination and the negative influence of misused rights. The answers might be found in the historical process of differentiation/integration of the family, and the increasing balance between generations, despite the initial dependence of small children. The process of individualization means that, increasingly, every family member has a legitimate equal right as a party particularly concerned with accomplishment of his own interests, and that the web of community institutions will lend their support or, at least, not actively oppose him in his endeavours. Not to be forgotten is the free spirit of equal rights in the twentieth century which is the future of humanity. The result, therefore, is a new conception of the special position and treatment of children.[5]

REVIEW OF INTERNATIONAL AND REGIONAL DOCUMENTS PROTECTING THE RIGHTS OF CHILDREN WHICH CROATIA HAS ACCEPTED

The Republic of Croatia has accepted a number of international and regional documents protecting the rights of children.[6] More accurately, ex-Yugoslavia, of which Croatia was a part, ratified those documents. In 1991, Croatia declared independence from the federation and was recognized as a sovereign and independent country. Those arguments which do not contradict the Croatian Constitution[7] were automatically applied to Croatia by the right of succession,[8] in accordance with the rules of international law on succession.

Specifically, Croatia is committed to the Universal Declaration of Human Rights (1948)[9] where children's rights are specifically defended in Articles 25 and 26, and The Declaration of Children's Rights (1959) in which children were, for the first time, afforded the rights *sui generis* and, as such, are protected. Furthermore, Croatia has ratified the Convention of Children's Rights of the Republic of Croatia (1989)[10] which, in the context of this chapter dealing with abuse and neglect of children, is significant for the provisions in Articles 19 and 20.

The proposal has been put before Croatia to sign The International Declaration for the Survival, Protection and Development of Children,[11] which represents a basic global appeal for securing a better future for children and which focuses on the dangers of raising children (war, violence, poverty, hunger, homelessness, illness and so on). The international documents in which one part protects the rights of children, and by which Croatia is bound, include The International Pact of Citizens and Political Rights (1966) which the former Yugoslavia ratified,[12] and which is now applicable to Croatia. Of special interest in the context of this chapter is the provision in Article 24. Also the International Act of Economic, Social and Cultural Rights[13] is significant for Articles 10 and 12.

Also important for Croatia are the following regional documents (multilateral agreements): The European Convention on Adoption of Children (1967), the European Convention on the Rightful Status of Children Born out of Wedlock (1975) and the European Convention on Recognition and Enforcement of Decisions Concerning Custody of Children and Restoration of Custody of Children (1980).[14] A suggestion is also before the Croatian legislature to sign the European Convention on the Exercise of Children's Rights which was submitted for ratification in January 1996. This Convention specifically outlines children's rights in court cases (irrespective of whether the court or other legal authorities are the decision-making organs).

The importance of those international agreements in Croatia's legal system is evident in Article 134 of the Croatian Constitution: 'international agreements which were introduced and ratified in accordance with the Constitution, and published, become a part of the internal legal system of the Republic and by rights supersede other existing laws. They can only be changed or repealed in the same way they were established or by agreement with the general rules of international law.'

ABUSED AND NEGLECTED CHILDREN IN CROATIAN LEGAL THEORY AND PRACTICE

Child abuse and neglect as a part of family violence

Family violence[15] is one part of the total violence in society. The word 'abuse' is generally understood as a misuse of power in relationships which are not based on equal terms. Victims of family violence are most likely to be children, women and older family members; violence is either physical, sexual or mental and emotional abuse. Each type of abuse may be either 'active' or 'passive'.

Research by the Attorney General of the Republic of Croatia found that 'only' 3 per cent of young children and 10 per cent of adolescent are victims of violence.[16] However, in cases of sexual abuse, 30 per cent are adolescents. This family violence mainly occurs in larger urban areas. It is assumed that rural areas are more conservative and isolated and, therefore, there is more pressure to cover up such violence. This is not difficult since the prevailing attitude is that they are 'only' children – children who cannot adequately protect themselves and who have no idea that they have legal recourse against physical abuse, verbal aggression and violence in general from their closest family members. It is supposed that the number of actual cases of child violence which remain unreported is quite high.

In the last few years, 2053 children in the Republic of Croatia have been victims of family, physical and sexual violence: 1140 persons have been victims of sexual violence only, out of which number 583 have been minors, some 270 children being even below age 14. In as many as 85 per cent of cases, sexual violence has been made on children by their own parents, relatives, family friends or those whom children knew very well and trusted. The most harmful and most serious consequence of such violence is the fact that it mostly remains unknown; the intimate and closed family circle usually hinders an investigation, and brutal violence becomes an illusion, an accident and thus an affliction.[17]

The state trusts parents (adoptive parents or guardians) to be responsible (to care) for their children and imposes standards to limit the parent's abuse and neglect of children. However, outside the realm of the parent's responsibilities, there is a wide range of misconduct, large and small failures, 'moderate beatings', cursing, loneliness and so on.

Legal intervention in the relations between parents and children is, above all, very restrained, cautious and, most often, very slow. When intervention does occur, parents very often blame society in general for neglect, bad housing and living conditions, unemployment, post-war trauma syndrome, loss of partner in the war, displaced or refugee status, difficulty in adapting to new circumstances and conditions and so on.

The truth is that it is impossible to attribute the incidence of child violence in the family only to failure of an individual offender, in this case the parent or guardian. Abuse can always be explained within the context of specific social, economic, cultural, ethical and other factors. If to that is added some mental predisposition by the offender, and sometimes by the victimized children (for example in hard-to-educate children), there is abuse and neglect of those who are weaker and 'handy'; that is, children. It makes no difference how much avoidable suffering is observed in post-war Croatia; there are still increasing chances of domestic violence, primarily directed towards the children. There can be no excuse for violence or the offender.

Characteristics of two crimes: abusing and neglecting minors

The Croatian Penal Code[18] includes three criminal laws which protect minors from three types of standard criminal offences: (a) unlawful acts committed against minor members of the family, (b) unlawful acts committed at the expense of personal dignity and morals of minors, and (c) other unlawful acts committed at the expense of minors. The abuse and neglect of minors is included in (a) and standardized by the provisions in Article 101 of the Croatian Penal Code.

Of all criminal offences committed against minors and adolescents, abuse and neglect are the gravest and second most common criminal offences committed against children and youth in Croatia.[19] They comprise 18 per cent of all criminal offences against minors and every second offender is given an unconditional prison sentence.[20]

In determining characteristics of the abuse and neglect of children, Croatia's judicial law and legislature differ on three aspects: (a) neglecting to care for minors, (b) neglecting to bring up minors properly, and (c) abuse. 'Neglecting to care for minors' includes not providing the basic needs such as food, care, love, good health, clothing and housing. Any lapse in parental responsibilities may be equally caused by not acting or acting.

'Neglecting to bring up minors properly' means failing to provide the basic essential guidance necessary for a child's upbringing or for preventing deviant behaviour; the constant absence of any action which may encourage or promote the minor's development; or performance and development of activities which may directly or indirectly endanger the upbringing of a minor, and which may result in educational abandonment, asocial behaviour or criminal behaviour.

'Abuse' is an intentional use of a degree of physical or psychological suffering and pain. When it comes to judging specific instances, it depends on the circumstances. Therefore infrequent slight physical harm is not considered abuse if it is groundlessly delivered and if the perpetrator had previously conducted himself in a manner aiming to educate a minor properly. Intensity of physical discomfort is properly evaluated by taking the age and physical development of the minor into consideration. Psychological harm and shock are more often represented in the form of abuse than is usually thought and, consequently, their effects on the development of minors are often more serious and of longer duration than with physical injury. For instance, terror and everyday psychological shock caused by violent outbursts of drunken parents come under the heading of abuse which often causes illness, neurosis, stuttering and bed-wetting, and which, as a rule, has detrimental effects on the upbringing of children, who often run away from home, exhibit rowdy or disorderly behaviour, talk in a vulgar fashion and, in every way, are disturbed, as indicated by their conduct.

Frequently, insulting and humiliating minors is also regarded as psychological abuse. As a rule, it is a case of being offensive and humiliating, not in the heat of the moment, but rather by expressing extreme intolerance towards minors.[21] Where pedagogical or disciplinary measures are undertaken in child-rearing these will not usually be considered as abuse. It is the misuse of parental rights, imposing impossible, unreasonable, unnecessary demands along with inflicting psychological and physical harm.

Besides physical and psychological suffering, abuse, unfortunately, includes one more component – sexual abuse of children. Croatian law unequivocally protects the sexual integrity of persons under 14 years of age, that is minors. In the case of minors between the ages of 14 and 18, a criminal offence is committed only if the minor was sexually abused under the circumstances which are subject to punishment and by an adult (rape, coercion, exploitation, harassment and so on). The law against having intercourse or committing unnatural sex acts with a minor (Croatian Penal Code, Articles 87 and 88) has been broadened to include aggravating circumstances under which obscene acts are qualified as a crime (Article 89). Item 2 of this Article deals with lesbian acts with a minor which are also criminal offences. The broadening of laws protecting children has brought about the creation of new criminal categories relating to immoral and lascivious behaviour with children (Article 90), as well as with unconsenting adolescents (Article 91).

These are the terms of *de lege lata* in the Croatian Penal Code. It must be mentioned that, in May 1996, this proposal to the Croatian Penal Code was put before the legislature. At the time of writing this chapter, major changes to the Croatian Penal Code were not anticipated, but the existing law does not allow for changes that would impose fines. For example, for harsh (that is more serious and constant) neglect in caring for and raising the minor, the parents or guardians who jeopardize the health and happiness of that minor can be sentenced to a term of between three months to three years in jail (Croatian Penal Code, Article 101, Item 1). It has been proposed that the law be amended to read: 'a fine or jail sentence up to three years' (Proposal of Croatian Penal Code, Article 213, Item 1). Such a change has, in fact, been suggested for the majority of all penalties for the maltreatment of minors. Also prohibited is the exploitation of minors for pornographic purposes (Proposal of Croatian Penal Code, Article 196) and acquainting minors with pornography (Proposal of Croatian Penal Code, Article 197). These are new additions to the Penal Code.

The abuser and the victim

The offender in the case of adolescent abuse and adolescent neglect is always a parent, whether married or not, including a stepfather or stepmother, adoptive parents, or guardian or other person responsible for supporting and caring for the adolescent. The 'other person' means a child counsellor or anyone else to whom the adolescent is entrusted for custody and care.

As regards the perpetrator, it is necessary to provide evidence of premeditation to have the offence sanctioned by law. This means that the abuser has to be aware that his attitude towards, and the manner in which he treats, the adolescent constitute a grave neglect of his responsibilities regarding proper custody and care for the adolescent, or just the adolescent abuse. Probable reasons for the child's parent or guardian being abusive or neglecting include the following: (a) animosity of either spouse/partner to the other; (b) animosity towards the child (for example, the child was unwanted from the very beginning, irrespective of his behaviour; (c) the child may be a 'nuisance' to his parents who are only concerned with unscrupulous and selfish individual satisfaction. A tribunal proceeding currently under way in the County Court, Split, has revealed that a mother and stepfather beat their 18-month-old baby to death because they could not watch a TV programme; their excuse was that they had been disturbed by the baby's crying while they watched TV; (d) in certain cases, there is absence of any form of animosity but just senseless (wrong) ideas about child raising and exaggerated expectations (for example, there are many cases of severe child abuse for minor misdeeds, intended to correct the behaviour: severe beating, extinguishing cigarettes on the child's head or genitals, and so on); (e) such misconduct was once attributed to mental and other abnormalities of the offenders (sadistic, sex-abusive individuals who tried to explain their misdeeds as 'educative methods'); and (f) a high proportion of child abuse and, particularly, child neglect cases primarily suggest the existence of unfavourable social conditions which may influence the incidence of other forms of delinquency (alcoholism, prostitution, avoiding work, and so on).

A study released by the Social Welfare Study Centre, Zagreb University School of Law, aimed to show the profile of an abuser[22] based on a sample comprising two groups: Group 1 included parents from the general population in Croatia whose children were elementary school pupils (grades 1–6) and Group 2 was made up of parents whose children were on file in the Croatia-based Social Welfare Centre's list because of troubled psychophysical development in the family, particularly child abuse and child neglect. On the basis of data compiled from the ranking list of child abuse and child neglect, the parents were classified into groups of 'abusers' and 'neglectors'. The data were obtained from 11 major Croatian communities in 1994.

Results of the research were as follows. According to the figures, mothers are more often abusers and neglecters of their children than fathers. They make up more than two-thirds of the group of abusers and neglecters and more than three-quarters of the group of parents from the general population. There is also statistically significant evidence that parents from the group of abusers and neglecters were on an average older than parents from the group from the general population. A statistically significant difference also appeared in respect to their marital status: 90 per cent of parents from Group 1 and 56 per cent from Group 2 were married; others were either divorced, widowed, single parents or cohabiting. It is interesting that there were more stepmothers and stepfathers in Group 2 than in Group 1.

The educational background was higher in the group of parents from the general population. The average mother and father from this group was at least a high-school graduate. The average mother in families registered for child abuse and child neglect had completed elementary school, and the father trade school. The employment status was also significantly different. Half the mothers from Group 2 and a quarter of those from Group 1 had no jobs. The proportion was similar for fathers.

With regard to stress-related conditions, particularly associated with war in the region, it is evident that displaced and refugee families and those having a husband or son participating in the war were more common in the group from the general population. There was also a significant difference in the average income level per household, which was lower in Group 2.

Among the parents from Group 1, there were twice as many (58 per cent) who had their own apartment. While families in Group 1 had, on an average, one- or two-room apartments, those from Group 2 lived in two- or three-room apartments. However, the apartments occupied by families from Group 2 were in greater disrepair (poor maintenance, broken furniture, and so on).

Family dysfunction associated with social pathology was more significant in Group 2, despite the fact that problems of alcoholism, prostitution and delinquency were also reported in Group 1. Parents' chronic diseases and disabilities were found in a relatively small proportion in the group of parents from the general population (2 per cent, 5 per cent); in Group 2, mothers accounted for 20 per cent and fathers 10 per cent.

Average verbal aggression between parents in the year of the study was 'a common occurrence but less than once a month' in Group 2 and 'once a year' in Group 1. Average physical aggression among parents from Group 2 occurred 'twice or three times a year', while in Group 1 it 'never' occurred. Obviously, the occurrence of physical aggression among parents was higher in the group of abusers and neglecters. However, there was no difference between the groups as to physical abuse of children reported by the parents themselves. The average child physical abuse in the course of that year was reported as 'twice or three times a year' in Group 2, which was frequently identical in Group 1. However, this statistic is tenative because the parents themselves responded to the questions.

The abusive/neglecting families also exhibited a higher level of social isolation (rare or no visits by friends, neighbours and so on).

Even though this group analysis of two groups of parents, of which one involved abusive and neglective parents and the other parents from the general population, was based on discriminative variables, it was possible to approximate an offender's profile. The victim is always an adolescent, an 'object' of institutional care, with the family and law wanting to protect that adolescent fully. Such protection may also apply to a person under extended parental care (who is of legal age and who, owing to physical and/or mental problems, are not capable of living independently). These problems are dealt with, not only in the Penal Code, but also in the Law on Marriage and Family Relations (hereinafter LMFR)[23] (Article 91).

From the results of the research by the Study Centre,[24] it may be concluded that, in regard to the average number of minors, abusive/neglectful families (from Group 2) appear not to be significantly different from the general population parents (Group 1). In regard to child sex abuse, males were more often abused and neglected than females, which was also confirmed in some earlier research.[25]

Child abuse and child neglect are most often discovered at the six to 14 age levels, when children attend school. In pre-school children, it is more difficult to determine consequences of abuse because they are mainly confined to the home, with the exception of cases where gravely injured children were brought to hospitals for medical treatment.

While the groups did not exhibit significant differences in the number of chronically ill and disabled children, statistically significant differences appeared at school achievement level: the average achievement in abusive/neglective families was good or fair, whereas in cases of children from the general population it was excellent or very good.

The consequences of child abuse and child neglect are as follows: such children, more often than their peers (persons of the same age), exhibit behaviour problems and socialize with difficulty; they are more often involved in criminal offences; they are aggressive and self-destructive, anxious and insecure; their morality is deviant; and relations with peers are very bad. At the national level, about 25 per cent appear to have committed some criminal offence, 39 per cent avoid work, 57 per cent exhibit problem behaviour at school, 34 per cent leave home, 20 per cent are alcoholics and 11 per cent account for other forms of socially irresponsible behaviour.

Considering the town of Split, the second largest city in Croatia, it is evident that, of 280 children with behaviour problems who were registered in 1996 and sanctioned by a variety of measures, there are only nine who have not committed any criminal offence so far. However, out of 329 children with behaviour problems who were part of the social-welfare programme, either as old wards or newcomers, 301 experienced addiction-related problems (34 were addicted to alcohol, 216 were light drug addicts and 51 had been heavy drug users since early childhood).[26] All of them are angry and unhappy young people and it is hard to say that anyone can help them at all. It is too late to teach them true family values which they were deprived of when they needed them the most. They lack parental care and love and help from the community.

Also, the abused and neglected children suffer from post-traumatic stress disorders and the symptoms of this specific stress condition (thoughts which awaken memories, nightmares, outbursts of anger, sleeping difficulties, loss of concentration and so on). These symptoms are particularly common in children abused sexually inside or outside the family.

Long-lasting consequences of violence in childhood are numerous. It is well known, for example, that 80 per cent of sufferers from mental disorders have been abused or suffered similar traumatic experiences in childhood. Adults who witnessed violence between parents or were the victims of violence during childhood are more likely to abuse their spouse and/or children.[27]

The purpose of this chapter is not to describe the overall range of consequences but to focus upon only the basic harm arising from this problem. Accordingly, it is worth mentioning the Croatian Penal Code which defines the instances when abuse and neglect of an adolescent is qualified as a criminal act (Article 101, Item 3). The consequences may be (a) grave injury to a child's mental and/or physical health (in this regard, it is necessary to determine that gross negligence was committed: otherwise, the act is qualified as grave physical injury) (Article 41, in conjunction with Article 101, Items 1 and 2); (b) criminal activity; (c) prostitution; and (d) other forms of socially irresponsible behaviour. It is always essential to determine the cause–effect relationship in child abuse/neglect and its consequences. Abuse and neglect of minors are not necessarily the exclusive cause of their deviant behaviour. They are usually only a common concomitant of antisocial behaviour.[28]

As long as 300 years ago, John Milton said, 'Child shows the man, as morning shows the day.'[29] As a rule, no-one can expect an abused or neglected child to become a loving, caring spouse and/or parent. The victims carry forever their memories of maltreatment, first by their family, then by society itself. They are inevitably the hallmark of their future. Each exception to this rule should make us very happy.

Family law provisions relating to child abuse and neglect within the family circle

Parental right is established at the moment of birth. Its meaning is defined in the Constitution of the Republic of Croatia, which says: 'It is the duty of parents to raise, support and educate children and they are given the right and freedom to make their own decisions how to care for the children. The parents are responsible for recognizing the children's rights for their full development in harmony with their personality' (Article 63).

Parents are charged by society with the responsibility of properly bringing up their children. With these duties, the parents are also given rights, which, however, may be limited or taken away in cases when certain requirements prescribed by law are not met. The Law on Marriage and Family Relations (LMFR) of the Republic of Croatia clearly defines the rights of parents and their limitations, and when these parental rights can be taken away in order to protect the children's rights.[30]

One of the measures enforcing the limitation of parents' rights is stripping the parent of custody and the bringing up of the child (Article 88) which can be ordered on the presentation of sufficient evidence of the following: (a) a greater degree of neglect in the child's upbringing, (b) neglect in the child's education, or (c) jeopardizing proper upbringing. The actual meaning of the above has been already discussed.[31] The body authorized to initiate this procedure is the Centre for Social Services. By enforcement of Article 88 of the LMFR, the parents' right to retain custody of their child is revoked. Also, in accordance with this provision of Article 88, the Centre for Social Services is charged with the responsibility of deciding where the child will be placed for care. This clause has no effect on other parental rights and responsibilities, so the parents' duties remain to support, represent and manage the child's property. If there is no apparent danger to the child, the parents to whom the social welfare agencies denied custody and care for the child may also visit and communicate with the child.

Though not explicitly regulated, the parents may claim that their right to custody should be restored provided that sufficient evidence is produced that they are able and ready to take over the responsibility for properly rearing the child. If they are successful, the Centre is charged with the responsibility of making frequent home visits in the beginning in order to ensure that parents are fulfilling their responsibilities in respect to the proper care and nurturing of the child, and to prevent recurrence of irresponsible parental behaviour.[32]

Deprivation of parental rights represents the most severe sanction of the family law with the aim of protecting the child's well-being and interests.

This sanction may be ordered only by a court decision made in an extrajudicial procedure and in the manner prescribed by law (LMFR, Article 76) and for the following reasons: (a) misuse of parental rights (abuse, cruelty, vulgarity); or (b) gross neglect of parental responsibilities (indifference, disregard for the child's basic needs, abandonment and so on).

In addition to prosecuting parents for child abuse, cruelty, abandonment and so on, there is an urgent need to protect the children from irresponsible parents with a variety of measures established under the family law. The right to initiate a child's removal from the family is given to the other parent, if he or she has a parental right, the social welfare agency or the public prosecutor. This mandate of the Attorney-General is of great assistance since it attempts to balance the criminal proceedings against parents with the family law child-protective measures.

The social welfare agencies are given not only the right, but also the duty, of initiating the legal procedure for deprivation of parental rights when certain requirements for such actions are applicable. Besides, if social workers discover that the child is at risk because of misuse of parental rights or harsh neglect of any parental responsibilities, they are duty bound to urgently undertake all steps available in order to protect the child (LMFR, Article 94). The purpose of this clause is to give authorities a preventive measure aimed at protecting the child's interests by giving serious consideration to counselling of parents so as to prevent more harm and/or dysfunction (for example, if the court orders the removal of one child because of parental abuse, and if another child is left with the parents without any type of control).[33]

By virtue of the court decision, the parents are deprived of their parental right for an indefinite time. However, this decision cannot be enforced if, meanwhile, the child comes of full legal age, or marries and is deemed fit to work before reaching full legal age. In these instances the parents' right is terminated.[34] Those parents who are stripped of custody are also deprived of all incidents contained in this right. They remain responsible only for contributing to the child's support.[35] If both parents are deprived of this right, or it applies only to one parent and the other is unknown, depriving of capacity (to perform a legal act), the child is treated as a minor without parental support and, thus, falls under the welfare system (LMFR, Article 199).

There is a possibility for the parents to regain their parental right, of course, in cases where the reasons for ordering this limitation do not exist any longer (for example, when an alcohol-addicted parent complies with court-ordered treatment, or finds a job and pursues his duties in an acceptable manner). Although the LMFR does not explicitly regulate who has the right to initiate restoration of the parental right, it is assumed that it is any person or authority who was authorized to initiate deprivation of parental rights. This also includes the parent who was deprived of this right. But it is not sufficient that he is willing to reassume responsibility for the child; he should also give evidence of compliance with the prescribed requirements.

According to Croatian legislation, this is a *de lege lata* condition. However, a new draft of the LMFR was proposed on 29 November 1996. In contrast to the existing law, which is focused on the protection of parental rights, the new proposal for the protection of the child's legal interests and well-being is instead given priority, with the new draft advocating the child's rights and child welfare (see Articles 85–118 of the draft). Responsibilities in a broader social environment are raised to a higher level on behalf of children's rights. For the first time in legislation, it is clearly defined that the responsibility of each individual is to report the violation of children's rights to competent authorities, particularly for all forms of physical and mental violence or maltreatment, neglect and indifference, abuse or exploitation; child sex abuse is explicitly included (see Article 108 of the draft). Clearly established in the draft are standards to regulate the meaning of misuse of parental rights and duties, and neglect of parental rights and duties (see Article 114). Child sex abuse is defined overtly, which leads to one of three optional qualifications of a punishable act for misuse of parental rights and responsibilities (see Article 114). According to the draft, limitation, as well as termination, of parental rights is further proposed, provided that certain requirements are met. Also the family, primarily the parents, are expressly charged with responsibilities for protecting their children against any form of abuse, maltreatment or humiliation by others (Article 91).

It is evident that the proposed draft of the new family law in Croatia offers many good and more favourable solutions on behalf of children than are provided by the existing law. It also reflects a growing trend in Croatian legislation towards compliance with various international documents dealing with children's rights.

Review of child abuse and maltreatment of children in general outside the family circle

Although this chapter is focused on child abuse and neglect inside the family, where these problems most frequently occur, also worth mentioning are cases where children are victimized outside the family circle.

The truth is that, according to information received by the Centre for Social Services, Department of Work and Child Welfare Department, many child abuse cases outside the family remain unreported. Meanwhile, reporting of abuse in society has recently increased dramatically in the daily news and professional publications. Schools more often appear to be scenes of the releasing of teachers' frustrations. It is hard to say whether the reasons for such misconduct lie in the difficult economic and social status of teachers in Croatia or whether it is post-war trauma which might have affected some teachers more than others. Other reasons might be found in their psychological, cultural or ethical profile; or it may simply be that this problem has started to be discussed openly, which was not the case in the past.

One of the most alarming cases, which was recently reported and alerted the people in Croatia to the problem, concerned a pupil from one of the elementary schools in Zagreb who was reported to have been seriously injured by his schoolteacher. The pupil was slapped so hard by the teacher that he suffered permanent hearing damage, besides a brain convulsion. There is also the case of a physical education teacher who was sent to court for raping a schoolgirl and repeatedly molesting her colleagues. Psychological torture is more difficult to identify and far more difficult to prove, both in and outside the family. Any form of physical abuse has an impact on a victim's psychological well-being.

Schoolteachers usually find justification for the use of corporal punishment by saying: 'The others used to do the same to me', or 'Yes, I did it, and that is the "only" reasonable method of discipline which is allowed.'[36] Also worth mentioning is a recently reported case of a physician, a child's surgeon, who was charged with the repeated rape and molestation of two young female patients. It is hard to evaluate the existing situation in nurseries, kindergartens and children's homes and to give firm conclusions on the occurrence of similar incidences. In the preceding cases it was easy to gather sufficient evidence on child abuse because they involved schoolteachers and physicians, who are for the most part caretakers of older children who know how to help themselves.

It is interesting to note that half of the cases of abuse of children have been reported by social workers and rather less by citizens. Far fewer are reported by police, while physicians, nursery teachers and schoolteachers almost never intervene. Questions are raised as to whether the perpetrators of abuse are extremely cautious or child caretakers in kindergartens, schools and hospitals are blind in general.

The importance of early detection, reporting and prevention of child abuse and neglect

In principle, children who are exposed to abuse and inhumane behaviour are not able to take advantage of child protective services either because they are too young to be aware of their rights or, in the case of older children, because they are afraid of reporting an adult on whom they are dependent.

Therefore the conviction of most prosecutors that only a small number of cases of suspected child abuse and neglect are reported is quite justified.

For this reason, priority for an effective reduction of the occurrence of child abuse in Croatia will be given to the following:

- serious treatment and evaluation of child abuse and neglect which represent violation of basic human rights and the rights of children who are most vulnerable in the family;
- redirection towards prevention of child abuse and neglect, instead of efforts to eliminate, treat medically or prosecute after the event. Generally, repression will be applied as the last option;
- clear definition at the state level of the role of primary, secondary and tertiary protection services against child abuse and neglect;
- close cooperation and interaction between governmental and non-governmental officials and child welfare workers at all levels, from state departments to local services;
- interdisciplinary cooperation at all levels of prevention and treatment.

This requires clarification of the meaning of primary, secondary and tertiary protection.[37] *Primary prevention* refers to those approaches that are applied to a population in general as well as to professionals in order to develop awareness of all possible forms of child abuse and neglect and to inform and educate the public on the range of services available in the local community and broader social environment. Other important child abuse educational options are TV and radio programmes, written materials, lectures and so on. Primary prevention concerns efforts directed at telling the public to whom, where and how to report child abuse and neglect. There still remains a lot to do in order to promote various child-caretaking homes, that is, foster homes which, besides playing a humane role, are three times more cost-advantageous and effective form of child custody than institutional child care. There are currently 14 such institutional homes, providing services for 1200 children. There are many other possibilities for the implementation of various educational programmes, through schools and the mass media, which greatly assist in the struggle against numerous prejudices such as 'the parents are masters of their children'. Focused activities are the best method to teach people about their rights and all types of protection in order to prevent harmful outcomes. The introduction of these programmes can help develop responsible parenting.

Secondary prevention refers to the earliest possible detection of risks for a particular condition of abuse and neglect and timely intervention in order to protect the children. This form of prevention includes methods of teaching the public how to report on all types of abuse and neglect to the court, social services, health professionals and schoolteachers. It also helps the public to be aware of the importance of timely reporting abuse inside and outside the family. In addition, it ensures the appropriate training of professionals involved in such activities and encourages targeted high-risk families to refer their problems to child protection officials locally and in the broader community.

Tertiary protection refers to identification of the condition. It includes psychosocial and rehabilitation treatments for victimized children as well as those intended for parents aimed at preventing the recurrence of violence (investigations have showed that 65–70 per cent of violent parents may become responsible parents after appropriate treatment). These interventions should be understood as attempts to be more supportive of the victimized children and to seek medical treatment instead of a repressive approach to the perpetrators of abuse, with an introduction of compulsory psychosocial programmes for abusive and neglecting parents. All interfamily relations should be carefully assessed. For example, an intervention proposing removal of the child from the family should be preceded by a well-grounded and clearly defined plan of action and a detailed assessment of the child's family circumstances and their effects on abusing the child. This protection also assumes evaluation of the effectiveness of the preventive strategies applied by social workers and enforced by law on dysfunctional families, as well as regulation of the processes ordering investigation and prosecution in the manner which is least painful for the victimized child.

CONCLUSION

The legislature of the Republic of Croatia is in final discussions about adopting new criminal laws and also laws covering family relationships. These proposed laws concern protecting the legal interests and welfare of children. They are designed to inspire hope and strengthen beliefs in a better and brighter future for Croatia's children. The legislature has exerted maximum effort to avoid the shortcomings in the current laws and, therefore, the inadequate protection of abused and neglected children in practice in Croatia. It is believed that the enforcement of these laws will intensify all possible forms of preventive protection of children and emphasize treatment instead of punishment of the abusers and neglecters, although this will not mean that the law will lose its effect. It is hoped that it will never again happen that more than 50 per cent of all cases of abuse and neglect go unreported, mainly because of the silence of neighbours, teachers, guidance counsellors and school physicians, a situation quite unthinkable in Europe.

In the proposals of this new law, children's rights have been sufficiently recognized and accepted, so that it is to be expected that Croatia may adopt practical statutes for protecting these rights, using Sweden and other Scandinavian countries as models and introducing an Ombudsman.

Croatia recently established the State Institute for Protection of Families, Maternity and Children,[38] which has the responsibility of meeting the challenge of ensuring that all children are afforded the rights to which they are entitled. Only by applying efficient mechanisms to protect children and their rights can Croatia reach an acceptable level of legal representation and progress in the relationship between adults and children.[39]

It is justifiably anticipated that these new laws will bring about new hope of creating a happy childhood and future for most children in Croatia.

NOTES

1. Mary Cholmondeley and Diana Tempest, 'Fanciullo', in F. Palazzi and S. Spaventa Filippi (eds), *Il libro dei mille savi* (Milan: Ulrico Hoepli, 1967) p.320.
2. There is a lot of written material on the role childhood plays in forming an adult. See, for example, Ivan Furlan, *Man's Psychological Development* (Zagreb: Filozfsko-Teoloski Institut, 1991), Mladen Zvonarevic, *Social Psychology* (Zagreb: Filozfsko-Teoloski Institut, 1981), Dragica Plasaj, *Child Development within the Family* (Zagreb: Filozfsko-Teoloski Institut, Ivan Koprek, *Family Life in the Year of the Family* (Zagreb: Filozfsko-Teoloski Institut, 1994) pp.109–30.
3. Antonija Zizak, 'Does the Family Have a Place in Institutional Care?', *Our Family Today* (papers presented at a conference in Opatija, 28–30 Nov. 1994; and see R. Soisson, *Social Ecology and the Context of Care* (Burich: FICE, 1995) pp.129–44.
4. For more details, see Nikola Viskovic, *Animal and Man – Contribution to Cultural Zoology* (Split: Kajizevai Krug, 1996) pp.431–2.
5. For more details, see Dubravka Hrabar, 'Children's Rights in Family Relations', doctoral thesis, Zagreb Law School, 1991, p.20.
6. Juraj Hrzenjak, *International and European Documents on Human Rights* (Zagreb: Informator, 1992).
7. *Narodne novine*, no. 56/1990, 22 Dec. 1990.
8. Constitutional decision on sovereignty and independence of the Republic of Croatia (*Narodne novine*, no. 31/1991, item III); also see Mira Alincic, Ana Bakaric-Abramovic, Dubravka Hrabar and Nenad Hlaca, *Family Law* (Zagreb: Informator, 1994) p.32.
9. This Declaration was ratified by Croatia in 1971 (*Narodne novine*, no. 7/1971).
10. Convention published in Sluzbeni list of Yugoslavia, no. 15, 21 Dec. 1990 and ratified by the Law on Ratification in the National Assembly of Yugoslavia, 18 Dec. 1990, P. no. 13. 06. This became law in Croatia on 8 Oct. 1991.
11. This was agreed upon at the Summit on Child's Rights, 30 Sept. 1990.
12. *Narodne novine*, no. 7/1976. Pact enforced 23 March 1976.
13. *Narodne novine*, no. 7/1971. Pact enforced 3 Jan. 1976.
14. See Mira Alincic, 'European Conventions on Child Protection and Croatian Family Legislation', *Woman*, 50 (1–2): 24–41, 1992.
15. 'Family' is defined as parents and children only, without any other relatives.

16 According to Croatian legislation, a child is defined as being under 14 years of age and an adolescent between 14 and 18 years of age. See 'Republic of Croatia Penal Code', *Narodne novine*, no. 32/93 and revisions published in *Narodne novine*, no. 38/93.
17 Zvonimir Separovic, *Family Violence* (Dubrovnik: 1988) p.8. See also Marina Janjic-Komar, 'Children's Rights', *Social Policy*, **XLII** (11–12): 289–91, 1987.
18 *Narodne novine*, no. 32/93.
19 Most frequent is the failure of parents to support children (70 per cent) and, as a rule, this responsibility usually falls to men (96 per cent).
20 Zvonimir Separovic, *Victimology* (Zagreb-Beograd: Pravini Fakustet Zagreb, 1987) p.168; Marina Ajdukovic, 'Family Violence – Legal, Psychological and Social Factors', *Our Family Today* (Zagreb: Ministry of Labour and Social Welfare, 1994) pp.11–12.
21 Franjo Hirjan and Mladen Singer, 'Adolescents in Criminal Law', *Globus* (Zagreb: Globus, 1991) pp.268–72.
22 Nina Pecnik, 'Abused and Neglected Children in the Family', *Our Family Today* (Zagreb: Ministry of Labour and Social Welfare, 1994) pp.244–57.
23 *Narodne novine*, no 51/1989.
24 See Pecnik, op. cit., note 22, pp.247–9.
25 Ksenija Turkovic, 'Violent Behaviour towards Children', *Family Violence* (Dubrovnik: Pravini Fakustet, 1988) pp.85–98.
26 Data provided by Centre for Social Services, Split, 3 Feb. 1997.
27 See details in Marina Ajdukovic, 'Family Violence – Legal, Psychological and Social Factors', *Our Family Today* (Zagreb: Ministry of Labour and Social Welfare, 1994) p.10.
28 F. Bacic and Z. Separovic, *Criminal Law (Special Part)* (Zagreb, 1992) p.135.
29 J. Milton, *Paradise Regained*, IV; F. Palazzi and S. Spaventa Filippi (eds), *Il libro dei mille savi* (Milan: Ulrico Hoepli, 1967) p.321.
30 *Narodne novine*, no. 51/1989.
31 See p.82.
32 M. Alincic, A. Bakaric-Abramovic, D. Hrabar and N. Hlaca, *Family Law* (Zagreb, 1994) pp.236–7.
33 See Alincic *et al.*, op. cit., note 32, pp.241–2.
34 Ibid., p.242.
35 LMFR (Article 240).
36 See details in Z. Separovic, 'Criminal Law Protecting Children and Adolescents', *Our Law*, **37** (7–10): 148, 1983.
37 See details in M. Ajdukovic, 'Family Violence – Legal, Psychological and Social Factors', *Our Family Today* (Zagreb: Ministry of Labour and Social Welfare, 1994) pp.13–16.
38 Law on establishing the structure and extent of authority of state departments and state administration (see Articles 18 and 26) (*Narodne novine*, no. 72/1994).
39 See D. Hrabar, 'The Child in the Family – Legal Aspects', in *Our Family Today* (Zagreb: Ministry of Labour and Social Welfare, 1994) p.131.

6 The Definition of, and Legal and Management Responses to, the Problem of Child Abuse in England and Wales

Christina Lyon

INTRODUCTION

For the last 25 years, the vexed problems associated with the issue of child abuse have rarely been out of the public eye in England and Wales.[1] Since the publication in 1973 by Shropshire County Council of the *Report of Inquiry into the Circumstances Surrounding the Death of Graham Bagnall (and the Role of the County Council's Social Services)*[2] there have been over 70 public or private enquiries into the deaths or abuse of children at the hands of parents, foster parents, residential care workers or others providing for the care of children in residential schools, and scarcely a year has gone by when there has not been at least one enquiry being held and making a report either to local government authorities or central government authorities. The most recent official enquiry into abuse of children concerns what is now referred to as 'institutional' abuse which is alleged to have taken place at a number of North Wales children's homes throughout the last quarter of a century and the Tribunal of Inquiry is still hearing evidence at the time of the writing of this chapter. Complementary to this, the last government ordered, in June 1996, the establishment of a more general enquiry into the lives and experiences of children placed in the care of local authority social services departments, usually as a result of having experienced some abuse within their birth or immediate families. The report of this government enquiry chaired by Sir William Utting and entitled *People Like Us*[3] is just the latest in line to reveal that such children continue to face appalling sexual and physical abuse from staff, foster parents and other children, and, like its predecessors, it makes a series of recommendations, a number of which can be found in previous enquiry reports.[4] The catalogue of child abuse seems never to close and at the time of putting the finishing touches to this manuscript, the police child pornography squad was coordinating widespread raids across England on a considerable number of establishments, from private homes to top English public schools, with a view to tracking down the organizers and perpetrators of a large-scale child pornography ring and a pop star had been questioned about child pornography material having been found upon his computer when he took it into a well-known computer retail store.[5]

Such serious attempts by the police to attack the vice of child pornography evidences official willingness to pursue the perpetrators of such abuse in order to provide greater protection for children who may have been the victims of abuse by reason of the production of such material and for those who may also become victims by being exposed to the publication of such material. That the new possibilities opened up by the new communication technologies may expose children to forms of abuse to be viewed in a widely accessible medium has already prompted a number of European governments[6] to try to prevent such publication as being in contravention of principles of public morality. Such actions, however, have not been without criticisms from those who, from a civil libertarian standpoint, argue that such attempted restrictions are unconstitutional.

The attempts made by the government in England and Wales to provide for the protection of children from abuse has, therefore, to be viewed against a backdrop of the problem needing to be tackled not only within individual small families but in institutional settings, as well as, in some cases, on a global and international scale.[7]

Social attitudes to the phenomenon of child abuse can be influenced by a range of factors: from the diversity and multiculturalism of the society under review in which different cultural or ethnic groups may perceive some practices as abusive whereas others do not, and vice versa, to laws which, as a result of a tacit agreement between the people and the government, reflect a consensus view as to the type of abusive behaviour which will be made the subject of censure and attract the sanctions of either criminal or civil law, and to media exposure and censure of behaviour which might not previously have been thought of as actually, or potentially, abusive. Prompted by concerned groups within the community, massive media exposure of a particular problem can lead to a coming together of both the community's and the government's view that behaviour previously thought acceptable or, indeed, denied should be outlawed, and such has been the experience in England in relation to such important matters as violence towards women, race and sex discrimination.

The most wide-ranging investigation into issues associated with child abuse was recently concluded by the National Commission of Inquiry into the Prevention of Child Abuse and Neglect.[8] After considering the evidence of the many thousands of individuals as well as hundreds of governmental and non-governmental organizations, children's charities and other representative bodies in the community, the Commission concluded, along with all the major children's charities in England, that corporal punishment of children by parents in the child's own family is behaviour which should now be ranked and defined as child abuse.[9] Given that the right to administer 'reasonable chastisement' to one's child has for so long been protected by the law, that this 'right' is strongly supported both by previous governments and by the new one, and that the reaction to the most recent finding of the European Human Rights Court in respect of the case of *A* v. *The United Kingdom*[10] was the government's immediate press release indicating their 'respect' for the 'right' of parents to exert discipline by smacking their children, it would appear that the outlawing of physical chastisement of children by their parents in England may be an uphill task. No doubt, however, such was felt to be the case by those who originally embarked on the campaign to outlaw husband's rights to hit their wives and the practice of race and sex discrimination.

English society's attitude towards the corporal punishment of children in their families is in many ways as ambivalent as the attitude of English society towards its children generally. The notion that children are the property of their parents and that children should be seen and not heard is still evident in many parts of our society and, indeed, prompted Thomas Hammarberg to observe that 'it was the Committee's experience that difficulties arose whenever a "reasonable" level of corporal punishment was permitted under a State's internal law'.[11] To draw an analogy, no-one would argue that a 'reasonable' level of wife-beating should be permitted. His conclusion was that the 'United Kingdom position represented a vestige of the outdated view that children were in a sense their parents' chattels'. It was, therefore, his and the Committee's view that the notion of a 'permissible' level of corporal punishment was best avoided. The response of the English media to the suggestion that, as a result of the case of *A* v. *The United Kingdom*,[12] English law would be put under scrutiny with regard to the issue of corporal punishment has meant that this is back in the forefront of people's minds and may prove over the next year to be the real test of whether English society really can be described as being dedicated to the eradication of child abuse at the heart of its society, that is, the family. English law currently sends out a very mixed message to children, in that corporal punishment has been outlawed in state-funded schools or for state-funded pupils in private schools since 1986,[13] and must not be 'inhuman' or 'degrading' where it is administered for privately funded pupils in private schools.[14] It is soon to be outlawed in all schools.

Although the last government acknowledged that the use of corporal punishment in state schools or for state-funded pupils sent out the wrong message to children and, in addition, that it was difficult to regulate and control, it nevertheless attempted at the same time to signify respect for parental choice in selecting private education which did allow corporal punishment. This certainly appears to indicate that previous government thinking on the issue of corporal punishment was muddled, and the reaction of the new government to the case of *A v. The United Kingdom* reveals that it, too, is suffering from the same problem of confusion and muddled thinking over this particular issue.[15] It seeks, on the one hand, to express its horror about the particular circumstances of the case where a boy who was repeatedly beaten by his stepfather was acquitted by the criminal courts on a charge of actual bodily harm and yet asserts that this has nothing to do with parents who exert discipline by smacking their children when they misbehave. The government minister is quoted in the press release as indicating that the government respects that right, and as further stating that 'the overwhelming majority of parents know the difference between smacking and beating'. But this is by no means clear and there are many in England who find it extremely difficult to reconcile the notion that the government has outlawed hitting children in schools while continuing to assert that hitting children in the home is right.

It is also the case that children and young people throughout England find it very difficult to reconcile the notion that acts which would be regarded as criminal assaults if committed on adults, even within a family setting, are recognized by government and by the law as being an aspect of parental rights deserving of special protection and continued defence by government ministers. The censure of the UK for permitting parental physical punishment of children represented by the case of *A v. The United Kingdom* is not, however, the only form of international pressure being exerted on the government in England. Within Europe, successive recommendations of the Committee of Ministers of the Council of Europe, to which the government is party, have condemned all corporal punishment. Within the European Union, prominent parliamentarians who have taken initiatives related to women and children and violence are strongly opposed to physical punishment in families and see its prohibition as an essential Europe-wide reform.

Whilst it is clear, therefore, that the attitude prevalent in English society is not necessarily one which even perceives that there is anything wrong in parents hitting their children, there have been considerable efforts made at both legislative and professional practice level to attempt to deal seriously with all manifestations of what is more commonly accepted as constituting child abuse. There have been major legislative reforms, not only in relation to the law governing state intervention in family's lives in order to prevent the incidence of child abuse but also in the field of criminal law,[16] to ameliorate the effects on children of having to give evidence in criminal cases. Both central and local government agencies have published a plethora of guidance on best practice for all the various professional agencies concerned in trying to prevent child abuse and, as was pointed out earlier, successive child abuse enquiries have highlighted human fallibility in respect of awareness of relevant procedures and guidelines or practice that could be deemed to be in compliance with the notions of best practice. Indeed, one academic commentator has been prompted to note that 'the child protection system in Britain has been distorted by its reliance on public investigations into cases that have gone wrong and it lacks coherent and consistent goals and programmes as a result'.[17] The vast array of guidance issued by different government departments and by different institutions at local level mean that, inevitably, children are not assisted by the fragmented and conflicting policies, values, objectives and responsibilities revealed therein. As a result, children suffer from the lack of a powerful and coordinating government voice. As the National Commission pointed out, where there is cooperation, this is often despite, rather than because of, the existing systems. The Commission further noted that law, regulations, structures and policies must be harmonized with a concept of the 'whole child' in mind.[18]

It is proposed in this chapter to consider the various definitions of child abuse offered in both the law and professional practice guidance in England, to reflect upon the extent of child abuse as characterized by such definitions, to consider and evaluate both the civil and criminal law responses to the problem of child abuse and, finally, to reflect upon management responses to the problem and to consider necessary legislative and policy changes which must be made if England is to provide a safer life experience for its children and young people.

THE DEFINITION OF CHILD ABUSE IN ENGLAND AND WALES

The term 'child abuse' is one which is widely used in England by ordinary members of the public, the media and even official government publications.[19] But it is not a phrase which is actually to be found in either English criminal or civil law provisions governing what may be deemed to be potentially abusive behaviour towards children. In its *First Report to the United Nations Monitoring Committee* in 1994,[20] the UK government claimed that the Children Act 1989 ensured that children were protected from *all* forms of abuse and neglect *as delineated in Article 19* of the United Nations Convention on the Rights of the Child. Article 19 provides that governments should take all appropriate legislative, administrative, social and educational measures to protect the child from *all* forms of physical or mental violence, injury or abuse, neglect or negligent treatment, maltreatment or exploitation, including sexual abuse, while in the care of parents, legal guardians or any other person who has the care of the child. From what has already been said in the introduction, however, it is apparent that English law does not provide protection against *all* forms of physical violence, injury or abuse while in the care of parents or legal guardians, since parents, legal guardians or anyone else having the responsibility for the care of the child is allowed to engage in reasonable physical chastisement of the child.[21] Whilst it is apparent that 'reasonable physical chastisement' exercised by a parent, guardian or other person with the care of the child will not constitute ill-treatment, the question left hanging in the air is what constitutes 'reasonable' physical chastisement. The stepparent of the child A in *A* v. *The United Kingdom* was actually acquitted of an offence under s.1 Children and Young Persons Act (CYPA), 1933, since the magistrates found his conduct in inflicting punishment on his stepson by beating him with a cane so as to leave wounds requiring hospital attention to be 'reasonable'. The stepparent was thus acquitted of any criminal offence albeit that the minister, in his press statement released on hearing the initial determination of the Commission, indicated that the stepfather's actions had been 'plainly abusive'.

One of the major difficulties in trying to understand how the concept of child abuse may be understood in England lies in the failure, even in the Children Act 1989, to lay down standards of care which children in this jurisdiction can expect from their parents. The Children Act 1989 defines 'parental responsibility' as 'all the rights, duties, power and responsibilities and authority which by law a parent of a child has in relation to the child and his property'.[22] Nothing further is said to define *what these are*, or *how* they should be exercised. The Act nevertheless provides local authority social services departments or the NSPCC with the power to intervene in families to remove children where it can be shown that 'the child is suffering or is likely to suffer significant harm' and that this is 'attributable to a lack of *reasonable* parental care' or 'the child is beyond parental control'.[23] 'Significant' is defined by reference to a comparison of the child's health and development with that of a 'similar' child;[24] harm can encompass *ill-treatment* or the *impairment* of health and development; health encompasses physical or mental health; and ill-treatment includes 'sexual abuse and forms of ill-treatment which are not physical'.[25] It should be noted that the definition of 'significant' can scarcely be said to give any sort of guidance to parents, in that the characteristics of a 'similar child' are not given and, more critically, 'reasonable', 'abuse', 'ill-treatment', 'impairment' and 'development' are not further defined and thus fail to give clear legislative guidance either to parents and carers or to those who may have to intervene in families in order to protect children.

The Children Act 1989 clearly does not lay down the standards of care which children in this jurisdiction can expect from their parents, nor does it exist to guide or to educate parents themselves. In this sense, it also fails to comply with the provisions of Article 18(2) of the United Nations Convention on the Rights of the Child which states that 'state's parties shall render appropriate assistance to parents and legal guardians in the performance of their child rearing responsibilities'. Since no clearly defined positive duty in relation to the care which parents should exercise in bringing up their children is laid down in the legislation, and there is a complete absence of any further statutory guidelines comparable to those which exist in Scotland,[26] it is therefore the case that a negative but ill-defined issue takes precedence, and emphasis is laid on the fact that both civil child protection proceedings and criminal proceedings may be instituted if a child is 'suspected of suffering' or is 'actually suffering from *significant* harm'.[27]

The use of the term 'significant' in relation to the harm suffered by the child, is, as has been noted above, defined by reference to a comparison of the child's health and development with that of a 'similar' child. This therefore necessarily imports into the concept of child abuse some notion of comparative and evaluative judgment on the part of professionals coming into contact with the family, who have to determine, in accordance with these notions, whether it can be said that *significant harm* has occurred to the child. The professional is expected to draw on their own experience of the health and development of similar children, and the definition of 'significant' can scarcely be said to give any guidance at all to parents, particularly those who have no other children, any more than it does to professionals, some of whom may be young, without children and recently qualified and who may lack any very great experience or knowledge in relation to the health and development of 'normal children'. The lack of guidance given to all those who must interpret the phrase 'significant harm' in the Children Act may then give rise to problems, as do the terms 'reasonable', 'abuse', 'ill-treatment', 'impairment' and 'development'.[28] It should also be noted that the provisions relating to 'significant harm' do not comply with the demands of Article 19(1), since that article is unequivocal in stating that appropriate measures must be taken to protect the child from *all forms of abuse* and does not qualify this in any way with regard to the degree of harm. The Children Act 1989 demands, however, that the harm must be 'significant' and the difficulties attendant upon establishing this are well illustrated by the struggles which the courts have had in interpreting this phrase.[29] Considerable attention has focused on the notion of 'significant harm',[30] but little critical comment has been developed on the issue of the measurement of significance, how this relates to Article 19(1) and how parents, guardians or other carers are to be enabled to make some sense of the standard of care which is expected from them under this piece of legislation.

The Children Act 1989 contains other measures designed to protect children from abuse, all of which demand a consideration of the terms used in s.31 and which depend upon how the notion of significant harm is construed. Thus, under the provisions of s.1 Children Act 1989, the court is directed to have regard to a list of factors which include 'any harm which a child has suffered or is at risk of suffering'[31] whenever the court is considering whether to make, vary or discharge orders with regard to the residence of or contact with a child or with regard to the exercise of parental responsibility in respect of that child,[32] or when the court is considering whether to make, vary or discharge orders placing the child in the care or under the supervision of local authority social services departments, where it has been determined that the child has suffered or is likely to suffer significant harm attributable to an absence of reasonable parental care or control.[33]

Given that the definition of harm contained within the civil law of England is somewhat problematical for professionals to interpret, let alone parents, it is not surprising that official government departments charged with the task of overseeing the well-being of children determined that further guidance was necessary in order to elucidate this area for all the professionals who might be involved in working together on suspected cases of child abuse. Thus the Home Office, the Department of Health, the Department of Education and Science and the Welsh Office have on two separate occasions[34] issued guidance which contains detailed consideration of what may be understood to constitute 'child abuse'.[35]

Working Together is a very significant document in that it consolidates previous guidance procedures for the protection of children from abuse and recommends developments aimed at making these more effective. The document takes into account the requirements of the Children Act 1989 and lessons learned from a succession of inquiry reports,[36] as well as examples of good practice provided by a number of agencies. The document has in effect become a working bible on inter-agency cooperation and, whilst it acknowledges that before local authority social services departments or the NSPCC may initiate care proceedings under the 1989 Act they must have regard to the notion of 'significant harm' as developed and expanded upon in s.31 Children Act 1989, nevertheless there are other steps which generally precede the taking of legal proceedings and for which clear guidance criteria were necessary in order to regulate practice all over the country.

Where concerns about children surface in different agencies, workers in those agencies are entitled to call together their colleagues from other agencies to meet in what is generally referred to as a 'child protection conference'. In such a conference it is anticipated that all the professional agencies concerned with the protection of children or working with the particular child in a family will have their representatives present and that the parents of the child will generally also be present. The concerns which the individual professionals have are then fully aired and the parents given the opportunity to give their explanation for any 'harm' which the child may have suffered. *Working Together* implicitly acknowledges that the notion of significant harm, even as laid down in s.31, is not really adequate for the purposes of all the professionals who might be concerned with child protection and so it sets out clear criteria intended to guide the professionals in a child protection conference, particularly when they may be considering placing the child's name on a child protection register.

The purpose of a child protection register entry is to signal to anyone who may consult the register[37] that there have been discussions in a child protection conference concerning the welfare of the child and that that concern has reached such a level that the professionals have agreed that the child's name should be entered on the register. The register is generally held by the local social services department as custodian of the register, and any of the professional agencies who may have concerns about the child are then entitled to consult it. Placing a name on a local child protection register thus provides an easy and quick reference system for professionals in England concerned with identifying children at risk and it also promotes coordination of inter-agency plans to minimize that risk. If, however, formal proceedings need to be taken, obviously the professionals involved will have to fit the particular circumstances of the case into the definitions provided in s.31 Children Act 1989. Nevertheless, the expanded definition of child abuse provided by the criteria listed as a precondition for entry on the child protection register are extremely useful in providing a much clearer definition of what may be understood to be abuse in the eyes of professionals concerned about child protection in England.

As has been noted above, the inclusion of a child's name on the child protection register in England will only occur following a child protection conference, the exception being when a child on another local authority's register moves into the area. Such children will be registered immediately pending the first child protection conference in the new area.

Both the requirements for registration and the actual categories of abuse for registration produced in *Working Together* are set out below.[38] The document first sets out that, before a child can be placed on the child protection register, the conference must decide that there is, or is a likelihood of, significant harm leading to the need for a child protection plan. It goes on to state that 'one of the following requirements needs to be satisfied':

1. There must be one or more identifiable incidents which can be described as having adversely affected the child. They may be acts of commission or omission. They can be either physical, sexual, emotional or neglectful. It is important to identify a specific occasion or occasions when the incident has occurred. Professional judgment is that further incidents are likely; or
2. Significant harm is expected on the basis of professional judgment of findings of the investigation in this individual case or on research evidence. The conference will need to establish so far as they can a cause of the harm or likelihood of harm. This cause could also be applied to siblings or other children living in the same household so as to justify registration of them. Such children should be categorised according to the area of concern.

Working Together then sets out the various categories of abuse for registration which constitute a welcome and expanded definition of abuse which was necessary in order to provide adequate guidance for professionals. It should be noted, however, that few, if any parents have access to this material so as to understand in more detail what may be seen by professionals as constituting child abuse. It should also be pointed out that the guidance in *Working Together* can only be seen to be just that and it certainly does not close the categories of abuse which might be considered. Indeed, the document contains further guidance on other aspects of child abuse which may necessarily encompass the categories listed as forming the basis for registration.[39] Thus *Working Together* provides that the categories which it lists should be used for the purpose of the register and for statistical purposes and emphasizes that these categories are intended to provide definitions as a guide for those using the register and that in some instances more than one category of registration may be appropriate. It points out that this will need to be dealt with in the protection plan, that statistical returns will allow for this but that multiple abuse registration should not be used simply to cover all eventualities. The guidance thus makes it clear that it would be wrong to enter children under all categories on the register and that it is far better to focus on a particular reason for entry on the register in order to concentrate the attention of the professionals on the particular nature of the child abuse being identified. The categories defined are as follows:[40]

> *Neglect*: The persistent or severe neglect of a child or the failure to protect a child from exposure to any kind of danger, including cold or starvation, or extreme failure to carry out important aspects of care, resulting in the significant

impairment of the child's health or development, including non-organic failure to thrive.

Physical injury: Actual or likely physical injury to a child, or failure to prevent physical injury (or suffering) to a child including deliberate poisoning, suffocation and Münchhausen's syndrome by proxy.[41]

Sexual abuse: Actual or likely sexual exploitation of a child or adolescent. The child may be dependent and/or developmentally immature.

Emotional abuse: Actual or likely severe adverse effect on the emotional and behavioural development of a child caused by persistent or severe emotional ill treatment or rejection.

This guidance which is issued for professionals working in England can be contrasted with that issued in Scotland,[42] which many professionals south of the border have found to be extremely useful and to which they make frequent reference.

The Scottish document more fully defines the various types of abuse and instead of listing, for example, non-organic failure to thrive as a result of the significant impairment of the child's health or development without further expanding upon what is meant by the term 'non-organic failure to thrive', it provides an explanation which runs to some paragraphs. English professionals are not, however, referred to the Scottish document and thus must rely upon their own knowledge base to alert them to the fact that there may be fuller explanations in other documents. Given that expanded definitions exist in the Scottish document, it would seem that the Department of Health in England, which is currently working on revisions to the *Working Together* document, should take note of the nature of information contained in the Scottish document and provide similar information in the English one. It should also be noted that the very limited definition of sexual abuse contained in the English document is also expanded upon at greater lengths in the Scottish document and examples are given of what activities may be comprised in the term 'sexual abuse'. Very importantly, in the light of concerns recently surfacing in England, the activity of encouraging children to become prostitutes or activities involving the sexual exploitation of or between young people is also specifically encompassed within the Scottish definition of sexual abuse.

It is clear from a consideration of the UK government's report to the UN Monitoring Committee that the government felt that the need to protect children from sexual abuse in England was adequately provided for by the terms of the Children Act 1989. This would appear to be because the then Conservative government perhaps focused rather more on the issue of child sexual abuse occurring in the domestic, or perhaps even institutional, setting as principally envisaged by the terms of Article 19, rather than by responding to the demands of Article 34, which demands that 'State's Parties should protect children from sexual exploitation and abuse including the exploitative use of children in prostitution or other unlawful sexual practices and involvement in pornography', and goes on to state that 'state's parties must take all appropriate national, bilateral and multilateral measures to prevent such exploitation and abuse from occurring'.

The problem of child prostitution in England has been opened up by a number of studies and the idea of seeing prostitutes in England solely as women or girls has now shifted to include men and boys.[43] The reasons why children and young people may be caught up in prostitution are many and diverse, but a large number of the children involved will have been in the care of social services residential institutions from which they have fled or they may have experienced high levels of abuse in the domestic setting in families or foster families, which again has prompted them to seek a life on the streets. In 1989, the Children's Society published a study of young people at Britain's first refuge for runaways, the 'Safe House' in central London.[44] Key findings from this research indicated that there was a high incidence of abuse amongst those who ran away and resorted to prostitution and an over-representation of young people from residential care among those working on the streets in London. Numerous other surveys have identified that many of the young people who entered prostitution did so well before the age of 16 and had resorted to providing sex for money as a survival strategy.[45] Unfortunately, in this area of child prostitution, attention has tended to focus rather more on dealing with both the abused and the abuser as criminal offenders. A number of those involved in working with young prostitutes, however, have asserted that police and social services should work together much more closely to deal with these child prostitutes as though they were dealing with child abuse victims and those children who would normally be characterized under s.17 Children Act 1989 as being in need.[46]

While a number of those who have engaged in research in this area, including Lee and O'Brien[47] and Barrett *et al.*,[48] would undoubtedly argue that what is required is an overhaul of the relevant legislation in this area, what is also required is detailed guidance, such as that contained in *Working Together*,[49] to take account of the difficulties posed by the problem of child prostitution; the necessity to coordinate more closely the legislative provisions of the Children Act 1989; and a more enlightened policy approach to deal with child prostitution evidenced by commentators such as Edgington, who is himself a police officer. Such an approach to the problems of child prostitution in terms of the sort of guidance produced in *Working Together* has been drawn up by Nottinghamshire Social Services as part of their *Children in Need – Policy Procedures and Practice Guidance* issued in December 1996. An addition to *Working Together* along the lines set out in the Nottinghamshire document, using family support measures contained in such provisions as Part III Children Act 1989, would enable separate provision for children and young people, who have been subject to sexual exploitation in particular, to make their exit from such a lifestyle more structured within the terms of an official response under the Act.[50]

Emotional abuse as defined by *Working Together* is also somewhat lacking in terms of a full definition. Again, the Scottish document runs to some four paragraphs and explores specific examples of the nature of behaviour engaged in by parents or care givers which could be described as amounting to emotional abuse. No such guidance exists in the English document, but professionals and lawmakers are now becoming increasingly concerned with the issue of the impact of domestic violence witnessed by children on their emotional and behavioural development.[51] The fact that the lawmakers have become rather more concerned with the issues of domestic violence and its impact on children has been seen very recently with the enactment of provisions in Part IV Family Law Act 1996 which provide for much greater protection of children from the impact of domestic violence, although it remains to be seen whether these provisions work out fully to the benefit of such children.[52] The new provisions contain directions for the court to consider whether greater harm will be done to children in not making orders than would be done in making an order and, clearly, where this balance of harm test is satisfied, the orders available for protection, not only of partners but also of children, should be issued under the provisions of Part IV.[53]

While much of *Working Together* is clearly concentrated on guidance for professionals dealing with allegations of abuse arising from a domestic setting, there are nevertheless clear acknowledgments that abuse may take place in institutional settings including residential homes run by social services or other private organizations providing for the care of children away from their parents, often pursuant to a care order obtained under the provisions of s.31 Children Act 1989. The type of abuse will generally have been encompassed by the provision as defined in paragraph 6.40.

Working Together does, however, helpfully also define the notion of organized abuse. This is described[54] as 'a generic term which covers abuse which may involve a number of abusers, a number of abused children and young people and often encompasses different forms of abuse. It involves to a greater or lesser extent, an element of organisation'. The document goes on to state:[55] 'a wide range of activity is covered by this term, from small peadophile or pornographic rings, often but not always, organised for profit, with most participants knowing each other, to large networks of individual groups of families which may be spread widely and in which not all participants will be known to each other'. It then explains that 'some organised groups may use bizarre or ritualised behaviour, sometimes associated with particular belief systems'. Thus forms of organized abuse may or may not involve the use of satanic rituals and it is incorrect to simply classify ritualistic and organized abuse as one and the same form of child abuse.[56] *Working Together* goes on to stress that research suggests some caution in sharp distinctions between types of abuser and points out that knowledge is growing in this area of abuse and that the Department of Health had commissioned research into its frequency and characteristics.[57]

Since there is a total lack of clarity in terms of the guidance given to parents in relation to the standard of care which they should exercise in relation to their children it is, therefore, the case that both civil child protection law and the criminal law tend to focus upon the identification of 'harm' or 'injury'. It is often the case that both civil and criminal proceedings may arise out of the same facts, for example, where chastisement may be deemed to have gone beyond what is deemed to be 'reasonable', or where ill-treatment has gone beyond what might be deemed to be trivial and an offence has been committed under various provisions of either the offences against the Person Act 1861 or under s.1 Children and Young Person's Act, 1933. Where sexual abuse is suspected, not only may civil child protection proceedings ensue but prosecution may follow under the provisions of the Sexual Offences Act, 1956 as amended. In all such cases the child victim faces the possibility of system abuse on top of the other types of abuses already identified.

Criminal prosecution will only ensue if the police and Crown Prosecution Service are satisfied that there is admissible, substantial and reliable evidence that a criminal offence known to the law has been committed by an identifiable person. As is made plain by the Code for Crown Prosecutors,[58] a bare prima facie case is not enough, and the service must apply the test as to whether there is a realistic prospect of a conviction. Thus, in relation to children, the inevitable question will be asked as to whether a child witness is going to be both a credible and reliable witness. Will the child stand up to rigorous cross-examination by barristers for the defence? Despite much increased police involvement in child abuse investigations, research studies, as well as anecdotal evidence, suggest that successful prosecutions are rare. For example, Moran Ellis[59] revealed prosecution rates of 12 per cent and 7 per cent in sexual abuse cases at two different research sites, and Creighton's study in 1992[60] reported that criminal proceedings occurred in 17 per cent of the sexual abuse cases out of a sample of 1732 and significantly, perhaps, in 9 per cent of the sample of 2786 physical abuse cases in the period between 1988 and 1990. Once the case is within the criminal justice system, the dynamics of adversarial criminal trial demand that the defence lawyers seek to undermine the credibility of child witnesses, label them as liars and constantly belittle them. The low conviction rates achieved send out very mixed messages to children who have plucked up the courage to speak out and the links between the civil child protection and criminal adult prosecution processes may ultimately result, in some cases, in the child being returned to the abusive household. The situation may be further compounded by an acquittal in criminal proceedings or a decision by the police not to proceed with the prosecution, leading to the child being very much on their own in the civil child protection process and a more onerous burden of proof being demanded in relation to proving that child abuse may have taken place, more especially when the allegation made is supported only by the evidence of one child and even where the judge who hears the parties in person is of the view that the child is telling the truth.[61]

When situations like these occur it is clear that the very system which has supposedly been designed to protect children is in turn actually abusing the children itself. This is now generally referred to as 'system abuse' and the National Commission characterized it as occurring whenever 'the operation of legislation, officially sanctioned procedures or operational practices within systems or institutions, is *avoidably* damaging to children and their families' (emphasis added).[62] As a result of the work of various researchers contributing to the Commission and on the basis of the evidence which it received, the Commission noted a range of examples of system abuse ranging from a lack of differentiation of treatment as between children and adults as witnesses or victims in the criminal justice system or were in receipt of punitive or harsh treatment in the penal refugee or asylum systems; where services were unavailable because they did not exist or were inadequate or were inaccessible through lack of information, location, or through insensitivity to race, culture or gender; where services were so poorly organized, managed, monitored or resourced that they permitted unskilled and unsafe environments in day, residential and family care settings; or where they permitted repressive and abusive regimes to develop;[63] and where they do not detect and deal with abusive individuals who infiltrate organizations and services for children;[64] or where there are unnecessarily intrusive procedures or practices which undermine children or their families. The identification of this varying range of system abuse as delineated by the Commission was, as indicated, drawn from the evidence presented to it, but was also derived from the work of members of the New South Wales Child Protection Council.[65]

After consideration of the various definitions of the different types of abuse which might be perpetrated upon children provided by such documents as *Working Together* or *Child Protection in Scotland*, and after hearing and considering the written and oral evidence offered to them, the National Commission of Inquiry into the Prevention of Child Abuse decided that it would offer a wider definition than that currently found in official documents. In its report, the National Commission[66] found that agreed definitions of child abuse are important for two reasons: first, to establish a general framework within which policy designed to prevent child abuse can be developed and assessed; and secondly, to provide a set of technical definitions for identifying actions or circumstances which are taken to be abuse to children and which are needed for statutory, legal, statistical, procedural and research purposes. The Commission nevertheless acknowledged that there is some uncertainty or even disagreement amongst professionals and the public over what constitutes child abuse and that different professional disciplines do not always work to the same definitions of abuse. The Commission points out that, despite the fact that there may be broad agreement at the extremes over what is harmful to children, there is a sizeable grey area about which there is confusion.

The Commission poses the rhetorical question as to whether a single instance of harm, which appears unlikely to be repeated, should be regarded as abusive in the absence of any evidence that any long-term damage has been or is likely to be done. It identifies the fact that these considerations have important implications for assessing whether a child is at risk, the 'diagnosis' of abuse, and the appropriateness of official intervention. Bearing in mind that differences of emphasis are inevitable when people with strongly held views are dealing with such an emotive issue as child abuse, the Commission concluded that a single definition of abuse, however extended, could not meet the twin requirements of providing a general framework for the common understanding of abuse and a set of technical terms for identifying abusive acts. The Commission therefore established a very broad definition of abuse for general use but within that considered the various technical definitions offered in official guidance, which could be used by professionals. The range of technical definitions included within this description are precisely those which have been considered here incorporating references to the concepts of 'significant harm'[67] and 'children in need'[68] as well as drawing on the definitions contained within the English and Scottish professional guidance documents.[69]

The broad definition adopted by the National Commission was that 'Child abuse consists of anything which individuals, institutions, or processes do or fail to do which directly or indirectly harms children or damages their prospects of safe and healthy development into adulthood.'[70] The definition adopted stemmed in part from an appreciation of the lack of any shared understanding between individuals who have been abused, professionals and policy makers, as became clear from a study of the letters, sent in mainly from survivors of abuse, to the Commission and analysed by one of the Commission's research teams. All of these express the view that professionals do not fully understand what constitutes child abuse and that, while the more conventional descriptive terms of sexual, physical and emotional abuse and neglect experienced by children are abuse, they also interpreted a broader range of potentially harmful actions, such as bullying, the deliberate subjection of a child to danger and a lack of concern for children's rights, as child abuse. It was also the case that many victims placed greater emphasis on the long-term emotional consequences of abuse than on the immediate effect of physical injury or sexual assault. The victims also linked abuse to its impact upon personal relationships within the family, partly defined by what sense the child makes of what is happening to him or her. In other words, the victim's definition of child abuse related not only to the abuse itself but also to its context and its longer-term impact on the individual and the family concerned. This, for the National Commission, was a key component of the wider definition of abuse which it proposed. As the Commission point out,[71] the definitions and perceptions of child abuse held by people who wrote of their experiences did not relate neatly to the definitions provided in legislation and in government guidance. The Commission noted that the importance which these survivors attach to the emotional impact of abuse is not reflected in child protection registrations and that in terms of defining abuse greatest weight is generally given to the views of professionals. The Commission goes on to note that the victims also indicated that 'official definitions' exclude certain forms of abuse that can have damaging consequences. Thus the emotional impact on children who witness violence was mentioned many times by the correspondence but is not yet officially acknowledged in any formal definitions and the Commission recommends that these differences in perception need to be addressed in both policy and professional practice.

The definition of child abuse and the operationalization of such definitions are clearly critical in the development of strategies for preventing child abuse and the National Commission concluded that its wide definition of abuse was one which would lead to a greater focus upon prevention, albeit that it could be supplemented by the set of technical definitions already in use but revised and improved upon in the ways which have been identified in this part of this chapter.[72]

The National Commission was fully aware that its very broad definition of child abuse would be seen by many to be unacceptably wide and indeed media response to the Commission's report, particularly in the tabloid press, and even from government ministers, was typically derogatory. The response of the then government minister, John Bowis, was that 'child care workers need clear advice on the signs of abuse, not vague definitions which are in danger of being misinterpreted'. That the government minister should have failed to see the aim of the Commission in proposing a broad definition so as to shift the focus away from intervention when things go wrong, and much more heavily on trying to prevent abuse from occurring in the first place, was perhaps not surprising. That such a reaction could be mirrored in the response from his successor to the Commission's ruling in *A v. The United Kingdom* is nonetheless extremely disappointing for those who had high hopes of New Labour and of a prime minister who had stated that, whilst he had smacked his children, he had always regretted it and had always thought that there could have been better ways of dealing with the particular situation which had provoked his angry response. Other media reaction to the Commission's report, particularly in its portrayal of emotional abuse, was similarly derogatory and it is clear that the English public, through its media, clearly perceive child abuse as principally being constituted by the grosser forms of physical or sexual assault upon children. Given the Commission's broad definition, it is interesting to consider the extent of abuse in England at the current time.

THE EXTENT OF ABUSE IN ENGLAND

It is important to note that, in England, official statistics record cautions and convictions for crimes *against* children but do not record the complaints made *by* children about potential offences. In the area of the civil law, the official statistics record the numbers of care and supervision order proceedings and applications for emergency protection orders made in respect of children and also list the number of children who are considered sufficiently at risk of significant harm from abuse to be placed on a local authority child protection register.

In so far as criminal convictions are concerned, English statistics do not record the age of the victim and thus for some sexual crimes, such as rape, and for most offences involving physical violence, the total number of such cases where the victim was under 16 is not revealed by the official statistics. If one looks at the categories of abuse as technically defined by such documents as *Working Together*, then, for the category of physical injury, it should be noted that for most violent crimes there is no separate category of offence where the victim is under the age of 16, and the statistics showing violence against those under the age of 16 do not tell us very much. Convictions and cautions, however, number just under 500 for the year 1994 but since, as indicated, these official figures exclude most violent crimes, there must be a severe under-reporting of the number of people found guilty of, or cautioned for, violent offences against children.[73] Death resulting from child abuse may also be recorded in a number of different ways, whether through criminal statistics, in local authority studies, through child abuse death enquiries, by the Office of Population Centres and Surveys or by confidential enquiry into stillbirths and deaths in infancy. As the National Commission identified, the problems of collating these statistics, and the reluctance of professionals to make a diagnosis of death by abuse, further results in an under-representation of such deaths in official statistics. Very few deaths are recorded as infanticide.[74] Statistics from 1992 show that 38 infants under the age of one year died from abuse and further reveal that children under 12 months of age are six times as likely to be killed in this way as children aged one to four years.[75] Creighton[76] points out that infants and toddlers are more 'at risk' of homicide than any other age group, but that this has been the case for the last 20 years. In the UK in 1992, the statistics also show that 103 children under the age of 16 were victims of homicide, which equates to nine offences per million children.[77] More recently, Falkov has reported that roughly 120 child deaths are notified to the Department of Health each year.[78] It appears to be the case from the statistics that children are more likely to be killed in their own home by members of their own family (including step-parents) than anywhere else or by anyone else.[79] It would appear, however, that in England and Wales the numbers of fatal child abuse are relatively low, showing little year by year fluctuation.[80] As indicated earlier, child protection registers cover children considered to be at risk of abuse if there already is, or is likely to be, 'significant harm', and for whom a protection plan has been developed by the relevant local agencies. At the end of March 1995, just under 35 000 children in England, that is, approximately one in every 300 children, had had their names put on a local child protection register. Yet even this figure is not a true picture of the real situation, since it only presents a situation on a particular date. During the year ending 31 March 1995, for example, more than 60 000 children's names had been placed on English registers, although on 31 March itself there were under 35 000.[81] In addition, it must be recognized that children who are registered represent only a minority of those referred to social services authorities and other child protection agencies in England and Wales. In 1991/92, an estimated 160 000 children were referred to social services in England, with up to 120 000 family visits and 40 000 social services child protection conferences, resulting in around 24 500 children and young people being placed on English registers.[82]

In England, suspicion of physical injury was the most common reason for registration, accounting for two in five of children on registers, followed by neglect, then sexual abuse, with emotional abuse the smallest category. As was pointed out by the National Commission, the chance that a child will be placed on the register depends on definitions and interpretations which vary in different parts of the country and on thresholds determined by local circumstances, practice and resources.[83] For example, the registration rate for 1994/95 in Sunderland and Tyneside, in the north east of England, is four times higher than in Gloucestershire and Hampshire, in the south west of the country.[84] The Commission also points out that the figures on child protection registers cannot possibly be seen to be an estimate of the true extent of abuse in England because the figures only record the child protection process and *not* the number of children who are abused. Not all children on the registers have been abused, since some are registered because they are deemed to be 'at risk'. Another important point to note is that child protection registers principally record cases of abuse within families where urgent action is needed and generally exclude cases of abuse by people outside the family when it is deemed that the family can protect the child. It is also the case that, simply because a child is not placed on the register, this does not necessarily mean that no abuse has occurred. In addition, it is inevitably the case that the registers exclude the large numbers of children who do not come to the attention of social workers but who have exactly the same experience as those who are registered.

When children have been placed in the care of the local authority, one would hope that this would mean the children would then be safe, but again figures revealed by the Department of Health show that, in England on 31 March 1995, just under one in five, or 18 per cent of children on child protection registers were actually living in local authority approved foster homes, local authority children's homes or voluntary homes or hostels.[85] As has been stated, the children who are registered represent only a small minority of those referred to local authority social services and other agencies. An analysis of the figures relating to child protection registers reveals that the main reason for approximately 25 000 children being on child protection registers during the 12 months to March 1995 was excessive physical punishment administered by parents, generally arising from the parents' inability to cope with the child's behaviour.[86] Evidence from various surveys done in the United Kingdom suggest that the extent of severe physical harm within the home may be much greater and that each year an estimated 150 000 children are harmed by what may be classified as severe physical assault, that is, punishment leaving severe bruising or marks on the child.[87]

As far as sexual abuse is concerned, the official statistics in England reveal approximately 4000 convictions and cautions for sexual offences against children in 1994.[88] Of these, 274 were for 'gross indecency with a child' and 2204 for indecent assault on a female person under 16'. In the year to 31 March 1995, some 17 000 children were on the registers under the category of sexual abuse,[89] but various surveys done in the United

Kingdom suggest that up to 100 000 children each year experience harmful sexual encounters and that well over a million adults may still be suffering from the consequences of sexual abuse into adulthood.[90] As is the case with other countries, most sexual abuse of children in England is committed by males. However, surveys of the child protection register statistics show that approximately one-third of sexually abused children are assaulted by an adolescent or pre-adolescent.[91] Criminal statistics from the Home Office covering the whole of the United Kingdom during 1989 revealed that, out of the 10 729 persons found guilty or cautioned for sexual offences, one-third were aged 20 or younger, but a number of these young people will have been charged with offences related to child prostitution. That the problem of child prostitution is a growing one is further indicated by Home Office figures which show that there has been a significant number of cautions and convictions relating to children under 18 involved in prostitution. Between 1989 and 1995, a total of 2380 cautions were issued and 1730 convictions were secured against those under 18 in England and Wales.[92] From the figures available to the Home Office it appears that there was a 40 per cent rise in cautions and convictions relating to children aged 16 and under between 1989 and 1994. The figures on cautioning and convictions of children (that is, those under 18) include a caution issued against a 10-year-old, 52 convictions secured against girls under 16 and 52 convictions against boys under 18. It should further be noted that such cautions and convictions were registered despite the fact that girls under the age of 16 cannot in law consent to sexual intercourse and boys under 18 cannot in law consent to homosexual sex.[93] The convictions were thus secured in many cases because, in reality, prostitution itself was not being prosecuted but other associated behaviour such as soliciting, loitering, living off immoral earnings and other related offences. It would appear, therefore, that the convictions secured against children and young people in these circumstances relate not to their sexual exploitation as such, but more to their conduct occurring in a public place.

The statistics and figures on emotional abuse and neglect are far more difficult to obtain or to estimate than in the areas of physical and sexual abuse. In England for the year up to 31 March 1995, 4554 children were put on the child protection register under the category of emotional abuse, whilst the figures for those on the register owing to neglect amounted to 11 185. Dealing first with the issue of neglect, the figures for the year ending 31 March 1995 disclosed that during the course of that year some 18 500 children had actually been placed on the register because of concern over neglect, but the National Commission noted that many practitioners and researchers have expressed concern that this significantly underestimates the real extent of neglect.[94] The Commission suggests that this 'neglect of neglect' can partly be explained by problems of definition and, as a result of the uncertainty over definition, thresholds for intervention may be changed in line with available resources. Whatever the reason, the Commission concludes that the indications are that many more children than are registered for neglect are left 'bumping along the bottom' until something assessed as a higher risk, such as physical or sexual abuse, stimulates action.[95]

As far as emotional abuse is concerned, whilst the figures officially recorded on child protection registers would seem to be quite low, the view of the National Commission was that at any time some 350 000 to 400 000 children (that is, 3 per cent of the UK's total child population) live in a home environment which is consistently low in warmth and high in criticism.[96] Surveys reveal that a significant minority of adults describe their relationships in childhood with their parents in extremely negative terms and a disturbingly high proportion of adults interviewed in Creighton's survey,[97] nearly one in two adults (45 per cent), stated that as a child they had witnessed some physical violence between their parents and one in 10 had witnessed it constantly or frequently. Not only may these children develop behavioural and other problems but they themselves become vulnerable to physical violence and other abuse, and other studies have revealed that in about one in four cases of child abuse there is also domestic violence within the family as a whole.[98] Yet another study in England demonstrated that, in three out of five cases where children had suffered physical or emotional abuse or neglect, their mothers were also subjected to violence by their male partners.[99] In addition to those categories which relate to sections of the child protection register in England, the National Commission identified other, what they referred to as 'in need', categories. This is in line with the Commission's focus on *prevention* of abuse and recognizes that children who might officially be classified as 'in need' under the definition provided in the Children Act 1989 may actually run into several million. Thus it notes that, within the UK as a whole, there are reckoned to be some 4.3 million children living in poverty,[100] 350 000 children with disabilities, 130 000 children with a record of offending, 600 000 children who are bullied, generally at school but also in residential institutions, 62 000 children in institutional care generally under the aegis of local authority social services, and 40 000 child carers.[101]

As can be seen from the above, it is extremely difficult to produce precise figures on the extent of child abuse in England. Under-reporting is a feature of all forms of child abuse in England, as it is in other countries, and there are always judgements to be made about what in any one situation will actually qualify for the description 'child abuse'. It is, however, clear that the number of children involved in harmful or potentially harmful situations is extremely high and apparently growing all the time, and there is evidently a pressing need for the government to improve the statistical information upon which effective policies and strategies for the prevention of abuse could be based.

THE LAW RELATING TO CHILD ABUSE

The civil law

As has been noted earlier, the provisions in the civil law for dealing with the problem of child abuse in England in its many forms are laid down in a small number of statutes. The principal provisions governing state intervention in families' lives in order to protect children are to be found in the Children Act 1989.[102] Provisions of that Act may also be used to protect children who are experiencing domestic violence, whether as witnesses or at first hand, but where a parent is being relied upon to take action and state intervention by social services is felt to be unnecessary new provisions dealing with domestic violence are to be found in Part IV Family Law Act 1996. This came into force on 1 October 1997, and by s.52 and sch.6 effects further amendments to the Children Act 1989,[103] providing for the courts to grant exclusion orders excluding an adult party from the family home where they constitute a threat, at the same time as the court grants emergency protection orders under s.44 or interim care or supervision orders under s.38 Children Act 1989.

Section 17 Children Act 1989 places a duty upon local authorities in England and Wales 'to safeguard and promote the welfare of children within their area who are in need and so far as is consistent with that duty to promote the upbringing of such children by their families by providing a range and level of services appropriate to those children's needs'. The phrase 'child in need' is defined later in the section,[104] so that a child is taken to be in need if he or she 'is unlikely to achieve or maintain, or to have the opportunity of achieving or maintaining a reasonable standard of health or development without the provision for him/her of services by the local authority; Or the child's health or development is likely to be significantly impaired or further impaired without the provision for him of such services; the child is disabled'.

The Act further expands the definition of 'child in need' by reference to the concept of health, development and disability, in that development is defined as including 'physical, intellectual, emotional, social or behavioural development; "health" means physical or mental health'; and 'A child is defined as "disabled" where he is blind, deaf or dumb or suffers from a mental disorder of any kind or is substantially and permanently handicapped by illness, injury or congenital deformity or such other disability as may be prescribed.'

The duties contained within the main body of the Children Act 1989 are further expanded upon in the very important schedule 2.[105] It should be noted that the use of the word 'appropriate' in the main section leaves it to local authorities to determine the range and level of services which are appropriate to children's needs. The problem with this is that there is no entitlement to services identified and all the evidence has shown[106] that most local authorities have been forced, in consequence of a shortage of resources, to focus on safeguarding children's welfare. This has meant that most effort has gone into dealing with families who are already causing concern to social services and where some abuse or neglect of children has already occurred. Few if any resources, in reality, are left for local social services departments to concentrate on prevention. Under the amended provisions of schedule 2 of the Children Act, however,[107] local authorities have now been required to produce Children's Services Plans and, as a result of the messages emerging from *Child Protection – Messages from Research*,[108] it would appear that local authorities should be directed towards focusing more attention on providing support services generally to families in need, rather than allegedly focusing on crisis management, highly expensive, complex and fraught child abuse investigations and what had been alleged to be unnecessary court proceedings. As a result of the publication of the research document, a debate, emanating from the Department of Health, ensued about the desirability of a 'lighter touch' in child protection practice. It should be emphasized, however, that this does not imply a greater tolerance of abuse but relates to the manner in which child protection procedures are followed by professionals. It is also clearly important that, if the official government department supervising local authority responsibilities to children is seen to be emphasizing the findings of the research, it should also be providing the necessary resources to local authorities to concentrate efforts in equal measure into the prevention of abuse. The question of the proper resourcing of all family support and child protection work undertaken by local authority social services is one constantly to the fore in discussions with practitioners conducted by those concerned with this problem.[109]

As has already been indicated, schedule 2, part I expands upon the local authority duties in relation to children in need provided in the main body of the Act by, amongst other things, requiring local authorities to take reasonable steps to identify the extent to which there are children in need within their area; to take such steps as are reasonably practicable to ensure that those who might benefit from the services receive the information relevant to them; to take reasonable steps through the provision of services under the Act to prevent children within their area suffering ill-treatment or neglect; to inform another local authority if it is understood that a child who is at risk or is actually suffering from abuse will be moving to the area of another authority; to reduce the need to bring care or supervision order proceedings with respect to children in a local authority's area; and, finally, so as to emphasize the point that children who abuse are, potentially, equally to be viewed as 'children in need' as are those children who are abused, the local authority is also required to take reasonable steps designed to reduce the need to bring criminal proceedings against children within its area and to take reasonable steps to encourage children within its area not to commit criminal offences.[110]

While it may be noted that preventive work in relation to child abuse seems apparently to have been elevated by the 1989 Act to the top of local authority's child protection agendas, ensuring that a range of services such as day nursery places, play group places, child minding facilities, family aides, family centres, respite care, short holidays and access to various education and health facilities might variously be provided, nevertheless, the reality on the ground is that managers within local authority social services, who are essentially seen as the gatekeepers of resources, constantly have to emphasize to field social workers that budgets are severely cash limited and that services must be carefully rationed and aimed at high-priority cases. Inevitably, such high-priority cases will tend to be those where the child has already been identified as suffering or at being at serious risk of suffering ill-treatment or neglect. Inevitably, also, this means that true preventive work proves extremely difficult, if not impossible, because of cash problems.

As to the real costs associated with the problem of child abuse in England and Wales, the National Commission of Inquiry establish three separate studies to gain some idea of the financial costs of dealing with abuse and its effects.[111] As a result of the three studies established by the National Commission, it came up with a cautious estimate of the indirect costs of child abuse in the whole of the UK to £1 million per year, a figure which the Commission felt was likely to be an underestimate.[112] The Commission noted that one conclusion to be drawn from a sum of this size is that there must be substantial funds which could be transferred to support the prevention of abuse while, on the other hand, it recognized that, until preventive work can be better established, it would be unacceptably risky to diminish formal child protection work. The conclusion was that, inevitably, this would mean that some extra resources would be required in the short term to enable the necessary preventive work to be developed, but that, if successful, this should in turn lead to a substantial reduction of what would otherwise have had to be spent on dealing with the effects of abuse.[113] Unfortunately, while everyone involved in local authority financial arrangements can see the wisdom of this sort of approach, finding the necessary resources in an era of constant cutting of social services budgets is an impossibility. The 'cut and more cut' approach therefore positively hinders a more preventive approach being adopted and thus in turn is likely to contribute to continued greater abuse of children.

In addition to the range of services already identified as possibly being provided under the provisions of the Children Act, the main body of the Act also refers to the service of accommodation for children and young people being provided by local authorities where a child in need has no-one with parental responsibility for him, he is lost or abandoned, or the person who has been caring for him is prevented, whether or not permanently and for whatever reason, from providing him with suitable accommodation or care.[114] This provision goes on to state that a local authority may provide accommodation for any child within their area, even though a person who has parental responsibility for him is able to provide him with accommodation, if they consider that to do so would safeguard or protect the child's welfare.[115] Before a local authority provides accommodation for such children, however, it must, so far as is reasonably practicable and consistent with the child's welfare, ascertain the child's wishes and feelings with regard to the provision of such accommodation and give due consideration to them, and may not provide such accommodation if there is someone with parental responsibility who is willing and able to provide accommodation for the child and objects to the local authority making such provision.[116] These provisions were intended to underline the general principles implicit in the Children Act that local authorities would work with parents in partnership to ensure the best outcomes for their children. All the guidance produced for social workers and other professionals in the context of child abuse stresses that, wherever it is possible to promote and protect the welfare of the child by leaving him in his family, this approach is to be preferred to damaging and possibly unnecessary removal.[117]

These provisions, taken together with the philosophy of working in partnership with parents, would appear to be working well when one considers the steady fall in the numbers of children being looked after by social services departments in England (a reduction from 92 270 in 1981 to 49 000 in 1995). This has been accompanied by an even steeper reduction in the numbers in residential care (down from 37 069 in 1981 to 8200 in 1994) revealing that the percentage of children placed with foster carers has significantly and steadily increased. One must also be careful to note that the fall in the numbers of those children recorded as being in care also disguises the fact that each year many thousands of children run away from care and the number of children living on the streets has increased by almost exactly the number representing the decrease of children recorded as being in residential care. This may be coincidental but is nevertheless an interesting fact. One of the other difficulties with the children who are now generally looked after by the local authority is that, as the DoH has recognized,[118] these children include a higher concentration of the most difficult cases. While the DoH has recognized that these may be the more difficult children, there has been no recognition on the part of central government that more financial support must be given to local authorities in order to support the increasing expenditure by them on providing for difficult children in residential care. As the report by Sir William Utting demonstrates,[119] local authority provision for children's residential care has repeatedly been subject to cuts in resources, with the consequent disasters in terms of child abuse controversies centred on children's residential care in England and Wales.

As to the law relating to the identification, reporting, investigation and initiation of legal proceedings, this is also generally to be found in the Children Act 1989. As far as identification of child abuse is concerned, a range of professional guidance exists for all professions who may come into contact with children and should be able to identify signs in the child to alert them to the possibility that the child is being abused.[120] In addition to practice guidance being issued to enable professionals to identify signs of child abuse, quite extensive training has taken place for professionals to enable them to be able to identify signs of abuse.

As far as the reporting of child abuse is concerned, English law, unlike that of 47 states of the USA, does not provide for the compulsory reporting of child abuse. The idea of a reporting law has been discussed in England,[121] but it was determined that it would not be appropriate to proceed with such a proposal. There is therefore no legal duty laid upon members of the public to report suspicions or knowledge of incidents of child abuse. Nevertheless, every encouragement is given to the public to ensure that, if they provide such information, anonymity will be protected. As has been emphasized by the highest court in the land,[122] the private promise of confidentiality must yield to the general public interest and in the administration of justice truth will out, unless, by reason of the character of the information or the relationship of the recipient to the informant, a more important public interest is served by protecting the information or the identity of the informant from disclosure in a court of law. The House of Lords concluded in *D* v. *N.S.P.C.C.* that the public interest of ensuring the protection of children was greater than the public interest of ensuring that the whole truth be told, and it thus refused to allow the disclosure of any details relating to the original informant in the particular case.

Under the present law, only local authority social workers, the NSPCC and the police have a duty to report suspicions that a child is in need of protection. Other professional groups working with children, while not subjected to any mandatory reporting law as such, have nevertheless found that their own professional associations' guidance seeks to impose such duty upon them. For example, the Standards Committee of the British Medical Council in November 1987 expressed the view that, if a doctor has reason for believing that a child has been physically or sexually abused, not only is it permissible for the doctor to disclose information to a third party, but it is also his duty to do so.[123] Similar guidance also exists for senior nurses, health visitors and midwives[124] and, although the 1992 guidance does not make a duty to disclose explicit, it is nevertheless implicit throughout the document wherever it discusses the relevant actions of nurses, health visitors and midwives in responding to suspicions about child abuse. That document makes reference[125] to the United Kingdom Central Council's 'Code of Professional Conduct for the Nurse, Midwife and Health Visitor' and to an advisory paper on confidentiality published in April 1987, where the advice is rather more explicit:

> in all cases where the practitioner deliberately discloses or withholds information in what she thinks is the public interest, she must be able to justify the decision. These situations can be particularly stressful, especially where vulnerable groups are concerned, as disclosure may mean the involvement of a third party, as in the case of children or the mentally handicapped. Practitioners should always take the opportunity to discuss the matter fully with other practitioners (not only or necessarily fellow nurses, midwives and health visitors), and if appropriate to consult with a professional organisation before making a decision. There will often be ramifications that are best explored before a final decision as to whether to withhold or disclose information is made.

It will be noted that such advice falls some way short of a stringent duty advised in the *Guidance for Doctors*.

Other professional staff, particularly those in the education service, may also be deemed to be in the front line as far as initial identification and referral processes in child abuse cases are concerned. Local education authorities all over England have, in compliance with local (ACPC) guidelines, issued education staff with an explanation of the Children Act and the procedures which may flow from the referral of a case of suspected child abuse, but large numbers of teachers in the public sector report little or no knowledge of the detail of the Children Act on child protection matters or of relevant procedures. Their general view is that they would try to refer the matter to the head teacher or, if there is one, and there should be, to the teacher with responsibility for the liaison with social services over child protection matters. Whilst the local education authorities (LEAs) are responsible for staff and the education service, such as teachers, education welfare officers, educational psychologists and youth workers, they have no responsibility for the private sector. This instead falls on social services departments, who should ensure that education establishments not maintained by the LEA are aware of the local inter-agency procedures, and that the governing bodies/proprietors of these establishments should ensure that appropriate procedures are in place, seeking advice as necessary from social services. It has also been thought advisable in England and Wales that all educational establishment procedures should also cover circumstances where a member of staff is suspected of abuse of children. The DoE in England and Wales has now issued two quite lengthy circulars,[126] and these emphasize that all teachers should be alert to signs of abuse and know to whom they should report any concern or suspicions.

As far as police reporting of concerns about child abuse is concerned, this stems from their primary duty to protect members of the community and to bring offenders to justice. As will be seen later,[127] the police have special powers to take action in emergencies, but where they have concerns about the possibility of child abuse which is of a non-urgent nature, they would be expected to notify such concerns to social services.

Finally, whilst identification and reporting of concerns about child abuse may come from any of the professionals in any of the agencies referred to and may come through to a social services department, the police or the NSPCC, referrals may also come from children themselves or from members of the public, or those working with children and families who are not accustomed to dealing with child protection matters, such as youth workers or priests. *Working Together* points out:

> All referrals, whatever their origin, must be taken seriously and must be considered with an open mind which does not prejudge the situation. The statutory agencies must ensure that people know how to refer to them, and they must facilitate the making of referrals and the prompt and appropriate action in response to expressions of concern. It is important in all these cases that the public and professionals are free to refer to the child protection agencies without fear that this will lead to uncoordinated and/or premature action.[128]

As events in Cleveland, Rochdale and the Orkneys have demonstrated, a balance needs to be struck between taking action designed to protect the child from abuse and at the same time protecting him or her and the family from the harm caused by unnecessary intervention.

The issue of reporting can also become difficult when it is the case that children are making allegations against those supposedly in positions of care over them. This most notably involves the situation when children make allegations against teachers in their schools or, when in the care of the local authority, they make allegations against care staff. Children as well as teachers and care staff in England need to be confident that such allegations will be dealt with in a proper fashion. It would appear to be the case, from anecdotal evidence obtained from children in schools and from successive government inquiry reports in relation to children in residential accommodation, that children still do not feel confident about approaching those in authority, more particularly where they are seeking to make a complaint against those who are supposed to be looking after them.[129]

Once suspicions of child abuse are reported to the local authority from whatever source, then, under s.47 Children Act 1989, the local authority is required to make or cause to be made such enquiries as it considers necessary. The purpose of such enquiries is to enable the local authority social services departments to determine whether they should take any action to safeguard or promote the child's welfare. It should also be noted that a local authority may receive information about the possibility of a child suffering or being likely to suffer significant harm, from a court welfare officer who may be engaged in providing a report to the court in family proceedings under Part II Children Act 1989, or the local authority may receive a direction from the court itself to conduct an investigation as to whether there is a need to institute care or supervision proceedings.[130]

The duty placed on local authority social services to investigate in cases of suspected child abuse is the same no matter where that abuse has occurred or by whom it has been perpetrated. Thus, whilst *additional* special procedures may be invoked where children are abused in residential settings, outside the family home, in foster placements or in schools, the first duty upon the local authority is to engage in an investigation under s.47, which may well include taking steps to involve the police.[131] This is certainly the case if, at any point in the early stages of the investigation by social services or the NSPCC, it becomes apparent that there is the possibility of a criminal offence having been committed against the child. It may be the case, of course, that the police have been involved in some way, either in the initial referral or in the early stages of investigation following referral, but it is deemed to be essential that there is an early strategy discussion between police and social services in order to plan the investigation properly and, in particular, the role of each agency and the extent of joint investigations.[132]

It is the responsibility of the agency receiving the referral to initiate this and, throughout the early stages of the investigation, both police and social services in England have to keep in mind that it may be necessary to invoke both civil child protection proceedings and criminal proceedings against the potential perpetrator. Interviewing the child victim or the child or adult perpetrator must be conducted in accordance with the established codes of practice and current case law in England and Wales. As far as interviewing child victims are concerned the *Memorandum of Good Practice* on video-recorded interviews with child witnesses for criminal proceedings should be followed wherever such interviews are being video-recorded.[133] Problems associated with using the *Memorandum*, which followed on from the recommendations of the Pigot Committee, have been identified,[134] and there have been repeated calls for all the recommendations of the Pigot Committee to be implemented in order to improve all aspects of the criminal justice system when responding to the problems posed by the perpetration of abuse on child victims.[135]

The provisions in s.47 Children Act 1989 which go on to deal with processing the investigation by social services provide that enquiries must, in particular, be directed towards establishing whether they should make any application to a court or exercise any of their other powers under the 1989 Act, which could include any of the preventive measures described earlier. A determination to pursue legal proceedings for a care or supervision order under the provisions of Part IV of the Children Act 1989 or for any of the emergency orders such as an emergency protection order or for a child assessment order under Part V Children Act 1989 should only be reached after full discussion with all the concerned professionals involved, as well as with the parents in a child protection conference. This round-the-table discussion has been referred to earlier,[136] and is the subject of detailed guidance issued in *Working Together*.[137] The case conference's only decision-making power is to place a child on the child protection register, as discussed earlier, but, following a consideration of all the circumstances of the case, and where it is felt necessary to do so, proceedings for orders under Part IV or V of the Act may be recommended to social services for them to initiate the proceedings in the courts. The threshold criteria which must be satisfied before the court will respond by the making of such orders include that one must be able to establish to the court's satisfaction on the balance of probabilities that a child is suffering, or is likely to suffer, significant harm; that this is attributable to the absence of reasonable care on the part of the child's parents; *or*, that the child is beyond parental control; *and* that making an order is better for the child than making no order at all.[138] The interpretation of various phrases within the threshold criteria has given rise to the development of a considerable body of case law since the implementation of the Children Act 1989 in October 1991 and thus, as described earlier, the courts' attention has focused on the meaning of the phrase 'significant',[139] on the meaning of 'similar child' for the purposes of interpreting significant harm,[140] and on the meaning of the phrase 'is suffering';[141] there has also been discussion in the courts as to the relevant standard of proof which should apply.[142]

Despite the fact that the workings of English common law have always necessitated the interpretation of phrases in statutes by judges, there is concern that decisions such as that in *Re H* can send out extremely negative messages to children who have finally plucked up the courage to complain, especially when they are fearful of abuse which has occurred to them being further perpetrated on younger siblings, as was the case in *Re H*. What was felt by many to be the higher threshold criteria laid down in the Children Act 1989 has also prompted many members of the judiciary to express concerns that children might formerly have been better protected under the old law than they may now appear to be under the provisions of the Children Act 1989. Such feelings as are expressed by the judiciary are nevertheless difficult to substantiate, especially given that one of the primary philosophies of the Children Act 1989 was the promotion of partnership with parents and, in furtherance of the spirit of the United Nations Convention on the Rights of the Child, the promotion of the child's upbringing within his or her own family so far as this was consistent with the child's welfare.

It is nevertheless the case that there has been a significant drop in the number of cases taken before the courts by local authority social services for care or supervision orders. Once the various criteria outlined above are satisfied, the court, having considered that it would be better for the child to make an order than not to do so, can then choose which orders to make under the Children Act, including the making of care orders which will place the child in the care of the local authority and give the local authority day-to-day parental responsibility for the child,[143] or the making of a supervision order which will leave the child in the home with the parents or other carers, but will provide for local authority social workers to have direct monitoring of the child's situation. Under the provisions of the Children Act 1989, the court may also make orders under s.8 providing for the child to live with other relatives or even friends, and to have contact with other parties, or may issue prohibited steps orders and specific issue orders in relation to the exercise of other aspects of parental responsibility over the child. It should be pointed out that the court cannot make a residence order and a care order together, as the one cancels out the other.[144]

Although, clearly, it is the intention of the legislature to provide that upon the making of a care order a child should then be safe from further abuse, experience has demonstrated that in England and Wales this is not necessarily the case. Children who are accommodated either with foster parents or in residential homes run by local authorities or private agencies are also at risk even in these settings, as has been identified earlier, and it has become a matter of major concern to the new government that reports such as that of Sir William Utting[145] and the probable findings of the forthcoming Inquiry into Children's Homes in North Wales will reveal a catalogue of abuse in respect of children who desperately needed to be protected, having already experienced abuse in their own homes.

Given that there are risks in removing children from their own homes, various recommendations were made to government that other civil law provisions, specifically those dealing with domestic violence, might also be reformed so as to provide greater protection for children who might be at risk of abuse either directly through suffering at the hands of violent perpetrators in the family home or indirectly through witnessing such violence. Thus the reforms providing for the addition of exclusion orders to emergency protection orders and interim care or supervision orders issued under the Children Act, effected by means of the reforms contained in the Family Law Act 1996,[146] should mean that children will not be subject to unnecessary removal, but the willingness of local authorities to allow such children to remain in their homes permanently will clearly depend upon the willingness of the other partner to obtain non-molestation and exclusion orders on a permanent basis under the provisions of Part IV Family Law Act 1996. Whether or not social services are convinced that the partner is so prepared, and that she will be prepared to enforce such orders under the enforcement provisions contained in the new legislation, remains to be seen, but at least the provisions are now there.

In addition, in relation to the problem of domestic violence, as was noted earlier, the new provisions of Part IV Family Law Act 1996[147] provide that the interests and welfare of children in the domestic violence setting now have to be considered and, where the balance of harm test is satisfied in respect of them, then the court must make the relevant orders. Enforcement of such orders, however, as was pointed out previously, critically depends upon the willingness of the adult partner providing for the day-to-day care of the child to enforce such orders, and such willingness is not always already forthcoming. It is also the case that, under the Family Law Act 1996,[148] a child under the age of 16 can apply for an occupation order or a non-molestation order, provided the child has the leave of the court, which will be given where the court is satisfied that the child has sufficient understanding to make the proposed application. This provides a so called 'Gillick-type test'[149] for allowing the court to consider whether they should allow children to apply for occupation orders or for non- molestation orders under the Act. Unfortunately, the Act itself does not provide any process by means of which children could obtain information or assistance in seeking to obtain orders under the Act. As is the case with so many provisions of English law which purport to give children rights, this is likely to be more illusory than real, given the lack of information which so many children have about the law which may be relevant to them in England and Wales.

Criminal law provisions

The principal provision in criminal law designed specifically to protect children from abuse must be seen as being that provided by s.1 Children and Young Persons Act, 1933.[150] Under this,[151] any person who is at least 16 years of age, and has responsibility for any child or young person under that age, who wilfully causes or procures that child to suffer assault, ill-treatment, neglect, abandonment or exposure in a manner likely to cause the child unnecessary suffering or injury to health,[152] will be liable to criminal prosecution. Section 1(7) of the Act[153] provides a description of the persons who may be held liable for committing the prohibited types of conduct stipulated in s.1(7):

1. Any person who has parental responsibility for the child or young person; or is otherwise legally liable to maintain him; and any person who has care of him shall be presumed to have responsibility for that child or young person.
2. A person who is presumed to be responsible for a child or young person by virtue of the preceding provision shall not be taken to have ceased to be responsible for him by reason only that he does not have care of him.

These provisions were amended by the Children Act 1989 in order to incorporate the important principle of parental responsibility for the child and it can be seen that the provisions emphasize the role not only of the person having actual care of the child at any time but also of the person having parental responsibility. As was pointed out earlier,[154] the civil law, importantly, does not lay down any guidelines as to the standards of care which parents should exercise in the upbringing of their children, and the criminal law in turn is similarly lacking in clarity, in that it creates a single offence dealing with various forms of cruelty, some of which are defined within the body of the statute itself but the majority of which have, yet again, had to be interpreted by reference to case law developed by the judges over a number of years. Even where some further definition is offered in the statute, for example in relation to the concept of neglect,[155] as is the case with the concept of 'neglecting a child in a manner likely to cause injury to his health',[156] it is still the case that the courts have had to interpret other words used in this sub-section, such as 'wilfully', 'ill-treatment', 'neglect', 'abandonment' and 'exposure'. These terms and the expanded definition provided by judicial interpretation will now be briefly considered.

It should be noted that the word 'wilfully' in s.1(1) CYPA, 1933 qualifies all five actions or omissions under this provision and thus makes it clear that any offence under s.1 requires a state of mind on the part of the offender directed towards the particular act or failure to act which constitutes the *actus reus* and warrants the description 'wilful', as was seen in the leading House of Lords case, *R.* v. *Sheppard*,[157] which is the leading authority on the interpretation of the term 'wilful' in criminal statutes. In that case, the House of Lords held that a man 'wilfully' fails to provide adequate medical attention for a child if he either (a) deliberately does so, knowing that there is some risk that the child's health may suffer unless he receives such attention; or (b) does so because he does not care whether the child may be in need of medical treatment or not. It further appears, from the case of *R.* v. *Hayles*,[158] that a carer's conduct might fall within more than one of the statutory categories listed in s.1(7); thus neglect might also, in certain circumstances, be described as ill-treatment under the provisions of the section.

Section 1 Children and Young Persons Act, 1933, as referred to above, thus lists five types of cruel conduct which may overlap with each other. The types of ill-treatment referred to are assault, ill-treatment, neglect, abandonment and exposure, and it is now proposed to consider these briefly. It should be noted that physical assault involves 'any unlawful interference with a person's body which causes the apprehension of harm, whether or not there is physical violence'. It should be noted, therefore, that merely causing the child astonishment or disgust would not be assault within the meaning of the section. As far as assault under the specific provisions of s.1(1) is concerned, it is clear from the case of *R.* v. *Hatton*[159] that, for an assault to fall within this section, there must be something more than a mere common assault. The section provides that not only must there be 'wilful assault' but it must also be committed 'in a manner likely to cause the child unnecessary suffering or injury to his health'.

As far as 'ill-treatment' is concerned, there is no definition of this term in the Act, but it may be assumed that it is intended to cover wilful ill-treatment, and that bullying or frightening would suffice, or any course of conduct calculated to cause unnecessary suffering or injury to health. There is no need to prove an assault or battery, but clearly a series of assaults, even though not coming within the scope of the assaults envisaged by the section, might amount to wilful ill-treatment. It is, however, to be noted again that it is a defence that the alleged ill-treatment consisted in reasonable correction by a parent or other person having lawful control of the child.[160]

As far as the term 'neglect' is concerned, Lord Diplock stated, in giving the leading judgment in *R.* v. *Sheppard*, that:

> the actus reus of the offence with which the accused were charged in the instant case, does not involve construing the verb, 'neglect' for the offence fell within the deeming provision[161] and the only question as respects the actus reus was did

the parents fail to provide medical aid which was in fact inadequate in view of the child's actual state of health at the relevant time.

This is a pure question of objective fact to be determined in the light of what had become known by the date of the trial to be the child's actual state of health at the relevant time. If the answer to this question is 'yes' then by virtue of the deeming provision the actus reus, namely neglect in the manner likely to cause injury to health, was established but it still has to be proved that the neglect was 'wilful'.[162]

It was held in the case of *R. v. Ryland*[163] that the word 'neglect' sufficiently alleges the inability of the parents to provide for the child and that it was not necessary for the indictment to allege specifically that the parents had means. The old cases on 'means' however, are of less importance in the welfare state era. A failure to resort to the assistance authorities for the means of maintaining a child where a parent cannot do so out of his own pocket would presumably amount to neglect.[164] Where a father who earned a sufficient wage did not pay over to his wife enough to clothe and feed the children properly, it has been held to be no defence for the father, when charged with neglect, to say that by resort to the assistance authorities the mother might have obviated the effects of his neglect.[165] Evidence of the possession by the accused of such means at a date before the neglect as would presumably not be exhausted at the date of neglect is some evidence of the possession of means at the date of neglect.[166]

Refusal to permit an operation may be, but not necessarily, such a failure to provide medical aid as amounts to wilful neglect causing injury to health. The question is one of fact to be decided upon in each case upon the basis of the evidence;[167] as to a deliberate omission to supply medical or surgical aid on conscientious grounds, the case of *R. v. Senior*[168] should be referred to. In this case the parents were members of the 'Peculiar People', a religious sect which did not believe in medical interventions, but on a charge of neglect under the statute, the child's father was held liable because he knew that the child's physical suffering would be alleviated by the treatment but had deliberately refrained from having recourse to it because he thought that to do so would be sinful as showing an unwillingness to accept God's will in relation to the child.

As far as the concept of 'abandonment' is concerned, in *R. v. Boulden*,[169] after the children had been abandoned first by their mother and then by their father, the court held that the criterion to be employed was: did the parents take all reasonable steps to ensure that the child had been received into care? The fact that the father had left them alone unattended with only a small quantity of food, in this case, was sufficient to constitute 'abandonment' of his children.

As far as the meaning of the word 'exposure' is concerned, the courts have indicated that the exposure need not necessarily consist of the physical placing of the child somewhere with intent to injure it.[170] In the case of *R.* v. *Whibley*,[171] five children had been left at a juvenile court and it was held that this action was unlikely to cause them unnecessary suffering or injury to health, since this was not a place which would expose them to injury. The courts have further held that wilful exposure under s.1(1) CYPA, 1933 does not extend to exposure to risk.[172] A father took his eight-year-old son and five other boys onto a piece of timber on a disused section of the London docks and entered them into deep water, but none of them in fact suffered harm. If injury had in fact been suffered by the boys then the father would have indeed been deemed liable. What the court seemed to be saying in this case is that liability under s.1(1) will surely have to depend upon whether a risk actually materializes and the children actually suffer some degree of harm or injury.

It can be seen, therefore, that under the interpretation given to various offences which might be committed under s.1 CYPA, 1933 the courts have been determined to protect children from a wide variety of possible offences which might be perpetrated and are also alive to the risks which might be posed to children in allowing spurious defences to be developed in relation to any charges which might ensue. It should also be noted that, following the concerns of a number of children's charities such as the NSPCC, and a number of expressions of judicial concern, the maximum penalty on conviction of indictment under s.1 CYPA, 1933 was increased from two years' imprisonment to 10 years by the provisions of the Criminal Justice Act 1988.[173] This change was a very important factor in signalling to parents generally, but also to the police and other child welfare agencies, that the government was taking the case of child abuse under these provisions extremely seriously.

Under the Offences against the Person Act, 1861 it is further provided that anyone who unlawfully abandons or exposes any child under the age of two such as to endanger the life of the child or to cause or risk permanent injury shall be guilty of an offence and upon conviction may be liable to a term of imprisonment not exceeding five years. This criminal offence was clearly created to try to prevent children from being abandoned in situations where they could suffer considerable and possibly fatal harm, but prosecution for such an offence may well depend upon the circumstances of the case, particularly where, in a number of situations today, young girls under the age of 16 having babies may well leave them in a place where they hope the child will be found. Generally speaking, the authorities will stress their need to trace the mother, not for the purposes of prosecuting her but out of concern for the welfare of both the child's mother and the child.

It should be noted that where there is perceived apprehension of harm by a child then, in addition to possible liability under s.1 CYPA, 1933, people guilty of perpetrating or attempting to perpetrate such harm on a child may be charged with alternative offences, such as that of common assault under s.42 Offences against the Person Act, 1861 or common assault and battery under s.39 Criminal Justice Act, 1988. In cases of more serious harm being perpetrated against the child, there are similarly offences of assault,[174] unlawful and maliciously wounding,[175] and causing grievous bodily harm to the child.[176] These provisions are of course equally applicable in relation to offences against adults. Such charges may be made in addition to a charge being brought under s.1 CYPA, 1933.

As far as sexual offences perpetrated on children are concerned, there are a range of specific offences in relation to children provided for by the Sexual Offences Act 1956 to 1996. The wide-scale problem of child sexual abuse, and the fact that some recognition is now being given to the fact that child prostitution is a situation in which the child participants should be seen more as victims than as offenders, has meant that both the current and previous governments have indicated a stricter approach to perpetrators of sexual abuse on children. The criminal law currently provides for a series of offences under the Sexual Offences Act 1956 which either specifically relate to children[177] or contain special provisions within them relating to offences committed on children.[178]

Prior to 1993, it was presumed that a boy under the age of 14 could not be guilty of rape as he was presumed to be incapable of committing this offence,[179] but since the Sexual Offences Act 1993 this presumption has been abolished and there now appears to be no automatic presumption that a boy of any age will be incapable of committing the offence of rape. It must therefore be assumed that, where the provisions of the Sexual Offences Act 1956 to 1996 use the word 'man', this does not necessarily import the notion of someone being over the age of 18 but rather imports the idea of a person having the qualities of a member of the male sex and therefore being a male by gender. The same is true of words used in the Sexual Offences Act relating to women, although there are specific offences with regard to unlawful intercourse with a girl under the age of 13,[180] and the offence of unlawful sexual intercourse with a girl under the age of 16.[181] The creation of such special offences in respect of girls under the age of 13 and under the age of 16 recognizes the potentially vulnerable situation of girls under these ages, although in the case of an offence under s.6 it will be a defence for the man if he is under the age of 24 to prove that he had reasonable cause to believe that the girl was over the age of 16, provided he has not previously been charged with a similar offence. Another offence which specifically protects females, although it is not specifically age-related, is that under s.10 Sexual Offences Act 1956 which provides that it is an offence for a man to have sexual intercourse with a woman whom he knows to be his granddaughter, daughter, sister or mother, and it is further a criminal offence for a man to incite to have sexual intercourse with him a girl under the age of 16 whom he knows to be his grand-daughter, daughter or sister.[182]

As far as the protection of boys from sexual abuse is concerned, these are again principally to be found in the Sexual Offences Act 1956. Thus s.12 of that Act provides that it is an offence for a person to commit buggery with another person otherwise than where the act takes place in private and both parties have attained the age of 18. Section 13 of the Act prohibits acts of gross indecency between males in public and also the procuring of the commission by a man of an act of gross indecency with another man, and certainly where the males who are being procured are under the age of 18 the person doing the procuring will be convicted of an offence.

It is further an offence of a woman of the age of 16 or over to have sexual intercourse with a man whom she knows to be her grandfather, father, brother or son. This section thereby creates the offence of incest by a woman.[183]

Under ss.14 and 15 of the Sexual Offences Act 1956, the offences of indecent assault on a woman and indecent assault on a man are established and both provisions provide that neither a girl nor a boy under the age of 16 can in law give consent to prevent any act which would otherwise be an assault.

The Sexual Offences Act 1956 also contains a range of provisions dealing with prostitution which again are intended to protect women, including the offence of causing a woman to become a prostitute,[184] the procuring of a girl under the age of 21 to have unlawful sexual intercourse in any part of the world with a third person,[185] and the causing or encouraging the prostitution of a girl under the age of 16;[186] that Act also provides for it to be an offence for a man knowingly to live wholly or in part on the earnings of prostitution, which in this case refers to women prostitutes.[187]

There are also various provisions in the Sexual Offences Act 1956 dealing with offences which may be committed on boys, including the offence of a man persistently soliciting or importuning in a public place for immoral purposes,[188] and, by the Sexual Offences Act 1967, the offence of living off the earnings of male prostitution.[189] As was noted earlier,[190] there is now a great deal of concern amongst those working in social services and the police that children involved in prostitution should not be being dealt with themselves as criminal offenders but should rather be treated as 'children in need' under the provisions of Part III Children Act 1989. There are, however, a number of difficulties which face the police, including the difficulty, particularly with girls involved in prostitution, of actually identifying them as children, more especially when they give false names and details and obviously false ages. Richard Edgington indicates[191] that, instead of treating young prostitutes, be they boys or girls, as offenders, the police should approach the situation more as if they were dealing with child abuse victims. Edgington asserts that the advantage to the police in treating young prostitutes as victims would be that the joint investigatory approach would further assist enquiries into the circumstances surrounding the introduction of the child to prostitution and may reveal evidence of any person compelling the prostitution who might, in addition, be considered to be an abuser and therefore be rigorously pursued using these provisions of the criminal law. Edgington further notes that the medical examination normally undertaken of victims would in such circumstances necessarily focus on evidence of sexual activity, but may well provide evidence of assault, which would tend to assist further the investigation of pimps and procurers.

At the same time as trying to protect young people from potential sexual abuse by creating offences under the Sexual Offences Act, the government in England has also tried to deal with adults from the UK who may seek to go abroad to commit sexual acts upon children. Thus, in a range of measures, legislation has made it an offence to conspire to commit, or to incite another person to commit, certain sexual acts against children abroad,[192] and has further provided that the commission of any sexual offences, as defined under the provisions earlier described, in a country or territory outside the United Kingdom will constitute a sexual offence under the law of England and Wales in the same way as it would do if it had been committed in England and Wales.[193] The extension of the territorial reach of English criminal law by s.7 Sex Offenders Act 1997 so that the sexual exploitation of children committed abroad could be penalized here was in response to a very vociferous and well informed lobby who had sought this extension under the original 1996 legislation. In extending the territorial reach, the 1997 Act follows the lead given by the USA, Australia, New Zealand and Sweden who, by July 1996, had, already passed such extraterritorial legislation penalizing child sex tourism, and is in line with others, including Canada, Italy and Ireland, who had either begun to legislate or had committed themselves to so doing. In providing for such legislation, the government in England has complied with its obligations under Article 34 United Nations Convention on the Rights of the Child.[194]

Other offences specifically seeking to protect children from sexual abuse by being involved in indecent conduct or being portrayed in indecent photographs include offences under the Indecency with Children Act, 1960;[195] under the Protection of Children Act 1978[196] the Criminal Justice Act 1988[197] and also the Sexual Offences (Protective Materials) Act 1997. This last measure was seen as particularly important when it was revealed that inmates in prison were obtaining access to materials relating to the prosecution of offenders held in remand or those who were conducting appeals in respect of sexual offences against children. This Act allows the defence and others to gain regulated access to such materials but also provides for the creation of offences if an unauthorized person gets hold of such material.

It can be seen, therefore, that strenuous attempts have been made by the legislature in England to try to deal with problems arising from the sexual abuse and exploitation of children, but that there is still some way to go, particularly in relation to dealing with child participants in activities such as prostitution.

Given that a large number of offences involving the physical, sexual or other abuse of children are committed by people in England and Wales in any one year, and that this may include assaults and sexual abuse on children committed by other children,[198] it is clearly important that some attempt is made to keep track of the activities and movements of such individuals who may pose a very real threat to children in the future. In the past, both the Department for Education and the Department of Health have held lists of people who had been convicted of offences towards children in order that those seeking to employ them might seek access to information in order to gauge the risk which such individuals might pose if they were employed in positions where they would have to work with children. As can be seen from the inquiries relating to child abuse in Leicestershire and in North Wales, even where such records are kept, perpetrators seeking employment in children's settings may well be able to evade the protective net by using alternative names and employment details. Alternatively, it may be the case that records are simply not kept up-to-date or that, where individuals may have been cautioned for certain offences, those details are not adequately recorded.

Great uncertainty has also surrounded the situation with regard to obtaining relevant criminal records and the responsibility of the police in responding to requests for what are known as 'police checks' on individuals who may be employed in settings involving close work with children. In an attempt to ensure that there is greater uniformity of approach to these issues, but also greater protection afforded to children, the government in England has recently enacted provisions in the Police Act 1997 which will allow prospective employers to insist on a prospective employee providing a 'criminal conviction certificate', which will record convictions held on central police records which are not 'spent' under the Rehabilitation of Offenders Act 1974. A system of registration to be administered by the Criminal Records Agency is created for employers and licensing bodies working in areas which require access to certain *additional* types of pre-employment information because of the sensitive nature of the work (for example, certain licensed activities, work with children, young people or vulnerable adults under this Act).[199] Organizations like social services, charitable organizations, independent schools and the like will be subject to a Code of Practice on the use of information,[200] and will be liable for offences of improper disclosure.[201]

In an even greater effort to provide protection for children, the Act provides that joint applications may be made by a prospective employee and the registered person for two further types of check: 'criminal record certificates'[202] and 'enhanced criminal record certificates'.[203] These provisions provide greater protection for children in that a 'criminal record certificate' will include both 'spent' and 'unspent' convictions under the 1974 Act and further, and very importantly, will also disclose details of police cautions. An 'enhanced criminal record certificate' will include all of the details on the criminal record certificate, together with information from a local police force record check and details of minor convictions and cautions *and other 'non-conviction information'*.[204] These provisions are really quite radical in terms of the amount of information which may now be provided to prospective employers and such extensive enquiries as will now be possible may well reveal alternative names being used by an individual. The creation of a central system of administration under the aegis of the Criminal Records Agency is also important to ensure uniformity and to signal to prospective employers the degree of seriousness which the government and police authority are now attaching to the position of those employed in the task of looking after the nation's children in any setting.

The Secretary of State for Health in England and Wales, Mr Frank Dobson, declared, following the publication of the findings of Sir William Utting's Report,[205] that it had presented 'a woeful tale of failure at all levels to provide a secure and decent childhood for some of the most vulnerable children and that elementary safeguards were not put in place or were not enforced' and that he would 'chair a Ministerial task force to ensure that all provisions designed to protect children were rigorously enforced'. It remains to be seen how rigorously the provisions regarding 'criminal conviction' and 'criminal records certificates' and 'enhanced criminal records certificates' will be enforced to protect the nation's children in the future. Evidence to the National Commission of Inquiry into Child Abuse and Neglect found that in many situations people were being employed in settings which involved the care of the children where police checks had not been completed or, indeed, where reference had not been made to the consultancy lists provided by the Department of Health and the Department for Education.[206] Whether or not the new agency will be able to perform the functions with which it has been charged will depend on the government being prepared to match resources to its own words.

In a further attempt to protect children from those people who have been convicted or cautioned in respect of specific sexual offences against children, the last government enacted the Sex Offenders Act 1997 which requires such individuals to notify details of their names, addresses and any subsequent changes to the police force in whose area they are living. This Act also provides that, where a person has used one or more other names then he must notify each of the aliases which he uses to the police so that they may be aware of all his potential movements. The Act provides that it is an offence to fail to comply, without reasonable excuse, with the demands of the Act in relation to the notification of such information to the police, which can attract a fine or imprisonment for a term not exceeding six months. The most serious notification requirements relate to those who have received a sentence of imprisonment for life or for a term of 30 months or more, or who have been made the subject of a hospital restriction order. These persons are required to notify the police for an indefinite period and the period under which other persons remain under an obligation to notify the police of their details reduces according to the severity of the sentence imposed upon them for their previous offences.[207] Registration of those subject to the Act's requirements was supposed to have been completed by 30 September 1997.[208] Concerns about the civil liberties aspects of this type of legislation seem to have been overborne by the concerns of those responsible for the care of children, including their parents. This Act represents another attempt by the government to protect those who may be subject to abuse by making parents and other concerned adults aware of the presence within the community of individuals with a tendency to perpetrate sexual offences against children. On the other hand, there are some concerns, not only from the civil libertarian viewpoint but also from the humanitarian viewpoint, about the effects on the lives of those who might be trying to attempt a return to normal life in the community and who are undergoing treatment for their problems. This is again an area which will repay further continued close attention.

Recent changes in court procedures within the criminal justice system

A number of points as to the conflicts posed by the different demands of the civil child protection process and the criminal offence investigation process has been noted earlier, but the government has sought, through various legislative provisions, to ameliorate the conditions facing child victims having to give evidence about the abuse which they have suffered. Although, as a result of the Pigot Committee Report,[209] a number of changes were made to the processes of the criminal justice system in England dealing with the problem of difficulties faced by child witnesses, it should be noted that the system still has a considerable way to go before it can be described as substantially contributing to the prevention of child abuse and neglect. At the moment, the suspicion is that it contributes to child abuse and neglect.[210]

The Criminal Justice Act 1988 provided for the reception of evidence by television link in certain cases in order to reduce the stressful effects of a court appearance upon child witnesses in alleged child abuse cases, and the reforms effected by the Criminal Justice Act 1991 have meant that English courts have used video- and tape-recorded evidence with increasing frequency. Since 5 January 1989, evidence by children can be given as normal in the court room, but children can also now be allowed to testify from a room outside the actual court room and evidence may also be given by a satellite link where a witness is outside the UK.[211]

The Criminal Justice Act 1991 took the Criminal Justice Act 1988 reforms even further in the realm of video or live television links and has made admissible (in most cases) prerecorded interviews with child witnesses in place of live evidence in chief. A video-recording is thus admissible where the child is not the accused; the child is available for cross-examination (if the proceedings get that far); and rules of court requiring disclosure of the circumstances in which the recording was made had been properly complied with.[212]

A video-recorded interview is admissible at all stages at the crown court and in the youth courts for sexual offences and offences of violence and cruelty against children. Where any particular court does not possess live link facilities, the hearing can be moved to a court which does, even if that involves going outside the area for which the court acts. Live television links are available to any young person who has to be cross-examined following the admission of video-recorded evidence. A video-recording of an interview between an adult and a child who is not the accused, or one of the accused, is admissible if it relates to any matter in issue in the proceedings.

The recording of an earlier investigative interview with a child victim/witness is not admissible as a matter of course. It has first to be shown to a judge who has the power to declare it inadmissible in certain designated circumstances and if it is felt that it should be excluded in the interests of justice. Thus, before the recording may be given in evidence, leave of the court must be obtained and this will not be granted where the child witness will not be available for cross-examination, or where any rule requiring disclosure of the circumstances in which the recording was made has not been complied with to the court's satisfaction, or where the court is of the opinion, having regard to all the circumstances of the case, that, in the interests of justice, the recording ought not to be admitted.[213]

The court is allowed to exclude only that part of a statement which it is not in the interests of justice to admit, but the court is asked to consider whether any prejudice to the accused or one of the accused might result from showing the whole or most of the recorded interview. The construction of the provisions indicates that all three conditions must be satisfied before leave can be given.[214] Once such a recording has been admitted, the child should not be examined in chief on any matters covered in the recording, although examination of the child on other matters not covered in the recording is permitted, and this may be done through the live video link.[215] Any statement (which may include drawings and models, since a statement may include any representation of fact, whether made in words or otherwise)[216] disclosed in such a recording shall be treated as if given by a child in oral testimony in the witness box. Thus it shall not be regarded as hearsay simply because it is a recording.[217] It should be noted, however, that any statement made in a recording by a witness will not corroborate any other evidence given by that witness.[218]

Under the third condition provided for in this section,[219] the video-recording may be ruled out if it is not in the interests of justice to view it. The tape would, therefore, need to be of sufficient clarity in sound and picture quality in order for the court to view it as prima facie viewable.[220] The most obvious cases warranting exclusion might be where there are inadequacies in testimony amounting to evidence insufficient to satisfy a criminal prosecution, or the inclusion of inadmissible materials such as hearsay narrated by the child, or allegations of similar offences which have not been the subject of charges and which would not be admissible under the similar fact rule.[221]

It is the case, therefore, that children may still be called as witnesses and may have to undergo the trauma and ordeal of cross-examination in open court. Amendments moved in the House of Lords (on the basis of recommendations by the Pigot Committee Report) to allow the prosecution to have the right to apply for a child witness to be examined and cross-examined at a pre-trial out-of-court hearing, which could have been video-recorded and shown to the court, did not survive. Two main objections were taken to this form of pre-trial examination, in that it was said to be impracticable, unrealistic and logistically difficult to prepare cross-examination, particularly if it was supposed to be carried out long before the trial and especially if it meant that the child would not be recalled to give evidence, even if new material were discovered; and that, if the child could be recalled for cross-examination at any time during the trial, this would in effect prove to be more stressful to the child and might prolong the agony and distress of the whole occasion for the child.

Nevertheless, the advances represented by the Criminal Justice Act 1988 and 1991 are to be commended as representing a clear attempt to reduce the possibility of system abuse. Other major steps forward to improve the experiences of children appearing as witnesses have included the preparation of the *Child Witness Pack*, which consists of information and advice for parents and carers, an activity book for child witnesses aged five to nine and a book for witnesses aged 10–15.[222] It is to be hoped that this excellent pack could now be updated to provide additional guidance to children with regard to their ability to review video testimony which they may have provided and further that it should be updated in the light of children's experiences within the court system. Unfortunately, the resources to enable this to be done have not yet been made available.

In early 1997, the NSPCC, with the cooperation of the Judicial Studies Board, produced an important video, 'A Case for Balance', aimed at instructing judges in particular, but also barristers participating in criminal cases, of the ways in which child victim witnesses should be treated in court.[223] This video graphically illustrates how the adversarial process involved in the criminal justice system in England can lead to the serious abuse of child victims presenting themselves to give evidence in court or even on a live video link. The video encourages judges to take a much more involved and interfering approach when they believe that barristers are bullying a child or even engaging in tactics in which they would normally engage when cross-examining an adult witness. Nevertheless, the experience of children appearing as witnesses in the criminal courts is not one which is felt to encourage other children similarly to offer such evidence and media reports of the way in which children have been treated in courts only serve to accentuate this to other young people. It is clear that a great deal more needs to be done in England to support child witnesses. There have been one or two specialist witness support schemes operating in different parts of England for the support of child witnesses, but these are by no means widespread and many of them suffer for lack of funding. Such schemes are seen to be vital in supporting child witnesses and thus in securing convictions for perpetrators of child abuse and must be widely established all over England if children are to have any confidence at all in the criminal justice system.

Information about the criminal justice system as a whole and about the relationship between criminal prosecutions and civil child protection proceedings is not readily available to children who are the victims of child abuse and neglect. Children and young people themselves feel that greater care should be taken to explain the different purposes of the two systems, since many feel betrayed, and personally to blame, if a criminal prosecution fails to result in a conviction because their evidence has been called into question. Basic explanations that the standards of proof in criminal trials and in civil proceedings are different can often do wonders for the child. On the other hand, there are still major problems for the child and sometimes an appalling lack of judicial sensitivity to the problems which children will face at the conclusion of criminal and civil proceedings where their evidence appears not to have been believed.[224] In civil child protection proceedings there will often be, in England at least, a special representative of the child's interests known now as a litigation friend, who is an independent person generally qualified as a social worker, and who will explain to the child in civil child protection proceedings what is or will be going on in court and will endeavour to explain the whole process. There is no such comparable special representative for the child who has to experience the criminal justice system, unless this is made available through the child witness support schemes. This is because the child is not seen as a party to the proceedings and thus, where there are no special child witness support schemes in operation, the child will often only have the support of the non-abusing parent if the child is still living within the family, or, where the child has been removed, the support of social workers. Social workers have not been trained to deal, in such situations, with the problems raised by the intricacies of the criminal justice system. Given that there will be cases where the child has to appear in court, or has to undergo cross examination, the child will only be able to participate fully if she or he is prepared for the process and given support throughout. Such support is not available at present within the system in England and Wales, and it was the view of the National Commission that children should have some support available to them when undergoing this process. Thus, whilst some recent changes to the law have undoubtedly improved the situation with regard to the experience of children giving evidence of abuse within the criminal justice system, there is still much that remains to be done.

MANAGEMENT AND STRATEGIES FOR THE MANAGEMENT OF CHILD ABUSE IN ENGLAND

As has been pointed out earlier,[225] child abuse comes to the attention of the authorities in England and Wales usually through the child disclosing the abuse to a parent, teacher, health visitor or some other concerned relative or person with whom they have contact or by a third person directly observing actual abuse or the consequences of abuse upon a child. As was also noted earlier,[226] a range of guidance has been issued to professionals who might come into contact with children experiencing abuse, advising them on the course of action which they should adopt. Once a report of abuse is made to the police, social services or the NSPCC, there is a duty to conduct a further investigation in order to determine whether criminal or civil proceedings or possibly both should be pursued in the courts.

Social services authorities in England and Wales and the police, together with the range of other possible professionals who may be involved, are subject to quite detailed guidance on the subject of inter-agency cooperation issued in the important document, *Working Together*.[227] Despite what some might have seen as the crisis of confidence in social workers and constant widespread media criticism, it is nevertheless the case that, throughout the whole period in which child abuse has been centre stage in England, social workers have been seen to be those exercising primary responsibility in this area. Thus, *Working Together* recommends the employment of specialist child protection coordinators to oversee the various child protection systems established in all areas of the country and the structures which support the coordinators' role really date back to the findings of the Maria Colwell inquiry in 1974.[228] While the social services have a key coordinating role, this is supported by the presence of the Area Child Protection Committee which consists of senior managers of all agencies within the area of a particular social services department who might be involved in child protection work, as described earlier, and thus should have representatives of the social services, police, health, education, housing and probation departments as well as independent members. The principal function of the ACPC is to supervise the child protection system operating in a given area and monitor its operation. It also has responsibility for issuing procedural guidance to all practitioners in addition to that distributed by government departments, which it does through local ACPC handbooks, and also for identifying and meeting the training needs of the various personnel involved in the child protection system.

In order to promote the availability of information in respect of children who might be causing concern, child protection registers are now maintained generally by social services for the specific purpose of informing anyone who might have a professional concern about a particular child that their concerns may well be justified and that they should consider going on to call a child protection conference. As was indicated earlier,[229] a child protection conference may be called by anyone from any of the relevant agencies who may have a concern about a particular child, and *Working Together* further provides guidance as to the people who should attend such conferences. This will include the parents, together with the parents' representatives, if this is felt to be necessary by the parents, and also the child or children, if this is felt to be appropriate.[230]

The government department with overall special responsibility for child abuse is the Department of Health, and this government department has been to the forefront in issuing a vast range of guidance to all the professionals who might be involved with child abuse since the first issue of *Working Together* in 1988. Following upon implementation of the Children

Act 1989 and the variety of guidance issued pursuant to that Act by the Department of Health, social work and other health professionals now have available to them a positive plethora of guidance.[231] In addition, the Department of Health has provided various reports in relation to the implementation of the Children Act since 1991,[232] and has commissioned a series of research projects on various aspects of the implementation of the Children Act and on issues associated with the workings of previous legislation in this area. These have been subsequently reported upon in an impressive series of research reports.[233] The way in which the Department of Health has monitored the performance by local authorities of their duties under the Children Act 1989, and the criticisms and proposals which it has put forward as a result, have really been quite encouraging, but much remains to be done. As was noted earlier, little guidance exists for parents, in contrast to the quite considerable volume of guidance which now exists for professionals who might seek to intervene in families in order to protect children. It should be seen as critically important that the legislation guides parents and, indeed, children themselves in the standards of care which should be expected of all those providing for the care and upbringing of children.

Since it is clear that guidance needs to be available for parents bringing up their children when family conditions are favourable, it would also appear to be the case that effective strategies must be adopted for managing the problem of domestic violence as it affects families in the last stages of breakdown. Thus the new Family Law Act 1996 which reforms the current law of divorce contains some worrying features for partners and children suffering from domestic violence. The provisions on the reform of the divorce law are not yet in force nor are they likely to be in the near future, but the drive towards family mediation prior to filing for divorce and the extended cooling off period for those with children may entail greater risk and distress for weak, abused partners and potentially also for their children. The privatization of child abuse in this sphere of the law is one which has caused many considerable concern and could justify further research and investigation as we move towards implementation of the new law.

Where it is the case that, for whatever reason, children are removed from their own family settings into the care of the local authority social services department, it is still felt to be the case that the provisions allowing for children to complain about their treatment either in foster or residential care are extremely weak. It would still appear to be the case that children do not possess confidence in systems which have been put in place to protect them. If, having suffered from abuse in the home, they are then placed in residential or foster settings where they are further abused, we can have little cause to be surprised at their lack of confidence.[234] It was naively asserted by the Minister of State at the time of the implementation of the Children Act that s.26(3) of that Act, which provides for children to make representations using a complaints procedure, would adequately safeguard children against the sort of practices that have led to major child abuse inquiries, particularly those centring on abuse of children in residential care. Yet, as can be seen from the recent report by Sir William Utting,[235] this has manifestly not been the case and children's voices have continued not to be heard within the system. This is even despite the detailed guidance provided by documents such as *Working Together* with regard to the situation where complaints are made by children within the care process itself. Children and young people in England and Wales do not have any confidence in such representation systems as are offered by the civil law in legislation such as the Children Act and, even more importantly, as has been demonstrated earlier, when children do seize the initiative and actually complain to the police, the criminal justice system offers them little opportunity for protection and exposes them to the trauma of the adversarial dynamics inherent in the English criminal justice system. It might be suggested, therefore, that a proper balance has yet to be struck within the English criminal justice system between the interests and safety of our children and the interests of the accused, and within the civil system as a whole between the interests of adults working within the system and the safety of children who might seek to complain.

CONCLUSIONS

It should be apparent from all of the foregoing that much has been done in England to try to improve the position of children who are experiencing abuse in whatever form and in whatever setting, but that much remains to be done in order to protect children in England from such abuse. Amongst the range of measures which should be considered by the legislature one might include the following:

- the incorporation of the principles of the United Nations Convention on the Rights of the Child and the European Convention on the Exercise of Children's Rights to take direct legislative effect within the jurisdiction of the UK as a whole;
- a clarification of the legislative provisions on parental responsibilities towards children and legislative guidance providing positive proper standards of care to which reference might be made by parents and by children themselves;
- the amendment of the law on physical punishment of children so that children are made subject to the same protection under the criminal

law as adults in England and Wales. The mixed messages which are conveyed to children by the current ambivalence of the law are not defensible and the provisions in s.1(7) Children and Young Persons Act, 1933 should be repealed;[236]
- expanded explanations in leaflet form of legal provisions such as s.26 Children Act 1989 which provide children with rights but which do not provide them with access to relevant information, advice, consultation and representation on their theoretical rights, and certainly have not guaranteed children protection from abuse in its many different guises;[237]
- the taking of steps to make both the criminal and civil justice systems much more accessible to, and comprehensible by, children who may be involved as witnesses as a result of their having been abused. Consideration should be given to providing a nationwide child witness support scheme for all situations in which children act as witnesses and the necessary resources should be made available to support this;
- the appropriate level of input of additional resources into local authority budgets since, as has been repeatedly shown by successive local government and central government enquiries, the huge range of duties cast upon local authority social services in relation to the protection of children from abuse cannot be properly developed on current, and continually cut, budgets. To force local authorities to choose between one type of service for one group of children or another type of service for another group and to prioritize according to the risk which the children suffer is an intolerable situation. A decision has to be made by central government that adequate resources to allow for the appropriate degree of protection to be offered for all children at risk of suffering abuse will be made available;
- measures to ensure that much more will be done to give children confidence in the system's ability to respond to their concerns about actual or potential abuse. The message given out by professionals, across the system, and indeed by the criminal justice system itself, is that, if a child does find the courage to speak out, this will not necessarily mean that a successful prosecution will result, or, more importantly, that a safe outcome for the child is guaranteed. Children in England must be given much more information and assurance about their continued safety in order to enable them to appreciate that it is still important that they should speak out, even if the criminal prosecution of those responsible for abuse committed upon them may not always follow or, where it does, will not always be successful. The same is true of the civil justice system and steps must be devised to ensure that the

child who makes complaints is not put at further risk if it appears that such complaints cannot be substantiated with the lesser degree of proof required in civil child protection proceedings;[238]
- coordination between central government departments and even between local government departments where the lack of such has led to situations in which children have not been adequately protected from abuse in much stronger and more directed England. A classic example of this is to be found in the situation concerning child prostitutes. Local examples of good practice in relation to this problem may be found, but it is clear that there is a role for a central coordinating body charged with concerns exclusively in respect of children. There should therefore be a Minister for Children,[239] and, in order to ensure the adequate performance of both central and local government with regard to its duties towards children, England would be well advised to institute the office of a Children's Rights Commissioner or a Children's Ombudsperson.[240]

As in so many areas of life in English society today, the vexed problem of child abuse demands an input of both economic and human resources and it is the test of central government's commitment to eradicate the abuse of children to answer whether it is prepared to supply the necessary amount of resources to achieve this end.

NOTES

1. Under the Interpretation of Statutes Act 1978, the term 'England' is always taken to include a reference to Wales, as the two countries have a common legal system. Henceforward, therefore, in the text of this chapter, whenever the term 'England' is used it should be taken to include Wales.
2. Shropshire County Council (1973).
3. *People Like Us* (London: HMSO, 1997).
4. See, for example, the report of the Committee of Inquiry under the Chairmanship of Norman Warner, whose report was entitled *Choosing with Care* (London: HMSO, 1992).
5. See *The Times*, 24 and 25 November 1997.
6. See, for example, the attempts by Germany and Belgium to criminalize publication of such material on the Internet.
7. For the most recent example of an attempt by the government to deal with child abuse perpetrated by English adults abroad, see the Sex Offenders Act 1997 considered below at page 134.
8. See *Childhood Matters – The Report of the National Commission of Inquiry into the Prevention of Child Abuse – Summary Report* (London: NSPCC, 1997).
9. *Childhood Matters – Report of the National Commission of Inquiry into the Prevention of Child Abuse* (London: HMSO, 1996) vol. 1, para. 1.4.

10 See European Commission of Human Rights, Application No 25599/94. *A* v. *The United Kingdom Report of the Commission* adopted 18 September 1997 and published 17 November 1997. The Court decision is reported at [1998] 2 FLR 959.
11 See the UN Monitoring Committee on the Rights of the Child, 8th Session, Summary record of the 205th Meeting held at the Palais des Nations, Geneva, Tuesday 24 January 1995, at para. 63.
12 See European Commission of Human Rights – Application No. 25599/94 A. against the United Kingdom – Report of the Commission (adopted on 18 September 1997 and published Friday 7 November 1997).
13 See S.47 Education (No. 2) Act 1986, now S.548(1) Education Act 1996.
14 It should further be noted that Thomas Hammarberg stated that he could not grasp the justification for the different treatment meted out to pupils in privately and publicly funded schools. That state of affairs, he said, seemed to contradict the laudable principle mentioned in the delegation's opening statement that there was no place for corporal punishment in the United Kingdom's system. See Committee on the Rights of the Child, 8th Session, Summary record of the 205th Meeting, at para. 64.
15 See Press Release, Department of Health, 'Government to Clarify the Law on Parental Discipline', Friday 7 November 1997.
16 See Criminal Justice Acts 1988 to 1996, inclusive.
17 See M. Walton, 'Regulation in Child Protection – Policy Failure?', *British Journal of Social Work*, **23**: 139–56, 1993.
18 See *Childhood Matters – Summary Report*, op. cit., note 8, p.8.
19 See, for example, *Child Abuse – A Study of Inquiry Reports 1973–1981* (London: DHSS/HMSO, 1982) and *Child Abuse – A Study of Inquiry Reports 1980–1989* (London: Department of Health/HMSO, 1990).
20 See UK Government, *First Report to the United Nations Monitoring Committee* (London: HMSO, 1994).
21 See above and also note the provisions of s.1(7) Children and Young Persons Act, 1933.
22 See s.3(1) Children Act 1989.
23 See s.31(2) Children Act 1989.
24 See s.31(10) Children Act 1989.
25 See s.31(9) Children Act 1989, emphasis added.
26 See Children (Scotland) Act 1995, s.1.
27 See s.31 Children Act 1989, emphasis added. If harm has been occasioned to a child which under the civil law provisions would be deemed to be 'significant', this would almost certainly justify consideration being given to criminal prosecution under s1(1) CYPA, 1933 or for offences under the Offences against the Person Act, 1861 or the Sexual Offences Act, 1956.
28 See s.31(9) Children Act 1989.
29 See, for example, the House of Lords decision in *Re H and R* [1996] 1 FLR 80.
30 See, for example, M. Adcock, R. White, A. Hollows *Significant Harm* (Croydon: Significant Publications, 1991) and J. Thoburn, M. Brandon and A. Lewis, 'Need, risk and significant harm', in N. Parton (ed.), *Child Protection and Family Support* (London: Routledge, 1997) pp.165–93.
31 See s.1(3)(E) Children Act 1989.
32 See the court's powers to make specific issue orders and prohibited steps orders in respect of children under s.8 Children Act 1989.
33 See s.31 to s.36 Children Act 1989.
34 1988 and 1991.

35 See *Working Together* (London: Department of Health, 1988) and *Working Together under the Children Act 1989 – A Guide to Arrangements for Inter-Agency Co-operation for the Protection of Children from Abuse* (London: HMSO, 1991).
36 See, for example, *The Report of the Inquiry into Child Abuse in Cleveland in 1987* (London: HMSO 1988) Cmnd 412 and *The Report of the Inquiry into the Removal of Children from Orkney in February* 1991 (London: HMSO, 1992) HOC 195.
37 Generally, only other professionals who may have concerns about the child and who wish to check whether these concerns have been previously recorded.
38 See paras 6.39 and 6.40, *Working Together* (Home Office, Department of Health, Department of Education and Science Welsh Office, 1991).
39 See, for example, the definition of organized abuse which will encompass the different forms of abuse listed at para. 6.40 and which is itself defined at para. 5.26.2.
40 See *Working Together*, op. cit., note 35, at para. 6.40.
41 Adult, suffering from Munchausen's Syndrome characteristically present themselves at the hospital with symptoms of physical disease and may have undergone many operations. They appear to seek the security and support of a medical environment. In Munchausen's syndrome by proxy, the adult uses the child to obtain medical attention by creating medical symptoms in the child, often induced by highly dangerous procedures such as attempted suffocation or poisoning, or ensuring that a series of invasive tests and/or operations are carried out on the child.
42 See *Child Protection in Scotland – Management Information* (Edinburgh: Scottish Office, 1992).
43 See N. Davies, 'Children of the Night', *Guardian*, 29 August 1994, S. Lonsdale (1994) 'Unfair Play on the Game', *Independent*, 31 July 1994; D. West, *Male Prostitution* (London: Duckworth, 1992); C. Foster, 'Male Youth Prostitution', University of East Anglia, Social Work Monographs, 1991.
44 See C. Newman, *Young Runaways – Findings from Britain's first Safe House* (London: The Children's Society, 1989).
45 See M. Stein et al., *Running – The Risk* (London: Children's Society, 1994).
46 See R. Edgington in D. Barrett (ed.), *Child Prostitution in Britain – Dilemmas and Practical Responses* (London: The Children's Society, 1997).
47 See *The Game's Up – Redefining Child Prostitution*, (London: The Children's Society, 1995).
48 See op. cit at note 44.
49 Currently being revised by the Department of Health (DoH).
50 See later for a discussion of more of the management issues associated with this type of response.
51 See A. Mullender and R. Morley, *Children Living with Domestic Violence* (London: Whiting and Birch, 1994); see also M. Hester and L. Radford, *Domestic Violence and Child Contact Arrangements in England and Denmark* (1996) Representing Children pp.155–162. For a more detailed report, see M. Hester and L. Radford, *Domestic Violence and Child Contact in England and Denmark* (Joseph Rowntree Foundation 1996); also the *Report of the Commission on Children and Violence* published by the Gulbenkian Foundation (London: Turn Around Distribution Ltd, 1995).
52 See later in terms of the actual provisions of the law.
53 See respectively s.33(7), s.35(8), s.36(7), s.37(4) and s.38(5) Family Law Act 1996.
54 See *Working Together*, op. cit., note 35, para. 5.26.1.
55 See ibid., para. 5.26.2.
56 See further, on this, C.M Lyon and S.P. De Cruz, *Child Abuse*, 2nd edn (Jordans, 1993).

57 See Jean La Fontaine, *The Extent and Nature of Organised and Ritual Sexual Abuse: Research Findings* (London: HMSO, 1994).
58 See the *Code for Crown Prosecutors*, Crown Prosecution Service, January 1992.
59 See 'The Investigation of Child Sexual Abuse: An Executive Summary', University of Surrey, 1991.
60 See S. Creighton, *Child Abuse Trends in England and Wales 1988–1990* (London: NSPCC, 1992).
61 As in *Re H. and R.* [1996] 1 FLR 80 HL.
62 See National Commission of Inquiry into the Prevention of Child Abuse, *Childhood Matters*, vol. 1 (London: HMSO, 1996) at para. 1.15.
63 See B. Kahan and A. Levy, *The Pindown Experience and the Protection of Children: The Report of the Staffordshire Child Care Inquiry 1990* (Stafford: Staffordshire County Council, 1991).
64 See the Leicestershire Inquiry, the Ty Mawr Inquiry and the North Wales Children's Inquiry.
65 See J. Cashman, R. Dolby and D. Brennan, *Systems Abuse: Problems and Solutions* (Sydney: New South Wales Child Protection Council, 1994).
66 National Commission of Inquiry into the Prevention of Child Abuse, *Childhood Matters*, vol. 1 (London: HMSO, 1996), paras 1.1 to 1.3.
67 See s.31(2) Children Act 1989.
68 See s.17(1), (10) and (11) Children Act 1989.
69 The English document is *Working Together*, op. cit., note 35; the Scottish document is *Child Protection in Scotland*, op. cit., note 42.
70 The Commission acknowledges that this definition is derived from the work of D.G. Gill, *Violence against Children*, (Cambridge, Mass.: Harvard University Press, 19970).
71 See *Childhood Matters*, vol. 1, op. cit., note 66, para. 121.
72 The author should point out that she was the author of that part of the National Commission's Report which deals with the law in England, Wales and Northern Ireland produced in Volume 1 of *Childhood Matters*, pp.263–333, and many of her conclusions were relied upon by the Commission in setting out its own views on the law.
73 See statistics from the Crime and Criminal Justice Unit, Home Office and Home Office, *Research and Statistics* (1994).
74 The unlawful killing of a child by its mother in the first 12 months of the child's life under the provisions of s.1 Infanticide Act, 1938.
75 See *UK Child Homicides in 1992* (London: Central Statistical Office, 1994).
76 See S.J. Creighton, 'Fatal Child Abuse: How Preventable is it?', *Child Abuse Review*, 4: 318–28, 1995.
77 See op. cit., note 75.
78 See A. Falkov, *Study of Working Together Part 8 Reports: Fatal Child Abuse and Parental Psychiatric Disorder* (London: DoH, 1996).
79 See P. Reder, S. Duncan and M. Grey, *Beyond Blame: Child Abuse Tragedies Revisited*, London: Routledge, 1993); and K.D. Browne and M.A. Lynch, 'The Nature and Extent of Child Homicide and Fatal Abuse', *Childhood Abuse*, 4: 309–16, 1995.
80 See Creighton, op. cit, note 76.
81 See Department of Health, *Children and Young People on Child Protection Registers Year Ending 31st March 1995, England* (London: Department of Health, 1996).
82 See Department of Health, *Child Protection: Messages from Research*, (London: HMSO, 1995).
83 See *Childhood Matters*, vol. 1, op. cit., note 66, para. 2.8.

84 See ibid.
85 See Department of Health, op. cit., note 81.
86 See ibid.
87 See S. Creighton and N. Russell, *Voices from Childhood: A Survey of Childhood Experiences and Attitudes to Child Rearing among Adults in the United Kingdom* (London: NSPCC, 1995). See also M.A. Smith, 'A Community Study of Physical Violence to Children in the Home and Associated Variables', poster presented at the International Society for the Prevention of Child Abuse and Neglect; V European Conference, Oslo, Norway, May 1995.
88 See Crime and Criminal Justice Unit, Home Office, *Research and Statistics*, 1995.
89 See Department of Health, op. cit., note 81.
90 See L. Kelly, L. Regan and S. Burton, 'An Exploratory Study of the Prevalence of Sexual Abuse in a Sample of 16–21-Year-Olds', University of North London, 1991; also A.W. Baker and S.P. Duncan, 'Child Sexual Abuse: A Study of Prevalence in Great Britain', *Child Abuse and Neglect*, 9: pp.457–67, 1985.
91 See L. Horne, D. Glasgow, A. Cox and R. Callum, 'Sexual Abuse of Children by Children', *Journal of Child Law*, 3: 147–51, 1990.
92 See Home Office, *Action Against the Commercial Exploitation of Children* (London: Home Office, 1996).
93 See post, p.132.
94 See *Childhood Matters*, vol. 1, op. cit., note 66, para. 2.31.
95 See ibid.
96 See *Childhood Matters*, vol. 1, op. cit., note 66, para. 2.26.
97 See op. cit, at note 87.
98 See J. Gibbons, S. Conroy and C. Bell, *Operating the Child Protection System* (London: HMSO, 1995).
99 See E. Farmer and M. Owen, *Child Protection Practice: Private Risks and Public Remedies* (London: HMSO, 1995).
100 Confirmed by recent European figures and also by the *Report on Income and Wealth* by the Joseph Rowntree Inquiry Group (London: Joseph Rowntree Foundation, 1995).
101 See *Childhood Matters*, vol. 1, op. cit., note 66, table 2.2, p.17.
102 See ss.17–26; ss.31–42 and Parts V to XI Children Act 1989.
103 By inserting new sections 38A and 38B, and s.44A and s.44B into the Children Act 1989.
104 See s.17(10) Children Act 1989.
105 See s.17(2) Children Act 1989 and sch.2, Part I Children Act 1989.
106 See Children Act Reports, 1992 onwards, published by the Department of Health (London: HMSO).
107 See para. 1A, sch.2, part I, Children Act 1989 as amended.
108 See Department of Health 1995, op. cit., note 82.
109 See *Childhood Matters – Summary Report*, op. cit., note 8; also *Childhood Matters*, op. cit., note 66.
110 See sch.2, part I, paras 1(1), (2), (4), (7) Children Act 1989.
111 See *Childhood Matters*, vol. 1, op. cit., note 66, ch. 4.
112 See *Childhood Matters – Summary Report*, op. cit., note 8, p.13.
113 See ibid.
114 See s.20 Children Act 1989.
115 See s.20(4) Children Act 1989.
116 See s.20(6) Children Act 1989.
117 See *Protecting Children: A Guide for Social Workers Undertaking a Comprehensive*

Assessment (London: DoH, 1988); *The Care of Children – Principles and Practice in Regulations and Guidance* (London: HMSO, 1989 ch. 2, paras 5–8); see also *Child Protection – The Messages from Research* (London: DoH, 1995).
118　See *Children Act 1989 Report* (London: DoH, 1993).
119　See *People Like Us*, op. cit., note 3.
120　See, for example, practice guidance issued by the NHS, *What Every Nurse, Health Visitor and Community Nurse needs to know about the Children Act 1989* (London: NHS, 1991); for education staffs see Circular 10/95 'Protecting Children from Abuse' issued by the Department for Education; for social services workers throughout England and Wales, their own authorities will produce child protection handbooks either themselves or under the auspices of local Area Child Protection Committees (see Post).
121　See DHSS, *Review of Child Care Law* (London: HMSO, 1985) para. 12(4).
122　See *D v. N.S.P.C.C* [1997] 1 All ER 589, HL.
123　See *Diagnosis of Child Sexual Abuse: Guidance for Doctors* (London: DHSS, 1988), p.12.
124　See DoH, *Child Protection – Guidance for Senior Nurses, Health Visitors and Midwives* (London: HMSO, 1992).
125　See para. 13.2.
126　See DFE Circular 10/95, *Protecting Children from Abuse: The Role of the Education Service* and Circular 11/95, *The Misconduct of Teachers and Workers with Children and Young Persons Working Together under the Children Act 1989* (London: Department of Health, 1991).
127　See post, p.124.
128　See *Working Together*, op. cit., note 126, para. 5.11.1
129　See B. Kahan and A. Levy, op. cit., note 63; A. Kirkwood, *Management Responses to Complaints and Evidence of Abuse, Malpractice and Other Related Matters in Leicestershire in the Light of the Trial of Frank Beck and Other Child Care Officers for the Period 1973 to 1976* (Leicester: Leicestershire County Council, 1993).
130　See s.37 Children Act 1989.
131　See *Working Together*, op. cit., note 126, paras 5.19–5.24.5.
132　See further, on this, C.M. Lyon and S.P. De Cruz, op. cit., note 56, chs 2–5 and figure 2; see also N. Parton, *Governing the Family* (London: Macmillan, 1991) ch. 5, especially pp.127–9.
133　See Home Office and DoH (London: HMSO, 1992).
134　See *The Child, the Court and the Video – A Study of the Implementation of the Memorandum of Good Practice on Video Interviewing of Child Witnesses* (London: Social Services Inspectorate, 1994).
135　*Childhood Matters – A Summary Report*, op. cit., note 8, pp.19–20.
136　See page 103.
137　See *Working Together*, op. cit., note 126, ch. 6 generally.
138　See s.31(2) Children Act 1989 and s.1(5).
139　See *Newham L.B. v. A.G* [1993] 1 FLR 281, especially the comments of Sir Stephen P. Brown.
140　See *Re O* [1992] 1 FLR 815; also *Re M* [1994] 2 FLR 541.
141　See *Northamptonshire C.C. v. S* [1993] 1 FLR 554; also *Re B* [1993] 1 FLR 815 and *Re M* [1994] 2 FLR 577.
142　See *Re H* [1996] 1 FLR 80.
143　See s.33 Children Act 1989.
144　See s.91 Children Act 1989.

145 See note 3 above.
146 See s.52 and sch. 6 Family Law Act 1996.
147 See above.
148 See s.43.
149 See *Gillick v. West Norfolk and Wisbech Area Health Authority* [1986] AC 112.
150 This provision can be seen as the direct lineal successor to the very first provisions protecting children from cruelty to be found in the 1889 Protection of Children from Cruelty Act.
151 As amended by the Children Act 1989.
152 This includes injury to or loss of sight, or hearing, or limb, or organ of the body, and any mental derangement.
153 See s.1(7) CYPA, 1933.
154 See above, page 100.
155 Thus, under s.1(2)(a) a parent or other person legally liable to maintain a child or young person, or the legal guardian of a child or young person, shall be deemed to have neglected him in a manner likely to cause injury to his health if he has failed to provide adequate food, clothing, medical aid or lodging for him, or if, having been unable otherwise to provide such food, clothing, medical aid or lodging, he has failed to take steps to procure it to be provided under the enactments applicable in that behalf.
156 See note 146.
157 See [1981] AC 394 HL.
158 See [1969] 1 QB 364
159 See [1925] 2 KB 322, CCA.
160 See s.1(7) CYPA, 1933 and see discussion above page 97.
161 See s.1(2)(A).
162 See earlier discussion on the meaning of 'wilful' at page 128.
163 (1867) LR 1 CCR 99.
164 See s.1(2).
165 See *Cole v. Pendleton* (1896) 60 JP 359.
166 See *R. v. Jones* (1901) 19 Cox CC 567.
167 See *Oakey v. Jackson* [1914] 1 KB 216.
168 [1899] 1 KB 283.
169 See (1957) 41 Cr. App. R. 105.
170 See *R. v. Williams* (1910) 4 Cr. App. R., 89.
171 [1938] 3 All ER 777.
172 See *R. v. Gibbins* [1977] Crim. Law Review 741.
173 See s.45(1) Criminal Justice Act 1988.
174 See s.47 Offences against the Person Act 1861.
175 See s.20 Offences against the Person Act 1861.
176 See s.18 Offences against the Person Act 1861.
177 See, for example, s.5 and s.6 Sexual Offences Act 1956.
178 See, for example, s.15 Sexual Offences Act 1956.
179 See *R. v. Waite* [1892] 2 QB 600.
180 See s.5 Sexual Offences Act 1956.
181 See s.6 Sexual Offences Act 1956.
182 See s.54 Criminal Law Act 1977.
183 See s.11 Sexual Offences Act 1956.
184 See s.22 Sexual Offences Act 1956.
185 See s.23 Sexual Offences Act 1956.

186 See s.28 Sexual Offences Act 1956.
187 See s.30 Sexual Offences Act 1956.
188 See s.32 Sexual Offences Act 1956.
189 See s.5 Sexual Offences Act 1967.
190 See page 106.
191 See 'Policing Under-aged Prostitution: A Victim Based Approach', in D. Barrett (ed.), *Child Prostitution in Britain – Dilemmas and Practical Responses* (London: The Children's Society, 1997).
192 See s.1 and s.2 Sexual Offences (Conspiracy and Incitement) Act 1996.
193 See s.7 Sex Offenders Act 1997.
194 Article 34 provides that states parties undertake to protect the child from all forms of sexual exploitation and sexual abuse. For these purposes, states parties shall in particular take all appropriate national, bilateral and multilateral measures to prevent the inducement or coercion of a child to engage in any unlawful sexual activity; the exploitative use of children in prostitution or other unlawful sexual practices; or the exploitative use of children in pornographic performances and material.
195 See s.1(1), indecent conduct towards a young child.
196 See s.1, indecent photographs of children.
197 See s.160, offence of possession of indecent photographs of children.
198 See, for example, *Children who Sexually Abuse Other Children* (London: National Children's Homes, 1991).
199 See s.112 and 120 Police Act 1997.
200 See s.122.
201 See s.124.
202 See s.113.
203 See s.115.
204 See ss.113 and 115 Police Act 1997.
205 See *The Times*, Thursday 20 November 1997, 'Children in Care Still Suffering Appalling Abuse'.
206 See Department of Health, *Child Abuse – Notified Persons List*, and Department of Education, *List 99*.
207 See s.1 Sex Offenders Act 1997 Table.
208 The date by which all such offenders were supposed to have registered with the police; the understanding was that fewer than a third of all potential registrants had actually registered their details with the police, but both police and probation services in England are understood to be working together to try to ensure full registration of such details since otherwise, yet again, children, young people and others may be at risk from the presence of such offenders in the community without their being aware of the proclivities of such individuals.
209 See T. Pigot, *Report of the Advisory Group on Video Evidence* (London: Home Office, 1989).
210 See *Childhood Matters*, op. cit., note 66, p.19.
211 See s.32 Criminal Justice Act 1988.
212 See s.32(A) Criminal Justice Act 1988 inserted by Criminal Justice Act 1991.
213 See s.32(A)(3)(A) Criminal Justice Act 1988 as amended.
214 See s.32(A)(4) Criminal Justice Act 1988 as amended.
215 See s.32(A)(5).
216 See s.32(9).
217 It should be noted that hearsay evidence, that is evidence given by one person of what

another person has said, is not generally admissible in criminal proceedings in England and Wales.
218 See s.32(A)(6)(B) Criminal Justice Act 1988 as amended.
219 See s.32(A)(3)(a).
220 See Home Office and DoH, *The Memorandum of Good Practice on Video Recorded Interviews with Child Witnesses for Criminal Proceedings* (London: HMSO, 1992).
221 See D. Birch, 'Children's Evidence', *Criminal Law Review*, p.271, 1992.
222 See *Child Witness Pack* (Home Office, Department of Health, Child Line, NSPCC and Gulbenkian, 1991).
223 See 'A Case for Balance' (NSPCC, 1997).
224 See quotations from *Re H and R* [1996] 1 FLR 80 HL.
225 See page 123.
226 See pages 102–5.
227 See *Working Together under the Children Act 1989*, op. cit., note 35.
228 See B. Corby, 'Inter-Professional Co-operation and Inter-Agency Co-ordination', in K. Wilson and A. James (eds), *The Child Protection Handbook* (London: Bailliere Tindall, 1995) pp.214–15.
229 See page 125.
230 See *Working Together*, op. cit., note 63, ch. 6, para. 6.15.
231 See DoH, *Guidance on the Children Act 1989*, vols 1–10 (London: HMSO, 1989–91).
232 See Department of Health, *Children Act Reports* (London: HMSO, 19991–5).
233 See *Child Protection – Messages from Research* (London: DoH, 1996).
234 See C. Lyon, 'Children Abused within the Care System: do current representation procedures offer the child protection and the family support?', in N. Parton (ed.), *Child Protection and Family Support* (London: Routledge, 1997).
235 See *People Like Us*, op. cit., note 3.
236 Some reform might be anticipated in this area in response to the decision in *A.* v. *The United Kingdom*. See discussion earlier page 97.
237 This has been particularly the case with regard to children being accommodated by local authorities under Part III Children Act 1989.
238 See *Re H and R*, op cit., note 224.
239 See, for example, J. Lestor, 'A Minister for Children' in B. Franklin (ed.), *Children's Rights – Comparative Policy and Practice* (London: Routledge, 1995), pp.100–107.
240 See M. Flekkøy, 'The Scandinavian Experience of Children's Rights', in B. Franklin (ed.), op. cit., note 239; England would thus be following the lead of such countries as Sweden, New Zealand and Costa Rica.

7　Dealing with the Problems of Sexual Abuse of Children in Finland

Sirpa Taskinen

PREVALENCE OF CHILD ABUSE IN FINLAND

Child sexual abuse began to be discussed as a social phenomenon in Finland at the beginning of the 1980s. The National Boards for Social Welfare and Health then invited experts to a seminar to discuss the matter in the light of some test cases. The seminar agreed that a study should be made of the prevalence of sexual abuse and that the authorities should give instructions for examining children and preventing abuse.

In the years 1983 and 1984, a total of 132 confirmed cases of abuse, with a further 222 suspected cases, came to the attention of the authorities, according to an enquiry circulated to all social and health care officials.[1] (It should be remembered that at that time there had been no public discussion of sexual abuse in Finland). The phenomenon gained wider public attention at the end of the 1980s as information spread through television and the press. The first television programme particularly aroused great controversy, with many shocked viewers calling a TV hot-line immediately after the programme. Afterwards, reports of suspected sexual abuse began to increase.

In 1990 and 1991, a total of 1000 cases of suspected child sexual abuse came to the attention of social and health care officials. The number of reported cases had tripled in seven years. Of these, 30 per cent, about 150 a year, were regarded as certain. Possible cases (but with doubt remaining) amounted to 47 per cent. Investigation was discontinued in 8 per cent of the cases, while 15 per cent were totally unconfirmed after social and welfare investigation. It should be noted that, where allegations involved divorce situations, almost a quarter (24 per cent) were evaluated as unfounded.[2] As there were so many cases with no evidence, it can be assumed that, nowadays, the majority of serious molestations come to the attention of the authorities. However, only in 170 cases out of 1000 suspected cases, were charges ever laid. The research does not reveal the reasons for this.

According to a 1988 youth survey, among 15-year-olds, 7 per cent of girls and 3 per cent of boys had been subjected to sexual molestation. In most cases this had occurred outside the family. In 0.5 per cent of cases there had been sexual experience between father/stepfather and daughter, and the same number of boys had had sexual experience with an adult male. This was one of the most extensive surveys in the world, with 7000 respondents who represented the entire 15-year-old age group.[3] A similar study in Sweden gave the same figures (girls 7 per cent, boys 3 per cent), omitting those who had witnessed indecent exposure.

Finnish and Swedish abuse statistics would thus seem to be somewhat lower than in many countries. There are, in fact, several factors in Finland that can be regarded as inhibiting abuse. Among these are parental and family guidance which increase the awareness and interest of both parents in the development of their child, and in which the well-being of the child is monitored. Finland also has a high standard of female education and opportunities for women's financial independence, so that they need not submit to ill-treatment of their children.

Sexual abuse of children is a problem with legal, child welfare and therapeutic dimensions. A balance between the interests and needs of the children, their families and different professionals is rather difficult to reach.

LEGAL FRAMEWORK

The legislation on sexual abuse of children in Finland dates back to the Swedish–Finnish Law of 1734, which acknowledged wormen's rights to physical integrity. By this law, the sexual exploitation of a girl under 12 years of age was considered a rape which was punishable by death. Sexual intercourse with an older girl was dealt with as illegal extramarital carnal knowledge.

During the Russian era, in 1866, the death penalty was withdrawn and replaced by imprisonment. The sexual exploitation of a girl of 12 to 16 was punished more severely than other extramarital affairs. The penalties were increased again in 1899. Finland became independent in 1917, and consequently, the constitution and most of the legislation were reformed. In 1926, the penalties for sexual abuse were broadened to apply also to the abuse of boys. Acts of unchastity with minors under 17 were punishable. Again in 1952, the Penal Code was reformed and sanctions became more severe. The crimes were divided into three categories according to the age of the child: children under 12, children from 12 to 14, and children from 15 to 16. The penalties for the last mentioned group were tightened again two years later.

The present regime on Offences Against Morality, Chapter 20 of the Penal Code, came into force in 1971. Homosexuality as such was decriminalized, but the age limits of protection against homosexual acts are higher (18 to 20 years) than for heterosexual acts (16 years). Exhortation to homosexual activity, however, remained a crime, although in practice there have been no cases taken to courts on this basis.

The present law is quite complicated. The level of penalties depends upon the following:

- the age of the child (children under 14, children from 14 to 16 and, if the perpetrator is a teacher or in some other position of authority to the younger person, 18). In homosexual acts, the age limit is 18 and, if the offender is in the position of authority, 20;
- the sex of the child (heterosexual/homosexual acts);
- the age of the offender (young or older than 16; in homosexual acts, younger or older than 20);
- the relationship of the offender to the child (own child, descendant of own child, (half-) brother, (half-) sister; also whether the child is subordinated to the offender's authority, for example in a school);
- the seriousness of the act (from a mild act of impropriety to penetration; the use of violence, exceptional cruelty or brutality).

The sanctions vary from a fine (in mild acts of impropriety, or if the child is over 14 and the intercourse has been consensual) to imprisonment of six months to 10 years (aggravated acts). Attempted offences are also punished. However, minors under 16 are not punished, nor are the persons involved where they are of almost the same age. Homosexual acts by persons younger than 20 are treated more leniently.

The growing awareness of child sexual abuse has revealed many shortcomings in the law, such as the problems of definition of the acts, the existence of too many age limits, and the difficulty of getting some of the crimes prosecuted. The decisions by courts in relation to sanctions in matters concerning physical integrity and child sexual abuse have been heavily criticized. Although the maximum penalties as such are in line with other sanctions, the courts have been mostly using the lower end of the scale. The mean penalties for rape (involving adults) have been one year, for improper acts with a minor, 18 months, and for aggravated sexual offences against a minor, 37 months.

The Finnish Penal Code is currently being reformed in its entirety. A government Bill on sexual offences was brought before Parliament in 1997. The regulations described above have been totally rewritten. The main alterations concern the terminology, the systematology of the law, and the age limits. Sanctions for exhortation to homosexual activity are to be removed from the law. Also new areas of criminalization have been proposed. Offering money for sexual intercourse with an adolescent under 18 is proposed as a criminal act (under the present law, only procuration is criminalized). The selling of child pornography has already been prohibited and now the possession of such pictures is to be punishable too.

Criminal sexual acts are rape, aggravated rape, forcing into intercourse, forcing into a sexual act, sexual exploitation, sexual exploitation of a child, aggravated sexual exploitation of a child, buying sexual services from a minor and procuration. Even though the terms have been modernized, the definitions remain problematic. For instance, it was necessary to define *sexual intercourse* as penetration into another person's body by a sexual organ. Previously, some lawyers did not consider that anal penetration should be regarded as sexual intercourse. The definition of a *sexual act* necessarily remains wide. In the Penal Code, it is defined as an act which is aimed at sexual excitement or satisfaction and which is for the persons involved and the situation, sexually essential.

An intense public debate regarding the proposals has been going on, especially about the scale of sanctions, incestuous relationships, the role of the public prosecutor and the criminalizing of child pornography. In general, the scale of penalties has remained the same as before. It must be noted that more than one crime may be considered at the same time; for example, an activity may be charged as both rape and aggravated sexual exploitation of the child, and sanctioned accordingly for both of them. As stated earlier, the problem of 'too lenient penalties' does not reside in the law but in its application.

The first proposal of the working party drafting the Act provoked major criticism. It was proposed that *incest* should be decriminalized because there are few grounds for defining voluntary sexual acts between adults as crimes. As to the children, the biological relationship is less relevant than the harm done by the offender (the father or step-father or the new, unwed partner of the mother). The process of prosecution should not depend on the biological relationship of the offender and the child, as is the case at present.

The images which this proposal created were, however, quite extraordinary. Even quality magazines were envisioning fathers asking for sexual services from their children. When it was made clear that minors would be protected in any case, there were fantasies that fathers would bring up their girls in such a way that they would be happy to go to bed with them on their eighteenth birthdays. Although these fears are far-fetched, it was thought they corresponded with public morality, which insisted that incest remained a crime. In the Government Bill, however, incest does not appear under the section of Sexual Crimes, but under Crimes Against Public Order. For decades, hardly any cases of incest between adults have been brought to court.

In the present Act, the public prosecutor may not bring charges for an act where the offender is not a biological relative of the child, but the custodians have the right to decide whether the act should be brought to police attention. This has created problems in cases where the offender is the new partner of the mother, and she is frightened to have him charged. In the government Bill, these problems are not solved in a satisfactory way, since it is still possible not to bring charges if the parents do not proceed. Parliament has still to consider a proposal that the public prosecutor should be mandated to act in all sexual crimes against minors.

The criminalization of possession of child pornography is included in the government Bill. There have been many public campaigns demanding this, especially after the unfortunate deaths of the paedophile cases in Belgium. The police, however, see problems in the definition of acceptable limits, especially in the case of drawings, and there are also resource problems.

GUIDELINES FOR SOCIAL AND HEALTH PERSONNEL

The main problem in dealing with suspected sexual exploitation of the child does not lie in the legislation. The Penal Code, as described above, is about to be reformed. The Child Welfare Act gives the welfare authorities the right to intervene if a child is maltreated. What has come to be the most difficult part of the process is the investigations. Are the professionals dealing with the suspected abuse trained will enough? Can their impartiality be trusted? Do they have adequate methods to reveal the exploitation? Or do they believe too readily the accusations, say, of a divorcing mother?

Looking back, it has not been for the good that investigations in child sexual abuse cases in Finland have mostly been by personnel in social and health centres, family guidance clinics and hospitals. In the 1980s, it seemed that these professionals, who were dealing with other of the children's problems, would be the best persons to carry out child sexual abuse investigations. Besides, it was thought that, since the suspicions often arose on the basis of the symptoms of the child's behaviour, the social workers, psychologists and psychiatrists would be the best experts to interpret them. But problems have arisen because these experts do not have forensic training, and the police have insufficient knowledge or understanding of the children or their problems.

Social and health care workers are placed in a conflicting role when the expectation is that evidence will be gathered for the purpose of a criminal investigation. Their main objective is to help children and families, and putting an offender in jail is not necessarily the best help for the child. This may be one of the explanations for only a few of the cases being brought to the attention of the police. Also the gathering of evidence has proved a problem. Social workers, psychologists and psychiatrists are not accustomed to weighing the credibility of their clients, nor is the objective truth the main concern in therapeutic work. In crime investigations, however, they are faced with the demand to find evidence 'beyond reasonable doubt'. This is a strange situation for people who have been trained to understand and accept clients' subjective truths.

The first guidelines given to social and health care workers for recognition, investigation and treatment of child sexual abuse were drawn up in 1986. Because Finnish social and health care is largely in the hands of local authorities, it was possible to send them to almost all the relevant services. In broad outline, the guidelines, updated in 1994, are as follows. Identification of child sexual abuse is linked to the United Nations Convention on the Rights of the Child in which signatory states are committed to protecting their children from all forms of sexual exploitation and abuse.[4] Determining sexual abuse is a difficult task. Abuse easily triggers various defences within professionals themselves: blindness to the problem (under-reaction); over-eagerness to blame a child's problems on abuse (over-reaction); feelings of helplessness and anxiety (professional regression). Unless these are dealt with, they will quickly lead to conflict, both with the family and among colleagues. The anxiety caused by child abuse is, however, an important motivator. It prompts the authorities to work towards understanding the situation and helping the child and others involved.

ABUSE DETERMINED BY CULTURE

It is important for all professionals to be clear on the cultural and historical background of what is regarded as sexual exploitation. Patterns of abuse and incidence found in different countries depend, for instance, on how abuse and the offender are defined, on protective age limits for children, how representative the samples are, and so on. In Finland, for example, we do not regard seeing children naked as abusive, because Finnish sauna culture regards this as natural.

There have been cultures where abuse has at least been tolerated, if not necessarily permitted. Later, abuse began to be regarded as morally wrong, as a crime or a deviant activity. Today it is known that sexual intercourse between children and adults harms the child in many ways. In the guidelines, the phenomenon is described as a problem with three aspects: juridical, child protection and therapeutical. The role of social and health care is to give support and help to all parties.

The factors and reasons behind sexual abuse can be related to many levels, social, situational and familial. There is no simple 'purely individual' or 'purely social' explanation. There are many social factors that make sexual exploitation possible. Many social institutions are based on hierarchies where people have unequal value. Extreme hierarchical thinking leads those who are strong to regard it as their 'right' to dominate the weak and to use other people to satisfy their own needs. In particular, the concept of male superiority over women and children is directly related to exploitation.

All manner of glorification and acceptance of violence – war is an example – increases the likelihood of sexual exploitation. Lack of information on childhood development and rights allows people to turn a blind eye to the phenomenon. Child sexual abuse can also mean economic exploitation. Child prostitution and pornography are million-dollar businesses, so their perpetrators have significant financial power. Often, too, double standards are found, with people visiting child brothels far from home and apparently living normal lives in Finland.

Abuse is often related to situations in which people face external pressures or problems within the family. It happens in all social categories, though families with social, financial or emotional difficulties are over-represented. Women and children, too, can be abusers, but the majority of known cases are male: in Finland, 92 per cent of the offenders are men. The abuser has often been the victim of abuse.[5] He or she often has a difficult background and has not received compassion or learned how to give it.

RECOGNIZING AND REPORTING ABUSE

The guide for social and health personnel describes in great detail how to recognize abuse in various situations. At the same time, it warns that no single symptom can be regarded as a sign of abuse. The situation must always be investigated as a whole. The child herself may talk about the exploitation, but most often it is an adult who deduces it, either from symptoms displayed by the child or from some other circumstance. Sometimes it is the abuser himself who reports the matter to the police. Procedures in these different cases vary. Generally, however, it is recommended that the child undergo both psychological and physical examination, the family is examined as a whole and the suspected abuser is confronted and interviewed. Special attention is paid to analysing the credibility of all parties.

The guidelines give detailed instructions for the writing of statements, since this has proved to be a major stumbling block. For the social and health personnel, giving evidence to a court means entering unfamiliar territory, writing in a 'foreign' language, to be understood by lawyers. The doctors are expected to offer their diagnosis with an assurance that they sign it 'through honour and conscience'. Is the court doubting their honesty when it asks for some 'evidence' to corroborate their statement? It has proved necessary to point out that, with a view to guaranteeing the receipt by the decision makers of all relevant facts of significance concerning the child, the statement should pay attention to the following factors.

1 As detailed information as possible shall be given of the places and times of investigations, of the persons who performed these, as well as of those who prepared the statement in question.
2 The background of the case, together with the situation in the family, should be analysed.
3 The report of the situation which has led to the investigation shall be as detailed as is possible.
4 An exhaustive list of investigation observations shall be included.
5 Conclusions shall be justified by concrete examples.
6 All this shall be written using an understandable standard language.

Recently, the courts have reported that the statements have been much more acceptable for their processes than was the case earlier. Problems still exist about the way investigations are made. A particular problem is the prevalence of leading and suggestive questions put to children: these may annul the whole report.

HELPING FAMILIES

In Finland, the Child Welfare Act gives wide possibilities to help children and their families. Different forms include (a) influencing situational factors (financial support, a day care place or finding an apartment,and so on), (b) supplying social support and controls (such as support personnel and home help) and (c) by altering the family structure, for example with therapy. Very often families also split up. Taking the child into care is not the first step.

The preferred measure is to remove the suspect from the family, and this is allowed by Finnish law.

Putting the child in care may make him/her feel that he/she is the guilty party. If the child is sent away and the suspected abuser remains, some other child may become the victim. Children taken into care have proved to be extremely difficult to look after. One problem in child care homes is that these children may sexually molest other children. Thus 'protection of a child' by removing him or her from home may endanger the safety of other children.

In Finland, individual, group and family care has been developed for children and members of their family. Care of abusers is still in its infancy but, for example, two prisons have engaged in this activity. Especially useful has been a course designed for foster parents, in which they are taught to help abused children.

PUBLIC REACTIONS

There were no serious problems in convincing the general public in Finland about the existence of the phenomenon of child sexual abuse. Difficulties in this field have, however, appeared in the form of some over-reactions. Some people with good intentions have been all too eager to find sexual abuse behind any problems of any child. We know all too well the situation in some countries, where false accusations of abuse have resulted in a backlash: the credibility of anti-abuse actions has been lost owing to excessive interventions, and even children in real need of help are not getting any.

In the vast majority of cases, matters in this field have been dealt with in an appropriate manner in Finland. However, one or two complicated cases recently in the headlines have been creating serious problems. Doubt has been raised about whether the professionals really help children or whether they are only defending their own status and acting against the families in a way that also harms the children. In response, professionals working with children react readily with accusations of 'backlash' or of 'undervaluation of the sufferings of the children', even to an objective criticism of the faults in investigations.

Most disputed cases in Finland, as elsewhere in the world, would seem to have at least two of the following situations in common:

- over-sensitive diagnosis,
- leading questions and disputed interpretations,
- the suspect is a well known figure in the community,
- suspicion of exploitation of more than one child, which may have ritualistic features,

- a working method that emphasizes legality and child protection instead of helping the child,
- conflicts between professionals.

Many of these problems can be eased through providing information and training. The last problem is perhaps the hardest to approach. There are many factors involved.

CONFLICTS BETWEEN PROFESSIONALS

Contradictions between different schools of thought gain in acuteness whenever a new provocative subject or field of activity is discovered. These contradictions mostly have the effect of furthering the development of professional practice. Usually, discussions are necessary and fruitful. However, providing help for children and their families in cases of suspected sexual abuse is a most delicate matter. It is aggravated and made even more complicated by professional differences of opinion if they are brought before the public. While public discussion is necessary and important, we should consider carefully what belongs in the public and professional domains. The conscious motivations of those participating in the discourse seem fair enough: all are concerned to promote the children's best interests, with honesty and high professional standards. But then the question arises of how to deal with the unconscious motivations, such as the hunger for power, self-assertion or a thirst for revenge.

It is a well-known phenomenon that, in dealing with difficult family problems, different professionals involved may start repeating these problems *by proxy*. Some parties start behaving like the child who panics: they do not know what to do, or urge instant interventions without proper consideration. Some parties act like the non-offending spouse who closes her eyes in the hope that nothing has happened and that it is not necessary to intervene. Some, again, unconsciously repeating the dynamics of the abusing person, do not pay any attention to the feelings of others, criticize everything that is done and upbraid other professionals. They believe that theirs is the only right way to think and proceed.

The dynamics behind sexual abuse, and the accusations of abuse as well, contain psychological dynamics relating, not only to sexuality, but at least as much to the use of power. This derives from the very core of the phenomenon: sexual abuse, like all forms of violence, is a form of misuse of power. The competition between professionals may lead to narcissistic situations where a person constantly asks: 'Mirror, mirror on the wall, am I not the best expert of them all?' In extreme cases, when a person is not conscious of his or her motives, much harm can be done in the name of the best interest of the child.

Those in the social and health professions are mostly well aware of their need for more knowledge and skills in the field of child sexual abuse. However, it is not enough to obtain more information on these matters, because the abuse of children is a highly provocative subject for all of us, relating to our emotions and very deep personal feelings. For people dealing with such difficult problems, gaining control of these feelings is a positive necessity. Training professionals to know themselves may well prove to be the best help for children.[6]

NOTES

1 Heikki Sariola, *Lasten seksuaalinen hyväksikäyttö Suomessa – Selvitys viranomaisten tietoon vuosina 1983–1984 tulleista lapsiin kohdistuneista hyväksikäyttötapauksista*. Lastensuojelun Keskusliiton julkaisu 79 (Helsinki: Lastensuojelun Keskusliitto, 1985).
2 Jorma Antikainen, *Lasten seksuaalinen hyväksikäyttö* (Child sexual abuse. English summary). Ammatilliset haasteet ja työorientaatiot, dissertation, University of Tampere, Tutkimuksia 46. Helsinki: Stakes, 1994.
3 Heikki Sariola, *Lasten väkivalta- ja seksuaalikokemukset*. Lastensuojelun Keskusliiton julkaisu 85 (Helsinki: Lastensuojelun Keskusliitto, 1990).
4 See Article 19. On children's rights in Finland, see David Bradley, 'Children's Welfare, Children's Rights and Political Economy in Finland', *International Journal of Children's Rights*, 6: 1998.
5 Heikki Sariola and Antti Uutela, 'The prevalence and content of family violence against children in Finland', *Child Abuse & Neglect*, 16: 1–21, 1992; Heikki Sariola and Antti Uutela, 'The prevalence and content of child sexual abuse in Finland', *Child Abuse & Neglect*, 18: 827–35, 1994.
6 See, further, Sirpa Taskinen, *Lapsen seksuaalisen riiston ehkäisy ja hoito*. Helsinki Sosiaalihallituksen julkaisuja 13/1986, Lääkintöhallituksen julkaisuja 87/1986; Sirpa Taskinen, *Lapsen seksuaalisen riiston selvittäminen ja hoito* (Helsinki: Stakes, 1994).

8   Child Abuse and the Law in the Federal Republic of Germany: Current Situation and Prospects*

Stefan Heilmann and Ludwig Salgo

INTRODUCTION

Child abuse is one of the most controversial topics of public debate in Germany today, not only in the media, but in professional discussions involving jurists, psychologists, and social workers. This is not surprising: any legal system which does not at least attempt to take adequate measures to ensure the best possible development for children[1] will find itself under large-scale critical assault, given extra force by the enormous interest shown by the media and the general public in the terrible and depressing stories of abused children.[2] In this chapter, by 'child abuse' is understood any form of mistreatment to which children may be subject,[3] including:

- physical abuse ('child abuse') – blows or some other violent act;
- neglect – doing nothing when proper parental care requires the taking of concrete actions and decisions;[4]
- emotional abuse – characterized principally by the rejection, terrorizing or isolation of the child;
- sexual abuse – the involvement of the child in adult sexual activities.

Child abuse is neither an exclusively historical nor an exclusively modern phenomenon. Over the centuries, children have always been subject to abuse, although its nature and extent have probably been different at different peri-

* Translated by James Patterson.

ods.⁵ The historical manifestations of child abuse, which unfortunately may still be found almost everywhere at the end of the twentieth century, supposedly the 'century of the child', range from murder, abandonment, injury and other impairments to health, to the exploitation of child workers, the sexual exploitation of children, and corporal punishment. In Germany, child protection and the provision of social services for young people came to be accepted as public duties only gradually: welfare laws in this connection were enacted towards the end of the nineteenth century, and remained in force for a short time after the coming into force of the *Bürgerlichen Gesetzbuches* or Civil Code on 1 January 1900 (compare Article 135, Introductory Law of the Civil Code, old version). Government action to combat cruelty to children goes much further back, however.⁶ Since the coming into force of the Civil Code – civil law child protection is basically contained in Book Four (Family Law) of the Civil Code – the legislature has sought, by means of a wealth of further codifications, to establish child protection as a duty of the state. The main focus of this legislative activity was the Youth Welfare Act of 9 July 1922, which has since been superseded by the Child and Youth Services Act (*Kinder- und Jugendhilfegesetz*, or KJHG) of 26 June 1990, in force since 1 January 1991. The latest outcome of these legislative endeavours is the Law 6 on the Reform of the Criminal Law (*6. Gesetz zur Reform des Strafrechts*), in force since 1 April 1998, the legislation on the Protection of Witnesses and the Child (*Zeugenschutzgesetz*), in force since 1 December 1998 and the Child and Parent Law Reform Act (*Gesetz zur Reform des Kindschaftsrechts*, or KindRG),⁷ in force since 1 July 1998.

The German Constitution (Basic Law) of 23 May 1949 has a decisive influence on legislation, jurisdiction and jurisprudence, particularly in the field of family law. The authority of the constitution and of the Federal Constitutional Court, whose task it is to interpret it, and whose decisions are legally binding, is enormous.⁸ For our purposes, the most important point in this connection is that the Basic Law (art. 6, para. 2, sentence 2) establishes child protection as a duty of state with constitutional force.⁹

The extent of child abuse in the Federal Republic of Germany cannot be accurately determined, since no national surveys are available. It is true that a range of figures exist, but they derive from sources which have a special interest or which have too narrow a focus: for example, crime statistics compiled by the police or statistics concerning criminal convictions. All these figures together do not even come close to portraying the real extent of child abuse: 'The question concerning the extent of abuse therefore cannot at present be seriously answered.'¹⁰

While the 1980s were characterized mainly by the women's movement's removal of taboos from the discussion of family violence, and by the alternative child protection which had come into being during the 1970s, in recent years, in connection with a number of sensational trials, judicial proceedings have increasingly become the focus of public debate, above all in respect of the fact that the principles of a constitutional state and procedural guarantees for the benefit of the accused in a criminal trial appear to constitute barriers to the effective protection of the victim. In the meantime, a growing number of jurists and legal policy makers have come to the conclusion that these tasks are no longer antagonistic or irreconcilable opposites, although the harmonization of these central principles in terms of criminal procedure has not yet made much progress. Although the goals of the Child and Parent Law Reform Act announced by the former government say a great deal about the 'improvement of the rights of children', and proclaim that 'child welfare must be promoted in every possible way',[11] in the text of the laws which have in fact been adopted little evidence of these intentions may be discerned. Despite government statements to the contrary, the parents, and relations between them, have been the central focus of the most recent developments.

LEGAL ASPECTS OF CHILD ABUSE

German law knows no comprehensive piece of legislation from which legal consequences and penalties for child abuse may be derived. Furthermore, there are three codifications which are of particular importance for the non-constitutional judgment of child abuse cases: the Civil Code (BGB) in the field of civil law, the Child and Youth Services Act (SGB VIII/KJHG) and the Penal Code (StGB) in the field of public law. This non-constitutional legislation is, as it were, overlapped by the requirements of constitution (*Grundgesetz*) in respect of the manner in which government bodies approach cases of child abuse.

Provisions of constitutional law

The Basic Law of 1949 – the German Constitution – occupies a unique position in the German legal system. This manifests itself in the fact not only that the legislature is bound to the constitutional order, but also that executive power and jurisdiction are subject to the law, and so to the Constitution (art. 20, para. 3, Basic Law). Article 1, para. 3, Basic Law, moreover, lays down a particular obligation on the part of government bodies in respect of the basic rights laid out in Articles 1 to 19. This special interpretation of the Basic Law is upheld through the activities of the Federal Constitutional Court (compare art. 92 to 94, Basic Law), which as a consequence of this function is known as the 'Guardian of the Constitution' (*'Hüter der Verfassung'*).[12] Should any non-constitutional legal regulation (for example, those of the Civil Code, the Child and Youth Services Act or the Penal Code) appear to contradict the provisions of the Basic Law, the Federal Constitutional Court, when called upon to give judgment, has, among other things, the authority to declare the regulation in question null and void. This decision, like other decisions of the Federal Constitutional Court, binds all other constitutional bodies of the Federal Government and of the *Länder*, as well as all courts and authorities. Particularly in the field of family law, the Federal Constitutional Court has already determined on several occasions that a particular non-constitutional enactment does not meet constitutional requirements.[13] It is against this background that the constitutional regulations of art. 2, para. 1, in association with art. 1, para. 1,[14] art. 2, para. 2, sentence 1,[15] and art. 6, paras 2 and 3, Basic Law must be viewed;[16] their significance in relation to the legal requirements concerning state procedures and sanctions in cases of child abuse should not be underestimated.

In 1968, the Federal Constitutional Court stressed that the child, as an independent bearer of fundamental rights, has a claim on the protection of the state.[17] The German Constitution does not know any explicit fundamental rights of children, but each child is 'a being possessing its own human worth and the right to the development of its personality in the sense of art. 1, para. 1 and art. 2, para. 1, Basic Law'.[18] While a truly human existence demands that the individual human being not be degraded to the level of a mere object,[19] the right to the free development of one's personality entails that one be brought up within a healthy physical and emotional environment.

On the basis of the right to freedom from bodily harm (art. 2, para. 2, sentence 1, Basic Law) the state has a duty of protection which is further underpinned by the 'state guardianship' (*Staatliches Wächteramt*) of minors established in art. 6, para. 2, sentence 2, Basic Law. Child abuse constitutes in every sense a violation of these constitutionally guaranteed rights of children.

The 'state guardianship' laid down in art. 6, para. 2, sentence 2, Basic Law must also orient itself in terms of these provisions. The state must make sure that the above-mentioned rights of children are not infringed, to the extent that they are able to develop into responsible members of the community in accordance with the conception of humanity contained in the Basic Law.[20] The care and upbringing of their children is both the natural right of parents and their highest duty (art. 6, para. 2, sentence 1, Basic Law); nevertheless, cases of child abuse oblige the state, against this constitutional background, to intervene, sometimes to the point of removing the child from its birth family and withdrawing it from parental care.[21] What kind of action the state takes in a particular case of child abuse will be decisively influenced by the principle of reasonableness (*Grundsatz der Verhältnismäßigkeit*). This principle of jurisdiction and jurisprudence, derived from art. 20, Basic Law, says that any kind of state action must be appropriate ('appropriateness') to achieve the desired outcome – in this case, the protection of the child – no other, less intrusive means capable of achieving the same result being available ('necessity'), and that the said action must be commensurate with the weight and significance of the relevant basic right ('reasonableness').[22] The taking of the child into care and the withdrawal of parental custody will, against this background, be regarded as *ultima ratio*, which finds its non-constitutional confirmation in s.1666 Civil Code.[23] Nevertheless, in some sets of circumstances, these measures are unavoidable.

Civil Law

The authoritative codification in the field of civil law is the Civil Code; in Book Four of this legislation are also found the authoritative regulations concerning the civil law assessment of child abuse. The regulation of procedural law is contained in separate pieces of legislation and divided up in a confused manner. This is one of the greatest weaknesses of the German family law system, and one which the most recent reform of legislation on children has not eliminated.[24]

The central regulations of civil law child protection are ss.1666 and 1666a Civil Code, which represent a non-constitutional realization of state guardianship, which has constitutional status (art. 6, para. 2, sentence 2, Basic Law). In accordance with these regulations a court (after 1 July 1998, the family court – hitherto, the guardianship court) can, when either the physical or the emotional best interests of a child are endangered, take the measures necessary to safeguard them, if the parents either cannot or will not do so themselves. The fault of the parents does not enter into it.[25] Child abuse forms, not only historically, but even today, the undisputed core of s.1666 Civil Code.[26] As a result, all manifestations of child abuse can without difficulty be subsumed under the requirements of s.1666, para. 1, Civil Code: physical, emotional or sexual abuse carried out by parents is to be regarded as 'improper exercise of parental care' in the sense of s.1666, Civil Code and – also when these actions are committed by a third party – as endangering the best interests of the child. Finally, neglect is explicitly grounded in the wording of s.1666, para. 1, Civil Code.

The decisive precondition of all possible variants of this general clause of civil law child protection is the imminent endangerment of the best interests of the child. The vague legal concept of the 'best interests of the child' is therefore the 'heart' of the rule.[27] It fulfils essentially three important functions.

1. With this vague legal concept a condition is formulated in terms of which every imaginable form of endangerment of the best interests of the child can be construed.
2. At the same time, the rule becomes a port of entry for extralegal experiences, and so for the latest findings of psychology, pedagogy, paediatrics, and so on.[28]
3. Finally, this decisive criterion codifies a number of fundamental values: precedence shall be given to the interests of the child before all other interests,[29] as well as to the just solution of an individual case before the fulfilment of general rules.[30]

The status of the wishes ('Wille') of the child in the interpretation of the child's best interests remains uncertain. The wishes of the child undoubtedly influence not only the question whether the conditions for having recourse to judicial proceedings of s.1666 Civil Code are present, but also the kind of measures to be taken. What is decisive in this connection is that civil law child protection in fulfilment of state guardianship should also ensure that the child has the possibility to develop into a responsible member of society. To this end the wishes of the child must be adequately taken into consideration in any proceedings concerning it.[31] To be sure, the age of the child must play an important role in the assessment of the significance of its wishes, although the wishes even of younger children must be taken seriously in judicial decision making.[32] The wishes of the child enter into the proceedings through the (obligatory) child hearings provided for under the law since 1980 (see s.50b Law on Matters of Uncontentious Jurisdiction [FGG]),[33] as well as through the guardian *ad litem* explicitly provided for under the law from 1 July 1998 (see s.50 Law on Matters of Uncontentious Jurisdiction).

When deciding whether the best interests of the child are endangered in the sense of s.1666 Civil Code, the judge finds himself called upon to balance the interests of the child, the rights of the parents and the interests of society. According to precedent '[there] must [be] an imminent danger that, if the situation is allowed to develop further, the emotional or physical best interests of the child shall, with reasonable certainty, be subject to substantial harm'.[34] To be sure, the classification of a particular mode of behaviour, whether practised by the parents or by a third party, as child abuse implies that the child's best interests are thereby under threat.

Should the family court affirm the existence of the conditions of s.1666 Civil Code in a particular case of child abuse, it must take the 'requisite' measures. In principle, the nature of the measures in question is at the discretion of the court. The aim of judicial intervention is the prevention of any harm to the child. The deliberately indeterminate formulation of the law (which speaks only of 'requisite' measures) gives the court considerable leeway,[35] requiring it to proceed, not routinely, but in accordance with the circumstances of each individual case. The choice of possible measures ranges from admonitions, or cautions, to conditions which must be complied with, and orders and prohibitions. The withdrawal of individual aspects of parental care (for example, the right to determine place of residence, or personal custody) or of parental care altogether, is also a possibility.[36] Should the court withdraw an aspect of parental care or personal custody in its entirety from only one of the parents, parental care shall become the sole responsibility of the other parent (s.1680 Civil Code). If the court withdraws parental care from both parents entitled to custody of the child, a guardian must be appointed (ss.1773, 1774 Civil Code). Finally, if an aspect of parental care is withdrawn and not transferred to the other parent, a special guardian or curator must be appointed (s.1909 Civil Code). Guardianships or curatorships are frequently administered by the youth office, as so-called *Amtsvormund-* or *Amtspflegschaft*, guardianship or curatorship undertaken by the youth office (compare ss.1791b, 1915 Civil Code).

If the child should be endangered, not by the parents, but by a third party, the court has a wide range of measures at its disposal in order to deal with the problem. The range of permissible measures is, however, determined by the constitutional principle of reasonableness, which must in theory be observed in respect of all judicial measures; as far as the specific measures 'separation of the child from the parental family' and 'withdrawal of personal custody' are concerned, their non-constitutional substance may be found in s.1666a Civil Code. The nature of the measures to be imposed is determined not only by the extent of the endangerment of the child's best interests; in the area of application of s.1666a Civil Code it is guaranteed that the measures there cited shall be considered only *ultima ratio*: in particular, the removal of the child from its usual environment is justified only when the social services are unable to avert the danger within the family. The Child and Youth Services Act is the focal point in this connection (see next section). Section 1666a Civil Code, a regulation which has been part of civil code family law since 1980, has effected a linking of civil law and social law child protection. As a result, family or guardianship courts must deal with the social services in accordance with Part VIII of the Code of Social Law (Child and Youth Services Act).

As a rule, the court will make an emergency protection order (a so-called 'provisional ruling') on the basis of the need for immediate intervention which frequently exists in cases of child abuse, and generally at the instigation of the Youth Office.[37] All of the above-mentioned judicial measures can therefore be taken within the framework of an emergency protection procedure for which it is sufficient that fulfilment of the conditions of the provisional ruling is 'credible'.[38] For this purpose, in order to take measures for the protection of an endangered child, a lesser degree of judicial conviction is required than in the case of a final ruling. A statutory basis in German procedural law for the making of an emergency protection order in civil law child protection proceedings will be sought in vain; this form of emergency protection order is made exclusively by judicial order. The inadequacy of the current legal situation in relation to the procedural law form of emergency protection procedures in cases of civil law child protection manifests itself in two aspects: the period for which provisional rulings are effective, and the question of the contestability of such judicial decisions.

In principle, provisional rulings are effective for an unlimited period and are invalidated only by the final decision. There is no statutory time period after which a provisional ruling becomes automatically invalid. The courts do have a constitutional duty to put a time limit on provisional rulings,[39] but they have generally failed to observe it in practice. This is a most undesirable state of affairs, since emergency protection orders in civil law child protection proceedings in Germany are frequently valid for periods which, due to the particular characteristics of the younger child's sense of time and related circumstances, result in the pre-emption of the final decision; for example, the removal of an abused child from its family and its placement with a foster family: the subsequent removal of the child from the foster family may often be out of the question if enough time has passed for it to have become attached to the foster family (compare s.1632, para. 4, Civil Code).[40]

The question concerning the contestability of a provisional ruling has so far been dealt with unsatisfactorily in judicial practice, since the view has been taken that these emergency protection orders can be appealed without any statutory time limitation (s.19 Law on Matters of Noncontentious Jurisdiction). With the coming into force of the Child and Parent Law Reform Act, however, there is reason to rethink the matter of the contestability of provisional rulings, since the legislature has granted a different status in procedural law both to the time limitations on appeals and to younger children's sense of time. Provisional rulings must therefore in future be contested, on the analogy of s.621e, para. 3, sentence 2 in association with s.516 (Code of Civil Procedure), by means of an appeal within one month.[41] These rules are to apply directly to final decisions in civil law child protection proceedings.

Judicial procedure is decisively influenced in this instance by the preconstitutional Law on Matters of Noncontentious Jurisdiction. This is characterized by the so-called 'inquisitorial' mode of proof (s.12 Law on Matters of Noncontentious Jurisdiction); that is, in principle, the court may itself make decisions concerning the institution of a proceeding (which in a civil law child protection proceeding can be simply proposed by the Youth Office or by a third party), the course of the proceeding, and the nature and extent of the taking of evidence (the calling of experts, and so on). Since 1980, however, separate hearings have been prescribed by statute: the court must hear not only the parents and the foster persons (ss.50a,c) but also the child (ss.50b). This hearing of the child should 'provide the court with a better understanding of its personality and situation, its needs and feelings'.[42] From 14 years of age, the child must always be heard personally; there is a compelling obligation to hear younger children too, however, if the 'inclinations, ties, or wishes of the child are important for the decision' (s.50b, para. 1, sentence 1). For this purpose, even three- and four-year-old children can be heard.[43]

Furthermore, the law prescribes that the Youth Office must participate; that is, that in every civil law proceeding affecting children the court must afford the Youth Office an opportunity to have its say (s.49a, para. 1, sub-para. 5 Law on Matters of Non-contentious Jurisdiction). This obligation on the part of the court to give a hearing corresponds to the Youth Office's obligation to participate (see s.50, para. 1, Child and Youth Services Act). The purpose of this involvement of the Youth Office is, among other things, to introduce into the proceedings the 'educational and social standpoints related to the development of the child' (s.50, para. 2, Child and Youth Services Act). The Youth Office can also be of assistance to the court in the investigation of the merits of the case. At the same time, the Youth Office is in no sense an auxiliary body of the court, but has its own position in the sense of a status *sui generis*.[44]

On 1 July 1998, an important procedural law amendment came into force: the explicit statutory introduction of a guardian *ad litem* in s.50 Law on Matters of Non-contentious Jurisdiction. Particularly in civil law child protection proceedings which involve intervention in parental child custody, there is a substantial conflict of interest between parents and children. For this reason the legislature provides in s.50, para. 2, sentence 1, sub-para. 2 Law on Matters of Non-contentious Jurisdiction that, 'as a rule', a guardian *ad litem* should be appointed for the child. Should the court decide not to appoint such a guardian, it must state its reasons (s.50, para. 2, sentence 2). With this a long reform debate concerning the need for a 'child counsel' in Germany finds its, to be sure only provisional, conclusion.[45] The concept behind the legislation is anything but convincing, however. We need consider only three aspects: (a) the legislature foresees no comprehensive programme of further training to prepare qualified persons for the difficult task of adequate interest representation; (b) the time of the appointment remains open, although experience from England and Wales has shown that the earliest possible appointment of someone to represent the interests of the child is essential if delays in the proceedings are to be avoided;[46] (c) in contrast to English law, there are no specific references to the fact that the guardian *ad litem* should help to circumvent delays in the proceedings. Finally, the duration of the proceedings is one of the central problems of German family law, not only in civil law child protection proceedings, but in proceedings under child and parent law in general.[47]

Similarly, in a civil law context, there is the question whether or when a physical or emotional punishment inflicted by parents on their children for the purpose of their upbringing (so-called 'chastisement') represents an acceptable exercise of the parental right to bring up their children or an instance of child abuse. The legislature settled on the following definition in its most recent reform of child and parent law: 'Humiliating methods of upbringing, particularly physical and emotional abuse, are unacceptable' (s.1631, para. 2, Civil Code, amended).[48] This solution must be considered a questionable compromise, because the question of the limitations of the parents' right to use corporal punishment has been one of the most widely discussed aspects of the latest legislation concerning children. The objective of this law is to make it clear that physical and emotional abuse can have no role in bringing up a child.[49] Physical abuse shall be understood to be 'any harmful or unreasonable action by means of which the best interests of the victim are impaired to anything other than a trivial degree'.[50] The opposition parties were unable to carry through their demand for a general prohibition on violence within the framework of the parent–child relationship ('Children must be brought up free from violence.')[51] In these terms a method of bringing up a child will be considered unacceptable when it reaches the threshold of child abuse; such a 'drawing of a line in the sand' will be difficult in individual cases. Children will have to suffer the consequences of the ambiguities and uncertainties which will result from this, although the government coalition regards this as the price which must be paid for a 'reasonable' parental right to bring up children.[52] If parents should happen to overstep the boundaries laid down in s.1631, para. 2, Civil Code the available sanctions are those already mentioned as laid down in ss.1666 and 1666a, Civil Code, and under some circumstances ss.223ff, 185, 239 and 240, Penal Code.

Finally, an abused child in principle can make civil law claims for damages and for pain and suffering (ss.823ff, 847, Civil Code) against the perpetrator, although hitherto these have rarely been invoked in practice.[53]

Child and youth services law

In cases of child abuse, child and youth services law has an important function. German law has undergone substantial amendment in this connection in recent times. Since 1 January 1991, the Child and Youth Services Act has applied, superseding the Youth Welfare Act of 1922, since the latter 'in many respects had ceased to be adequate to the needs of a changed society'.[54] The main focus of the Youth Welfare Act was a particularly severe conception of intervention, as a result of which so-called 'welfare' interventions and the legal position of the parents were very much to the fore.[55] The Child and Youth Services Act, however, to a great extent abstains from the authorization of intervention and limits itself primarily to statutory socioeducational provisions for children with problems.[56] If, in an exceptional case, intervention should come into question, it should be carefully planned and both time-limited and goal-oriented.[57] The professional standard for intervention has been raised considerably: openness towards the parents and their participation in decision making concerning the kind of assistance to be provided in bringing up the child are central concerns of the Child and Youth Services Act. This change of perspective corresponds to the constitutional requirement concerning the preventive protection of children and young people in respect of threats to their development.[58] The Child and Youth Services Act therefore makes available a wide range of forms of assistance in respect of which, in the present connection, assistance in upbringing (ss.27ff, Child and Youth Services Act) is of particular importance. This includes, among other things, the following: advice on upbringing (s.28), support in bringing up a child (s.30), socioeducational assistance (s.31), full-time foster care (s.33) and bringing up a child in a home or other supervised forms of residence (s.34). In an emergency or conflict situation children and young people, regardless of their age,[59] can, even without the knowledge of those responsible for their care, seek independent advice (s.8, para. 3).

In individual cases, however, endangerment to a child's best interests cannot, or can no longer, be adequately dealt with by means of assistance in its upbringing within the framework of the family, with the result that only crisis intervention for the sake of the child or young person will suffice. For such cases the Child and Youth Services Act – as an exception to its otherwise exclusively assistance-oriented stance – provides the authorities with the right to intervene to protect the child by taking it into care, at its own request (s.42, Child and Youth Services Act) or by issuing a care order (s.43). These norms therefore offer the Youth Office 'the possibility of immediate action for the protection of the child or young person in urgent and emergency cases'.[60] These regulations have particular practical significance in cases of child abuse. The Youth Office therefore takes over for a temporary period the right to determine the child's place of residence, as well as tasks related to its upbringing (s.42, para. 1, sentence 4, Child and Youth Services Act). In particular, the Youth Office must 'advise the child or young person in his current situation and offer him help and support' (s.42, para. 1, sentence 5, Child and Youth Services Act).

Taking into care comes onto the agenda, in the first place, when a child or young person asks for it (s.42, para. 2, Child and Youth Services Act) and, secondly, when the best interests of the child or young person are in imminent danger (s.42, para. 3). In both situations the Youth Office must immediately inform those responsible for the personal custody or upbringing of the child (s.42, para. 2, sentence 2). If these persons refuse to give their consent, the Youth Office must immediately procure a judicial decision concerning the measures required to ensure the best interests of the child or young person, when there is no question of handing him over to those responsible for him. Unfortunately, there is no time schedule for this radical form of intervention.

In addition to the basically assistance-oriented tasks of the Youth Office – although, as we have seen, in individual cases it also has at its disposal the authority to intervene – one of its fundamental functions is participation in judicial proceedings (s.50, Child and Youth Services Act).[61] The Youth Office has no general duty to have recourse to the court when a case of child abuse comes to its attention. The legal grounds here are constituted by s.50, para. 3, Child and Youth Services Act: accordingly, the Youth Office need have recourse to the court only when it believes such action to be necessary in order to avoid endangerment to the child. With this formulation, the legislature has made it clear that the Youth Office has its own decision-making competence in this field. Here also the Child and Youth Services Act departs from the approach of the Youth Welfare Act, according to which the Youth Office had an express duty to have recourse to the court (see s.48, sentence 2, Youth Welfare Act). An attempt by the German Federal Council to model s.50, para. 3, Child and Youth Services Act on s.48, sentence 2, Youth Welfare Act failed in the course of the legislative procedure.[62] The intention of the legislature was to give the Youth Office some leeway concerning judicial action, given the fact that it has other suitable measures at its disposal for the purpose of warding off threats to the best interests of the child.[63] At the same time, there is no question of a general priority being given to assistance at the expense of intervention in parental custody. Assistance can only be given priority in so far as it represents an appropriate means of preventing harm. This requires that no failed attempts have been made to eliminate the danger without resort to judicial intervention, or that it is clear that the latter would fail to achieve its aim. Should this be the case, the Youth Office must decide on the basis of an objective and professional assessment made in full consciousness of the facts. The Youth Office's assessment of the likely result of recourse to the court must play no role in this: the evaluation of the facts presented and the establishment of other decision-making grounds are matters for the court alone: they are outside the expertise of the Youth Office.[64] Should the Youth Office reach the conclusion that the limitation or elimination of the threat to the best interests of the child cannot be achieved without recourse to the court because the range of measures at the disposal of the youth services are no longer adequate to the task, it has a legal obligation to have such recourse. There is no obligation to notify the criminal prosecution authorities, however.[65]

Criminal law aspects of child abuse

When a case of child abuse comes to light, the question arises if and when – not to mention which – criminal sanctions should be taken against the perpetrator. In relation to a case of child abuse, the following criminal acts are particularly important:

- s.173, Penal Code (sexual intercourse between relatives),
- s.174, Penal Code (sexual abuse of charges),
- s.176, Penal Code (sexual abuse of children),
- s.176a, Penal Code (serious sexual abuse),
- s.176b, Penal Code (serious sexual abuse resulting in death),
- s.180, Penal Code (promoting the performance of sexual acts with or by minors),
- s.182, Penal Code (sexual abuse of young people),
- s.184b, Penal Code (prostitution which is liable to corrupt young people),
- s.185, Penal Code (slander/libel),
- s.221, para. 2, Penal Code (abandonment of one's own child or of a person committed to one's care for the sake of his/her upbringing),
- s.223ff, Penal Code (bodily harm),
- s.235, Penal Code (abduction of a minor),
- s.236, Penal Code (traffic in children),
- s.240, Penal Code (compulsion or intimidation),
- s.323c, Penal Code (failure to lend assistance).

In the wake of the public debate on tragic cases of child abuse and the increasing awareness of the extent of child pornography, the legislature reacted (among other things) by increasing the penalties for the relevant offences.⁶⁶ To that end, by means of Law 6 on the Reform of the Criminal Law (in force since 1 April 1998) a number of different criminal acts were newly inserted in the Penal Code (for example, ss.176a, 176b and 221, para. 2, Penal Code). In light of this, it seems that the criminal law is still regarded as a set of instruments for the purpose of combating child abuse, the hope still persisting that, by extending the number of criminal acts and increasing the range of punishments, the protection of children may be promoted. Nevertheless, the German legislature should be aware that effective child and youth protection cannot be achieved by means of the criminal law alone; this is a task also for society and the education system (compare BT-Drucks. (Bundestagsdrucksache: Federal Parliament Publication) 13/7087, p.2). Needless to say, the established criminal law protection of legal interests in this field, notwithstanding the fact that this protection is not always activated, should not be dispensed with. The mere existence of the criminal law protection of legal interests enhances the status of, and thereby stabilizes, the non-criminal law protection and assistance provided under civil and social law. It would be beyond the scope of the present discussion to consider in detail all the criminal acts mentioned. We will therefore pick out, by way of example, a number of problem areas of German criminal law in the field of child abuse.

Child abuse is subject to express criminal law sanction – in addition to the already mentioned criminal law legislation concerning sexual offences – under s.225, Penal Code, a regulation which, among other things, takes a different view of bodily harm when the victim is below 18 years of age and in a protective relationship (above all, parental custody) with the perpetrator.⁶⁷ Should the perpetrator be an 'ordinary' third party, without any particular legal, official or contractual relationship with the child, there is no particular qualification of the criminal act (such qualifications usually go together with an increase in the punishment).⁶⁸ This is even the case when the perpetrator is the cohabiting partner of the child's mother. German penal legislation makes no distinction in this connection concerning whether the victim is a child or an adult.⁶⁹ It is up to the court to take into account the particular features of an individual case when determining the penalty (s.46, Penal Code).

Particularly in the case of offences involving bodily harm, the view is still taken that the right of parents to bring up their child represents a ground of justification under criminal law. This consideration is fundamental for the legislature, which rejected an amendment of s.1631, para. 2, Civil Code which would have instituted an absolute prohibition on violence, among other reasons because this would have resulted in an undesirable extension of the criminal liability of parents.⁷⁰ This is not a particularly convincing stance, since it may well be asked whether the familiar 'smack' can be considered to constitute bodily harm in the sense of the criminal law.⁷¹ What is decisive, however, is that acknowledgement of the right to bring up one's child as a ground of justification under criminal law does not correspond to the notion of humanity embodied in the Basic Law, since it does not recognize the child as a full bearer of its own human worth (art. 1, para. 1, Basic Law) and personality (art. 2, para. 1, together with art. 1, para. 1, Basic Law). In this connection jurisprudence cannot close itself off from the human sciences, which are united in their agreement that, at least, corporal punishment is not appropriate for the purpose of bringing up a child, and may even be positively harmful.[72]

A wide-ranging discussion has flared up both in the media and among professionals concerning the criminal law relevance of neglect ('*Unterlassen*') in respect of child abuse. The dogmatic background here is the distinction between so-called direct and indirect cases of neglect ('*echte' und 'unechte Unterlassungsdelikte*'). Direct cases of neglect are crimes 'which amount to the violation of a prohibitive regulation and to the simple neglect of an activity required by law'.[73] An example of this is s.323c, Penal Code which subjects to criminal sanctions a failure to lend assistance. In these terms a neighbour could be punished for failing to act when he knows that child abuse is going on next door. In individual cases, considerably higher sentences can be imposed when criminal liability is allowed on the basis of an indirect case of neglect. Basically, any offence can be construed as a case of indirect neglect, although the chief requirement is that 'the person responsible for the neglect is bound as "guarantor" to act'.[74] The position of a guarantor can result from the law (this applies to the parents) and from a contract (this applies to doctors on the basis of the treatment contract), as a consequence of which punishment for child abuse on the basis of the criminal law regulations already mentioned can result, not only from a positive action, but also from neglect. The professional debate mentioned at the beginning took its decisive orientation from the question as to whether criminal law sanctions could be taken against the staff of the Youth Office when harm comes to a child currently in its charge. The background to this debate is provided by the death of a baby from emaciation and thirst in 1994, in which case there were extensive signs of neglect.[75] The crucial issue here is whether the responsible staff of the Youth Office are in the position of guarantors. This must be answered in the affirmative.[76] What is decisive is that the responsible persons have the task of protecting the physical, intellectual and emotional best interests of the child in question (see also s.1, para. 3, sub-para. 3, Child and Youth Services Act). They therefore have the 'position of guarantor due to the effective assumption of protection in favour of the child(ren)/young persons(s) taken into care'.[77] Criminal liability is not diminished just because the accused person is a trained social worker.[78]

The procedural law realization of substantive law provisions is just as significant for civil law as for penal law. In order that criminal proceedings be instituted, the public prosecution authorities must be informed. This information is generally communicated to the authorities by means of a complaint, which as a rule sets the criminal proceedings in motion at the same time. There is no obligation on the part of private persons to make a complaint as a consequence of a criminal act, however.[79] The principal argument brought against the institution of such a reporting obligation is that it could jeopardize the relationship of trust existing between doctor and patient, parent and doctor, or Youth Office and family.[80] In addition, criminal proceedings put the child under enormous pressure,[81] and criminal proceedings – unlike guardianship law or family law proceedings – are not oriented towards the best interests of the child, with the result that even an obligation to make a complaint on the part of third parties is problematic.[82] This is the case despite the hoped-for reduction in the pressures experienced in the course of questioning in criminal proceedings and improvements in respect of victim protection by means of the bill (which has in the meantime been passed) on the protection of witnesses. With this law, the Code of Criminal Procedure was amended. Among other things, a provision was included which makes it possible for the questioning of a witness who is under 16 years of age and the victim of a criminal act to be recorded on a sound or image recorder (s.58a, para. 1, sentence 1, Code of Criminal Procedure, amended version). This recording can be used afterwards during the judicial proceedings, instead of questioning by the judge (s.255a, para. 2, Code of Criminal Procedure, amended version). It is also possible, along the lines of the model which has proved successful in Great Britain, to conduct an examination of a witness in a trial by video, the presiding judge remaining in the courtroom throughout the questioning and communicating with the witness – who may be accompanied by a confidant or an adviser ('*Beistand*') – via a direct video link (compare ss.168e, 247a, Code of Criminal Procedure, amended version). By these measures, German law has finally taken cognizance of the established fact that the victims of criminal acts, particularly children, are generally subjected to considerable psychological pressures by the questioning which takes place in the course of criminal proceedings.[83]

The relation between criminal law protection and civil law child protection in Germany can best be described as relatively unclear. While, as already mentioned, civil law and youth service child protection concentrate on providing assistance to the child and associated matters when dealing with child abuse, the central issue in criminal proceedings is the conviction and sentencing of the perpetrator; the protection of the victim in such proceedings is still rather underdeveloped in German law.[84] A satisfactory clarification of cooperation between criminal and civil courts is yet to be made.[85] For example, in a case involving the sexual abuse of two girls – nine and 12 years of age, respectively, at the time of the offence – by the father, who admitted the offence in the course of a guardianship court proceeding, the relevant court rejected, rightly in our opinion, the request of the public prosecutor's office for the surrender of the case documents. In a nutshell, the guardianship court judge argued that she had demanded the information used in the guardianship court proceedings for the purpose of providing assistance and not for that of criminal prosecution.[86]

The possibly counterproductive effects on children of criminal proceedings have still not been sufficiently curbed in Germany, as a consequence of which a certain scepticism concerning criminal law has become widespread among those working in counselling services established by public bodies or volunteer organizations: at the very least, they have become more cautious about advising people to instigate criminal complaints concerning child abuse.

CONCLUSION

In the area of child abuse there is still a great deal to be done in Germany in relation to legal and social policy. Growing child poverty and high unemployment are making life more difficult for an increasing number of children. The legal machinery presented in this chapter is still in many respects well worth improving upon. Improvements in the help given to abused children over the last decade are due not least to community initiatives (the Child Protection League, child protection centres and the efforts of voluntary workers to help women, girls and children).

NOTES

1 By 'children', minors of both sexes are to be understood, unless age or gender are otherwise specified.
2 See Gisela Zenz, *Kindesmißhandlung und Kindesrechte* (Frankfurt am Main, 1979). She describes this reaction on the part of the general public as 'a new cultural acquisition of recent date', and complains of its ambivalence (p.57).
3 Compare Engfer, *Kindesmißhandlung* (Stuttgart, 1986) pp.10ff.
4 See Staudinger–Coester, *Bürgerliches Gesetzbuch*, 12 edn (Berlin, 1991) s.1666 Rn. 72.
5 For a comprehensive view of the historical development of child abuse, see Lloyd deMause, *The History of Childhood* (New York, 1974); Zenz op. cit., note 2, pp.19ff.
6 Compare, for example, s.90 Zweyter Theil, Zweyter Titel, Zweyter Abschnitt des Allgemeinen Landrechts für die Preußischen Staaten von 1794.

7   *Federal Law Gazette*, Part 1: 2942ff.
8   L. Salgo, 'Unerledigte Aufträge des Bundesverfassungsgerichts an den Gesetzgeber auf dem Gebiet des Familienrechts' (Unfinished tasks imposed by the Constitutional Court on the legislature in the field of family law), *KritV*, 262ff, 1994.
9   Article 6, para. 2, Basic Law: 'The care and upbringing of children are the natural right of the parents and primarily their duty. The state supervises the exercise of the same.' Article 6, para. 3, Basic Law: 'Children may be separated from the family against the will of the persons entitled to undertake their upbringing only pursuant to a statute, those so entitled having failed to perform their tasks satisfactorily, or in cases in which, for other reasons, the children are in serious danger of neglect.'
10 For a just approach to this, see Honig, *Verhäuslichte Gewalt* (Frankfurt am Main, 1992) p.34. This volume also contains further valuable comments on the problem of statistics, particularly the estimated number of unreported cases.
11 Introduction to the 'Reasons Given for the Law on the Child and Parent Law Reform Act', *Federal Parliament Publication* 13/4899: 1.
12 Compare Federal Constitutional Court Decision 1: 184, 195.
13 See particularly L. Salgo, 'The Family Justice System – The German Approach', in Ludwig Salgo (ed.), *The Family Justice System – Past and Future, Experiences and Prospects*, (Budapest: Collegium Budapest, 1997) pp.133f.
14 Article 1, para. 1, Basic Law: 'Human dignity is inviolable. To respect and protect it is the duty of all state authorities.' Article 2, para. 1 Basic Law: 'Everyone has the right to the free development of his personality insofar as he does not violate the rights of others or offend against the constitutional order or against morality.'
15 Article 2, para. 2, line 1, Basic Law: 'Everyone has the right to life and to physical integrity.'
16 See note 9.
17 Federal Constitutional Court Decision 24: 119, 144.
18 Federal Constitutional Court Decision, loc. cit.
19 See Federal Constitutional Court Decision 50: 166, 175 with further references.
20 Compare Federal Constitutional Court Decision 79: 256, 268.
21 Compare art. 6, para. 3, Basic Law.
22 Compare Herzog, in Maunz and Dürig (eds), *Kommentar zum Grundgesetz* (Commentary on the Basic Law), (Munich, 1996), Art. 20 Rn. 71 ff.
23 For more details, see 'Civil Law', below.
24 See Heilmann, *Kindliches Zeitempfinden und Verfahrensrecht* (The child's sense of time and procedural law), (Neuwied, 1998).
25 With the reform of the right of care in 1979 the legislature made it clear that even in the case of a failure of the parents which is not anyone's fault judicial intervention can be justified. All discussions concerning the requirement of parental fault in the variable elements of § 1666 Civil Code have so far been only of an academic character (compare Staudinger–Coester, § 1666 Rn. 12 ff.).
26 Zenz, op. cit., note 2, 83.
27 Staudinger–Coester, op. cit., note 4, s.1666 Rn. 56.
28 See Simitis, 'Familienrecht', in *Rechtswissenschaft in der Bonner Republik* (Jurisprudence in the Bonn Republic), (Frankfurt am Main: 1994) pp.431ff.; Coester, *Das Kindeswohl als Rechtsbegriff* (The best interests of the child as a legal concept) (Frankfurt am Main: 1983) pp.419ff.
29 Simitis, 'Das "Kindeswohl" – neu betrachtet' (A new look at the best interests of the child), in Goldstein, A. Freud and Solnit (eds), *Jenseits des Kindeswohls* (Beyond the best interests of the child) (Frankfurt am Main, 1974) pp.108f.

30 Staudinger–Coester, loc. cit.
31 Federal Constitutional Court Decision 55: 171, 179.
32 See Staudinger–Coester, ss.1666 Rn. 61 with further references.
33 See note 43.
34 Federal Court of Justice, *Neue Juristische Wochenschrift* (1956) p.1434.
35 Staudinger–Coester, s.1666 Rn. 132.
36 German law distinguishes between personal custody and care for the property of the child (*Personensorge* and *Vermögenssorge*) as components of parental care (s.1626, para. 1, Civil Code). Personal custody includes particularly the right and duty to care for, bring up and supervise the child, and to determine his place of residence (s.1631 Civil Code). A comprehensive overview of the nature of personal custody is provided in Staudinger–Salgo, *Bürgerliches Gesetzbuch*, 12th edn (Berlin, 1997), Commentary on s.1631 Civil Code.
37 For the conditions pertaining to provisional rulings, see especially Kahl, in Keidel, Kuntze and Winkler (eds), *Freiwillige Gerichtsbarkeit* (Jurisdiction over non-contentious matters), Part A, 13th edn (Munich, 1992) s.19 Rn. 30.
38 Gießler, 'Vorläufiger Rechtsschutz', *Ehe-, Familien- und Kindschaftssachen* (Provisional legal protection in marriage, family and parent-child cases), 2nd edn (Munich, 1993) Rn. 319.
39 Compare Heilmann, op. cit., note 24.
40 See L. Salgo, *Pflegekindschaft und Staatsintervention* (The fostering of children and state intervention) (Darmstadt: 1987). On s.1632, para. 4, Civil Code, see Staudinger–Salgo, s.1632 Rn. 42 ff.
41 Heilmann, op. cit., note 24.
42 Staudinger–Coester, s.1666 Rn. 160.
43 On child hearings, see particularly Fehmel's commentary on s.50b Law on Matters of Noncontentious Jurisdiction, in Baumeister, Fehmel, Griesche, Hochgräber, Kayser and Wick (Berlin, 1992), and Lempp, Braunbehrens, Eichner and Röcker, *Die Anhörung des Kindes* (Child hearings) under s.50b Law on Matters of Noncontentious Jurisdiction (Cologne: 1987).
44 See Wiesner-Mörsberger, *SGB VIII – Kinder- und Jugendhilfe* (Code of Social Law – Child and Youth Services), 1st edn, (Munich, 1995) before the commentaries on s.50 Rn. 55.
45 See L. Salgo, *Der Anwalt des Kindes* (The child counsel), 2nd edn (Frankfurt am Main, 1996).
46 Ibid., p.269.
47 For a comprehensive overview, see Heilmann, op. cit., note 24.
48 On the history of corporal punishment, as well as the legal situation before the reform, see Staudinger–Salgo, s.1631 Rn. 1 and 66 ff.
49 Federal Parliament Publication 13/8511: 65.
50 Ibid. A formulation, by the way, which was developed in judicial decisions and the literature on s.223 Penal Code (intentional bodily harm).
51 See the proposal forwarded by Bündnis 90/Die Grünen: Federal Parliament Publication 13/3341: 2. The new Government intends to formulate a bill in this direction.
52 Compare Federal Parliament Publication 13/8511: 65.
53 See, for example, the decision of the Düsseldorf district court (*Zeitschrift für das gesamte Familienrecht* [1998]:1426). The parents have to pay – beside the criminal sanctions (imprisonment) – 50 000 DM as compensation for immaterial damage, because they abused their daughter sexually.
54 Federal Parliament Publication 11/5948: 41.

55 See Wiesner-Mörsberger op. cit., note 44, Introduction, Rn. 15ff.
56 Ibid., Rn. 37.
57 L. Salgo, 'Die Regelungen der Familienpflege im Kinder- und Jugendhilfegesetz' (The rules of family care in the Child and Youth Services Act), in *Das neue Kinder- und Jugendhilfegesetz* (The new Child and Youth Services Act), ed. Wiesner and Zarbock (Cologne, 1990) pp.115ff.
58 See Wiesner op. cit., note 44, Introduction, Rn. 38.
59 Ibid., s.8 Rn. 41.
60 Ibid., s.42 Rn. 1.
61 On this see previous section.
62 Compare Federal Parliament Publication 11/5948: 138.
63 Wiesner-Mörsberger, op. cit., note 44, s.50 Rn. 76.
64 For another opinion, see ibid., op. cit., note 44, s.50 Rn. 84.
65 Ibid., s.50 Rn. 80.
66 See the law on the amendment of the Penal Code, the Code of Criminal Procedure, and other laws of 28 October 1994 (Law on the Combating of Crime), *Federal Law Gazette*, Part 1: 3168ff, as well as Criminal Law Amendment Act 27 of 23 July 1993, *Federal Law Gazette*, Part 1: 1346ff. On these reforms, see Tröndle, *Strafgesetzbuch und Nebengesetze* (Penal Code and Supplementary Statutes), 48th edn (Munich, 1997) s.130 Rn. 1 with further references. See also *Federal Law Gazette*, Part 1: 164ff.
67 See Tröndle, op. cit., note 66, s.223b Rn. 4.
68 For a justifiably critical view see Stumpf, *Opferschutz bei Kindesmißhandlung* (Protection of the victim in child abuse cases) (Neuwied, 1995) pp.190f.
69 Compare also Zenz, *Kindesmißhandlung und Kindesrechte* (Child abuse and children's rights), p.28.
70 Federal Parliament Publication 13/8511: 65.
71 Stumpf, op. cit., note 68, pp.197f.
72 On this see Staudinger–Salgo, s.1631 Rn. 73.
73 Wessels, *Strafrecht – Allgemeiner Teil* (Criminal Law – General Part), 26th edn (Heidelberg, 1996) p.208.
74 Ibid., p.209. Compare also s.13, Penal Code.
75 The statement of the facts and criminal law proceedings against the responsible social worker, as well as the discussion in the literature, are comprehensively treated in Bringewat, *Der Tod eines Kindes* (The death of a child) (Baden-Baden, 1997).
76 For a different opinion, probably that of Mörsberger, see 'Stichwort Garantenpflicht' (Keyword: Duty of Guarantor), in Mörsberger and Restemeier (eds), *Helfen mit Risiko – Zur Pflichtenstellung des Jugendamtes bei Kindesvernachlässigung* (Help at your own risk: on the obligations of the Youth Office in cases of child neglect) (Neuwied, 1997) pp.155ff.
77 Bringewat, op. cit., note 75, p.62.
78 Bringewat, op. cit., note 75, p.33 ('Criminal law orders and prohibitions do not spare even those possessing the highest level of expertise').
79 Roxin, *Strafverfahrensrecht* (Criminal Procedural Law), 24th edn (Munich, 1995) p.278.
80 Stumpf, op. cit., note 68, p.211.
81 On this see Zenz, 'Sekundärtraumatisierung von mißhandelten und mißbrauchten Kindern im gerichtlichen Verfahren' (Secondary traumatization of abused children in judicial proceedings), in Klosinski (ed.), *Macht, Machtmißbrauch und Machtverzicht* (Power, abuse of power, and renunciation of power) (Berne, 1995) p.91ff.
82 Marquardt, *Sexuell mißbrauchte Kinder und das Recht* (Sexually abused children and the law), vol. 1 (Cologne, 1993) p.91.

83 See BT-Drucks. 13/8990, p.1.
84 Compare Keiser, *Das Kindeswohl im Strafverfahren* (The best interests of the child in criminal proceedings) (Frankfurt am Main, 1998).
85 On this problem, see also Wiesner-Mörsberger, op. cit., note 44, Appendix s.61 Rn. 5.
86 Unpublished decision of the Hamburg Local Court of 13 February 1987 (114 VIII W 11 645 und 114 VIII S 16 648).

9 Child Abuse in Hungary

Klára Kerezsi

INTRODUCTION

'The icy atmosphere in the family' was the title of a recent newspaper report which dealt with child victims. It revealed a huge gap between our belief and reality. Instead of having a 'safe, loving and caring family', thousands of Hungarian children live in disturbed families. Today, when we see the continuously rising number of children 'at risk', we realize that something is wrong with our families. Thousands of children have daily experience of physical abuse or maltreatment. We encounter child beggars and child prostitutes on the streets every day. Criminal statistics show that children under 14 are committing more and more crimes

The question to be answered is: why does society fail to react to these problems and to the abuse committed against children? Why does society not respond to the tragedies of so many children? Why does the fact that there are perhaps as many as 300 000 children at risk not awaken the conscience of anyone besides the child protection professionals? My research suggests that we in Hungary have not as yet got to grips with the problem or found the appropriate ways of dealing with it.[1]

CHILD ABUSE AS A NEW PHENOMENON IN HUNGARY

In 1982 a researcher interviewed some children who were living in state care and asked what was the meaning of 'family life' for them. They answered with three phrases: 'physical abuse', 'money shortage' and 'alcohol'.[2] Agnes Losonczi found the same:

> Some 60% of the persons asked said that they were beaten ... 10 per cent of them saying they were beaten severely with straps, sticks, whips, wet ropes, rolling-pins ... There were homes where these punishments were carried out

with deliberate calculation or unrestrained anger and brutal cruelty and there were also places where violence was used as a special way of education, the child being given as many as twenty-five strokes or beaten until he bled ... There were homes where it was used to make the child understand better or prolonged until the father's hand got tired.

'I could be beaten because my father had not had a good day', because he had a 'very hard life', 'because he drank a lot' or because – and this is an understandable reason for these punishments – he was also beaten as a child or he was beaten by life itself, or in general his violence was a response to all that he had to endure in life.[3] Research carried out by the author at the National Institute of Criminology indicates that corporal punishment is a normal way of treating children, so that the regular experience of being punished in this way is regarded by them as the rule.[4]

The family should be a secure and caring community, but it may easily become the scene of the most brutal acts too. Recently, family violence has resulted in some children's deaths in Hungary. Commonly, as well, children die because their parents neglect to call doctors in time. The following are a few examples from Hungarian newspapers:

- *Népszabadság*, 18 November 1996: Parents failed to look after their three children (they were not fed or cared for and they were kept indoors) and the nurse was misled. The panel doctor attributed the swelled abdomen of the children to their prematurity and failed to notice their physical and intellectual underdevelopment. Andreas, the four-year-old boy, died of hunger, and the three- and four-year-old girls were saved only as a result of immediate medical treatment.
- *Népszabadság*, 21 December 1996: In a country town a man of 34 killed his six-year-old daughter and four-year-old son, just to take revenge on his wife.
- *Népszabadság*, 7 December 1996: A man wanted to take revenge on his brother and badly injured his brother's two-year-old daughter, who died as a result.
- *Kisalföld*, 27 December 1996: In a small country town a man of 37 shot dead his estranged wife and their seven-year-old daughter.
- *Népszabadság*, 13 December 1996: A father killed his six-year-old daughter in an extremely cruel way and then buried her in the woods. Two weeks later he said she had disappeared.

The loser in family violence is always the child. In families where fathers have limited communication skills violence, even extreme violence, is often the only known way of attempting to solve conflicts. And if violence becomes the only means of family communication, the danger of escalation is great, especially where there is a lack of social control. The dangers are especially great when traditional moral and family values are collapsing: anomie is rife and aggressiveness develops as well. There are no hopes of changing society in the short term.

Professionals working with children in state care talk more frequently about the many young women who have become victims of sexual abuse within their families. More and more revelations show that sexual abuse of children both in families and in institutions has taken place without anyone knowing about it. As the psychologist of a state care institute says: 'Studying the personal records of our children, I could find only 3-4 cases in which the physical or sexual abuse of the child was mentioned. But I personally know of 10-12 cases in which the children have themselves revealed that they have been sexually abused.'[5] As examples, she cites the following.

- Zs. was in state care from the time she was born, since her mother left her in the hospital. At the age of two she was sent to foster parents. At the age of three her foster parents got divorced and, from this time on, her foster mother became drunk more often and beat her regularly. When she was six years old, she was taken to hospital because she had been beaten, though the foster mother said it was an accident. At the age of nine she was given other foster parents, but violence continued. During PE, she undid her dress in such a way that the other children should not see the traces of violence. She spent her holidays at the farm of the brother of her foster mother. She was 12 when she was raped by him. She did not mention this to her foster mother, but she was reluctant to go to the farm any more. After some years she asked to be sent to a state institution.
- I. was brought up by her paternal grandmother and by her second husband. When the girl was nine years old she was raped by him. She told her grandmother, who – after her husband promised to change – accepted the truth of what had happened, but did not do anything about it. Five years later he again raped the girl. This time, the grandmother informed the police.[6]

CHILD ABUSE AND SOCIAL FACTORS

Despite the many child abuse cases in Hungary, the deaths and suffering of these children are not enough to raise public awareness about child victims. Since 1991 the number of children at risk increased sharply as the economic situation declined. Most families' living conditions have got worse and the unemployment rate has risen. Despite the many child abuse cases in Hungary, the deaths and suffering of these children have increased. The polarization of Hungarian society is great and the gap between the rich and poor has become very wide. Differences in income between the upper and lower social strata serve to demonstrate this: the upper level was only 3.9 times greater in 1980, but by 1993 this had increased to 5.9. As a result, the burden of the economically poorer has become greater, as have their psychological burdens, because people were not prepared for unemployment or to meet the difficulties of financial problems and the changes in their way of life. The living conditions of many deteriorated because the state's supportive network collapsed. Many could not attain even the minimum living standards. The number of families living below the subsistence level officially rose from 9 per cent in 1988 to 15 per cent in 1990.[7] (Previously there was no officially calculated minimum living standard, because the socialist system did not accept the existence of poverty at all.)

The proportion of children living below the poverty line is more than 40 per cent, as compared with the rate of 30 per cent in 1970.[8] 'Amongst children, the number of those in poverty is higher than any other group, with every third child at risk, the result of being brought up in larger families amongst the poor, with income being divided amongst the members of the family.'[9] According to a statement of the World Bank, 'The incidence of poverty ... rises steadily with the number of children and is especially steep in households with 2 adults and 4 and more children, and in households with 3 adults and 3 and more children. The corollary to these findings is that poverty among children is somewhat more pervasive than among the population at large.'[10] We have reason to believe that the situation of these families will further deteriorate in the years ahead.

Table 9.1 shows that the number of children at risk has nearly doubled in four years. However, the number of children in state care is declining. This can be seen in Table 9.2. Of those in care, 60 per cent are Romany children, although Romanies constitute only 5 per cent of the Hungarian population.

There have been conferences on child protection and a special issue of a journal on child protection; the police have created a new forum to discuss problems concerned with child sexual abuse; but even so, it is only professionals working in the 'front line' whose concern has been raised. Society as a whole seems to accept abuse as inevitable, and has become more tolerant of violence and neglect towards children.

Table 9.1 Hungary: children under 18 'at risk'

	All children	Children 'at risk'
1991	2 730 000	174 000
1995	2 600 000	320 000

Table 9.2 Children in state care

1975	34 818
1980	34 960
1985	33 101
1990	26 861
1995	24 600

WHAT DOES THE HUNGARIAN LAW SAY ABOUT CHILD ABUSE?

The legal means for protecting children can as a matter of practice be grouped into two parts: child protection by civil law and child protection by criminal law. In Hungary, state protection of children and youth applies to all children from birth to 18 who are 'at risk'. According to Hungarian law, a child can be considered to be 'at risk' when 'his care, education, physical, mental or moral development is harmfully influenced or hindered for any reason'.[11] The categories of 'physical, mental or moral development', established by the constitution, repeatedly appear in countless provisions of law, without giving a true sense of it or making the definition clear cut. For example, it is found in the Act on Family and Guardianship (1952, amended in 1974, 1986, 1990) as a cause of the termination of parental responsibility, and in the Criminal Code (1978) as the legal statement of crime of 'Endangering a Minor', as well as in a Cabinet decision (1986) as an inadequate way of bringing up children expecting state protection. Unfortunately, because this category ('to be at risk') is not clearly defined, there is scope for the state interventions into family life to become discretionary. Though in the child protection register authorities speak about four categories, (environmental, behavioural, financial and health-based), these registers are not sufficiently clear-cut to circumscribe the work of the child protection authorities. Table 9.3 lists the number of children 'at risk', categorized in this way.

Table 9.3 Children at risk in Hungary, by reason

	1989	1991	1993
Environmental	48 613	47 490	50 711
Behavioural	22 635	24 503	26 166
Financial	56 403	167 657	222 762
Health-based	2 346	3 249	4 175
Total	129 997	242 899	303 814

The Child Protection and Welfare Act 1997 defines what puts children at risk: 'actions, omissions or other circumstances, or the state as a result of these conditions, which can disturb, hamper or stop the physical, intellectual or physical or moral development of a child'.[12] Abuse can be categorized as endangering the physical and health development of a child, endangering his/her social integration or endangering his/her moral development.

If parents do not carry out their responsibilities in connection with bringing up their children, the court may limit or terminate their custodial rights. The courts can terminate parents' rights if the parents hurt or endanger the physical, intellectual or moral development of the child, or if the parents are condemned to imprisonment because of committing crimes against their children. The number of actions concerning termination of parental responsibility decreased considerably, from 729 in 1990 to 259 in 1994, though the number of children at risk increased by about 250 per cent in this period (from 129 997 in 1989 to 319 259 in 1994). So it is likely that the child protection authorities did not even start an action in many cases where it was appropriate. Public opinion accepts this state of affairs and this also influences the measures taken by the child protection authorities, as is shown in Table 9.4.[13]

Table 9.4 Measures taken

	1989	1991	1993	1994
Endangered minors	129 997	242 881	303 814	319 259
Rate of application of protective measures (per cent)	67.2	35.7	25.2	24.2

There has been an increase in the number of children at risk, but the number of protective measures taken to meet these problems has decreased, and, even worse, 80 per cent of the 24.2 per cent of protective measures amount to nothing more than the parents getting a warning. These statistics reveal both social attitudes and the lack of normative systems. They point to the dysfunctional nature of many families. These factors are linked to other deviance as well, especially alcohol abuse and crime.

In order to protect children when parents neglect or abuse them, the Criminal Code can also be used. Law is forced to play a double role in child abuse cases in Hungary, which sometimes causes conflicts. It must ensure that the child is protected and also bear in mind that child abuse is a crime, and that it might be in the society's interest to punish the abuser in criminal proceedings. The aim of the criminal law is to protect the physical condition and health of the children against violence and other abuse. Section 195 of the Criminal Code protects children where the perpetrator is a person obliged to look after them and is neglectful of his/her duties. These adults can be punished with up to five years' imprisonment, especially if the child's intellectual and moral development is endangered. According to a recent investigation, the child protection authorities are not enthusiastic about making a report to the police and initiating criminal procedures, and do so only as a last resort. This may happen even in cases where they are aware how dangerous the situation is.[14]

Criminal law should only be invoked in the most serious cases, when the parents have to be prosecuted. There is a big difference between the level of danger to a child which can be treated by child protection means and that which requires the use of criminal law sanctions. The line between the two has not yet been drawn with sufficient clarity in Hungary and this has led to cases of dysfunctional families having to be settled by the criminal law, when they could be managed adequately within the child protection system. The better we are able to define the limits of the child protection system and the criminal law, the more effective will be the impact. Indeed, a way might open up to solve the problems within the family itself or, if outside it, at least using non-coercive measures (see Figure 9.1).

CHILD ABUSE STATISTICS

Although there are many forms of child abuse in Hungary, two types of life situation seem to be most dangerous: first, the dysfunctional family, where the children live under constant threat of becoming victims of physical or sexual abuse or neglect and, secondly, the residential state care institutions, where the children are subjected to the risk of sexual abuse, of either a heterosexual or homosexual nature.

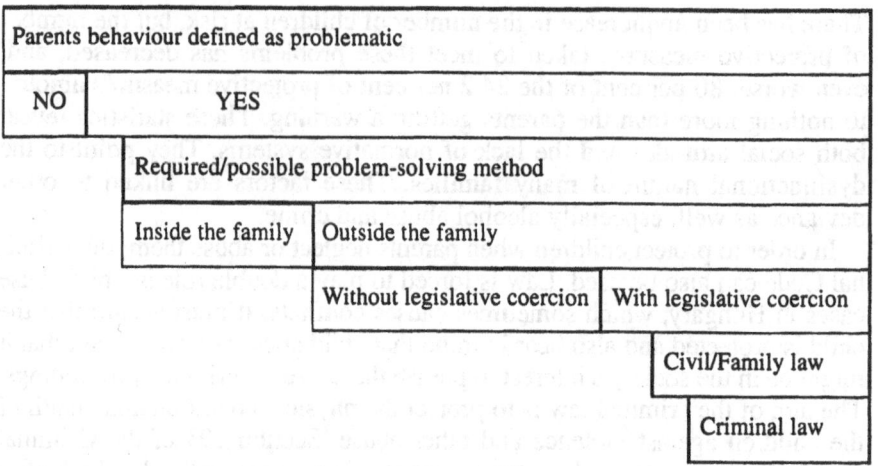

Figure 9.1 Child protection assessment

A survey of the period November 1994 to March 1995 on child abuse and neglect drew on the data of health service experts (general practitioners, paediatricians, nurses, kindergarten workers, hospital wards and so on). It found about 15 000 cases of child abuse a year. Of these, 25 per cent were physical, 20 per cent were emotional and 5 per cent sexual. A majority of the cases (48 per cent) were cases of neglect.[15] Social deprivation increases the number of children at risk. Where criminal activity is high, the number of child abuse incidents is also large. Criminal statistics reveal a decrease in the number of male and female adult victims,[16] but the number of children who are victims of criminal activity has increased. Of course, criminal statistics are unreliable as indicators of levels of offences committed. What is certain is that, in the year 1993, the criminal statistics in Hungary recorded 231 000 victims, among them 9786 under the age of 18 (4.2 per cent) and 20 per cent of these children were under 14. The proportion of victims of murder and manslaughter who are children was 7.2 per cent and in cases of serious bodily harm it was 9.6 per cent. Approximately 80 per cent of such crimes were committed by parents or step-parents. In 1995, the proportion of victims of sexual crimes who were children was 43.2 per cent. It may not be an exaggeration to suggest that the number of girls under 14 admitted to gynaecological wards as a result of sexual abuse (to have children, as a result of miscarriages, for abortions, to treat venereal disease and the like) is as high as 4000–5000 a year.[17]

There has been a rapid rise in reported criminal cases in Hungary. However, certain types of crimes have almost completely disappeared from criminal statistics. Two such criminal offences are 'endangering a minor' and the 'failure to pay maintenance'. These two offences together amounted to 4.6 per cent of all reported crimes in 1987, but by 1991 had decreased to 1.3 per cent. It is unlikely that these two offences actually declined, nor is it likely that they failed to keep up with the increase of crimes in general. A more probable explanation is that a considerable proportion of these crimes remains hidden. Authorities are more interested in what they consider to be the more serious forms of crime. This could be explained by failures within the child protection system and a lack of interest in the problems of children. But the situation is more complicated because the criminal justice system has changed and, as a result of liberalization with the end of communism, the criminal law has been forced to limit its activity. As a consequence of decriminalization, many people were removed from the ambit of the criminal law (for example, prostitutes and those who are workshy). New categories of criminal entered the system, for example those accused of computer crimes and new forms of economic crime, but this number was small in comparison.[18]

This process has also influenced the way Hungarians regard child abuse cases. The serious social problems which have been encountered made it more acceptable for children to be abused or neglected. So state interference in the lives of families was questioned at the same time. The ambivalence of the authorities may have decreased the number of criminal cases, but the serious problem of transition to a market economy and its impact on families actually increased the number of children at risk of abuse and neglect.

THE EMPIRICAL EVIDENCE

In Hungary, the first research on child abuse was carried out by the present author between 1988 and 1991 at the National Institute of Criminology. The aim of the research was not only to reveal the existence and amount of child abuse, but also to investigate the reasons why children were abused and neglected. The assumption was that with child victims the crime committed against them would have both immediate and longer-term indirect results. The way children behave can often be traced back to their upbringing. Equally, for an adult it is possible to understand behaviour in terms of violence suffered when a child.

There were data on 221 crimes in which 292 child victims were involved. Data included the crime files with details of the offences committed by parents or step-parents against children. In order to appreciate the long-term consequences of becoming a victim, interviews were conducted with 20 people who were victims of abuse 17–19 years previously. Some results of the research are presented below.

Referral

Before a case can come to the notice of professionals, someone has to define it as abusive. This might be the victim himself, the perpetrator, or more likely a third party. The data showed that approximately 30 per cent of the cases had been reported to the police by the welfare officer of the local government. Some 64 per cent of the cases revealed dysfunctional families. The symptoms, such as alcoholism of the parents and the regular abuse of family members, were also noticed by the school and the neighbourhood. It was common to find that public utilities had disconnected services of these families, an indication of their financial difficulties. Many families were not receiving allowances, and this was clearly a problem for such families which should have alerted professionals to the danger of crime. A quarter of the cases were referred to the police by one of the parents, who presented information against their partner in marriage or their cohabitant. The complainant was usually the wife, but often, after initiating proceedings, she changed her mind during the criminal investigation; or, during the period of investigation, she testified against her husband, but a few months later refused to testify again before the court.

There could be many explanations for this behaviour, but the most likely one is as follows. The standards of personal social services are very low in Hungary. All that exists is institutional care at one end and financial support at the other; there is hardly anything in between. Alcohol abuse and housing shortages are huge long-term problems in Hungary, which has the third highest alcohol consumption rate in the world. Alcohol treatments focus much more on health than on the social problem of the clients. Of the parents in the survey, 52 per cent were hard drinkers or alcohol abusers. It was of no use for the wife to present the police with information against her alcoholic and brutal husband, because there was no way of getting professional or effective help to solve her problems. She realized that she would not get the assistance of the personal social services by reporting the case to the police and she would remain without financial support, just as before. There is a widely quoted police saying that 'police have the legal right to intervene and use force within the home of the family if blood is being shed'. Families rarely receive effective help; instead they experience the ineffectiveness of the welfare services. Later on, if it came to court and the husband was sentenced to imprisonment or fined, the whole family's financial situation would change for the worse.

Of course, others' reasons for withdrawing from proceedings are intimidation by the husband and reconciliation between the couple.

Social status

Of those charged with crimes of abuse against their children, 72 per cent were men and 28 per cent were women. Among the families who put children at risk, the number of atypical families was above the average. These families were vulnerable and unstable. The parents were poorly educated, had few employment skills and were often unemployed. Abusive families in Hungary tend to be poor and to live in bad housing conditions. The survey confirmed the well-known fact that a family with many children is more likely to experience poverty. According to the survey, the proportion of the families with more than five children was very high (30 per cent); 83 per cent of the victims in the survey were children who lived in poverty. They lived often without heating or water in overcrowded temporary accommodation, facing eviction and often living as squatters. The financial situation of these families was aggravated by parental alcoholism and criminality.

Out of the 292 child victims, 48 per cent were boys and 52 per cent were girls. Using victimology studies to consider the crimes from the victim's point of view, the question can be raised as to whether the abuse could be predicted or not. In line with the results of surveys from abroad, our research indicated that there were certain kinds of physical and personal characteristics that predisposed a person to become a victim. We found that 30 per cent of the abused children had genetic or acquired health abnormalities or mental problems (such as a birth defect, prematurity, nervousness or bed-wetting).

In the second part of the survey we interviewed 20 people who had become victims in their childhood. The main emphasis of the semi-structured personal interviews was on their professional and educational careers, connections with their parents (who had perpetrated abuse against them), the occurrence of violence in their own families and the state of the relationships within their present family.

Educational and professional career

In the life of these 20 people, school was the first stage of social failure: having to repeat classes, unfinished studies, dropping out of schools. Dropping out of elementary school is in itself a factor that tends to marginalize people, and thus may be linked with subsequent deviance. As adults, they blamed the bad family conditions of their childhood for their failures at school. This is partly justified. Certainly, the family has a determinative role in forming the social status of the individual, as does schooling. In recent decades it has become obvious that the schooling system was not only unable to change the disadvantageous situation inherited from the family, but it often even served to conserve and reinforce it.

The majority of these victims failed to achieve any professional qualification as adults, because of their unfinished studies and failure at school. They worked as semi-skilled or unskilled workers. They started working at the age of 15 to 17 as unskilled workers. They applied for jobs and worked at different workplaces without any training. Although they realized that there was some connection between their former and present family situations, they did not do anything to change their own lives at all.

The system of family connections

According to the data in the survey, the habitual reaction of social services to solving family problems was/is to remove the child from his/her family. In order to act with authority, the welfare officer needs some legal training, but he or she rarely has it. Their wages are poor and the job has low prestige. Officers alone decide whether the child is at risk or not and whether he/she should be removed from his/her family. Other options open include warning the families, offering assistance or initiating proceedings against parents. But there is not even a precise definition of being 'at risk' when it is thought this applies. Nor is it clear how this is proved and what measures should then be taken. The most frequent procedure until quite recently was to remove the 'problem' child from his/her family and place him/her in an institution. In theory, a review should have been conducted annually in order to determine whether circumstances had improved: if they had, it was possible that the child could be returned. In Hungary, the real problem is that the families are expected to restore equilibrium in their lives by themselves, and there is no other real help for them. Moreover, the officers are generally responsible for several hundred families and this is not their only work. One result is that the yearly review of the families can become a pure formality.

It is the duty of the social services to promote the ties between the parents and children who are in state institutional care, even though the parents are not in favour of this. It is not an easy task to maintain family ties in such circumstances because of the lack of official help and support. Family problems cannot be solved by just taking the child away from his/her family. It has to be realized that the children who are taken into institutional care and deprived of their family receive little emotional support. They are physically taken care of, they get accommodation and clothing, but this care will never provide individual attention, emotional support and affection. It is galling that most of the children who have been taken into state institutional care remain there until they come of age. It is a new, sad tendency that the children do not want to leave the institutions on reaching maturity, because they have neither jobs nor any hope of getting accommodation.

The research data showed that a person who was a victim in her/his childhood was likely to face the same kind of conflict as an adult that their parents encountered, and that they also have no means of solving their problems. The family situation during childhood is not the only cause of this, but it is a major one.

Corporal punishment

Despite the public perception that the family is a happy, loving community providing a safe background for family members, research now indicates that violence within families is widespread. In Hungary, hitting children is socially accepted. The vast majority of parents hit their children at least occasionally and many of them do so frequently. It is common to use implements such as belts or canes.[19] Physical punishment is the habitual experience of children. Corporal punishment is a normal practice in many families. Children brought up in such a family environment can realize very soon that there is no hope of getting support and affection. Their aim is to avoid conflicts leading to violent situations in the family.

Conclusions

Some conclusions can be drawn from the survey. First of all, 'child abuse' can be considered as

- a social construction,
- a medical or social problem,
- a breach of the rights of the child, or simply as
- a crime deserving punishment.[20]

Our survey shows that there are two main consequences of severe dysfunctions within the family: the child becomes a victim, and/or he/she becomes a juvenile offender. So it is without question that crimes committed against a child within the family should be treated as a family problem. The question remains: what can be done to prevent abuse? The most important consideration is to offer help to abused and neglected children while not losing sight of the child's need for a family and the mutual interests of parents and children.

FAMILY COURT

The child care and youth protection network has always been criticized. Experts emphasize that the most serious problem of child care in Hungary is 'institutional irresponsibility'. The institutional system is overcentralized, each decision-making level is one step higher than it should be and still the system is disunited.[21] In the centre of the system stand the courts of guardians which belong to the network of local governments. Their jurisdiction ranges from preventative measures including accommodating the child in a residential home to removing the child from home and placing him/her under the state's protection. But connections between family care and social policy are lacking, with 'the courts of guardians concerned more with administration than the doing of effective work'.[22] An ideology of authoritarianism and legalism dominated the system until recently. This pushed social work intervention and prevention into the background. Furthermore, there was a belief that social work was by and large a charitable activity, the duty of the churches. This view is underlined by the absence of a law of charities in Hungary.

The Hungarian child protection system will be improved by the new Child Protection Act, but the Act omitted to say that only courts should be entitled to remove a child from his/her family. As a result, since 1 November 1977, the County Guardians' Office has been entitled to decide on these questions. (The civil courts are authorized to decide on the final termination of parental responsibility and on the questions of adoption.) The problem remains. It is my view that disputes between the state and citizens should be decided by a court independent of the executive. It would have been better to establish a separate family court. But Parliament, when passing the new Child Protection Act, did not consider this.

THE IMPROVEMENT OF THE CRIMINAL CODE

In the process of the codification of the criminal law in Hungary, it is necessary to reform the law relating to crimes committed against children. Everyone agrees that children have the right to be protected against sexual assault, but it is equally their right to have their physical integrity protected against physical punishment. But it is much more difficult to control the ways parents discipline children. The family can only be as democratic and civilized as society itself. There is clear evidence that major family crises or antisocial behaviour patterns are predictors of crime within the family. In 17.5 per cent of criminal cases in 1994, the offenders were related to the victims. In my view only child physical abuse and child sexual abuse should be punished as criminal acts, and child neglect should not be criminalized. There are better ways of teaching parenting skills than using the blunt instrument of the criminal law. The Act on Family and Guardianship and the Child Protection and Welfare Act should deal with the consequences of child neglect. They should offer guidelines for tackling this problem to the social and child welfare authorities. Until the passing of the new Child Protection and Welfare Act, many acts and numerous decrees regulated the tasks and institutions of child care. Fortunately, in this field, significant changes are expected in the near future. The new Act provides a complex network of law concerning child welfare and offers full protection of children's rights. One of the most important changes is that the separation of a child from its family will only be permissible when the risk to the child cannot be addressed in any other way, in particular by means of public assistance. This new way of thinking can only be applauded. Better things are expected of the new Child Protection and Welfare Act, which came into force on 1 November 1997.

NOTES

1. K. Kerezsi, *A védtelen gyermek: Eröszak és elhanyagolás a családban* (The unprotected child: Violence and Negligence within the Family) (Budapest: Közgazdasagi és Jogi Könyvkiad, 1995).
2. K. Hanák, *Tárasadalom és gyermekvédelem* (Child Protection and Society) (Budapest: Akadémiai Kiadó, 1996), p.130.
3. Á. Losonczi, *Artó-védö tarsadalom* (Harmful–Protected Society) (Budapest: Közgazdasagi és Jogi Könyvkiadó, 1995), pp.101–4.
4. K. Kerezsi, 'Bevezetés a kiskorúak sérelmére elkövetett büncselekmények viktimológiai értelmezésébe' (Introduction to victimological aspects of crimes committed against minors) (Budapest: KKT 25.k, KJK, 1996).
5. Zs. Szné Szilagyi, 'Szép gyermekkor?' (Nice Childhood?) in A. Volentics (ed.), *Gyermeki Jogok – Jogsértö felnöttel*, Gyermekvédelmi tanulmanyok 3. kötet (Budapest: FICE Kiadványok, 1996), p.48.
6. Ibid., pp.51–60.
7. K. Gönczöl, 'Anxiety over Crime', *The Hungarian Quarterly*, 34, Spring: 91, 1993.
8. P. Salamin, 'A létminimum és akik alatta élnek' (The minimum living standard and those who live under it) *Esély*, 4: 65, 1991.
9. R. Andorka and Zs. Spéder 'A szegénység Magyaroszagon 1992–1995' (Poverty in Hungary 1992–1995) *Esély*, 4: 25–52, 1996.
10. *World Bank Report*, Executive Summary (Budapest: World Bank, 1994), p.xi.
11. *Commentary to the Act of Family Law*, vol. II (in Hungarian) (Budapest: Közgazdasagi és Jogi Könyvkiad, 1988).
12. *A gyermekek védelméröl, valamint a szocialis és gyamhivatalokról szóló törvénytervezet vazlatos tartalma* (Draft of the Child Protection and Welfare Bill) (Budapest: Munkaanyag, Népjóléti Minisztérium, 1995).
13. E. Kovacs, 'A gyermekbantalmazas problémaköre a gyermekvédelmi, jogasz szemével'

(Problems of Child Abuse, as a lawyer sees them) in E. Barkó (ed.), *A gyermekbantalmazas Magyarorszagon* (Budapest: Népjóléti Minisztérium, 1995).
14 *Összefoglaló jelentés a kiskorú veszélyeztetése miatt indult eljarasok törvényességék vizsgalataró* (Report on investigation of legal procedure of crime 'Endangering a Minor') (Budapest: Legfőbb Ügyészség Gyermek-és Ifjúsagvédelmi Önalló Főosztaly, 1994).
15 É. Barkó (ed.), *A gyermekbantalmazas Magyarorszagon* (Child Physical Abuse in Hungary) (Budapest: Népjléti Minisztérium, 1995), pp.6–8.
16 This is mainly the result of decriminalization.
17 I. Vavró (ed.), *Tartas elmulsaztasa, kiskorú veszélyeztetése és megrontas miatt elitélt felnöttkorúak* (Sentenced Adults who committed crimes of Endangering a minor, Failure to provide maintenance and Debauchery) (Budapest: Igazsagügyi Minisztérium Kutatasszervezö es Elemzö Föosztaly, 1995).
18 K. Gönczöl, 'Kontrollalt devianciak és a bunmegelzési stratégia' (Deviance and crime prevention) in A. Erdei (ed.), *Tények és kilatasok* Budapest: Közgazdasagi és Jogi Könyvkiadó, 1995), p.203.
19 A. Losonczi (1995) in op. cit., note 18, p.104.
20 J. Christopherson, 'Child Abuse – What Can International Comparative Research Show?', presentation at the Conference on Child, Love, Law; Dundee, Scotland, 26–9 July 1992.
21 M. Lévai, 'Children's Rights and Child Welfare in Hungary', presentation at the Day Conference of the FICE on the Realization of the Rights of the Child in Extrafamiliar Care, Espoo, Finland, 26 August 1992.
22 I. Bernad, 'Nevelszülők, hivatásos neveloszulők és örökbefogadas' (Foster Parents, Professional Foster Parents, Adoption), *Child and Youth Care*, 1: 88, 1986.

10 Taking Stock of a Revolution: Child Abuse and the Law in Israel, 1989–97

Tamar Morag[1]

INTRODUCTION

In 1975, the Tel Aviv District Court convicted a woman for the attempted murder of her one-and-a-half-year-old daughter, in the course of which she inflicted major physical injuries on the child. In his verdict, the judge stated that 'this is not a widespread form of violence, and is seldom found in Jewish families'. The woman was sentenced to a suspended term of three years' imprisonment and placed on probation.

The prosecution considered appealing against the lenient punishment. In an internal memo addressed to his senior staff, Gabriel Bach, who was then the attorney general, set out his reasons for refraining from filing an appeal. On the one hand, Bach disagreed with the judge's view, as conveyed in the verdict, that offences of child abuse are rare in Israeli society. On the other hand, however, he attributed crucial weight to the mother's distress and to her chances of rehabilitation and, on these grounds, decided not to appeal.[2]

The verdict of the district court and the decision of the attorney general could constitute, in historical terms, an interesting vantage point for surveying the legal and social changes that have taken place in Israel concerning child abuse within the family. The verdict conveys an approach that had so far been prevalent in the Israeli legal system, namely, a basic reluctance to admit to the very existence of this occurrence in our midst. Although somehow conceding the existence and the seriousness of the events, the memo also reflects feelings of hesitation and ambivalence then prevalent in Israeli society regarding the use of strong penal measures for dealing with these acts.

The Israeli legal system, and Israeli society in general, have since undergone significant changes in their attitude towards child abuse. Despite the paucity of systematic data collection regarding the incidence of such acts, it is clear that we speak of a widespread phenomenon, of a scope apparently similar to that found in Western Europe and the USA.[3] In the legal and social circumstances characterizing current Israeli reality, a sentence of this type appears less plausible and, were it handed down, the attorney general would probably appeal against its leniency.

The vast changes characterizing present Israeli reality regarding child abuse within the family were sparked by the Law for Preventing Abuse of Minors and Helpless Persons enacted in 1989, and by the events leading to its enactment. This chapter examines the social and legal changes in this domain in Israel, including their scope, their causes, their achievements and their limitations. The Israeli case is particularly interesting because of its strong links to specific events relating to a particular girl who had been a victim of abuse, the accompanying social pressure, and the entire legislation process, including its social implications. All unfolded within a very brief time span.

THE LEGAL SITUATION OF CHILD ABUSE UNTIL 1989

Legal arrangements concerning child abuse divide into two main groups: penal laws, which aim to prosecute and punish offenders, and welfare laws, which aim to ensure the necessary legal options for intervening within the family and caring for the children.

In line with an approach entailing denial, repression and even an attempt to ignore child abuse, which are also manifest in the verdict mentioned above, Israeli society and Israeli law had, for many years, devoted scant attention to this issue. Even the few existing legal provisions, both in the penal and the welfare contexts, had been implemented only partially.

The Penal Code

Until 1989, the Penal Code included hardly any explicit references to child abuse within the family. The only offences in the criminal code explicitly dealing with child abuse within the family were those related to the neglect of minors, and an offence severely punishing a father having sexual intercourse with his minor daughter.[4] No specific offences were defined regarding other forms of incest or offences entailing physical or mental harm to children by their parents, nor did the penal code include any mention of 'child abuse'.

Also apparent until 1989 is an obvious reluctance to resort to penal measures in regard to child abuse offences within the family. This is evident, inter alia, in the behaviour of welfare agencies refraining from reports to the police regarding cases in their care,[5] and in the policy adopted by the police and the prosecution entailing the closure of most of these files on grounds of lack of public interest.[6] The courts were also party to this trend: they imposed light sentences on the few cases occasionally brought to trial, and even tended at times to be particularly lenient in regard to such offences.[7]

Child welfare laws

Most welfare laws, enabling intervention within the family to protect children at risk, were passed back in the 1960s.[8] The main law on this count is the Youth (Care and Supervision) Law, dating from 1960. This law creates the legal framework for the work of welfare officers, who are social workers empowered to act by virtue of this legislation, vesting them with authority to approach the juvenile courts requesting that a minor be declared 'a minor in need'. The court is then allowed to prescribe a series of measures, including removing minors from their homes and placing them in the custody of welfare officers, if the circumstances of the case are within the grounds set by the law. Note that child abuse within the family is not explicitly listed among the grounds set by the law justifying intervention in the family, which are formulated rather broadly and allow for intervention whenever 'a minor's physical or mental welfare is at risk'.

Section 2a of the Youth (Care and Supervision) Law, passed in 1974,[9] specified for the first time a duty to report cases of children at risk. The law was amended on the initiative of Alexander Russell, a British doctor who settled in Israel, and of Hanita Zimmering, one of the pioneers in Israel in the area of children at risk. According to this amendment, a duty to report was made incumbent on members of a limited number of professions, but no sanctions were stipulated for those violating this provision. The law required them to report to the welfare officer, but stated no duty to report to the police.

It is worth noting that, although the Youth Law was passed in 1960, it was not actually implemented until the 1970s. It was only then that the gradual appointment of welfare officers began, as required by the law. The duty to report, legislated as noted in the mid-1970s, had little public resonance and almost no effect on the working methods of the professions mentioned in its context. From conversations with people active in the field of social work in Israel during the 1970s and before, it was learned that the involvement with children at risk up to the 1980s was mainly in such fields as neglect, education for parenting and prevention of youth delinquency. Welfare services were almost oblivious to child abuse within the family and to acts of incest as real problems affecting Israeli society.[10]

The lack of social awareness was also reflected in the scattered media references to these issues, in the lack of any arrangements structuring the health and education systems to contend with these problems, and in the abstention of governmental agencies from any systematic data collection making it possible to gauge the scope of the problem.

THE LAW FOR PREVENTING ABUSE OF MINORS AND HELPLESS PERSONS: THE BACKGROUND TO THE LEGISLATION

Changes in legislation and public policy regarding children have been linked to the name and the story of a particular child in several countries. In Israel, the Law for Preventing Abuse of Minors and Helpless Persons is identified with the tragic death of three-year-old Moran Danmias from Tiberias.

Moran died on 9 February 1989, after being unconscious for five months as a result of injuries sustained through abuse by her uncle over several months. Against the background of denial and repression regarding child abuse, which had characterized legal and social agencies in Israel until then, the death of Moran Danmias came as a major shock. Moran's death was given extensive coverage in the Israeli media, culminating in a surge of feature articles on child abuse.[11] One of the hardest aspects of this incident was that the injury and abuse had continued for several months. Nevertheless, and although it is quite inconceivable that no-one had been aware of them, no report was filed with the welfare authorities.

Moran's death generated a public outcry, evoking in politicians a clear wish to react, and to act quickly. In the wake of this incident, two Knesset members from opposite ends of the political spectrum[12] tabled a joint bill prescribing a duty to report on children at risk, accompanied by penal sanctions against those failing to comply. This bill was the basis for a much broader amendment than that intended by the original proposal: Amendment No. 26 to the Penal Code, better known as the Law for Preventing Abuse of Minors and Helpless Persons, which was the name suggested by the Knesset members who had proposed it. Following motions submitted by several Knesset members,[13] a special sub-committee on child abuse was appointed, chaired by MK Yitzhak Levi.

Procedures for passing the Law for Preventing Abuse of Minors and Helpless Persons were exceptionally fast. Moran died on 9 February 1989. Motions for the agenda and the original bill, which were submitted to the

Knesset several days after her death, were given wide media coverage and enjoyed vast public support. The Levi Committee was established about a month after Moran's death, and submitted its conclusions at the beginning of August 1989. The bill went through a second and third reading on 28 November 1989.

CHANGES IN ISRAELI LEGISLATION SINCE 1989

The Penal Code

Amendment no. 26 to the Penal Code: 'The Law of Minors and Helpless Persons'[14]

The Law for Preventing Abuse of Minors and Helpless Persons is the most significant amendment to the Penal Code in the area of child abuse. The legislation aims to set down clear norms in two areas: the duty to report; and the criminality of the act.

The duty to report According to this amendment, a duty to report to a welfare officer or to the police is imposed on all persons who have reasonable grounds for believing that an offence has been committed against a minor by the person responsible for him or her. A special duty to report, with harsher sanctions for non-compliance, was imposed on professionals and on persons responsible for the minor.

The law also stipulates a duty of mutual reporting between welfare officers and the police regarding cases coming to their knowledge. Until then, the duty to report as set down by the Youth Law (a duty that, as noted, had hardly echoed in the public consciousness) had not required police involvement in cases brought to the attention of the welfare authorities.

In the course of the deliberations on the law, psychologists and social workers strongly objected to a legal duty to involve the police in every case, on the grounds that the automatic involvement of the police might hinder the treatment of both victims and assailants. As a result, several interesting provisions were included in the amendment, granting broader discretion to welfare officers concerning police involvement. Thus, for instance, the law states that welfare officers reporting to the police should enclose their own recommendations for action or non-action on each case. The amendment also ordered the establishment of regional committees, chaired by a representative from the district attorney's office and empowered to exempt welfare officers from their duty to report to the police about cases in which police involvement might be damaging to the minor.

Criminal offences The basic principle underlying the Law for Preventing Abuse of Minors and Helpless Persons is that injuring a minor is more serious than injuring an adult, and that injuring a minor who is a family member is more serious than injuring a minor who is not. Two special offences were stipulated in this regard: causing injury to a minor – a consequential offence; and abusing a minor – a behavioural offence. The legislator refrained from explicitly defining the term 'abuse', but stated that mental harm could also be considered a form of child abuse or of injury to a minor.

An additional amendment passed as part of this law dealt with the 'passive parent'. According to this amendment, a duty carrying a penal sanction is incumbent on all parents or persons responsible for minors. They must not only refrain from causing them any injury, but must also prevent injuries caused by the other parent or by other responsible persons. This legislative provision, touching on the highly sensitive issue of the role and responsibility of the 'other parent', also points to the penal deterrent approach chosen by the legislators in this amendment.

As for the offences included in this law, long imprisonment terms are stipulated. Thus, for instance, whereas the penal law dictates a three-year term of imprisonment for offences of assault and actual injury, this law imposes a seven-year prison sentence for injury to minors by the persons responsible for them.

In the context of the Law for Preventing Abuse of Minors and Helpless Persons, an amendment was also introduced into the 1955 Law of Evidence Revision (Protection of Children) which deals with children's testimonies, further acknowledging the scope and seriousness attached to child abuse.[15]

The extent to which the Law for Preventing Abuse of Minors and Helpless Persons constitutes a direct reaction to the death of Moran Danmias can be inferred, inter alia, from some of its provisions: the very duty to report, the definition of a broad group of family members as responsible for the minor (in Moran's case, the abuser had been her uncle), as well as the use of penal sanctions against the passive parent (in response to questions about the ability and the duty of close family members to terminate acts of abuse). The very fact that Moran Danmias died in circumstances that would be considered serious criminal offences according to any criterion and in any known legal system seems to have contributed to the change in the social and legal milieu, as manifest in the new penal norms established through this amendment.[16]

Amendment no. 30 to the Penal Code: defining criminal offences regarding incest

About a year after passing the Law for Preventing Abuse of Minors and Helpless Persons (Amendment No. 26), the Knesset adopted Amendment no. 30 to the Penal Code, dealing with incest offences. Amendment no. 30 continues and supplements Amendment no. 26.[17] It specifies special criminal offences in regard to incest, and rests on two principles: (a) sexual offences are to be punished more severely when they concern a minor within the family, in direct continuation of the provisions stipulated in Amendment no. 26; (b) some forms of sexual intercourse are not an offence if they do not involve members of the same family, but constitute a criminal offence if they do, owing to the special relationship of dependence and authority.

Since the enactment of Amendments nos 26 and 30, and as part of the same trend, additional amendments have been passed concerning children's evidence, and concerning the statute of limitations on sexual offences against children.[18]

Child welfare laws

From 1989 onwards, the penal law regarding child abuse underwent significant changes, reflecting a rather sudden shift in the public's awareness. In contrast, the Youth (Care and Supervision) Law, which is the main law dealing with the care of children at risk, remained substantially the same.

The sole important amendment concerning the Youth (Care and Supervision) Law during this period was adopted in 1991. The amendment empowers juvenile courts to issue removal orders against persons considered harmful under the Law of Violence Prevention within the Family.[19] This amendment to the Youth Law was urged by organizations dealing with women's rights and, following a request by the National Council for the Child, was extended to cover children too.

IMPLEMENTING LAWS DEALING WITH CHILD ABUSE

The Penal Code

In the Law for Preventing Abuse of Minors and Helpless Persons, legislators took a clear stand regarding the use of penal instruments in child abuse offences, stating that these offences are not only criminal but are particularly grievous. Indeed, the passing of the law and the amendments of the penal laws that followed in its wake marked the start of a revolution regarding the implementation of the Penal Code in cases of child abuse within the family.

As noted, the period preceding the passing of the law had been characterized by a reluctance to rely on penal instruments. Social perceptions regarding the criminality of these acts, and the policy endorsed by the police, the attorney general and the courts, have indeed undergone radical changes since the passing of the law, as emerges from the following: police data on decisions to open files and to prosecute; data from the attorney general on the decisions of the exemption committees; directives from the police and the attorney general regarding decisions to prosecute; and appeals and verdicts.

Data from the police[20]

With regard to police files opened for offences of bodily harm and child abuse within the family, excluding sexual offences,[21] as Figure 10.1 shows, the number of police files on child abuse cases shows a staggering increase since the passing of the law, strikingly illustrating the direct link between the passing of the law and the dramatic changes in the treatment of this problem. Figure 10.2 shows the corresponding trends relating to sexual offences and crimes of incest.[22]

Police decisions to close files are shown in Figure 10.3.[23] As this graph shows, the Law for Preventing Abuse of Minors and Helpless Persons is significantly linked to the sharp change in the policy endorsed by the police concerning the public's interest in prosecuting these cases.

Decisions of regional committees on exemptions from the duty to report[24]

As noted, the amendment had empowered regional committees chaired by a representative of the attorney general to exempt welfare officers from the duty to report to the police all the information brought to their knowledge. Generally, the number of requests for exemptions, in relation to the total number of cases reported to welfare officers, is very small.[25] Also the trend points to a clear decline, both in the number of requests for exemptions and in the number of decisions to authorize non-reporting. This is of special interest, given the strong objections to the suggested policy of automatic police involvement that professional agents had endorsed during the deliberations on the law.

It could be argued that both the small number of requests for exemptions and the limited number of exemptions granted can be partially ascribed to a normative change, affecting society in general and psychologists in particular, regarding the use of penal instruments to deal with these cases.[26]

Official directives

Police directives[27]   The comparison between police directives issued prior to the amendment to the law, in 1987, and those issued in 1992, is pertinent

Child Abuse and the Law in Israel, 1989–97 213

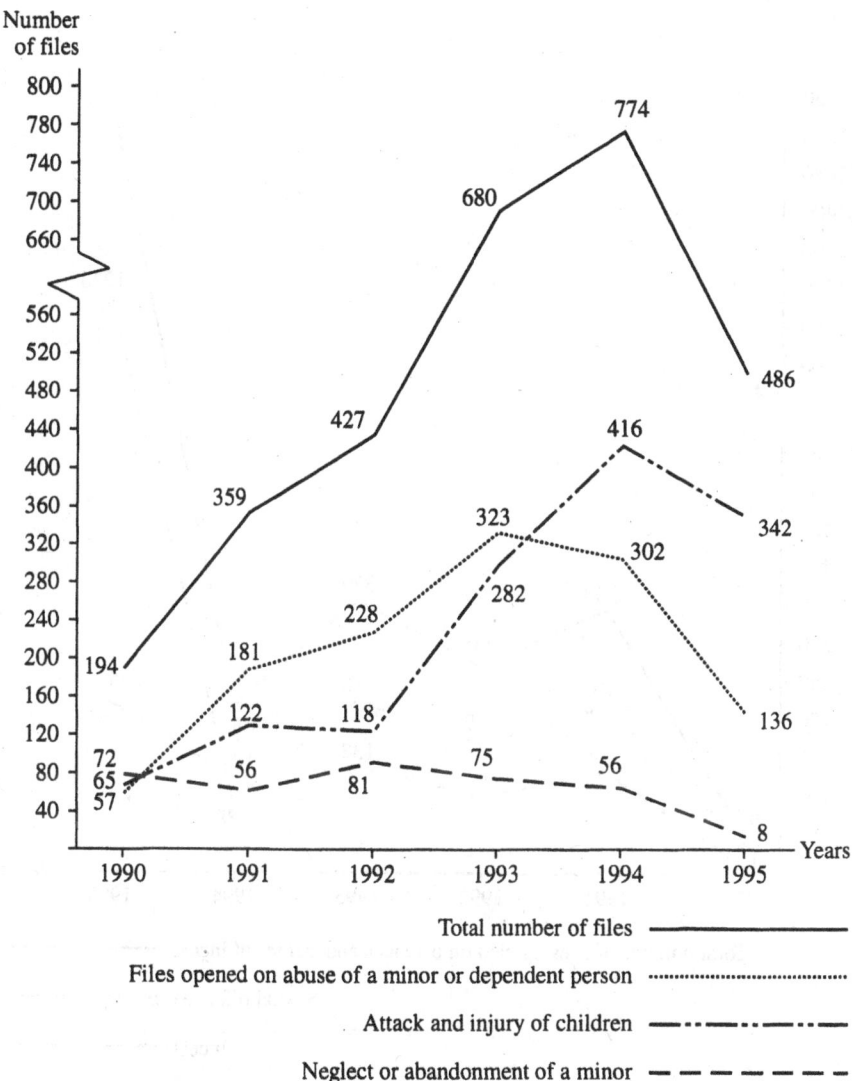

Source: Israel Police, National Headquarters, Statistical Unit.

Figure 10.1 Crimes against children within the family (excluding sexual offences) 1990–95: number of files opened (by type of crime)

214 *Overcoming Child Abuse: A Window on a World Problem*

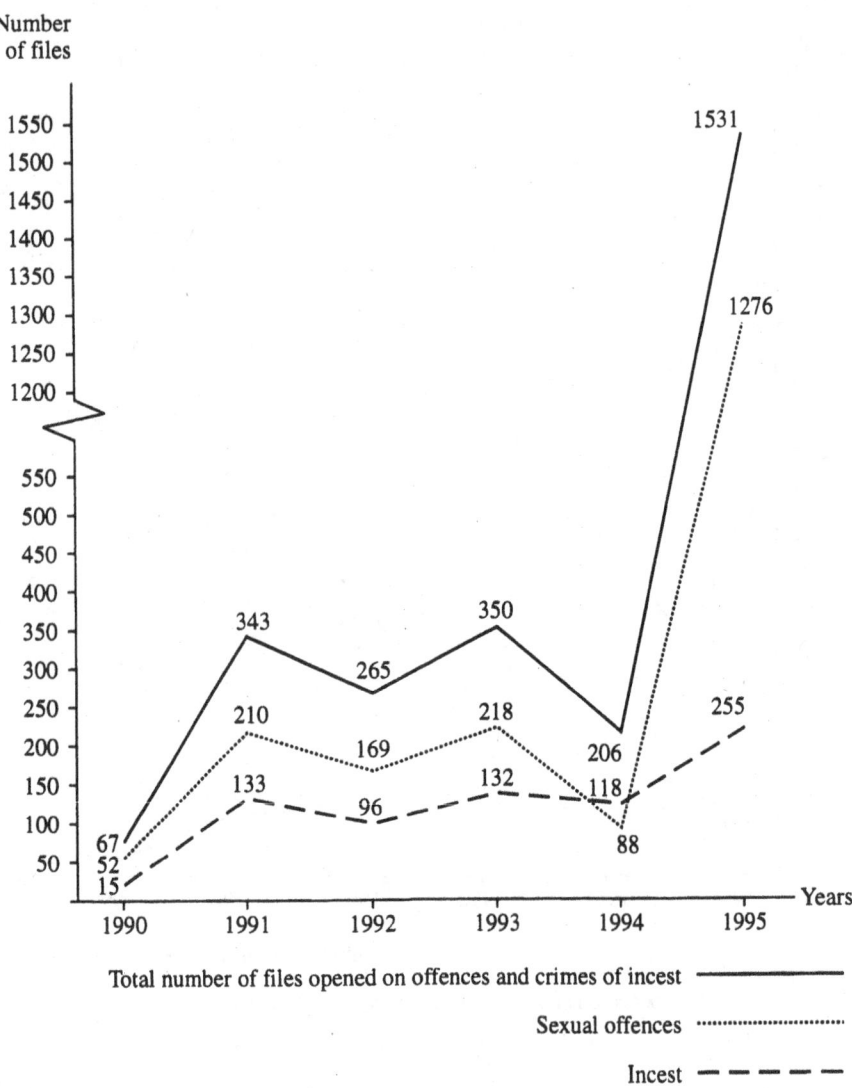

Source: Israel Police, National Headquarters, Statistical Unit.

Figure 10.2 Sexual offences and crimes of incest against children, 1990–95: number of files opened (by type of crime)

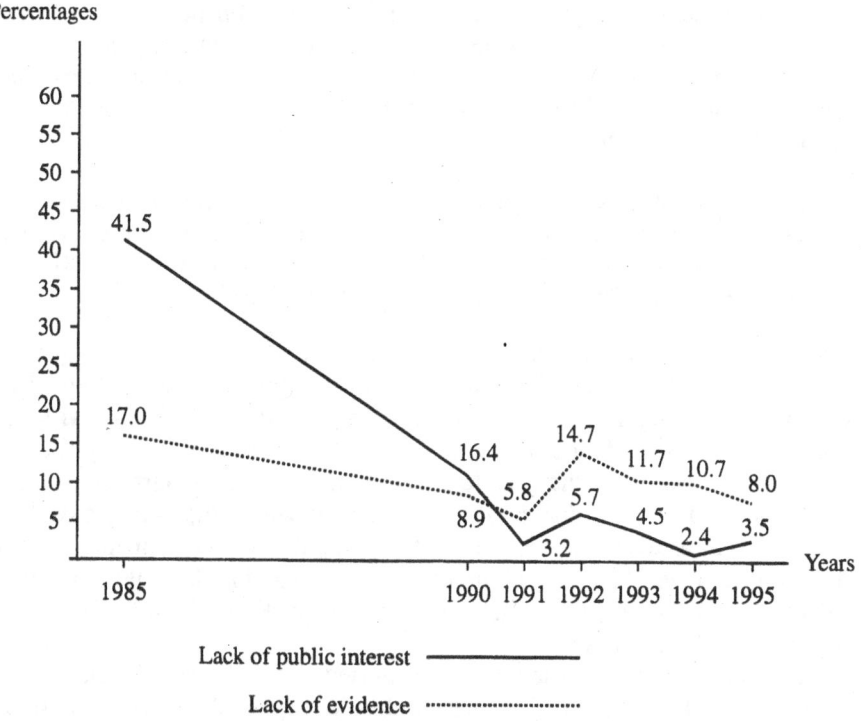

Source: Israel Police, National Headquarters, Statistical Unit.

Figure 10.3 Sexual offences and crimes of incest against children, 1985–95: percentage of files closed

to our subject. This comparison will also point to greater awareness of the very presence and seriousness of the problem, as well as to a normative change leading to the adoption of a penal–punitive approach in dealing with these offences. Thus, for example, whereas the 1987 directive had been entitled 'Police handling of *injuries* inflicted on children by their parents (battered children)', the heading of the new directive was: 'Police handling of *offences* of violence against minors within the family' (emphases added). The term in use in the 1987 directive is *'minor in need'*, a therapeutic term found in the Youth (Care and Supervision) Law, whereas the new directive adopts the term a *'minor who is the victim of an offence'* (emphases added), which is taken from a criminal context.

Whereas the 1992 directives are unequivocal in their perception of these acts as 'grave offences requiring special police intervention', the previous ones had indicated some unease in dealing with the issue, and hesitancy regarding the choice of the most suitable approach to it. Thus, for example, the 1987 directive states:

> The category of abused/injured child is hard to define, given an apparent spectrum ranging from a correctional beating and up to child abuse. Determining the incidence of these acts is not easy either, as actual knowledge about such cases among caring agencies, including the police, is incomplete.

The attorney general's directives The directive of the attorney general, issued on 22 September 1989, about a month after the first reading of the Law for Preventing Abuse to Minors and Helpless Persons,[28] deals with plea bargains in sexual offences and child abuse within the family. This directive opens as follows: 'In the last few years, an increasing number of cases concerning abuse of minors and sexual offences within the family have been exposed. These acts should be severely punished, keeping in mind public deterrence.' Several additional directives were issued in the following years, further reinforcing the view that severe penal sanctions should be sought in regard to such offences.[29]

In practice, as the attorney general reported to the Knesset Committee on Constitution, Law and Justice, the number of appeals filed by the attorney general on cases of child abuse has substantially increased.

Court decisions

It is obviously much harder to estimate or quantify changes in judicial attitudes. Nevertheless, and relying on a considerable number of recent judicial rulings and on conversations with judges and lawyers specializing in this field, it can be argued that court decisions tend to reflect the changes in the legislation. A general tendency to punish these offences more severely is now visible.

One radical example is a recent verdict by the Tel Aviv District Court on criminal case 21/96, dealing with a series of sexual offences against minors within the family, in which the defendant was sentenced to 24 years' imprisonment,[30] a sentence that 10 years ago would have been inconceivable. This tendency seems to have been effected in particular by the attitudes of Meir Shamgar, Supreme Court Chief Justice between 1984 and 1996, a period marked by the most significant changes concerning these issues. In several of his rulings, Justice Shamgar expressed strong censure of child abuse offences, claiming, for instance: 'I stress once again that, in order to eradicate acts as despicable as those described in this case, punishment must be severe and serve as a deterrent.'[31]

This reversal in the courts' attitudes, however, is far from complete. We can still find many verdicts reflecting the leniency and the ambivalence that had prevailed towards these crimes in the past, and concerning the use of penal instruments to contend with them.

Taking stock

The picture that emerges from an analysis of all the developments concerning the application of the penal law since 1989 points to one significant and substantial change: injury to children within the family is now viewed as a criminal act, of a particularly serious nature, deserving suitable punishment. Yet these positive developments were not accompanied by other steps, which could have been expected given the intensive penal concern with offences of child abuse. The reason might be that such steps require more subtle thinking and organization, or that the public pressure that resulted in legislative changes and harsher punishment was weaker in regard to the more complex aspects of the issue.

For instance, we have not seen in Israel any serious discussion of issues bearing on the treatment of assailants in child abuse offences. Almost no programmes have been set up for this purpose so far, nor has this issue become part of Israeli legislation. Questions bearing on the influence of criminal proceedings on child victims of offences still await due consideration by the Israeli legal system.

The welfare laws

The Law for Preventing Abuse of Minors and Helpless Persons, although enacted in a penal context, had an immediate impact on the care of children at risk. Its main effect was a relatively rapid restructuring of the welfare services, albeit incomplete, to cope with an immediate and staggering rise in the reports of children at risk.[32] This rapid restructuring, however, exacted a price: the focus was directed, almost exclusively, to the law's direct implications. Other and no less important courses of action, which had received more attention in the past, were thereby blocked and even somehow neglected.

After a period of turmoil and disarray, welfare services organized to face the consequences of the Law for Preventing Abuse of Minors and Helpless

Persons. The fact that the law had landed on them almost by surprise, without the welfare services being party to the legislation initiative, explains their reaction. As the implications of the new law, which no-one had apparently foreseen, became clear, some additional funds were necessarily made available after a relatively short time. Welfare services responsible for children at risk devoted most of their energy and their newly found resources to responding to the direct and short-term pressures created by the huge rise in the number of reports.

Thus, for instance, whereas the Ministry of Welfare had budgeted for the employment of some 160 welfare officers until the beginning of the 1990s, by 1995 it was employing more than 400.[33] Whereas no crisis centre for children had existed in Israel in 1990, five such centres were established in the years 1990–96, capable of absorbing children at risk on a short-term basis and caring briefly for children and their families. Comprehensive training programmes for welfare officers have been developed since 1992, laying stress on the teaching of legal aspects and on developing suitable working arrangements with the police and instruments of primary intervention within the family. At present, training programmes for welfare officers devote about a quarter of the time to the study of the Law for Preventing Abuse of Minors and Helpless Persons and its implementation.

Despite the initial confusion prevailing immediately after the passing of the law, the welfare authorities succeeded most impressively in restructuring their personnel and their resources. Since this reorganization was mainly a reaction to the legislation and its implications, which had surprised welfare agencies, a price was exacted in the treatment of children at risk, at least in the short term. Given the impressive achievements of the amendment to the penal law, and the relative success of the welfare services to deal with its implications, this cost has often been overlooked.

Up to the late 1980s, despite the widespread lack of awareness regarding the scope and the gravity of child abuse within the family, and perhaps because of it, emphasis had been placed on education for parenting, on preventing injury and neglect, and on treating abandoned children. These activities were largely dismissed when welfare agencies began to concentrate all their efforts in reacting to the changes in the penal law and their implications. Plans for developing services and treatment programmes drafted soon after the passing of the Law for Preventing Abuse of Minors and Helpless Persons were not implemented unless required as a first aid response to immediate needs arising from the law itself.

The 1989 Report of the Levi Committee is a reliable source for comparing areas in which services were developed from 1989 and areas in which they were not. The Levi report was prepared by a sub-committee of the

Knesset's Labour and Welfare Committee, which was established after Moran's death. Even before the legislation process of the Law for Preventing Abuse of Minors and Helpless Persons had been completed, the subcommittee made a series of recommendations concerning the care of children at risk, including suggestions for several bills that became the basis for all the amendments to the Penal Code and the Youth Law that were eventually passed.

It now emerges that the only recommendations that were actually implemented were those concerning disclosure, reporting, initial care, the legislation of the penal amendment, and those of its elements compelled by the law's immediate enactment. In contrast, recommendations dealing with more complex issues – concerning the establishment of interdisciplinary and interministerial teams, data collection, the development of preventive programmes, or programmes designed to ensure long-term care and rehabilitation of children and their families, or for dealing with the assailants – have been implemented only partly or not at all. Similarly, a provision within the Law for Preventing Violence within the Family allowing for the assailant's removal from the house, was hardly ever implemented when the victimized family member was a child rather than an adult.

Educational or health agencies failed to develop comprehensive programmes, notwithstanding the new public consciousness. Their reasons for this failure must be carefully examined, but it is quite plausible that these agencies were influenced by the social focus on issues related almost exclusively to the Law for Preventing Abuse of Minors and Helpless Persons. As a result of the marked and comprehensive effects of this penal legislation, together with the relative halt in the promotion of therapeutic and community approaches to child abuse, professionals in the field have recently become acutely aware of the need for an additional revolution dealing with prevention and treatment. This awareness, however, has mainly taken the form of demands for programmes and declarations that are not actually concretized.[34] The growing awareness regarding problems of child abuse, which rests on the revolution brought about by the penal law, on the absence of comprehensive therapeutic and community approaches and on the dearth of appropriate budgets, has led to extreme frustration among professionals.[35]

CONCLUSION

Gabriel Bach, who was attorney general in 1975 and wrote the memo quoted at the opening of this chapter, was eventually appointed to the Supreme Court. Whereas in the memo, written in 1975, he had tended to show great consideration for the defendant's personal distress, in a verdict written in 1994 his tone is different:

> We recognize the general problem of battered children, which is assuming distressing proportions, and whose victims and potential victims are entitled, above all, to protection. Very lenient sentences, which pay undue attention to the psychological hardships of the abusing parents and show them inordinate compassion, could foil the efforts designed to curb these offences.[36]

The difference between these two utterances by Bach J may epitomize the changes that Israeli society and its penal system have undergone in regard to attitudes towards child abuse.

This analysis of the sociolegal changes in Israel concerning child abuse raises a number of hypotheses or points for consideration, some of which may deserve further in-depth study.

1. The legislative change of 1989 is, in many ways, an unusual success story of the ability of legislation to change social reality. Success is manifest in increasing awareness of the existence and seriousness of the offence, in the social and legal internalization of the norm that views child abuse within the family as a particularly grievous criminal act, in the highly intensified exposure of such incidents and in the relative success of penal and welfare agencies in contending with the tremendous rise in the number of reported cases.
2. The nature of the legal change was largely dictated by the fact that it came in the wake of a specific event, massive public pressure and a rapid response of the political system to this concerted public pressure. On the one hand, and as a result of these circumstances, the legislative change in the penal code reflected the reaction to the public's outrage and trauma and focused on the 'simplest', most overt issues: the duty to report and the need for harsher punishment. On the other hand, public pressure was the very factor that facilitated far-reaching and effective change in a swift and easy stroke.
3. The relationship between law and society is of special interest in this matter. The legislative change in the penal code reflected the public mood in Israel. In turn, after its amendment, the penal code was itself capable of changing social approaches to acts of child abuse within the family, leading to their perception as grievous deeds carrying penal sanction.
4. The success of this initiative, at the legislative and operative levels as well as in the social and normative domains, can be partially ascribed to the unique character of Israel's social and political systems. Israel is a

highly polarized society, and this issue appeared capable of meeting a widespread need for uniting around shared goals. The 1989 bill was, as noted, a joint endeavour of both coalition and opposition parties, and enjoyed broad support among all members of the Knesset.

5 Legislation in the penal realm came in response to a public outcry demanding that all suspected incidents of child abuse be reported and that such offences be punished much more harshly. The fact that this was the background of the legislation could also be one of the reasons for the unbalanced and one-sided nature of this social and legal revolution.

6 The rapid pace that marked the legislation of the amendment to the Penal Code, its radical nature and its immediate implications forced the relevant agencies to focus almost exclusively on issues directly connected to the law. The 'revolution' that ensued regarding disclosure and punishment is yet to come as regards more complex but essential dimensions, such as preventive programmes, community care, establishing interdisciplinary teams, preparing educational programmes and treating the victims and their assailants.

7 The dynamics of the change, which we have pointed out, may lead us to conclude that a 'revolution' in such complex areas is a much harder and intricate process. The revolution that followed the criminal legislation, which was in keeping with public opinion, could unfold relatively swiftly and efficiently. In contrast, it seems that a 'revolution' bearing on aspects of care and rehabilitation cannot be as fast. The successful revolution we have witnessed both in the legal system and in social awareness has hindered, during its first stage, other positive developments regarding children at risk. The interesting question in the Israeli context is this: will this revolution, after it is finally 'digested', eventually lead to the development of those areas that have so far been neglected? These developments, if they take place, will be more gradual and better planned, and may ultimately result in another 'revolution', different but no less important.

NOTES

1 The Israel National Council for the Child actively promoted the legislation of the Law for Preventing Abuse of Minors and Helpless Persons discussed in this chapter, and lobbied extensively for its passing in the Knesset. The author was closely involved in this endeavour.

2 Memo from Attorney General Gabriel Bach to the District Attorneys, 28 April 1975. This memo deals at length and in detail with the district court's verdict on this trial (criminal case 675/75) and is the only document in my possession regarding the verdict

itself which, as far as I could ascertain, was never published and was eventually shredded.

3 Unfortunately, we do not yet have systematic data collection regarding the scope of these acts in Israel, and the partial statistics held by various agencies fail to match. Approximately two million children live in Israel. Partial statistics collected by the National Council for the Child and covering close to 75 per cent of the country show that 16 342 cases were reported to the welfare authorities in 1995: 4929 were reports of bodily harm, 968 of sexual assault, 2879 of psychological damage; 6391 of neglect and 1175 other cases. See Asher Ben-Arieh and Yaffa Zionit (eds), *The State of the Child in Israel: A Statistical Abstract* (Jerusalem: The National Council for the Child, 1996) (in Hebrew).

4 On the legal situation prior to the passing of the law, see Penal Code 1977, clause 345(b), on sexual intercourse between a father and his minor daughter, and clauses 361–2, on abandonment and child neglect. These were practically the only clauses in the Penal Code dealing with parental offences against children.

5 On welfare authorities refraining from reporting to the police, see *Report of the Knesset Sub-Committee On Child Abuse* (Levi Committee), August 1989: 'Statistics were presented to the committee showing the wide gap between the number of child abuse cases in the care of welfare authorities and the number of cases known to the police' (p.12).

6 On police policy concerning prosecution see Figure 10.1, and the accompanying text.

7 The following example illustrates the attitudes of the courts shortly before the passing of the Law for Preventing Abuse of Minors and Helpless Persons. This is a verdict by Judge Timan, from the Petach Tikva Magistrates Court, criminal case 896/90 (unpublished) which deals with a woman's indecent acts against her minor son between 1983 and 1989. The defendant was sentenced to a suspended prison term of 18 months for a period of three years. Although the verdict was issued after the passing of the Law for Preventing Abuse, the trial proceeded according to the previous law. The judge's arguments in the verdict are particularly interesting in our context. In explaining the lenient sentence, the judge stated that the woman had committed the offences 'only against her minor son' and not against other children. This justification runs counter to the spirit of the amendment, which actually demands harsher punishment for offences against family members.

8 The main laws in this regard are Youth (Care and Supervision) Law 1960, The Law on Adoption of Children 1981, the Law on Legal Capacity and Guardianship 1962, and the Law on Supervision of Institutionalized Care 1965.

9 This was the text of section 2a, as worded at the time: 'A medical doctor, a nurse, an educational worker, a welfare service officer or a policeman caring for a minor whose physical or mental health has been harmed, and who reasonably believe that this injury was caused by someone responsible for the minor, or because the person responsible for the minor is not competent to care for him or supervise him, or neglects his care or supervision, will report to the welfare officer.'

10 Information was gathered in interviews with Hannah Slutzki, the national welfare officer (5 May 1996), with Yitzhak Kadman, chief executive officer (CEO) of the National Council for the Child (15 April 1996) and with several experienced welfare officers.

11 For instance, Shimon Weiss, 'An infant was cruelly beaten in Tiberias for a year', *Hadashot*, 28 September 1988; Michal Kedem, 'We don't care, let him die', *Hadashot*, 7 February 1989; Moshe Pearl, 'A Family Connection,' *Hadashot*, 7 February 1989.

12 MK David (Dedi) Zucker from Meretz-Citizens Rights Movement, identified with the

left of the Israeli political spectrum, and MK Hanan Porat, from the National Religious Party, identified with the right. For the text, see bill 1947, dated 22 August 1989.

13   Motions were submitted by MKs David Zucker, Hanan Porat, Edna Solodar and Raphael Pinhasi. Following the debate on these motions, it was decided to set up a special subcommittee of the Labor and Welfare Committee to examine the issue of child abuse, chaired by Yitzhak Levi of the National Religious Party (hereafter the Levi Committee).

14   Penal Code (Amendment No. 26) 1989, Laws of Israel 1989, 10. For the wording of the legislation, see s.11 of the Penal Code, 1979, Injury to Minors and Helpless Persons, clauses 368a–368e, included as an appendix to this article.

15   According to the Law of Evidence Revision (Protection of Children) 1955, minors under 14 can be interrogated by a youth investigator. If the youth interrogator believes that giving evidence in court might be psychologically damaging to the minor, they are authorized to forbid the minor to testify. A cassette recording the minor's deposition will then be submitted to the court, and the youth investigator will testify about his or her impression of the minor's testimony and the method by which it was obtained. Prior to the Law for Preventing Abuse of Minors and Helpless Persons, this provision concerned only offences of sexual abuse. Following the passing of the law, it was extended to include offences of child abuse within the family. For an analysis of these provisions, see Tamar Morag, 'Children's Evidence in Child Abuse Proceedings under the Israeli Legal System', in F. Losel, D. Bender and T. Bliesener (eds), *Psychology and Law, International Perspectives* Berlin/New York: Walter de Gruyter, 1992).

16   On the clear connection between Moran's death and the beginning of public and legal concern with the case, see the report of the Levi Committee, which opens with the words: 'The girl Moran Danmias, aged three, is dead.' See also the article by Yitzhak Kadman, 'The Law for the Prevention of the Abuse of Minors and the Helpless – A Turning Point in the Attitude of the Israeli Society to Child Abuse', in J.H. Hattab (ed.), *Ethics and Child Mental Health* (Jerusalem: M.D. Gefen, 1994).

17   Penal Code, Amendment no. 30, Laws of Israel 1990.

18   On children's evidence, see Rules of Evidence (Interrogating witnesses) 1957, amended in 1997, which allows for the use of closed-circuit television when giving evidence. See also the 1982 Penal Code, clause 117, amended 1995, on obtaining testimony from a minor. On the statute of limitations concerning sexual offences in the family, see Penal Code (Amendment no. 47) 1996, which delays the statute of limitations in regard to sexual offences: whereas no action can be brought against an offender after 10 years have elapsed, the 10-year count concerning sexual offences against children begins after the victim has turned 18.

19   Para. 3a from the Youth (Care and Supervision) Law, Amendment 1991.

20   For the source of the figures in this section, see *The State of the Child in Israel: A Statistical Abstract* (note 3 above).

21   Ibid., table 13a.

22   Ibid., table 13c.

23   Ibid., tables 13b and 13c.

24   Ibid., table 14.2.

25   See above, note 2.

26   Although additional reasons could be adduced, such as the committees' inaccessibility and the development of alternative methods for working with the police, including recommendations by welfare officers to refrain from action on files of child abuse.

27   Police Directives 03.300.210 of 3 March 1987, and 03.300.210 of 1 July 1992.

28 Directive 8.2 by the attorney general on plea bargaining in sexual offences and offences of child abuse within the family, dated 22 August 1989.
29 Thus, for instance, directive 2.4 by the attorney general of 22 July 1993 on the prosecution's policy regarding offences of assault on a minor or a helpless person, and the attorney general's directives of 9 August 1993 and 14 October 1993.
30 See criminal case 21/96 and criminal case 272/95, *the State of Israel* v. *John Doe* at the Tel Aviv District Court, Strassnow, Hammer and Timan וו (unpublished). Further examples of stricter punishment appear in appeal 6163/95, *John Doe* v. *the State of Israel* (on 13 January 1997) in which the Supreme Court upheld a verdict sentencing the appellant to 20 years' imprisonment for raping two of his minor daughters and committing indecent acts against them, and in appeal 2620/93, *the State of Israel* v. *John Doe* (3) (1), sentencing the defendant to 20 years' imprisonment for sexually abusing his daughter.
31 Appeal 5237/93, *John Doe* v. *the State of Israel* (Supreme Court, *Takdin*, vol. 94 (3) 1994).
32 On this issue, too, only partial statistics are available. As an indication of the increase in the number of reports, we can use data found in the *Statistical Abstract*. Thus, for instance, in 1991, approximately two years after the passing of the law, welfare officers in Haifa dealt with 510 cases concerning such children; in 1993, 906 children; and in 1995, 1339 children. In Jerusalem, the 1991 caseload was 1309 children, rising to 1702 in 1995. We have no data regarding the caseload before the law was passed. An immediate and huge rise in the number of cases reported after the passing of the law is recounted by field workers active at the time. See the *Statistical Abstract* 1995, 1996.
33 Ministry of Labour and Welfare, Community Services Division, Children and Youth Service, *Annual Report 1994/1995*, ed. Yossi Corazim. No statistics are available on the number of welfare officers appointed prior to the passing of the law. This figure, however, might be misleading, since we are not referring to new positions or additional budgets that were allocated to welfare services, but rather to the conversion of existing positions of regular social workers into positions for welfare officers. Nevertheless, this figure still reflects the emphasis that welfare services did place at the time on the function of welfare officers, and their focus on the allocation of resources to this area.
34 Interview with Hannah Slutzki, note 10 above. As for declarations and programmes on this question, note that the Minister of Labor and Welfare, Eli Ishai, has recently stated that the area of children at risk is one of his office's first priorities. Moreover, following a request of the prime minister, a broad programme for treating children at risk has been developed. Programmes have so far remained at the declarative level, however, and have not yet affected budgets or actual practical steps.
35 A prominent example of the high level of frustration affecting welfare professionals can be found in a letter from Motti Winter, Head of the Child and Youth Service at the Ministry of Welfare, addressed to the directors of various other services at his ministry and to non-government organizations, dated 21 July 1997. In this letter, Winter states that the treatment of children at risk is undergoing a deep crisis, and calls for energetic action on the part of all those concerned to ensure the appropriate budgets. Of particular interest to our present concern is his call for a law on children at risk, ensuring their rights to treatment. He writes: 'As the director of the Child and Youth Service I believe that this area [children at risk] is in retreat and undergoing a deep crisis ... The worst downfall is in the community realm, where for several years we have been unable to provide any responses to the population of children at risk ... Thousands of children and their parents in the community require frameworks and community programmes – therapeutic centers, day foster care, pre-school programmes, treatment centers and

individual therapy for the children and their parents. These programmes have suffered terrible budgetary constraints and many have been closed.'
36 Appeal 3958/94, Supreme Court, *Takdin*, vol. 94 (4), 1994.

APPENDIX: PENAL (AMENDMENT NO. 26) LAW, 5750–1989

Replacement of section 323
1. Section 323 of the Penal Law, 5737–1977 (hereinafter: the Principal Law) shall be replaced with 'Duty of a parent or any person responsible for a minor'.

323. A parent, or any person responsible for a minor living in his dwelling and under the age of eighteen, is under a duty to provide the minor with sustenance, take care of his health, and protect him from abuse or bodily harm. This person will be decreed the cause of any consequences affecting the minor's life or health, as a result of a breach of the said duty.

Amendment of section 337
2. In section 337 of the Principal Law
(1) The subtitle shall be replaced with: 'Breach of duty by a parent or another responsible person'.

(2) In the main part of the section, after the words 'to take care of his health', the following shall be added: 'and protect him from abuse or bodily harm'.

Addition of paragraph F1 in Chapter...
3. In Chapter ... of the Principal Law, the following shall be added after paragraph F:
'Paragraph F1: Harming minors and helpless persons'.

Definitions
368a. In this paragraph, 'A person responsible for a minor or a helpless person' shall mean any of the following:

(1) A parent or anyone responsible for the sustenance, health, education or well being of a minor or a helpless person, under law, judicial order, implied or explicit contract, or any person thus responsible for a minor or a helpless person as a result of a lawful or unlawful action on his part.

(2) Any of the following relatives of a minor or a helpless person, eighteen years of age or older, who is not himself helpless: spouse of a parent, grandmother or grandfather, offspring, sibling, brother or sister in law, uncle or aunt.

(3) Any person with whom the minor or the helpless person dwells or permanently stays, who is eighteen years of age or older, provided that relations of dependence or authority exist between them.

'helpless person': any person who by reason of his age, illness or physical or mental disability, mental defect or any other reason cannot take care of his own sustenance, health or well being;
'action': shall include failure to take action;
'welfare officer': an officer appointed for these purposes by law;
'minor': shall mean as defined in the Capacity and Guardianship Law, 5744–1962.

Battering a minor or helpless person
368b. (a) Any person who batters a minor or a helpless person causing him substantial harm shall be liable to five years' imprisonment; if the assailant is the person responsible for the minor or the helpless person he shall be liable to seven years' imprisonment.

(b) If such offence as stated in subsection (a) had been committed thus causing the minor or the helpless person grave bodily harm, the assailant shall be liable to seven years' imprisonment, and if he was the person responsible for the minor or the helpless person, he shall be liable to nine years' imprisonment.

(c) For the purpose of this section, 'harm' means both physical and mental harm.

Abusing a minor or a helpless person
368c. Any person abusing a minor or a helpless person, physically, mentally or socially, shall be liable to seven years' imprisonment; and if the perpetrator is also the person responsible for the minor or the helpless person, he shall be liable to nine years' imprisonment.

Duty to report
368d. (a) If a person reasonably believes that an offence has been recently committed against a minor or a helpless person by the person responsible for him, he must report it as soon as possible to a welfare officer or the police; any person who violates this provision shall be liable to three months' imprisonment.

(b) A medical doctor, a nurse, an educational practitioner, a social worker, a welfare service worker, a policeman, a psychologist, a criminologist or any paramedical professional, a manager or any staff member in a care facility or an institution where the minor or the helpless person is staying, any one of whom during the performance of their professional duty and as a result of their profession or duty reasonably believes an offence has been committed against a minor or a helpless person by anyone responsible for them is under a duty to report this as soon as possible to a welfare officer or the police; any person who violates this provision is liable to six months' imprisonment.

(c) If a person responsible for a minor or a helpless person has reason to believe that another person responsible for the minor or the helpless person committed an offence against him, he shall report it as soon as possible to a welfare officer or the police; anyone violating this provision is liable to six months' imprisonment.

(d) If any of the following offences has been committed against a minor or a helpless person while staying in a care facility, an institution, or any other educational or care agency – sexual offence under sections 345 to 348, or the infliction of grave bodily harm under section 368(b) or abuse under section 368(c) – it shall be the duty of the manager, or any staff member in the said facility, to report it as soon as possible to a welfare officer or the police; anyone who violates this provision is liable to six months' imprisonment.

(e) Said duty to report under this section shall not apply to a minor.

(f) A welfare officer who receives such a report under this section shall deliver it to the police together with his recommendation to act or not to act regarding the report, unless granted permission not to deliver the report to the police by any one of the committees established by the Minister of Justice, for this purpose; the said committee shall be comprised of a District Attorney who will serve as the chairperson, a police officer – an inspector or of higher rank – and a district welfare officer.

(g) Upon receiving information under this section, the police shall pass it to the welfare officer, and take action after consulting the welfare officer.

(h) In this section, except for subsection (d), an 'offence' shall mean endangerment of life and health under section 337, sexual offence under sections 345–8, abandonment or neglect under sections 361 and 362 and battery or abuse under sections 368b and 368c.

Regulations
368e. The Minister of Justice after consulting the Minister of Labor and Welfare and with the approval of the Constitution, Law and Justice Committee of the Knesset, may promulgate regulations for the implementation of this paragraph.

11 Child Abuse in Japan: The Current Situation and Proposed Legal Changes

Yukiko Matsushima

There is a movie, *Kichiku* (Brute), directed by Yoshitaro Nomura, based on a book by Seicho Matsumoto, one of Japan's best-known authors.[1] In it, a childless couple were forced to take care of three children, who were the results of the husband's extramarital affair. The step-mother treats the children cruelly, and their cowardly father obeys her order to dispose of them. The step-mother kills the youngest child, aged about two, and disguises the deed as an accidental death. The second child, a four-year-old girl, is taken to a city and abandoned in a crowd by her father. The eldest, a boy about seven years old, is astute enough to spit out a poisoned cake given to him by his father and he cannot be abandoned because he is old enough to give his name and address. At a loss, his father pushes the boy over the edge of a cliff overlooking the sea. However, the boy is caught by a tree halfway down the cliff and is helped by a fisherman. Asked by the police who pushed him, the boy will not say the criminal's name. He covers up for the father who tried to kill him, but his belongings provide a clue to his identity and his father is arrested. When the police ask if this man is his father, he cries, 'No, I don't know this man. This is not my father.' In this last scene, the grudge against the father who tried to kill him and the feelings that prompted him to cover up for his father are intertwined. A problem which we now need to face up to, and which we will need to continue to face up to, lies in this last scene. Although it is simply called 'child abuse', abuse of children by parents is a serious problem that involves the complex mutual affection between parent and child. The issue of child abuse provokes public debate over the ideal relationship between parent and child and society's involvement in the problem.

INTRODUCTION

In June 1997, the Japanese Child Welfare Law was drastically revised for the first time since its establishment in 1947. The Child Welfare Law, inserted in the legal system as a special statute under the Law on Parents and Children (part of Book IV of the Civil Code), originated from the Anti-Child Abuse Law enacted in 1933. The Anti-Child Abuse Law was written to protect children from the whims of parents who in pre-war days had absolute control over children and who could force their children to beg, or sell them to show-tents or to brothels. Absorbing this Anti-Child Abuse Law, the Child Welfare Law was established in 1947 to protect the lives of the many children who were robbed by the war of parents and a place to live and were thrown out, hungry, into the streets. However, in the 50 years since the end of World War II, the environment surrounding children and families has changed remarkably. The birth rate has sharply decreased and the number of families with working parents has increased. As a result, the role of families and communities in bringing up children has deteriorated. Under such circumstances, the law was revised to re-establish the welfare system for children and families, which constitutes the environmental conditions required for easy child care and supports the sound growth and independence of children. However, as far as abuse is concerned, it cannot be said that the revised law solves all aspects of the problem: there are still many issues that need to be resolved.

In Japan, the Child Welfare Law has a direct and dominant role, and child guidance centres and other facilities occupy a central position in the welfare of children. Starting with an overview of the current state of child abuse and the surrounding issues in Japan, this chapter mainly describes the treatment of abused children under the Child Welfare Law. However, those who are directly involved in child abuse include the parents, siblings and other family members. Accordingly, the problems of child abuse lie directly in family life, mainly that of the parents and children. Attention should also be given to the strains of modern-day family life. While focusing on the Child Welfare Law, this chapter will suggest future revisions and approaches to solving the problem of child abuse by looking at the Civil Code provisions on parental rights which prescribe the relationship between parent and child.

DEFINITION OF CHILD ABUSE

According to definitions widely accepted in Japan, child abuse is non-accidental abuse by parents, or guardians substituting for parents, of children (under the age of 18). Child abuse is divided into four categories: (1)

physical abuse, (2) negligence or refusal of care, (3) sexual abuse, and (4) psychological or emotional abuse. This definition is based on child maltreatment at home as defined by the International Child Abuse Permanent Committee.

However, in practice, child abuse can be defined in different ways and it is difficult to give it a fixed definition. Current Japanese laws do not have a provision that officially prescribes 'what is child abuse'. For example, decisions as to whether children should be placed under the temporary protection of a child guidance centre, or whether children should be admitted to the facilities or entrusted to foster parents, or whether a family court should make a pronouncement on the loss of parental rights for child abusers, and decisions as to the presence or absence of 'abuse' and its degree are judged in the terms of individual cases and requirements. From the standpoint of the principle of *nulla poena sine lege*, concrete and clear definitions are needed to punish assailants. However, when looking at the recovery of children's human rights, definitions that have some flexibility can be more desirable.

As illustrated by the fact that the right to discipline children is included in the provisions on parental rights in the Civil Code,[2] Japanese people tend to think that the training of children is the responsibility of parents and a personal family matter and one that should not be carried out by public authorities. However, there is no clear definition to differentiate between discipline and abuse. Furthermore, abusive parents are often not aware that they are abusing their children and have no intention of having consultations with public facilities. Abuse does include cases by assailants other than parents, such as a juvenile crime which shook Japanese society,[3] the serial murders of little girls by a killer with abnormal tendencies,[4] and the suicide of a junior-high student distressed by bullying.[5] However, this chapter concentrates on abuse by parents or guardians substituting for parents.

THE CURRENT STATE OF CHILD ABUSE

In many cases, child abuse happens behind closed doors and the victims are too young to report the fact to the outside world. Accordingly, it is difficult to get an accurate figure of the number of actual cases of child abuse. Figures shown in the statistics of public organizations represent only the tip of the iceberg. One view holds that Japan may have more than 10 000 cases of child abuse a year.[6]

Survey

Typical surveys of child abuse were conducted by the Directors' Committee of National Child Guidance Centres. The first survey took six months, from April to September of 1988, and the second one from April to September of 1996. The following is the result of the surveys, based on a report by the National Child Guidance Centres released in March 1997.[7]

Number of abused children

During the six months from April to September of 1996, 2061 cases of child abuse were reported by 175 child guidance centres nationwide. Compared with 1039 cases found by the 1988 survey, instances of child abuse have doubled in the last 10 years. While this increase is in part the result of the increase in the number of child abuse cases, it is also attributable to the recent recognition by society of child abuse. Each child guidance centre reported an average of 12 cases, and the numbers reported by the centres ranged from 0 to 76. Calculating from the population figure for children from a national census, an average of 1.7 out of 10 000 children were abused.

Categories of abuse

Of the total of 2061 cases of abuse in the 1996 survey, 'physical abuse' occupies the largest share at 48.9 per cent, followed by 'improper care or refusal of care' (40.4 per cent), then 'psychological abuse' (5.9 per cent) and finally 'sexual abuse' (4.9 per cent). In the 1988 survey, 'improper care or refusal of care' (abandonment, neglect, refusal to allow school attendance and so on) ranked top at 62.4 per cent, while 'physical abuse' accounted for 26.5 per cent of the total. The recent survey which has 'physical abuse' at the top of the list shows that the number of cases of aggressive abuse that threatens the lives of children has increased.

Physical abuse	Improper care or refusal of care	Sexual abuse	Psychological abuse	Total
1007	832	100	122	2061

Sex

In terms of the sex of those abused, 50.6 per cent of abused children were boys, a slightly larger proportion than girls. When this is divided into each category of abuse, boys occupied 52.8 per cent in terms of 'physical abuse' and 53.7 per cent in 'improper care or rejection of care', while an overwhelming 96.0 per cent of victims of 'sexual abuse' were girls.

Age

In terms of age, nearly 80 per cent of victims were under the age of 12, with babies and infants between 0 and five years representing 41.5 per cent, and elementary schoolchildren of six to 11 years 36.4 per cent. Compared with the 1988 survey, the proportion of babies and infants being abused increased from 35.0 per cent and, in particular, 45.3 per cent of those receiving 'improper care and rejection of care' were babies. The figures for 'sexual abuse' include seven cases of the abuse of infants.

Period of abuse

In terms of duration, 'longer than one year and less than three years' ranked top at 27.8 per cent, followed by 'longer than three years'; this indicates that abuse continues over a relatively long period of time. 'Sexual abuse' in particular tends to continue over a prolonged period.

Abusers

Of 1626 cases, excluding those in which the identity of the abusers are uncertain, 'biological mothers' constituted 50.8 per cent of the abusers, 'biological fathers' account for 28.5 per cent, 'step-fathers' 4.8 per cent, 'adopted fathers' 4.3 per cent and 'step-mothers' 3.1 per cent. As for 'physical abuse', 'biological fathers' occupied 38.5 per cent and 'biological mothers' 28.7 per cent in the 1988 survey, while 'biological mothers' occupy 43.2 per cent and 'biological fathers' 30.8 per cent in the 1996 survey. 'Biological mothers' represent a larger proportion than 'biological fathers' in all categories except 'sexual abuse'. Nearly half of the total of 'sexual abuse' cases are perpetrated by 'biological fathers', showing an increase on the previous figure of 41.7 per cent. It should be noted that three cases of 'sexual abuse' by 'biological mothers' were reported.

Age and occupation of abusers

Of the abusers, 37.9 per cent were in their thirties, 30.3 per cent were in their twenties, and 23.2 per cent were in their forties, showing that younger parents occupy the largest proportion of the total. Of the young parents, only 29.8 per cent, less than a third, had a fixed job, and more than half were 'unemployed', 'often changing jobs' or 'part-timers', which indicates that they were living in unstable economic conditions.

Physical and mental status of abusers

Many abusers have physical or mental problems themselves. About 40 per cent of the abusers had disordered personalities, 10.9 per cent were 'alcoholics', 10.9 per cent were 'neurotics or suspected neurotics', 9.9 per cent were 'psychiatric patients or suspected psychiatric patients', 9.6 per cent had 'personality disorders' and 8.9 per cent had 'intellectual disorders'.

How abusers inflict abuse

Of the abusers, 64.9 per cent did not recognize that their acts were acts of abuse. On the other hand, it should be noted that some 40 per cent of the 'psychological abusers' recognize that their acts constituted abuse and sought support.

Recent trends of child abuse

The number of cases of child abuse has been increasing year by year,[8] remarkably so in cities. One recent serious problem is that many mothers who take care of babies and infants all day long do so alone in the city in an isolated family unit without any support from their busy working husbands, and they fall into infant care neurosis which leads to child abuse.[9] Some mothers start asserting that they do not love their own children: the myth of motherly love has started to lose its foundation. A 'chain of child abuse between generations' has also been identified. Those who were abused in childhood grow up to become parents who in turn abuse their children. One estimate is that 30 per cent of those with a history of childhood abuse turn into parents who abuse their own children. The proportion of previously abused parents abusing their children is higher than that for non-abused parents.[10] Under such circumstances, where there are many parents without a fixed job and where child abuse is not recognized by the parents, even if the abused children are protected temporarily, they repeatedly become victims of child abuse when they return home. In reconsidering child abuse as a family problem, separating abused children from abusing parents is not the only solution; the economic stability of their parents should also be addressed and the mental treatment or re-education of parents may be necessary.

ADMINISTRATIVE HANDLING OF ABUSE UNDER THE CHILD WELFARE LAW

Japan does not have an Anti-Child Abuse Law, which systematically prescribes child abuse, or something like the English Children Act that comprehensively describes the rights of children. In Japan each case is handled under the Child Welfare Law, the Civil Code and the Penal Code. Of these, the Child Welfare Law plays the central role, and provides the basic framework for the welfare of children. Here I shall describe the structure of the Child Welfare Law and the role of the administrative system in providing remedies for child abuse.

Child welfare facilities

Child welfare facilities which function as child abuse relief facilities are medical facilities, public health centres, family and child counsellors' offices, and child guidance centres. Of these, the child guidance centres, under the supervision and control of the Welfare Ministry, play the leading role. The child guidance centres, established by each prefecture and large city, act as central facilities active on the 'front line' with a total of 175 nationwide as of 1 April 1996. The main functions of the centres include: (a) providing consultation to families and others on children's problems; (b) conducting necessary research into children and their families and making a professional judgment in terms of medicine, psychology, education, sociology and psychological health; (c) providing guidance based on these judgments; and (d) giving children temporary protection, as required. Each child guidance centre has professional staff comprising doctors, psychological assessors, child welfare officers mainly engaged in casework, counsellors, child guidance officers mainly involved in the temporary protection of children, and nurses.

The process of administrative treatment

The process of supporting cases at the child guidance centres under the Child Welfare Law is as shown in Figure 11.1. Under the Child Welfare Law, the rescue of abused children starts with a report from guardians or finders to a child guidance centre. According to the findings of the research by the child guidance centre, a conference at the centre decides how to deal with an abused child. The measures include (a) guidance at home, (b) emergency temporary protection, (c) admission to the facilities with the

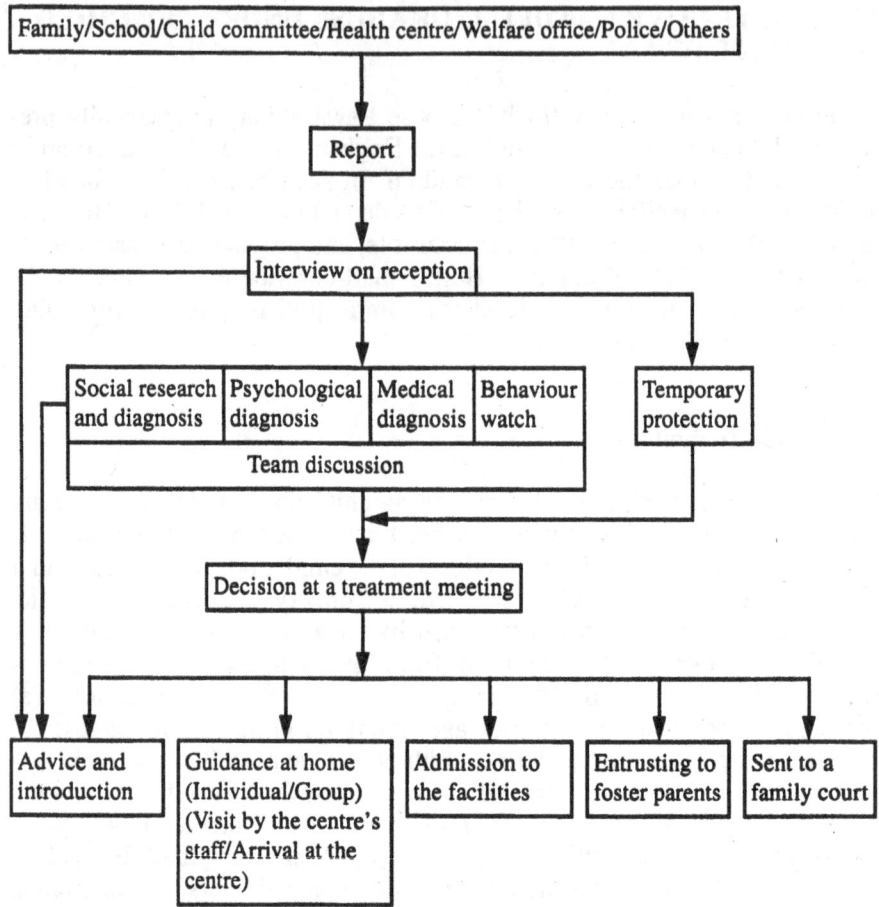

Figure 11.1 The administrative process

consent of parents, (d) admission to the facilities through Article 28 of the Child Welfare Law in cases where the parents do not consent to the admission, and (e) cases where the head of the child guidance centre makes a claim for the removal of parental rights.

Guidance at home

On receiving notice of a report of child abuse, the child guidance centre sends a case worker to investigate the case and a psychological assessor to interview the abused child to judge his or her physical and mental state. If it is not deemed an emergency case, the child is not separated from his or her family, and the family is given guidance on how to coordinate the relationship between the parents and the child. The Convention on the Rights of the Child provides that children, 'have the right to be cared for by parents as far as possible'[11] and that 'children shall not be separated from their parents against their will'.[12] Accordingly, the ideal solution is to eliminate abuse, with the child staying at home.

Since it is necessary to give guidance to guardians, the case worker who supports abusing families is required to make every effort to avoid a confrontation with them. However, since the guardians usually do not recognize the need for guidance, and as in most cases the case worker becomes involved with them through a report, special care is needed for an early approach to the family. Many of the families in which children are abused have difficulties, such as different types of stress, isolation from society, opposition to public organizations and a rejection of others. Accordingly, an ill-considered approach carries the strong possibility of provoking a reaction and can end with the opposite result to that required. When making their initial approach care workers should:[13]

- quickly collect as much information as possible on the family and child to understand the situation;
- determine from the child's damage and risk the degree of emergency;
- in the event of extreme emergency, give priority to separation and protection, such as temporary protection and admission in hospital, and take appropriate measures (some cases may require police involvement);
- consult relevant organizations and, if necessary, get them to make a quick judgment;
- maintain a position of helping the parents to solve their problems and avoid reprimanding or criticizing;
- if medical treatment is necessary, give it first priority. For later approaches, gather evidence (medical certificates and photos); and
- be flexible in approaching each case according to the parents' values and behaviour patterns.

Some cases may require a child guidance centre to cooperate with a public health centre and a welfare office. For example, a health worker may visit the family to give guidance on child care. If the family has financial problems, the welfare office will take measures to provide social security. If the mother is a child care neurotic, the child may require day care at a nursery school or kindergarten or the mother may require guidance treatment outside the home. Support from relatives such as grandmothers and grandfathers and support from the community will also be necessary to prevent isolation.

In Japan, it is a basic policy of the child guidance centre to give guidance at home, and it is considered that the separation of a child from his or her parents should be avoided as much as possible. Article 44-2 of the revised Child Welfare Law provides that a 'child and family support centre' be attached to welfare offices as part of the child welfare facilities. This provision allows the head of a child guidance centre to entrust guidance of children and their parents to the welfare office staff (Item 2, Clause 1, Article 26, and Item 2, Clause 1, Article 27 of the Child Welfare Law) and allows the centre to implement comprehensive coordination with child guidance centres and other child welfare facilities. It is expected to create a network of support for victims of child abuse.

Emergency temporary protection

In April 1995, many children who were living with their parents in the compound of Aum Shinrikyo,[14] a cult group, in Kamikuishiki Village of Yamanashi Prefecture, were rescued from the site by police officers. The police reported the matter to a child guidance centre because of the absence of an environment to enable the sound upbringing of children, and the director of the centre asked the police to rescue the children (on the basis of the duty of finders to notify the authorities of children requiring protection under Article 25 of the Child Welfare Law). On the day, 53 children were rescued by Yamanashi Prefectural Police and given temporary protection at Kofu Child Guidance Centre. Adding to these the children taken into protection in Tokyo and Gunma in May, the total number of children exceeded 100. This is the largest number of temporarily protected children in a single case in the history of child guidance centres, except for the protection of orphans immediately after World War II. According to a report by the child guidance centres which protected the children, the staff found that those children who had lived in the cult compound for a long time not only had physical disorders, such as anaemia or bronchial pneumonia, but were also poor in scholastic ability and had not acquired basic knowledge needed for daily living, such as taking meals, using the toilet and bathing.[15] The parents of the children, the cult followers, thronged the centre many times and demanded that it release the children, claiming their parental rights. Their demands were rejected. Claiming that temporary protection by a child guidance centre is illegal, the parents filed suit in court to demand habeas corpus. However, the suit was also rejected. Of the 112 children, 56 were taken into the care of relatives and those remaining entered child welfare facilities. The case, leads to a reconsideration of the questions, 'what is an appropriate upbringing for children?' and 'to what extent can the police and public authorities get involved in such cases?'

If the judgment is made that there is a possibility that the child will remain a victim of repeated abuse or will not be given proper mental and physical treatment if he or she stays with the family, the director of a centre may separate the child from his or her parents and place the child under temporary protection (Article 33 of the Child Welfare Law).[16] Temporary protection centres are attached to the central child guidance centre of each prefecture. At the centres, children under 18, except babies, are cared for and their behaviour is monitored around the clock by guidance staff and nurses. Most of them stay for two or three weeks, but the period is not fixed. The law does not require the consent of guardians for this temporary protection (Article 33 of the Child Welfare Law). The temporary protection of children rescued from the premises of Aum Shinrikyo is a good example. However, the Aum case is an extraordinary one. If a child guidance centre forcefully separates children from their parents for temporary protection, the parents turn against the centre, which makes it difficult for those at the centre to give the parents guidance. To avoid this scenario, protection is usually carried out with the consent of the parents or by giving them reasons which they can easily accept to persuade them to agree. However, without facilities to reform or educate abusive parents, children may again become the victims of abuse and risk losing their lives after returning home. In this case, they are admitted to the facilities for long periods. About half of the children temporarily protected return home and the other half enter child welfare facilities.

Admission to facilities with consent of parents

If the presence of abuse is confirmed during a period of temporary protection and it is judged that it is desirable for the child to be separated from his or her family for a certain amount of time, the process moves to the next step: admission to a nursery,[17] a child care centre[18] or other child welfare facilities,[19] or entrusting the child to foster parents (Item 3, Clause 1, Article 27 of the Child Welfare Law).[20]

Admission to facilities is carried out with the consent of parents or by a petition to a family court in the situation where parents do not consent to admission.[21] If parents fail to provide proper care for their children, admission to facilities is the next best solution for child guidance. However, problems are noted. First, where sexually abusive parents have strong feelings of attachment to their children, it is very difficult to persuade such parents to allow admittance of children to facilities. It is also difficult to persuade parents who believe in physical punishment or who are strongly opposed to public organizations to allow their children to be admitted. If parents change their minds and demand to take over care of their children, it is not easy for the facilities to oppose them, given the strong legal rights that parents have.[22] After admission of children to facilities, the child guidance centres try to restructure the relationship between parent and child by having children see their parents at the centre or stay overnight with their parents. However, the centres actually provide children and parents with no professional treatment programme. There is criticism that children, admitted for various reasons and living together as a group, are not given sufficient individual treatment (particularly in mental terms). This is partly attributed to a shortage of staff.

Admission to facilities by petition under Article 28 of the Child Welfare Law

If the parent refuses to give consent but the child needs to be separated from its family, the head of a child guidance centre may admit the child by petitioning a family court for approval to admit the child to facilities. However, the number of petitions filed by child guidance centres nationwide ranges from several to 10 or more a year, showing that this method is rarely used.[23] The reason is that the functioning of Japanese law basically differs from that of US law. In the USA, once a court gets involved in a case, it continues to supervise parental rights, gives directions for the treatment of parents and monitors developments. In Japan, on the other hand, the family court only makes a judgment on whether or not to give approval for admission to facilities, and the child guidance centre may voluntarily become involved in the guidance to parents. The centre tends to avoid confrontation with parents and it is difficult to confirm the facts supporting abuse; also it takes a long time (usually two or three months) to get a decision. Therefore this situation makes it undesirable for a child guidance centre to petition a family court. To take this step, the staff of a child guidance centre may enter the house of the child to obtain the necessary information (Article 29 of the Child Welfare Law). However, if the research in the house provokes a reaction from the parents, the relationship with the parents is damaged and it becomes difficult to give them guidance on improving the relationship between parent and child. Because of this problem, the right to on-the-spot inspection of houses has yet to be practically executed.

Another contentious issue is the extent to which the effect of approval by the family court for admission to facilities can limit parental rights. Is the effect limited only to giving approval for admission or are parental rights limited during the admission period? These questions are not clearly answered by the law. The family court assumes that the approval remains effective continuously, limiting parental rights for a fixed period of time. However, the end of admission depends on the decision of the child guidance centre. The extent to which parents can be limited in their involvement with their children is an issue that is difficult to handle in practice.

Petition for removal of parental rights by the head of a child guidance centre

If the petition in a family court for admission to facilities is not effective, the head of a child guidance centre may petition for removal of parental rights (Clause 6, Article 33 of the Child Welfare Law). Article 37 of the Child Welfare Law gives the head of a child guidance centre the right to take necessary steps for child welfare. However, in comparison with the strength of parental rights, it is only a limited proxy right. To match the rights of people with parental authority, the right to petition for removal of parental rights of people with parental authority and the right to demand the selection and rejection of guardians is approved as necessary, with the aim of supplementing the limited proxy right.

When the petition for removal of parental rights is made, a provisional order (provisional suspension of parental rights and selection of guardians) is available. Accordingly, it is possible to solve problems by first receiving an application of a provisional order and then obtaining other maintenance rights, such as a change in parental authority and designation of supervision rights. If the centre obtains a provisional order from a family court to choose the head of the child guidance centre which protects the child as the proxy substituting for people with parental authority, and to suspend the abusive parents' authority, the centre can oppose the demands of the parents to take over care of the child, even before the pronouncement of removal of parental authority.

However, petitioning for the removal of parental authority by the head of a child guidance centre is very rare. (The reasons will be described in detail when this chapter discusses the handling of parental authority under the Civil Code.) The power of the head of a child guidance centre is in practice weaker than that of people with parental authority.

LEGAL MEASURES AGAINST CHILD ABUSE

Measures under the Civil Code

Under the Civil Code, one measure is the forfeiture of parental rights for parents involved in child abuse. Article 818 of the Civil Code prescribes that

'A child who has not yet attained majority is subject to the parental rights of his or her father and mother.' The vital elements of parental rights involve the rights and duties of providing for the custody and education of the child (Article 820 of the Civil Code). In addition, and more specifically, the Civil Code prescribes the rights of the parents to designate the place of residence, the right to discipline, the right to permit employment, as well as the right of management of property and the right of representation (Articles 821 to 824 of the Civil Code).[24]

Article 834 of the Civil Code provides that the family court may declare the parental rights of a parent lost where he or she abuses those rights or fails to exercise them properly. Child abuse is no doubt a ground for such a declaration. The petition for the removal of parental rights may be made either by a relative of the child or by a public prosecutor (Article 834 of the Civil Code) or by the head of a child guidance centre (Article 33–6 of the Child Welfare Law). Thus measures have been taken to control acts of child abuse by threatening forfeiture of parental rights by parents involved in child abuse and, once such an act has occurred, to protect the child by separating it from a parent who places it at risk.

However, these procedures are subject to limitations and, according to the Annual Report of Judicial Statistics, between 1988 and 1995, such declarations were only made in about 10 of 90 to 100 cases where applications were made. There are several reasons for this number being so small. First, the family court is reluctant to make an order that a child should live separately from its parents. The court maintains a clear dogma that it is best to rear a child at home and that the mother is 'sacred'.[25] Therefore the appropriateness of forfeiture of parental rights is decided bearing in mind that the child is to be returned to the home of the parent sooner or later, even if the parent from whom the child has been separated is an abusive one. The reality of this world is that there are some mothers with little maternal love and that there are some fathers who would have sexual relations with their daughters. However, in many cases, such images of the parents and their children are beyond the general apprehensions of the court. Some judges have a preconception that no father could ever assault his own daughter and that no mother could ever abuse her own child. And when parents involved in child abuse cases appear before such judges, the judges may tend to trust the testimony of the parents or their attitude of apparent remorse and eventually dismiss the case.

Second, the reason why the number of cases brought by plaintiffs, particularly from the heads of the child guidance centres, is small, (one a year on average) is that the child guidance centre has two extremely contradictory missions within one institution: one is the mission to assist the family of a parent who abuses his or her child; and the second is to punish the parent who abused his or her child. It is the policy of the child guidance centre to help parents and children rebuild their relationship as a family and it tries to avoid at all costs categorizing parents as failed parents by initiating legal proceedings. There is a tendency for the child guidance centre to offer a soft-touch type of welfare-oriented assistance, where it tries to use persuasion with the relevant parent as much as possible. This is out of the fear that it would be difficult for it to provide future assistance if the child guidance centre and the parent fell into a hostile relationship. On the other hand, in the USA, compulsory separation will be exercised through judicial intervention. Education is then provided to the parents responsible for the protection of such children under the supervision of the court. In Japan, however, the head of the child guidance centre will make a decision to declare the removal of parental rights only after it has been found that no headway can be made by continuing to use the soft-touch type of welfare-oriented assistance. However, the centre is still reluctant to make applications, since the family court in many cases tends not to accept such a petition, even once made, for the reasons described above.

Third, Article 834 of the Civil Code lacks flexibility in that it only provides for the total removal of parental rights. This 'all or nothing' approach produces a reluctance in the minds of decision makers to make the declaration. Therefore many scholars and lawyers propose a system of 'temporary suspension of parental rights', instead of full-scale forfeiture of parental rights.

In addition to the above, the following points can be considered as reasons for the system of removal of parental rights under civil law not being sufficiently used.

1 The fact of child abuse is rather difficult to prove, since the event occurs behind closed doors.
2 There is a fear that a declaration of the loss of parental rights will prove to be a handicap to the child in the long term since the declaration will be recorded on his or her family register,[26] even though such a declaration would temporarily fulfil the welfare needs of the child.
3 It is difficult to find an appropriate guardian to bring up the child, since there are few candidates for guardianship after the loss of parental rights is affected.
4 Under the current Civil Code, a guardian is selected from private individuals who have no official status; consequently, the private individual will be recorded on the child's family register, and thereby the guardian is left open to private attack by the child's biological parent.

In the meantime, if the causes behind the forfeiture of parental rights have ceased to exist, the family court may, on the application of the party concerned or of any of that party's relatives, revoke the adjudication of the forfeiture of parental rights (Article 836 of the Civil Code). However, this leaves some difficult problems unsolved. For example, how can the alleged improvements in the attitude of the abusive parent be proved in cases where the parent and child are separated?

The following is a reported case of child abuse: the case of the adjudication made by the Hachioji Branch of the Tokyo Family Court on 16 May 1979.[27] In this case there was a couple, Man A and Woman B. Because their eldest daughter, X, was assaulted by Man A and forced to have a sexual relationship with him when she was in the second grade of junior high school, she and her mother, Woman B, left home around 1973. The marriage of the couple was annulled by a court in 1976 and Man A was given custody of their three children (son, eldest daughter and second daughter) since the livelihood of Woman B was unstable. However, Man A did not engage in work, using the excuse of being weak, and received public assistance under the Daily Life Protection Law. Being alcohol-dependent, he not only failed to protect his second daughter Y, but also forced her to have sexual relations with him, assaulting her as soon as she started the first grade of junior high school. After the son left home, Man A's forceful requests for sexual relations with Y became more outrageous until Y ran away from home; she asked her teacher at junior high school for help. The teacher notified the police and Y was placed under the protection of a child guidance centre through police action. However, Man A pressurized the centre into returning Y, on the ground of his parental rights over her. The head of the child guidance centre pleaded with the family court for a declaration of the loss of Man A's parental rights. In response to this, the family court first suspended the performance of his duties as the holder of Y's parental rights as a 'provisional disposition before the trial' and appointed the head of the Centre as the agent. Next, the family court adjudicated that Man A would lose his parental rights, determining that 'It is improper to let Y be subject to the parental rights of Man A, since it has been concluded that Man A abused his parental rights and abused Y unreasonably, and caused significant harm to her welfare.'

The above is a very rare case where the head of the child guidance centre petitioned for the declaration of the loss of parental rights and the petition was approved by the family court.

Measures under criminal law

Under criminal law, there are measures in which sanctions by punishment are prescribed so that child abuse or negligent non-interference can be prevented. For example, in cases where child abuse occurs, any recurrence of such an act will be prevented by punishing the parents involved in child abuse, charging them under criminal law with abandonment by a person responsible for the protection of the victim, infliction of bodily injury, infliction of bodily injury resulting in death, or rape.

Penalties under criminal law are as follows: for abandonment only, imprisonment with labour for a term of more than three months and not exceeding five years; for infliction of bodily injury on a child, imprisonment with labour for a term not exceeding 10 years; for infliction of bodily injury resulting in the death of a child, imprisonment with labour for a limited term of more than two years; and for rape, also to imprisonment with labour for a limited term of more than two years.

However, criminal sanctions against a parent who abused his or her child do not always serve the best interests of the child. This is because a child will continue to need its parent. For example, in a family where the child lives with one parent, if the father or mother is imprisoned, the child will immediately lose his or her place of abode through having no guardian (although in many cases the child will be taken in by relatives or placed in a facility). In cases of a suspended sentence or punishment by a fine, the parent who abused the child will continue to live with the child as before, and therefore the child will not lose its domicile. However, the risk will remain that such child abuse will be repeated. In addition, as child abuse is a crime conducted privately, and since many of the victims are babies or young children, it is often difficult to prove. Even if the child is of an age to be able to testify, the child will find such testimony difficult owing to fear of retaliation by his or her parent. Furthermore, if the child is repeatedly asked the same thing at different institutions, he or she might be psychologically harmed by such repeated questioning.

Consequently, there is naturally a limit to dealing with child abuse through criminal law, and we can say that it only plays an ex post facto measure in ending child abuse. In reality, criminal law does not play an important role in preventing child abuse.

REVIEW AND PERSONAL APPRAISAL OF THE JUDICIAL AND ADMINISTRATIVE PROCEDURES AGAINST CHILD ABUSE

Problems under the Child Welfare Law

Clear prescription concerning the child abuse

Article 34 of the Child Welfare Law enumerates many acts to which it is illegal to subject a child. However, when we look at them in detail, we find many things that have no bearing on present times, such as not letting a child engage in begging, or in acrobatics (circuses); therefore it is necessary to review this article. The most crucial problem lies in the fact that there are no words prohibiting child abuse: the words, 'no-one should abuse a child' are not found. In view of this, it is necessary plainly to prohibit and to provide a clear definition of child abuse.

Reinforcement of the duty of notice

The duty of notice, when any child requiring protection is found, is prescribed in Article 25 of the Child Welfare Law.[28] It is a duty imposed upon all people to report a child that has no guardian or is being cared for inadequately. However, there are no penalties for failing to report such a situation, therefore the legal force of the duty is weak.

This being the situation, for people of specified occupations the onus of reporting child abuse when it is noticed should be clearly prescribed, as prescribed in the reporting laws of the USA. More specifically, it is considered necessary to impose this duty of reporting upon those who are able to obtain information, or see the facts of the child abuse, through the performance of their jobs. Such people would include public health nurses, day nursery teachers, teachers, medical doctors, hospital nurses,[29] police officers, and the case workers of the welfare offices and the child guidance centres. They should be subject to fines if they fail to report abuse, but also they should be provided with immunity from responsibilities under criminal law and civil law even if the report so made later proves to be incorrect. In the USA, some harmful results of this reporting duty have recently been publicized.[30] However, there is an impression that Japan is 10 to 20 years behind the USA in terms of countermeasures against child abuse, and also that the existence of child abuse itself is not sufficiently recognized. At the same time, the perception in Japan is that child abuse is a family matter and that it is not desirable for the administration to intervene in family affairs. For this very reason, where there is an environment in which the issue of child abuse is latent, it is important to increase the onus on those who are in a position where they can easily see abused children to report suspected child abuse. Also it is important to confront people with the actual issues: the strengthening of the provisions concerning this reporting duty and the legislating of the associated immunity provisions should be considered.

Utilization of the authority to make on-the-spot inspections

Article 29 of the Child Welfare Law clearly prescribes that the commissioners for child welfare may enter a home as they feel necessary without a court order where there is child abuse taking place and may investigate the situation and question those involved. However, this right to make an on-the-spot inspection is not actually utilized. It is said that the reasons for this are to avoid the commissioner having to have an unnecessary confrontation with the parents. However, when we consider that it is crisis intervention at the point when the life of a child is endangered, the commissioner should make on-the-spot inspections because he should correctly understand the developing situation and collect the evidence by all means possible, even if this means a confrontation with a parent. It is essential that those in the child guidance centres are not afraid of confrontations with parents. In addition, the strengthening of the groups of case workers who are dealing with child abuse should be pursued. This includes increasing their number, as well as providing for their continuing education as specialists.

Reflections on the desires of the children

A revision made to Article 26, Paragraph 2 of the Child Welfare Law added the duty to listen to the opinions of the child at the time when measures are taken by the child guidance centre. This is one of the most important innovations of the recent changes in the law. However, the issue of whether a child can apply for admission to the child guidance centre by himself or herself was left untouched. The situation remains that admission to the child guidance centre is permitted only in cases where there is agreement by the person holding parental rights over the child or where there is an affirmative result from the family court hearing. However, there is no system yet established where the child himself or herself can directly petition the court for admission. In view of this, it is desirable that the right to petition for admission to the child welfare facilities is acknowledged if the child in question has the ability to make his or her own judgement. In addition, the release of the child from the centre is at the discretion of the head of the centre at present. In order to prevent an arbitrary release, it is desirable to have the release checked by another institution, and for those making the decisions to respect the desires of the child.

Problems under the Civil Code

Removal of the disciplinary right

The legal right to discipline a child, prescribed in Article 822 of the Civil Code, presents some questions pertaining to child abuse. The disciplinary rights of a child's guardian are clearly stipulated in Article 822, and this forms the legal ground for justifying corporal punishment by a child's guardian. If the family unit works properly, and the good sense of a father and mother can be relied upon, the right to discipline cannot in most cases be questioned. However, in cases of child abuse, the major problem lies in the fact that the right to discipline is being misused under the pretext of administering acceptable home discipline to the child. Added to this is the fact that many parents involved in child abuse do not have any awareness that they are abusing their children. The existence of the right to discipline under the Civil Code leads to a situation in which the safeguarding of human rights and the welfare of the child are hindered. Therefore the provisions of the disciplinary rights should be abolished.

Exercising the forfeiture of parental rights by stages

As described above, for various reasons, loss of parental rights is a measure that is not actively used to separate a child from an abusive parent. In view of this, the Japanese bar association and others are proposing the legislation of a system for 'temporary suspension of parental rights',[31] not the absolute forfeiture of parental rights. If the measures only temporarily suspend parental rights, the parent in question will not have any fear that he or she will lose his or her child and such parent should be more cooperative. In addition, from the standpoint of the administration, it will be easy to oppose a child's parent if there is a legal endorsement of such measures. The Law on Parents and Children under the Civil Code should perhaps be revised to allow a declaration of temporary suspension of the rights of protection where the holder of parental rights cannot exercise them or where the welfare of the child is significantly injured because the exercise of parental rights is inappropriate.

In connection with the above, the plaintiffs in a case where an application is made for a temporary suspension of parental rights should be the child himself or herself (having a stipulated age, for example 15 or older), a relative of the child, a prosecutor and the head of a child guidance centre. The opinions of both the relative of the child and the child should be listened to during the procedures. Also no record should be made in the family register regarding the temporary suspension of parental rights. Furthermore, interviews of the parent and the child should be temporarily prohibited. The domicile should be reported to the relevant facilities. Any disruption to providing medical treatment for the child should be prohibited. If such individual orders can be issued by the family court, responses to cases of child abuse can be made more speedily. For example, for parents who stubbornly oppose blood transfusions for their children because of religious beliefs, a temporary suspension of parental rights in regard to the 'prohibition of disruption to provision of medical treatment' will be made. And, if there are measures of temporary suspension of the parental rights with regard to the 'return home of a child from the facilities', the facilities, too, can oppose the return of the child to the parent or guardian with confidence. Looking at the rights of the defendants, consideration should be given to the interests of the person vested with parental rights in cases where it has become possible for the parent to protect and educate the child. In such cases, after the period of temporary suspension is over, the parent or guardian should be able to petition for cancellation of the declaration of temporary suspension. If it is clearly prescribed that the period of temporary suspension of parental rights and the renewal thereof shall be left at the discretion of the family court and that, in a case of emergency, the procedures require no examination, the family court will be able to act quickly and flexibly to different situations. Thus it can be expected that such measures will be utilized more actively.

If the time comes when there is a variety of measures that can be taken – where advice and assistance can be provided while leaving the child in his or her home, where parental rights can be temporarily suspended by the judicial institution, and where parental rights can be completely forfeited – the response of the authorities to cases of child abuse will be remarkably improved in terms of both speed and flexibility.

Measures should be decided that balance the infringement of the human rights of the child against the effectiveness or otherwise of the measures of assistance, including the declaration of the loss of parental rights. It would also be necessary to review and utilize the measures of loss of parental rights from the viewpoint of the best interests of the child.

Forming a network for relief institutions

If child abuse is discovered, it should be necessary for those concerned – the staff of the child guidance centre, specialists, case workers, police officers, public health nurses, medical doctors, lawyers and others involved in the issue – to get together and hold a network session so that information can be exchanged to solve the problem.

At the private-sector level, the importance of horizontal relationships has already been realized and the formation of networks has already been tried. The 'Child Abuse Prevention Association' was inaugurated mostly by those involved in medical treatment and by lawyers in Osaka in 1990; and in Tokyo, the 'Child Abuse Prevention Centre' was established in 1991. In addition to the above, many other networks were formed in Japan. In April 1996, the nationwide Society for the Study of the Prevention of Child Abuse was launched. Bar associations in different regions are involved in activities including telephone consultation services and interviews for children and parents. This involvement comes through the establishment of the 'Children's Human Rights Tel. No. 110' (Tokyo Bar Association); the 'Children's Human Rights Relief Centre' (Tokyo Bar Association); and the 'Consultation Window for Children's Troubles' (the Second Tokyo Bar Association).

Responding to such moves, in fiscal year 1996, the Ministry of Health and Welfare started at an administrative level a case management model project in eight child guidance centres around the country.[32] The project is designed to provide a comprehensive framework in which the child guidance centre will be able to deal with difficult cases through collaboration with a team involving the welfare offices, medical doctors, lawyers, police officers and people involved with public health centres. It is hoped that these model projects will be generalized and effectively used. In Japan today a realistic approach is being initiated on the issue of child abuse, if a little belatedly.

CONCLUSION

It can be said that the widespread recognition of the child abuse issue as a social problem in Japan is just a recent phenomenon. The first reason for this is that the total number of cases of children being abused has increased and the causes of child abuse have changed. It should be noted that child abuse is not caused solely by poverty, but by a complexity of assorted factors such as fewer children, an increasing tendency towards the nuclear family, a decreased sense of responsibility to nurture children owing to double-income lifestyles and the loss of the guardian function in some communities. The second reason for the issue of child abuse having become a social problem is the increased awareness of human rights. Particularly with the signing and ratification of the Convention on the Rights of the Child, momentum has been given to an increased recognition that a child should not be simply seen as an object that is to be protected by its parents or society, but rather that a child has its own human rights and should be respected as an individual. Although it is said that a child should not be protected simply as one of the weak, a child can maintain his or her life, in practical terms, only by the protection of his or her parents at home. The life of the child depends primarily upon the protective and nurturing function of the family. However, in concrete terms, the rapid increase in the number of divorces is accelerating the collapse of the family unit, and the family that should protect its children is actually collapsing. Now the widespread recognition is that the problem of child abuse can no longer be solved through relying upon the protective function of the family, or by enhancing that function.

In the recent revision of the Child Welfare Law, efforts were made to form a network of consultative and assisting systems in regions through establishment of the Child and Family Support Centre, while strengthening measures for fatherless families. However, practical field work places an emphasis on the protection of the family as a unit rather than the protection of individual human rights in the family, since the system is structured on the reconstruction of the family unit. Actually, despite the fact that the original extended family structure has dissolved (even the structure of the nuclear family has been deteriorating) and that different forms of families have been created, the doctrine of traditional family harmony cannot be completely wiped out and, as a consequence, the protection of the human rights of the child is subordinated.

Looking at the parent–child relationship from a legal perspective, parental rights are still the dominating influences on a child. In their origin, the laws of Japan stand on the premises that a parent is a reasonable and rational object and Japanese law does not consider the existence of undesirable parents. In addition, the perception of a child as an independent, separate entity is weak. These two facts make it difficult to give relief to an abused child. Without a system that directly hears the voice of the child, an abused child will be the victim while the parents will continue to waive the flag of parental rights.

The relief of child abuse is the relief of failed families themselves, where the parents are not correctly performing their protective functions. As described above, the sense of autonomy of the family is as strong as in the Japanese family in the past. There is a tendency to exclude intervention in family affairs by the state or society as an infringement of privacy. However, from the perspective of safeguarding the human rights of the child as an individual currently being abused, relief should be pursued by exercising the force of the law. Laws should have some flexibility to be able to react to individual situations. We should not simply be satisfied with the policy of the reconstruction of the parent–child relationship, which is the one that is currently being carried out in most practical casework studies.

What Japan needs is the creation of a comprehensive system of laws and policies that would enable the state to become positively involved in the issues of child abuse.

NOTES

1 Seicho Matsumoto, *Kichiku* (Tokyo: Shincho Bunko, 1965); *Kichiku*, Shochiku Home Video (1992).

2   Article 822 of the Civil Code prescribes as follows:

   '1. A person who exercises parental rights can, in so far as it is necessary, personally chastise his or her child, or can, with the permission of the Family Court, place it in a disciplinary institution.
   2. The period for which a child is to be placed in a disciplinary institution shall be determined by the Family Court within six months or less; however, such period may be shortened by the Family Court at any time on the application of the person who exercises parental rights.'

   However, there exists no such 'disciplinary institution' (the correctional institution of the past) so there are many people who consider that this article should be deleted since it is likely to be abused.
3   In May 1997, in Kobe, an incident occurred in which a 14-year-old boy killed an 11-year-old boy, cut his head off and left it in front of the gate of his junior high school. The incident shocked everyone. With this event as a catalyst, public opinion is calling as never before for a stricter revision of the current juvenile law.
4   The serial murders of young girls committed by Tsutomu Miyazaki from the summer of 1988 to the summer of 1989 also shocked the public.
5   In the case of the 'Nakano Fujimi High School Bullying' (Judgment of Tokyo District Court on 27 March 1992, *Hanrei Jiho*, No. 1378: 26), the court denied the school's liability in proceedings brought by the mother of a 14-year-old schoolboy who had committed suicide because of bullying. After that, many suicides by schoolboys and schoolgirls occurred as a consequence of bullying at school. In view of this, the essence of school education has been called into question: Japanese education is based on a results-oriented principle that could create psychological stress among children.
6   Child Abuse Prevention Centre, *Jido no Gyakutai ni tsuite – Wareware wa Nani wo Nasubekika?* (About Child Abuse – What should we do now?), CA Textbook No. 5, p.1, 1992.
7   'Zenkoku Jido Sodansho ni okeru Kateinai Gyakutai Chosa Kekka Hokokusho' (Report on Results of Investigation Concerning Child Abuse in the Household Conducted by the National Child Guidance Centre)', compiled by the Executive Office of the National Society of Heads of Child Guidance Centres, *Zenjiso*, **62**, Supplement, June 1997.
8   For example, according to a statistical report by the Ministry of Health and Welfare, the numbers of consultations conducted concerning child abuse in the whole country were 1101 for 1990; 1171 for 1991; 1372 for 1992; 1611 for 1993; 1961 for 1994 and 2722 for 1995. However, the above statistics do not include abandoned babies, failure to protect children and children being prevented from attending school.
9   *Kodomo Hakusho* (*White Paper on Children*), compiled by the Association for Child Protection (Tokyo: Sodo Bunka, 1996) p.288.
10 *21 Seiki Oyako-Ho e* (*Parent and Child Law for the 21st Century*) Shuhei Ninomiya and Fujiko Sakakibara (Tokyo: Yuhikaku, 1996) p.146.
11 The Convention on the Rights of the Child, art. 7, para. 1.
12 Ibid., art. 9, para. 1.
13 Society for the Study of the Prevention of Child Abuse, *Kodomo no Gyakutai Boshi* (Prevention of Child Abuse) (Tokyo: Toki Shobo, 1993), p.35.
14 Aum Shinrikyo shocked the whole of the country. Aum is a new religious cult and has many criminal and civil cases pending against it in the courts. It is suspected of manufacturing poison gas in its facilities, abducting and murdering the family of

lawyer Sakamoto in November 1989, the Matsumoto sarin incident in June 1994 and the Tokyo subway sarin incident in March 1995. Many believers of Aum were living together in the vast facilities of the religious group and their children were receiving special religious education from the teachers of the cult at these facilities, separated from their parents and not being allowed to go to school even though they were of school age.

15 Sadayoshi Kitamura, 'Aum no Kodomotachi no Ichiji Hogo' (Temporary Protection of the Children of Aum), *Seishonen Mondai* (Juvenile Problems), **42** (12): 21, December 1995.

16 According to the report on the results of the investigation conducted by the National Society of Heads of Child Guidance Centres in 1996, out of 2061 reports of child abuse, the number of reports concerning temporary protection was 844 (41.8 per cent). Classified by causes, 49.0 per cent of cases requiring temporary protection were of 'sexual abuse' and 48.4 per cent were of 'psychological abuse'; thus these two causes accounted for the great majority of cases.

17 The purpose of the nursery, the 'infant protection institute' is to provide a domicile for infants who have not reached two years of age, in cases where it is difficult to foster the infants with guardians. These infants are not only orphans: in recent years, infants with parents account for as much as 90 per cent of those admitted. According to June 1995 statistics, the number of infants protected in infant protection institutes throughout the country was 2552.

18 The child care centre is one of the child welfare facilities established for the reception and protection of children, other than infants who have no guardians, who are being abused and whose environment is not favourable. According to June 1995 statistics, the number of children protected in child care centres throughout the country was 25 237.

19 Depending upon the characteristics of the children, some of them may be admitted to facilities for the treatment of short-term emotionally handicapped children, others to various other facilities for handicapped children.

20 The ideal is that these abused children will be protected by foster parents and be given great affection, if possible. But in Japan at present there are very few candidates for foster parents. The number of children placed with foster parents, as of the end of 1994, was only 2475, which was less than one-tenth of those children left in the protection facilities.

21 According to the results of the report on the investigation conducted by the National Society of Heads of Child Guidance Centres in 1996, out of 2061 reports of child abuse, the number of children where it was considered necessary for them to be admitted to the facilities was 968. Of these, the proportion of children whose parents readily gave consent for admission was 51.2 per cent, and that for children whose parents gave consent after a special effort was made was 21.6 per cent, making the total for the two categories 72.8 per cent. The actual admission rate was 73.6 per cent. On the other hand, the proportion of cases in which guidance was given while the children remained at home was 18.3 per cent; the figures were 6.2 per cent for cases in which both consent and contact were rejected and in which difficulties in correspondence were associated, while 2.0 per cent of the cases were those in which no consent was obtained and admission was being sought through application to the family court.

Although the number of cases admitted was 649, almost half of these cases had problems at their homes after their admission. In the meantime, of the cases in which the reason for admitting the children was 'inadequate protection', there was a greater percentage of cases with indifference on the part of the parents, refusal to take the children home and cases where the parents' whereabouts were unknown.

22 According to the morning edition of the *Yomiuri* of 3 July 1997, the Ministry of Health and Welfare announced its policy of the active implementation of the Child Welfare Law by issuing a circular from the Child Household Bureau declaring that, 'The protection rights of the directors of facilities should have priority over those of the parents.' Because of this circular it is now easier for child guidance centres to confront parents who are abusing their children.
23 The number of petitions submitted to the family court for admission to the facilities during the period 1987 to 1994 was on average seven a year. The number of affirmative judgments was on average only five a year.
24 With regard to parental rights, see Yukiko Matsushima, 'Controversies and Dilemmas: Japan Confronts the Convention', in M.D.A. Freeman (ed.), *Children's Rights: A Comparative Perspective* (Aldershot: Dartmouth, 1996) p.129.
25 Atsuhiro Kinoshita, 'Gyakutai Mondai kara Kazoku wo Miru' (Child Abuse Issue from the Perspective of the Household), *Jiyu to Seigi* (*Liberty and Justice*) **47** (9): 84, September 1996.
26 The registration system of Japan is a detailed recording system of family relationships which is unique in the world and its importance and impact on the people of Japan are great. However, its nature is rather difficult to understand for people of other countries.
27 *Kateisaiban Geppo* (*Monthly Bulletin on Family Courts*) **32** (1): 166.
28 Article 25 of the Child Welfare Law prescribes: 'A person who finds a child who has no guardian or a child who is inappropriately protected by his or her guardian shall inform a welfare office or Child Guidance Centre about the child.'
29 In Japan a nurse (*kangofu*) usually works at a hospital. A public health nurse (*hokenfu*) is a public servant and works at a public health centre (which provides health care to those in lower-income groups).
30 For example, some reports indicate that half of the reports were proved to be groundless suspicion, such as cases in which teachers, medical doctors, public health nurses and others who were afraid of being charged with the violation of their reporting duties reported some cases involving only the slightest suspicions. In others, neighbours formed hasty conclusions, and in one case parents believed the fabricated story of a child who reported being abused by a schoolteacher. See op. cit., note 10, p.149.

For a book that introduced the reporting laws of the USA and tried to compare them with the laws of Japan, see Norio Higuchi, *Oyako to Ho* (*Laws of Parent and Child*) (Tokyo: Kobundo, 1988, pp.94–121.
31 For example, *Kodomotachi no Egao ga Miemasuka?* (*Can You See the Smiles of Children?*), Report of the Symposium of the Japan Federation of Bar Associations, p.77, 1991.
32 In addition to the above, *Kodomo Gyakutai Boshi no Tebiki* (*The Guide to the Prevention of Child Abuse*) was published under the supervision of the Child Household Bureau of the Ministry of Health and Welfare in March 1997 and distributed among institutions concerned with child welfare as well as educational, health and medical institutions. This illustrates that the administrative agencies are in recent years taking more positive measures towards the prevention of child abuse.

12 Child Abuse and Neglect: A Malaysian Perspective

Zaleha Kamaruddin

INTRODUCTION

The death of 17-month-old Norshafiqah Maswari in 1989 shocked the Malaysian nation,[1] and the fact that her injuries were afflicted under the care of a child minder was cause for concern. Enough concern to have Datuk Syed Hamid Albar, the Law Minister (as he was then) to study a proposal to make the death penalty mandatory for those convicted of causing the death of children through abuse.[2] But Norshafiqah's case is not the first case of child abuse to end in death. In 1990, baby Balasundram died of multiple injuries caused by his mother's boyfriend.[3] A year after that, two-year-old Mohamad Afiq also died after being brutally abused by his 28-year-old father.[4] These are a few of the incidents which were highlighted by the media, and, fortunately, it was these reported incidents which acted as the catalyst in prompting the government to introduce the Child Protection Act in 1991 (hereinafter referred to as the Act).[5] This Act is an epitome of Malaysian legislative prowess for it has transcended the boundaries of a mere description of the circumstances in which a child is in need of protection to a reasoned definition of the major aspects of child abuse itself. Since the introduction of this Act, numerous actions have been taken in an effort to curb child abuse.[6] Malaysian society has now become more conscious of this social problem. However, the extent of the problem throughout the country is not known.

This chapter examines four aspects. First, there is a brief historical background of the discovery of the social problem and how the problems are defined in Malaysia; second, the main areas of concern of child abuse are examined; third, the chapter considers how the legal system in Malaysia responds to child abuse, examining in particular the different approaches with which related institutions respond to the problems. The fourth aspect is the assessment of the success or otherwise of the measures being taken to solve the problem.

HISTORICAL BACKGROUND OF THE DISCOVERY OF THE PROBLEM

Malaysia, a multiracial country of 20 million people,[7] consists of three major races, Malays, Chinese and Indians, and a number of other races and tribes which have their own distinct social and cultural practices. Even the attitude towards children and child-rearing practices differs significantly from one race to another. As a developing nation, Malaysia has a relatively high child population of about 42 per cent, of which 52 per cent are males and 48 per cent are females; this also reflects a high dependency ratio.[8] The major socioeconomic consequence of a young population is a substantial demand for social services, especially regarding health, education and welfare.

Incidence of child abuse

Child abuse is not a new phenomenon in Malaysia, although public and professional awareness has only been awakened in recent years.[9] Datuk Ahmad Ragib's[10] statement that child abuse has been on the increase over the previous two years[11] confirmed that child abuse and neglect is a growing social problem. The higher incidence was not due solely to an increase in reports, but also to greater awareness among victims of their rights. However, any exact assessment of the number of cases is difficult to get because of the hideous nature of the crime in question. The Department of Social Welfare keeps a record of cases reported to it but those working in the field realize that this is only the tip of the iceberg, as most cases are not reported to the authorities concerned. One should also be cautioned against thinking that cases of child abuse and neglect in Malaysia are now decreasing. Dr Mohd Sham[12] warned that any figures on child abuse should not be taken at face value, as there were many unreported cases of abuse. He explained that, for misplaced reasons of shame, guilt and even pity for the culprit, the victims rarely speak out.[13]

Statistics collected and compiled by the Department of Social Welfare show that the Federal Territory of Kuala Lumpur records the highest incidence of child abuse in Malaysia. This figure confirms that, since most of the socioeconomic activities are concentrated in this major city, which leads to overcrowding in the slums and in the high-rise flats, it is inevitable that child abuse and neglect will occur, given the social and environmental conditions prevalent. The incidence will continue to increase unless these conditions are reversed.[14] The figures at present show a remarkable upward trend.

A few observations can also be made in respect of the figures shown in Table 12.1. First, these figures may not be truly representative of the realities of child abuse in Malaysia. The fact that there were fewer cases of abuse in the early 1980s does not necessarily mean that the problem existed only in negligible proportions during those years and has suddenly grown dramatically in recent years. Over the years, Malaysian social feeling has grown against child abuse and exploitation, which in turn has exerted increasing pressure on the law enforcement agencies to keep a closer eye on child abuse situations. The sharp increase in reported cases of child abuse can thus plausibly be referred to this factor. However, it cannot be determined conclusively whether the increasing incidence of reported cases and neglect is attributable to improvements in detection and reporting efficiency, or to increasingly declining standards of family care. Second, owing to the limitations inherent in the situation, child abuse cases remain drastically under-reported. Third, the cases reported are those with overt signs of abuse; many cases of emotional abuse and neglect remained undetected and unreported. The figures in Table 12.1, as they are, demonstrate clearly that child abuse has emerged as a serious social problem calling for remedial measures.

In another piece of research, it was pointed out that, although child abuse exists in all racial and income groups, the incidence is more pronounced among the Malays and low income earners.[15] These figures were consistent with figures documented by the Suspected Child Abuse and Neglect (SCAN) Team at the Kuala Lumpur Hospital.[16] According to statistics compiled by the SCAN Team, the victim's natural father has been the culprit in 24.5 per cent of all physical abuse cases reported between 1985 and 1996. The natural mother comes in next, at 19.1 per cent. In most cases , neither parent had any intention of deliberately hurting their child. However, in cases of sexual abuse, the most common culprit is neither parent, nor relative, but a miscellany of other people who come into contact with the child, for example, the child minder.[17]

A study on the personality profile of child abusers conducted at the Kuala Lumpur General Hospital and the University Hospital found that 40 per cent of the perpetrators interviewed had a diagnosable psychiatric disorder.[18] Another interesting study made by Dr Haliza showed that an infant child of a drug addict mother is a very high-risk candidate for abuse. She added that, although the present child protection system is assisting in identifying them, and providing short-term intervention, this system is still deficient in long-term monitoring and rehabilitation.[19]

Table 12.1 Child abuse and neglect cases, 1985–95

State	1985	1986	1987	1988	1989	1990	1991	1992	1993	1994	1995
Johore	6	4	19	18	16	25	75	115	134	127	134
Kedah	3	4	7	4	6	11	10	14	15	15	21
Kelantan	2	3	2	1	1	3	5	7	1	6	7
Melaka	0	15	11	22	14	33	29	6	73	47	73
N. Sembilan	7	4	9	11	5	21	24	31	16	54	74
Pahang	1	3	0	3	5	6	12	7	24	29	24
Perak	2	20	17	22	19	52	62	57	77	86	131
Perlis	0	0	2	4	3	2	4	2	3	6	8
P. Pinang	9	12	7	25	31	29	33	30	62	57	72
Selangor	15	55	28	41	50	120	356	245	269	250	246
Terengganu	0	1	2	0	0	1	12	13	24	17	21
W.P.K.L.	27	50	45	40	126	208	348	293	386	140	306
W.P. Labuan	NA	NA	0	0	0	0	0	0	0	2	0
Total	72	171	149	191	276	511	970	820	1,084	836	1,117

Source: Department of Social Welfare, Malaysia.

Categories of Child Abuse

There are many and varied types of child abuse and neglect, both physical and behavioural. However, for identification purposes, the Act sets out the circumstances under which a child is in need of protection. They are as follows:[20]

a. the child has been or there is substantial risk that the child will be physically injured or emotionally injured or sexually abused by his guardian;

b. the child has been or there is substantial risk that the child will be physically injured or emotionally injured or sexually abused and his guardian, knowing of such injury or abuse or risk, has not protected or is unlikely to protect the child from such injury or abuse;

c. the guardian of the child is unfit, or has neglected or is unable, to exercise proper supervision and control over the child and the child is falling into bad association, or is exposed to moral danger, or is beyond control;

d. the guardian of the child has neglected or is unwilling to provide for him adequate care, food, clothing and shelter;

e. the child has no guardian, or has been abandoned by his guardian and after reasonable inquiries the guardian cannot be found, and no other suitable person is willing and able to care for the child;

f. the child needs to be examined, investigated or treated for the purpose of restoring or preserving his health and his guardian neglects or refuses to have him so examined, investigated or treated;

g. the child behaves in a manner that is, or is likely to be, harmful to himself or to any other person and his guardian is unable or unwilling to take necessary measures to remedy the situation or the remedial measures taken by the guardian fail;

h. there is such a conflict between the child and his guardian, or between his guardians, that family relationships are seriously disrupted, thereby causing him emotional injury;

i. the child is a person in respect of whom any of the offences mentioned in chapter xvi of the Penal Code or any offence of the nature described in Part VI has been or is believed to have been committed and his guardian is the person who committed such offence or has not protected or is unlikely to protect him from such offence;

j. the child is —
    (i) a member of the same household as the child referred to in para (i) or
    (ii) a member of the same household of the person who has been convicted of the offence referred to in para (i),
    and appears to be in danger of the commission upon or in respect of him of a similar offence and his guardian is the person who committed or is believed to have committed the offence or who is convicted of such offence or his guardian is unable or unwilling to protect him from such offence;

k. the child is found begging.

Thus the circumstances where the law can intervene to provide state care and protection to an affected child are wide and varied. They range from such a neglect as would impede the child's development as a moral being to such serious situations as the commission of offences punishable by the criminal law. Once it is found that any of the circumstances described under (a) to (k) exists, it may be assumed that the child needs state protection.

The SCAN Team in its 1996 *Annual Report* lists six categories of child abuse:

a. Physical Abuse
Physical abuse is when parents or adults deliberately inflict injuries on a child. It includes hitting, shaking, squeezing, burning or biting. It also includes using excessive force when feeding, changing or handling a child. Giving a child poisonous substances, inappropriate drugs or alcohol and attempting to suffocate or drown a child are also examples of child abuse.

b. Sexual Abuse
Sexual abuse takes place when an adult forces a child to take part in a sexual activity, using the child to satisfy his or her own sexual desires. This can involve sexual intercourse, fondling, masturbation, oral sex, anal intercourse or exposing children to pornographic videos, books, magazines or other material.

c. Physical Neglect
Neglect occurs when parents fail to meet their child's essential needs, such as adequate food, clothing, warmth and medical care. Leaving children who are too young to look after themselves alone or without proper supervision is also an example of neglect.

d. Emotional Abuse/Neglect
Emotional abuse is when parents continuously fail to show their child love or affection, or when they threaten, taunt or shout at a child, causing him or her to lose confidence and self-esteem and to become nervous or withdrawn.

e. Street Child
A child who spends all or part of his time regularly on the streets. He may or may not have contact with his parents or guardians and may or may not go home at night.

f. Child Labour
A child who may be involved in hazardous employment or in one where his/her schooling and development is affected.

These definitions are used by the SCAN Team in the detection and identification of child abuse and neglect cases at the Kuala Lumpur Hospital. They are in line with what has been defined under the Act. The Act gives definitions of physical, emotional and sexual abuse. It provides as follows:[21]

(a) a child is physically injured if there is substantial and observable injury to any part of the child's body as a result of the non-accidental application of force or an agent to the child's body that is evidenced by, amongst other things, a laceration, a contusion, an abrasion, a scar, a fracture or other bone injury, a dislocation, a sprain, haemorrhaging, the rupture of a viscus, a burn, a scald, the loss or alteration of consciousness or physiological functioning or the loss of hair or teeth;

(b) a child is emotionally injured if there is substantial and observable impairment of the child's mental or emotional functioning that is evidenced by, amongst other things, a mental or behavioural disorder, including anxiety, depression, withdrawal, aggression or delayed development;

(c) a child is sexually abused if he has taken part, whether as a participant or an observer, in any activity which is sexual in nature for the purposes of any pornographic, obscene or indecent material, photograph, recording, film, videotape or performance or for the purpose of sexual exploitation by any person for that person's or another person's sexual gratification.

From the above, we can deduce that the definitions prescribed by the Act are more comprehensive than those given by SCAN. In fact, the circumstances prescribed by the Act under which a child can be said to be in need of protection and a definition of the composite parts of the elusive expression 'child abuse' would pose no problem to those who enforce the Act to act in a just and fair manner.[22]

THE MAIN AREAS OF CONCERN OF CHILD ABUSE

The Child Abuse Team at the University Hospital, Kuala Lumpur documented that, over the past few years, there has been an alarming rise in the number of children admitted for possible sexual abuse. A retrospective study (January 1993–June 1996) was conducted to examine the extent of sexual abuse locally. The study shows that children under 16 years of age (54 per cent), schoolchildren (61 per cent), those from a poor socioeconomic background (93 per cent) and Malays (53 per cent) were strongly represented. Most events occurred at night (59 per cent) while drug usage accounted for slightly less than 20 per cent of cases. Physical force was used in two-thirds of the cases. Similarly, two-thirds of the cases involved a single act of penetrative sexual assault and one perpetrator, with 45 per cent of the perpetrators being known to the victims. The study also showed that certain psychosocial factors are considered associated with risks of sexual abuse which can be remedied by early supportive psychotherapy.[23]

Dr Mary J. Marrett, in her report on sexual abuse in children seen at the University Hospital, stated that a significant number of abuses occur in the context of disrupted families, sometimes with multiple victims. Her experience also shows that it is uncommon to find any physical injuries, as many of the victims may be enticed with bribes, or threatened verbally, rather than there being the use of force and the victim being too frightened to struggle. Many cases involve molestation not amounting to rape, presenting with a consistent and highly suggestive history but leaving no physical injuries. The majority of cases are seen several hours or days after the event, so there is no fresh evidence available. Unfortunately, this lack of physical evidence often leads some members of law enforcement agencies and even relatives to the misconception that no assault has taken place, or that no harm has been done. Too often the focus shifts away from the effects on the child. Efforts are made to protect the perpetrator instead, hampering efforts to take remedial action.[24]

The present trend is that most of the rape cases are of an incestuous nature. Owing to the seriousness of this problem, a conference was held in 1995 to highlight the issues and the problems of management encounted when handling 'intrafamilial sexual abuse' cases, the effects of abuse on the child and the repercussions on the family involved. It was concluded that most cases are not brought to court because of the unavailability of corroborative evidence needed for prosecution. And, in court, the suspected abuser is often released, either because the abused child refused to testify or is too frightened to do so, or the testimony is not accepted as evidence.[25]

In relation to investigation, the police encountered more difficulties due to delays in reporting by the victims, reluctant witnesses and retraction of statements to police.[26] With the recent Federal Court decision in *Arupragasam v. PP*, where judges ruled that the prosecution has to prove its case beyond reasonable doubt before an accused can be called to enter his defence, the police will have to push harder in their investigation to obtain evidence to prove the guilt of the accused.[27]

The matter is further complicated by the fact that victims of sexual abuse are said to be examined by medical officers who have no training at all in clinical forensic medicine. It was further pointed out that medical examination of the alleged sexual abuse victim would require sound knowledge and experience, together with a clear understanding of relevant laws. These factors are essential in examining and interpreting the various findings. In addition, no suitable facilities are available to conduct an efficient and scientifically foolproof medical examination of sexual abuse victims. Examinations are usually carried out in a haphazard manner, without any uniformity, each doctor doing it his own way, which is not necessarily the correct way. Non-availability of a sexual examination kit is certainly a factor which hampers a proper examination.[28]

Another significant phenomenon in sexual abuse cases is under-reporting. This is due to societal discrimination against people who have been sexually abused. Lack of specialized 'one stop' centres for the sexually abused and cultural taboos in relation to 'losing face' are added factors of under-reporting. Therefore, unless the health care providers are sensitive to the problems faced by these patients, the provision of care may never be optimal.[29] Gill Raja contends that society has to overcome this problem by directing its energy to creating a supporting environment which encourages children to disclose abusive situations, shows understanding of their varied reactions and needs, and is willing to discuss the multiple factors which lead to people sexually abusing children.[30] Hospital University, Kuala Lumpur has done a commendable job by setting up since 1986 a multi-discipline team, called the INSAM (Intervention for Sexual Abuse and Molestation) team, to provide crisis intervention for victims, helping them to minimize their emotional and social stress while awaiting and receiving treatment.[31]

The Department of Social Welfare and a number of voluntary organizations have also established various institutions for children who need to be placed outside their families. Care in institutions includes the provision of basic care facilities, formal and informal education, social and recreational facilities, vocational training and spiritual and religious education aimed at total development in respect of physical, social, cognitive, emotional and moral qualities. In meeting the emotional needs of these children, the department has embarked on a programme of foster care and adoption, if it is necessary to provide better care and upbringing in an atmosphere of family life, which provide love, security and continuity of care.[32]

LEGAL RESPONSES

The Child Protection Act 1991 (the Act) came into operation in March 1992. It is based on the assumption that, although the child's welfare is a family affair, law must come forward to extend its protection in case of neglect and abuse. It is stated that the Act is comprehensive in coverage, and has incorporated detailed provisions with a view not only to protecting a child from direct physical, emotional or sexual abuse but also to saving the child from neglect in a wide variety of situations.[33]

The Act provides four basic innovations.

1. It defines the circumstances in which a child[34] will be entitled to state protection and care.
2. It provides for an administrative machinery for detecting and reporting cases of abuse and neglect, and taking care and custody of the abused child.
3. It defines what protection the state will give to a child who is abused or neglected.
4. It declares certain acts as punishable offences, and also prescribes the quantum of punishment.

Administrative machinery

The Act has made provisions for the establishment of an administrative machinery responsible for providing help in cases of need. This includes protectors, a coordinating council and child protection teams.

Protectors

The power to ensure that a child receives protection from abuse and neglect is vested in the hands of the police and protectors. Section 13 of the Act authorizes any protector who is satisfied on reasonable grounds that a child is in need of protection to take the child into temporary custody or present the child before a medical officer for medical examination or treatment if needed. The protector is also empowered under section 38 to search, after obtaining a search warrant from a magistrate, any premises for the purpose of ascertaining whether there is any child who is in need of protection or whether any offence punishable by the Act is being, or has been, committed. The protector may also use force if authorized by a magistrate. He can also arrest any person from such premises if they are suspected of having committed an offence. A protector is defined in s.2 as the director general, the deputy director general, a divisional director general of social welfare, Ministry of National Unity and Community Development, and the state director of social welfare of each state. In addition, under s.3, the minister may appoint any officer in the public service to exercise the powers and perform the duties of a protector.

Coordinating Council

The Act provides for the setting up of a council, to be known as the Coordinating Council for the Protection of Children.[35] The purpose of the council includes advising the minister in charge of the Ministry of National Unity and Community Development on various aspects of child protection. The council has the power and duty to design an effective management system throughout the country incorporating information channels for reporting cases of children in need of protection, to recommend establishment of services specifically oriented to meet the needs of children and families in need of child protection services, to coordinate the resources of such government departments involved in child protection, to develop programmes to educate people in the prevention of child abuse and neglect, and to supervise the management, operation and practice of child protection teams throughout the country. Apart from the director general, the council composition includes the deputy director general of the Ministry of National Unity and Community Development, the Ministries of health, education, human resources, information, representatives of the Attorney General and the inspector general of police, and also representatives of the states of Sabah and Sarawak.

Child protection teams

The Coordinating Council is required by the Act to establish, throughout the country, groups of persons to be known as 'child protection teams' for the purpose of coordinating locally-based services to families and children in need of protection.[36] The members of the team are the state director of social welfare or the district social welfare officer as chairman, a senior police officer and a medical officer who can organize preventive, rehabilitative and supportive services, for families and children who are in need of protection. Other functions of the teams are mentioned in the Child Protection Team (Procedures and Practice) Regulations, 1995.

In practice, the child protection team issues clear protocols on the procedure for management right from the time of contact of the medical staff with the children and parents at the Accident and Emergency Room and outpatient clinic. The cornerstone of the team approach to management is the team conference, which must take place before the discharge of a child suspected of abuse. Although the team members are from different disciplinary backgrounds, the focus on critical decisions enables them to work towards the best interest of the individual child while recognizing the strength and weakness of the family members and available social and community resources. The team also function as supervisors, with each individual team member having a different supervisory function. Members of the team may be called by the police to give evidence in some of those cases where the police may decide on legal action. With the close liaison with the team member who represents the police, team members are able to accept that, apart from the therapeutic role, the clinical team member can provide clinical evidence which can assist the police in their investigations. The child protection team gradually involved adolescents, including those managed by the medical social workers dealing with alleged rape and sexual molestation in the INSAM (intervention for sexual abuse and molestation) team and the University Hospital. In the 1980s, responding to the nation's increased recognition of preventive and legal actions, an additional Child Protection Committee, a sub-committee of the University Hospital Medical Advisory Committee, was formed.[37]

Another policy of the Act is that, whenever a case of neglect or abuse is reported, the child should be, as far as is practicable, removed from the custody of the parent or guardian in order to save the child from future neglect or abuse. The child should then be given into the custody of an appropriate person, and a court should determine whether the circumstances warrant imposition of any liability or punishment upon the parent or guardian. The question of custody arises at two stages: first, where the child has to be taken into custody for a temporary period pending decision by a juvenile court, and second, where the court feels that the child should be given back into the custody of the parent but needs protection under the care and custody of someone else.[38]

The protector or police officer, if satisfied that a child is in need of protection, may take the child into temporary custody, and place him or her in a place of safety until such time as the child can be brought before the juvenile court. But under s.14 of the Act, if the child is in need of medical examination or treatment then the child should be taken by the protector or police officer to a medical officer for treatment, and not to a place of safety. The protector or police officer may authorize treatment of the child if the illness, injury or condition is minor, but has to obtain the written consent of the guardian if the illness, injury or condition is serious. If it is not possible to secure consent, the protector or police may authorize treatment. The director general of social welfare is required under s.18 to have care and control of the child during the period of hospitalization. Upon discharge from the hospital, the child has to be placed in a place of safety until such time as he or she can be brought before the juvenile court.

A child taken into temporary custody has to be produced before a juvenile court within 24 hours of being so taken into custody. The rationale behind this measure is to allow the judicial authority within a short period to examine the problem and decide the following action. If a child is medically examined, treated or hospitalized, the requirement is that the child should be produced after the completion of such examination, treatment or discharge from the hospital. If it is not possible to bring the child to the juvenile court, the child should be brought before a magistrate, within 24 hours, who may direct that the child should be placed in a place of safety or committed to the care of a fit person until the time the child can be brought before a juvenile court.[39]

The juvenile court is given wide powers for protecting a neglected or abused child. The nature of protections given would depend on the degree of seriousness of the individual case. The court is directed to endeavour to obtain such information on the family background, general conduct, home surroundings, school record and medical history of the child as may enable it to deal with the case in the best interest of the child. The court may ask the guardian to furnish a written undertaking that he or she will in future exercise proper care and guardianship. Alternatively, the court may place the child in the custody of a fit person, such as a family member. It may also place the child under the supervision of a protector or some other person appointed by the court; or it may direct the child to be placed in a place of safety, for a maximum period of three years, or until the child attains the age of 18. The child may also be committed to the custody of a foster parent. But in all cases of custody, the maximum period cannot exceed 18 years. The court is also empowered to impose conditions or give directions as it may find appropriate for the purpose of ensuring the safety and the well-being of the child in respect of whom a custody order is made. Further, no order will be made by the court without giving the guardian a right to be heard.[40]

The minister is also empowered by s.49 to make regulations providing for the care, maintenance and education of children placed in the custody, care and control of a person, and for the duties of such person. Regulations may also provide for the control, care, detention, temporary absence, maintenance and education of children in places of safety, and for the procedure and practice to be followed by child protection teams.

Punishment

The general attitude of the public is that the abusers must be prosecuted and punished. The Third Asian Conference on Child Abuse and Neglect suggested severe punishment for those found guilty of sexual exploitation and child trafficking. Some of the members of Parliament who took part in the 1991 debate suggested that the abuser, upon conviction, be given a stroke of the cane.[41] But the reality is that only a few are prosecuted and fewer get convicted.[42] Among the factors that lead to the unsuccessful prosecution of child abuses cases are inefficiency and insufficiency of police investigations, violation of rights of the accused in terms of police procedure and investigation, lack of proper police documentation of facts, poor testimony on the part of the witnesses in court, poor expert evidence and unreliable or uncorroborated evidence tendered in court.[43]

The quantum of punishment under the Act depends on the gravity of the offence. Section 26 provides that 'any person who, having the care of a child, abuses, neglects, abandons or exposes the child in a manner likely to cause him physical or emotional injury or causes or permits him to be abused, neglected, abandoned or exposed shall be liable to a maximum punishment or fine of RM10,000 or imprisonment for five years, or both.' However, the court, in lieu of or in addition to the above punishment may order the person to execute a bond of good behaviour and also to undergo such counselling and psychotherapy as the court may specify.

Section 27 provides that any person who causes any child, or any person having the care of a child who allows that child, to be on any street, premises or place for the purpose of begging shall be liable to a maximum fine of RM5,000 or imprisonment for two years, or both. The Act also punishes trafficking in children. If any person takes part in any transaction, the object of which is to transfer the possession, custody or control of a child or to bring a child into Malaysia with fraudulent means, he or she shall be liable to punishment of a maximum fine of RM10 000 or imprisonment for five years, or both.[44]

A former Supreme Court judge is of the opinion that the court's role in such cases should be to impose comparatively heavy sentences of imprisonment on the offenders when found guilty of a crime against children. The sentences should reflect the public's abhorrence of such crimes, aided in most cases by coverage in the mass media.[45]

Other related laws

Besides the Act, there are a number of laws which contain specific provisions dealing with the protection, maintenance and well-being of children. Such legal provisions that are made to secure the interest of the children, are briefly as follows.

1. The Penal Code, 1960 contains several provisions aimed specifically at protecting the life and limb of children. It is culpable homicide to cause the death of a living child, and culpable homicide becomes murder if the act by which death is caused is done with the intention of causing death. Other offences include infanticide, causing miscarriage, preventing a child being born alive or causing it to die after birth, causing death of a live unborn child, exposure and abandonment of a child under 12 years by parent or person having care of him or her, concealment of birth by secret disposal of a dead body, kidnapping from lawful guardianship (male under 14 years and female under 16 years), selling a minor for purposes of prostitution for persons under 21 years, buying a minor for the purposes of prostitution, rape for women with or without consent under 16 years and if she is a wife under 13 years old. Offences involving bodily injury apply to children as they do to adults.
2. The Children and Young Persons (Employment) Act 1966 prohibits children from being employed in hard and hazardous work. The law seeks to protect working children from exploitation and lays down certain basic requirements as to the type of work in which a young person may be employed, hours of work, and working conditions.
3. The Guardianship of Infants Act 1961 (Revised 1988), which applies only to Peninsular Malaysia and does not apply to Muslims unless adopted by the legislature in a state, essentially determines the question as to who will be the guardian of an infant (any person below 18) in certain cases.
4. The Law Reform (Marriage and Divorce) Act 1976 empowers the relevant court to determine the question of the custody of a child in a case of parental divorce. The law further provides that, when deciding the issue of custody, the paramount consideration should be the welfare of the child.
5. The Married Women and Children (Maintenance) Act, 1950 (Revised 1981) provides that, where a person neglects or refuses to maintain his legitimate child, a court can order such person to make a monthly allowance for the maintenance of the child. The Married Women and Children (Enforcement of Maintenance) Act 1968 (Revised 1988) which complements the previous law, provides that failure to comply with the court's order empowers the court to make another order to attach that person's earnings, including wages, salary, any other emoluments, pension or gratuity.
6. The Adoption Act, 1952 protects and takes care of the interest of any adopted child. It also regulates the practice of adoption and protects the child from exploitation. Any adoption should be made through the court, where the law places certain restrictions to ensure total protection.

7 The Care Centres Act 1993 gives power to the government to regulate child care centres.

It appears from the above discussion that there are adequate laws to protect children from exploitation and abuse. But the need of the hour is to ensure the effective implementation of these laws.

CONCLUSION

Child abuse is nowadays being highlighted as an undesirable phenomenon of modern-day stressful living. It is one of the indicators that our traditional values are being eroded. The government's aim is to prosper without sacrificing the values we grew up with and to share them with our children. Therefore there is a dire need to strengthen family values, as the present progress in Malaysia has created influences which threaten the foundations of Malaysian society. Child abuse is a result of a very deep-rooted problem within a family. Therefore, unless we deal with the root problem, there will always be child abuse cases constantly reported. We have short- and long-term solutions. Short-term solutions are made to deal with the issue at hand, whereas long-term solutions aim to address the root problems within a family unit.

Short-term solutions

Multi-agency approach

Curbing child abuse requires a combined effort. It is not limited to a particular government department or individual. Concerted effort by all parties, from neighbours to government agencies, should promote a multi-agency approach so that all concerned would work together in addressing the problem. There should be better coordination and cooperation amongst the major agencies involved, especially health, social welfare and police. This cooperation should start the moment a case of child abuse is detected, with the initiative taken by the first agency involved. It is suggested that the medical team should coordinate the case when the victim is hospitalized, and the social worker should coordinate rehabilitation when the child is discharged. Multi-agency training of all staff members should also be organized to ensure an understanding of the importance of cooperation and coordination. Manpower should be increased, especially that of social workers, which is needed to handle the reported increase in cases of child abuse.

To ensure detection and proper management of abuse cases, it is suggested that a Suspected Child Abuse and Neglect (SCAN) Team should be set up in all hospitals throughout the country. Non-governmental organizations (NGOs) and child protection teams must be involved in the detection and the rehabilitation, counselling and follow-up of cases.[46]

Mandatory reporting

The suggestion of the mandatory reporting by the public in child abuse cases was made during the debate in Parliament. In response, the government argued that enforcement would be very difficult and stated that the free-of-charge TELEDERA service is sufficient for the public to make their reports. However, a conference attended by experts on child abuse stated that this is inadequate. The conference also passed a resolution that it should be made mandatory for teachers, social workers and police to report child abuse cases. Those failing to report should be fined RM1000 because, under the Act, only doctors are at present bound to report. The requirement to report applies where the medical practitioner believes that a child under treatment or examination is 'physically or emotionally injured as a result of being ill-treated, neglected, abandoned or exposed'. This is a very important section of the Act because it provides for an early detection of cases of child abuse and neglect. Furthermore, notification is made simpler by just filing a standard form. Under the same section, a government medical officer may take the child into temporary custody until such time as the temporary custody of the child is assumed by a protector or police officer.

The conference also pointed out that more than half of the children who died were not examined by medical personnel. It was suggested that medical personnel examine and determine the cause of all children's deaths. Child protection team members should be given special training so that they could spot an abused child immediately. It was also suggested that team members be allowed to recommend to the court the kind of punishment or treatment that an abuser should receive, as they were more familiar with case histories.[47]

To eliminate the element of fear and hesitation, reporting may be made mandatory, with legal immunity from prosecution and assurance of anonymity in appropriate cases for the reporter. Under s.46(5) of the Act, the identity of the medical practitioner who makes a notification shall not be disclosed in court unless the report is tendered as evidence or the maker of the report is called as a witness. This requirement, however, does not cover sexual abuse cases, since s.3 (c) defines sexual abuse as a distinct kind of child abuse. Where the case is reported by a medical practitioner, the courts should perhaps be required to attach more weight to the medical evidence than they would attach otherwise. This may have the effect of minimizing the chances of defence counsel treating a medical expert as a discreditable witness. Further, where a child has visible injuries and the prosecution's case is that these were caused by the guardian/parent, an amendment in the Evidence Act, 1950, shifting the burden of proof from the prosecution to the guardian/parent, may have useful results.[48]

Register for child abuse cases

At present, it is not mandatory to keep registers of child abuse cases. The 1995 Conference suggested that a nationwide confidential registry of children who are abused and their abusers should be maintained by the Welfare Services Department. The registry will be used to record and monitor child abusers and their victims and assist social workers and legal officers to decide on the type of punishment or treatment the parties should undergo. However, information in the registry will be confidential and only available to officers of the child protection team (which consists of doctors, social workers, police and lawyers). From the registry, it could be deduced whether the abuser is a first-time offender, so that further action could be recommended by the team. However, if the abuser turned over a new leaf and had a clean record for three years continuously, his name should be removed from the registry.[49]

The proposals also include compiling a data bank of abusers' profiles. It should be compiled collectively by all organizations dealing with social development to combat the rising number of abuse cases. The data bank would serve as an important source of information on factors that lead to such assaults. With such information, the trend and lifestyles of abusers can be traced, and what led them to abuse and what remedial steps to take to combat the problems can be determined.[50] While the government is proposing that these abusers receive psychiatric treatment, it should also consider whether there are enough psychiatrists and psychologists in the country.

There are also several factors that contribute to the less than optimal functioning of the medical practitioner in the child protection team. To have an effective team, adequate training, supervision, communication and remuneration of the team members is important. The multiple problems of child abuse and neglect and the need for multiple modes of intervention may lead to ineffective, uncoordinated management and follow-up unless every member of the team functions optimally.[51]

Training

The family practitioners or general practitioners need to refer to the SCAN Team for initial evaluation. Regarding the areas of training needs of the doctors, a questionnaire study by the Department of Social Welfare in 1993 showed that these practitioners should be equipped with knowledge on legal and medical matters, child psychology, general psychology, sociology and family functionings, and skills on handling abused and neglected children, confronting child abusers and counselling child abusers. Where the need arises, the medical practitioner has his therapeutic, educational supervising, research and advocacy roles. He has to be objective, especially when he has to differentiate between his role as a therapist to the child and to the parents who may be the abusers. Too much identification with the parents may place a child in danger if he or she is returned prematurely to a dangerous home environment.[52]

The Ministry of National Unity and Social Development is studying ways to prosecute men responsible for the birth of babies who were later abandoned. At the same time, a Child Adoption Scheme has been set up to appeal to expectant mothers who could not take care of their babies to contact the Welfare Services Department for assistance, while keeping their identities confidential. The Ministry had also set up hotlines for unwed mothers at various centres where they could seek advice and guidance to save a baby from being abandoned.[53]

In addition, a task force was set up in 1993, comprising representatives from the Home, Human Resources and Health Ministries, the police and the welfare services department, to monitor the problem of abandoned babies. Through the media's focus on child abuse, more people have been made aware of the importance of reporting suspicious cases and even criticized such wrongdoing. The establishment of a hotline for child abuse cases helped significantly to keep an eye on these cases as it has become more practicable and easy for the public to report them.[54]

Enforcement of the laws

It is doubtful whether child protection laws can ever be able to solve completely the problem of child abuse. What is certain is that, if a law is effectively enforced and its objectives are sincerely pursued, the incidence of neglect and abuse can be minimized. Public awareness campaigns, together with an effective enforcement of the law may, in course of time, bring about substantial change.

Besides enforcement, the legal system should assist in ensuring more 'victim-friendly' court proceedings. Resolutions made by the 1993 Conference on Child Abuse and Neglect include setting up special units based in hospitals to ensure proper legally accepted collection of evidence. They also suggested video-taping of the first interview to prevent unnecessary repeat interviewing. The police also play an important role, especially in interviewing the child. It is felt that, when interviewing a child, they must dispense with formalities, and not wear uniform. It is highly recommended that there be, as part of their training in the academy, an element on child abuse. The inspector general of police stated that police officers will be sent overseas to study laws on child abuse and gather information and experience of other countries relating to new ways of conducting investigation and prosecution to boost conviction rates.[55]

In court, the abused child should be interviewed in a special room adjacent to the open court, where he or she does not have to face the abuser, who is often the father or close relative, and the government is committed to look into the Evidence Act 1950 with a view to accepting evidence given by children.[56] One of the ways would be to amend the law; that is, to admit a child's sworn/unsworn testimony on video without the need for corroboration. It would be left to the discretion of the judge to decide on the truth of the child's testimony.

At present, the trial courts hearing cases of abuse against children vary according to the nature of the crime. If the offence committed carries a penalty not exceeding 10 years' imprisonment, it is heard in the magistrate's court. For life imprisonment, the cases will be heard in sessions court. The high court will only hear cases that carry the death penalty. According to Tan Sri Harun (a retired Supreme Court judge), this plethora of trial courts tends to distort the gravity of such offences, in the sense that the individual courts are not assisted with the social background material when hearing such cases. In particular, they are not furnished with reports of the background of the home and environment in which the child was brought up, or that of the offenders. The courts are not given the full picture; they only look at the injuries and the identity of the offenders. This is not enough. Tan Sri Harun suggested that the answer to these problems lies in the establishment of family courts presided over by experienced judges. In Malaysia, this level of the judiciary would be the sessions court, taking into account the decentralization of the judicial infrastructure in terms of location of such courts nationwide, the number of cases involved and the availability of judges. The family court should hear all types of cases involving the family: that is, on the civil side, family and personal law cases and, on the criminal side, all cases of abuse of children committed by adults. A family court, empowered with the concurrent jurisdiction will have a full and complete picture enabling it to be seized of the social problems that exist and are manifested by the crimes of violence committed on children. Such courts should be supported by specially trained probation officers to furnish reports on the background of the child victim and that of the offender in every case.

Tan Sri Harun also suggested that the judges of the family court should have the temperament, patience, understanding, appreciation and compassion to preside in such courts to deal effectively with the matters before them. However, the family court should be a separate court of the subordinate courts judiciary. To the public, it will be a single trial court to which they can have easy access in respect of all matters involving the family.[57]

Specially trained magistrates should also be appointed. It has been suggested that it is better for a court dealing with child abuse cases to have a panel, comprising the judge, the doctor who attended the child, the psychiatrist, the paediatricians, the police and the social welfare department personnel, to decide what is best for the child in terms of placement after trial. The proceedings should be amended in such a way that the child does not have to face further trauma. At present, the Welfare Services Department assists in referring victims and their families for 'intensive intervention' therapy. Post-conviction compulsory counselling should be imposed for those found guilty of child abuse. It is also equally important to rehabilitate them where possible, particularly in cases where they were parents of the abused child. Under s.26 (1) of the Child Protection Act, a child abuser is liable to a maximum fine of RM10 000 or five years' jail, or both. Although the maximum jail term is five years, the abusers might face heavier sentences, depending on the severity of the case.

Long-term solutions

There is a need to build up the people's inner strength by inculcating religious and moral values. One of the ways would be through life-long education. Couples wanting to get married should have pre-marriage counselling and periodic marriage counselling in the course of their married life. This should be made available within the community. Religious groups and social clubs have a part to play in organizing workshops and training sessions on topics related to family life, and to be held within the community.

The Information Ministry should play a more proactive role by using the media because it covers a wide range of society and is easily accessible to everybody. They should have more television programmes and community service advertisements on child abuse and neglect in order to increase public awareness. It is important to educate the people in view of the increasing number of such cases. The ministry is also capable of highlighting the root causes of the problem and can call for a change. However, child abuse should not be sensationalized and the ministry should ensure that the abused child and family not be identified.[58]

Schools are the best places to detect child abuse. School is the second home for most children. Studies have shown that a child more confidently confides in a fellow classmate than in anyone else. Teachers, by keeping an attentive eye and ear, will be able to detect a child abuse case and report it. Subjects dealing with family life should be introduced into the curriculum. There should be open sessions to encourage students to talk about situations in their homes. To promote better understanding of child abuse and to prevent its occurrence, it has been suggested that child abuse should be included in the school curriculum and in pre-marital courses.

The corporate sector also has a role to play in the prevention of child abuse. It is recorded that the third highest abuser is the baby-sitter.[59] Therefore the corporate sector should, as part of its incentive scheme, provide a crèche for young babies. It should also organize workshops in parenting skills and other family-related topics. When planning housing estates, town councils, housing development boards and district offices should include facilities for child care centres, recreational facilities, facilities to promote communal cooperation, counselling centres and medical clinics within the area. They should also provide facilities to encourage the fostering of better relationships amongst neighbours.

Finally, since children are the country's most important asset, in 1995, Malaysia ratified the United Nations Convention on the Rights of the Child. With the accession to the Convention, Malaysia has signified that it recognizes children's rights in the areas of children's survival, protection, development and participation. Malaysia's present concern for her children has surpassed the survival stage. Now the nation is more concerned with issues relating to protection, development and participation among children. The setting up of a National Plan of Action for Child Survival, Protection and Development of Children in the 1990s clearly indicates the nation's interest, readiness and commitment to the spirit of the Convention, as reflected in its goals and scope of actions. It is also consonant with the aspiration of 'Vision 2020', which aimed at creating a caring society represented by resilient and economically independent individuals.

NOTES

1. *New Straits Times*, 23 July 1989.
2. *New Straits Times*, 28 July 1989.
3. *New Straits Times*, 15 January 1990.
4. *New Straits Times*, 6 May 1991.
5. Although before that there were several studies made by medical practitioners which showed that this vicious crime has actually long been in existence, the whole issue of child abuse and neglect in Malaysia had only gained full momentum in the late 1980s, with the media playing a significant role in highlighting child abuse cases with a view to generating social consciousness in curbing the increasing trend.
6. The National Unity and Social Development Ministry even declared war on child abuse and child neglect.

7   Department of Statistics Malaysia, *Population and Housing Census of Malaysia: General Report of the Population Census, I*, edited by Khoo Teik Huat (Kuala Lumpur: Government Printers, 1995).
8   Ibid.
9   In 1986, the first national seminar on child abuse and neglect was organized by the Malaysian Council of Child Welfare and the Department of Welfare. At the end of the seminar, it was concluded that no single group of workers could handle child abuse and neglect on their own: each case would require the involvement of various professionals so that proper care and long-term attention could be given to the child and family in question.
10 Deputy Director of the Police Investigation Department.
11 *New Straits Times*, 18 July 1993.
12 Head of Paediatric Institute, Kuala Lumpur Hospital.
13 M. Sham Kassim, 'Epidemiology and Clinical Aspects of Child Abuse in Malaysia', *Journal of Malaysian Society of Health*, 11 (1):35, 1993.
14 M. Sham Kassim, 'Impact of Child Abuse and Neglect of Professionals in Developing Countries', *Jurnal Perubatan UKM*, 11: 65, 1989.
15 Abu Bakar Abdul Wahid, 'Child Abuse – New Perspectives', Seminar On Child Abuse, Kuala Lumpur, 1992.
16 Suspected Child Abuse and Neglect (SCAN) Team, *Annual Report*, 1996, p.14.
17 Ibid.
18 Kasmini Kassim, 'Personality Profile of Child Abuse', *Journal of the Malaysian Society of Health*, 11 (1): 43, 1993.
19 Haliza Shafie, 'Infants of Drug Addict Mothers', Symposium on Child Abuse and Neglect, Kuala Lumpur, 1995.
20 Section 2(2).
21 Section 2(3).
22 See also S. Augustine Paul, 'Child Abuse: The New Law', *Child Law Journal* 3: xxiii, 1991.
23 Alex Mathews, 'Sexual Abuse: Local data on the extent of problems and rate of judicial conviction of assailants', Symposium on Child Abuse and Neglect, Kuala Lumpur, 1995.
24 Mary J. Marrett, 'Sexual Abuse in Children seen at the University Hospital', Symposium on Child Abuse and Neglect, Kuala Lumpur, 1995.
25 *Proceedings of the National Conference on Child Abuse and Neglect, Intrafamilial Sexual Abuse*, Kuala Lumpur, 1995.
26 From 1993 to 1995, the police investigated a total of 5013 cases of sexual offences and only 1050, or 20.9 per cent, were solved.
27 ACP Dato Hassan, 'Local Data on the Extent of Problems and Rate of Judicial Convictions of Sexual Offences', Symposium on Child Abuse and Neglect, Kuala Lumpur, 1995.
28 Kasinathan Nadesan, 'The Need for a Sexual Offences Examination Kit', Symposium on Child Abuse and Neglect, Kuala Lumpur, 1995.
29 Rokiah Ismail, 'Care and Problems Faced', Symposium on Child Abuse and Neglect, Kuala Lumpur, 1995.
30 Gill Raja, 'Moving Beyond Denial, Anger and Shame: Creating A Supportive Environment for Sexually Abused Children', Symposium on Child Abuse and Neglect, Kuala Lumpur, 1995.
31 Zuraidah Abidin, 'Care and Problems Faced', Symposium on Child Abuse and Neglect, Kuala Lumpur, 1995.

32 Mailvaganam Pillai, 'Care and Problems Faced', Symposium on Child Abuse and Neglect, Kuala Lumpur, 1995.
33 Anwarul Yaqin, *Law and Society in Malaysia* (Kuala Lumpur: International Law Book Services, 1996), p.140.
34 Section 2(1) defines a child as a person under the age of 18 years.
35 Section 9(1).
36 Section 12(1).
37 For further details, see T.H Woon, 'From Child Abuse to Child Protection Committee', Conference on Child Abuse and Neglect, Kuala Lumpur, 1993.
38 See reference in note 33.
39 Section 20.
40 Section 22.
41 For further details on the debate, see Parliamentary Debate, 29 July 1991.
42 *The Sunday Star*, 23 August 1992.
43 Abu Bakar Munir, 'Child Abuse and the Law of Evidence', *Malaysian Law Journal*, 249, 1992.
44 Sections 33 and 34.
45 Tan Sri Dato Harun Mahmud Hashim, 'The Court's Role in the Protection of Children', Conference on Children's Rights, Kuala Lumpur, 1995.
46 For further detail, see *Proceedings of The Conference of Child Abuse and Neglect* (Kuala Lumpur, 1995).
47 Ibid.
48 Ibid.
49 Ibid.
50 Ibid.
51 See T.H Woon, 'Child Abuse in an Urban Centre in Malaysia', Conference on Child Abuse and Neglect, Kuala Lumpur, 1995.
52 Department of Social Welfare, Malaysia, *Child Abuse and Neglect, A Study of Cases Reported to the Department, 1991* (sponsored by UNICEF, 1993).
53 Ibid.
54 *New Straits Times*, 20 January 1993.
55 *New Straits Times*, 29 March 1995.
56 Ibid.
57 Tan Sri Dato Harun Mahmud Hashim, 'The Court's Role in the Protection of Children', Conference on Children's Rights, Kuala Lumpur, 1995.
58 *New Straits Times*, 24 October, 1993.
59 SCAN, *Annual Report*, 1996.

13 Protecting, Reporting and Supporting: Child Abuse and the Assessment of Risks in the Netherlands

H.E.M. Baartman and L. de Mey

INTRODUCTION

With regard to child abuse there are three different situations in which a choice must be made in the interest of a child. The first situation is one in which it is determined that a child is being abused. Here one must assess the risks of recurrence and decide whether steps must be taken for the protection of the child.[1] The second situation concerns a suspicion of child abuse. In this case one must assess the likelihood that child abuse is actually taking place and decide whether reporting is in the interest of the child. This applies particularly in countries where a legal obligation to report exists. In the third situation there is no suspicion of child abuse at all, but the risk that it might occur is higher than usual. Here one thinks of young, high-risk families. In this situation, one must assess whether offering the parents preventive help and support would serve the interest of a child.

In each of these situations one can make two types of errors. One might erroneously refrain from taking action (protecting, reporting, offering help) or one might erroneously take action. Erroneously taking action is an error of the 'false positive' type. Erroneously not taking action is an error of the 'false negative' type. The consequences of the two errors can differ in terms of their gravity. The consequences of 'false negative' action are, in principle, always serious, inasmuch as child abuse is taking place and/or continuing to take place and no one has taken action to prevent and/or stop it. The seriousness of the consequences of the 'false positive' type varies according to the degree to which the action taken was radical in nature. An intervention is more radical in nature the more it affects the authoritative relationship and/or the daily relationship between parent and child and the more it affects the privacy of family members. An unjustified protective measure, for example removing the child from the home, in principle has more serious consequences than an unjustified report, and the chance that an unjustified report will have serious consequences is greater than would be the case were superfluous help to be offered.

So all of these points mean that the more harmful the consequences of an incorrect assessment could be, the stricter the regulations which are called for. In other words, the more serious the consequences of an incorrect intervention could be, the narrower the margins of uncertainty must be. Conversely, the broader the margins of uncertainty, the less radical an intervention must be. Table 13.1 shows the difference in seriousness of the two types of errors in the three types of interventions.

Table 13.1 Type of errors, seriousness and interventions

	False positive	False negative
Protecting	+++	+++
Reporting	++	++
Supporting	+	+

Note: +++ = very serious; + = less serious.

In daily practice, the margins of uncertainty in each of the three interventions mentioned above are generally broader than is desirable. In addition, one notes that, in the realm of youth care and youth protection, much more energy is expended on protecting and reporting than on early stage preventive support. In principle, this is understandable. In a situation in which it is certain that a child is being abused, the consideration of whether some type of protection is necessary is unavoidable. This is much less the case with regard to the necessity of reporting in cases where child abuse is only suspected,[2] and it is even less true where child abuse is not occurring at all but may perhaps take place in the future.[3]

As we have stated, the broader the margins of uncertainty, the less radical the intervention should be. But at the same time one also notes that the chance of doing nothing at all is greater the broader the margins of uncertainty are. The result of this is that reports are often not made in situations where they should indeed have been made,[4] and that, when it comes to offering help to at risk families, one waits until it is certain that a child is being abused or neglected.

In this chapter we reconnoitre the margins of certainty in each of the three situations listed above. First, we discuss the factors which play a role in the failure of professional help and in the decision to take measures to protect a child. Then we discuss the factors which play a role in the decision to report; finally, we address the factors which increase the risk of child abuse and thus play a role in the decision to offer preventive help. We end with a brief concluding section.

RISK FACTORS AND THE DECISION TO PROTECT

Basically, a decision is made to take protective measures if voluntary help has failed or appears not to be feasible and the chance of recurrence appears great. What is involved here is usually an error of the false negative type (failing to protect). Here it is important that one be aware what the characteristics are of families upon whom professional help exerts little effect. Considering the differences between physical abuse and neglect, on the one hand, and sexual abuse, on the other, in terms of backgrounds and professional help, we concentrate, in this question, on physical abuse and neglect.

To estimate the chances of recurrence, the results of two types of research are relevant: (a) research into those characteristics of parents, children and families which increase the likelihood that professional help will not succeed, and (b) research into the characteristics of those families with regard to which a decision is made to take protective measures. In the first of the studies mentioned, what is concerned is a combination of three clusters of factors: facets of treatment form, for example frequency and length of treatment; facets of treatment content, such as intervention and strategies, and features of family, parents and child. Here we limit ourselves to features of family, parents and child, since in order to estimate the chance of recurrence these are the most important points.

Failure of help and recurrence

The possibility that help will fail and of recurrence appears to be greater the greater the degree of unemployment,[5] the greater the degree of housing problems,[6] the greater the degree of psychiatric problems in the parents,[7] the more unreasonable the expectations of the parents are towards their children,[8] the less the parents are able to interpret correctly the behaviour of their children,[9] the more they deny the abuse,[10] the less capable they are of establishing a relationship with others including a professional,[11] and the less they adhere to agreements made with a professional,[12] the more that reports of child abuse were made in the past,[13] and if the parents themselves were abused as children.[14] One finds little mention in the available literature on the subject about the characteristics of the children concerned. According to Herrenkohl *et al.*[15] and Cohn,[16] recurrences are more likely the younger the child is; according to Ferleger *et al.*,[17] the reverse is true. On the one hand, the younger the child, the more he or she demands of those raising him or her and the more vulnerable he or she is; on the other hand, effective help can be more difficult the more the problems have already existed for a long time and, therefore, the older the child is. And finally, although strictly speaking this does not concern a characteristic of parents, family or child, it has also been noted that the chance of successful help becomes slimmer the more the abuse has led to more serious injuries.[18]

Protection and out-of-home placement

Research has been carried out on the characteristics of the family, the parent and the child which increase the chance of child protective measures being taken. One may assume that a child protective measure in which a child is taken out of his or her home and/or where there is intervention in the authority of the parents will take place if voluntary professional help has not yielded the desired results. For example, according to a regulation in Dutch civil law, a Family Supervision Order can be imposed upon parents – which means that the parents must share their authority with a family supervisor – 'if a minor is growing up in such a way that his moral or psychological interests or his health are seriously threatened, *and if other means to avert this threat have failed or it can be foreseen that they will fail*' (emphasis added). Home-based treatment such as 'Homebuilding' and 'Families First' is one of the best known means of averting this threat.[19] Nelson,[20] and Yuan and Struckman-Jones,[21] have carried out research to determine how abusive families in which professional help was successful in preventing out-of-home placement differed from abusive families where out-of-home placement was not successful. In the families where a decision for out-of-home placement was made at some later point, there was a greater level of addictive behaviour in the parents,[22] they had more psychological problems,[23] they adhered less well to agreements with the professional,[24] an out-of-home placement had more often taken place in the past[25] and the parents had less insight into the problems in their family.[26] Furthermore, on the whole, more children from these families were likely to be placed out of their homes in the future.[27]

Schetky et al.[28] studied the characteristics of parents whose parental rights were terminated, describing such properties as the following: deficiency in capacity for empathy, viewing the child as a possession, abuse in own childhood, low self-esteem and poor cooperation with the professional. According to Dalgleish and Drew's[29] research, severity of abuse, inadequate parenting and the family's lack of cooperation appeared to contribute to the likelihood of out-of-home placement of the child in cases of abuse and neglect. The picture of the family where the chance of successful help is more limited than would appear to be the case as a result of the various studies appears, as a whole, to look like this. The concern here is with families with serious child-rearing problems, particularly in terms of insufficient sensitivity towards the child, serious relationship problems between, and individual problems of, the parents, and serious material problems, where the cooperation of the parents with the professionals is poor, and the abuse has led to serious injuries. This picture corresponds to the manner in which Jones has described untreatable parents: 'those who were seriously damaged as children and who appear to have little or no capacity to love, relate to others, or empathize with the child'.[30]

Characteristics of the parents and characteristics of the context

Some theoretical perspectives on the aetiology of child abuse and neglect focus strongly on features of the parents, while other models emphasize characteristics of the environment. It is notable that the above-mentioned factors which increase the chance of the failure of professional help and which appear to play a role in the decision to proceed to out-of-home placement (whether or not in combination with legal measures for the protection of the child), relate more to the characteristics of parents than to characteristics of the context. This is consistent with Belsky's buffer hypothesis,[31] which assumes that contextual risk factors have a greater negative influence upon the quality of child rearing the weaker the characteristics of the parent, for example in terms of empathy. So he attaches a greater significance to the characteristics of the parents than to the characteristics of the context. Thus knowledge of these individual characteristics appears significant in preventing errors both of the false positive type and of the false negative type. The chance of errors of the false positive type is perhaps greater the more contextual risk factors are overestimated, and the chance of errors of the false negative type is probably greater the more individual risk factors are underestimated. The degree to which one possesses knowledge of these individual factors depends upon the degree to which one is familiar with the family in question. This knowledge appears maximal the longer the professional help, even if it failed, lasted and the more intensive it was. But it is specifically the commitment of the professional to the parents which is thus allowed to grow which can cause one to adhere too long to a compassion strategy and to wait too long to switch over to a control strategy.

The Dutch confidential doctors' offices and false negatives

In 1972, the first four confidential doctors' offices (DCOs) were established in the Netherlands as organizations where (suspicions of) child abuse could be reported. Now there are 12. In addition to these DCOs there is also the Child Protection Board, set up in 1905, which can best be compared with the Social Services Department in Great Britain. The Board, which as a part of the Ministry of Justice is the gateway to civil child protection measures, is the other organization where child abuse can be reported. The DCOs are not a part of the Ministry of Justice, but, having in the past been part of one single private national organization, since 1995 they have been a part of 12 different private regional organizations of child care.

In 1995, the DCOs received 14 175 reports (compared with 430 in 1972). It is difficult to give the figures of the reports the boards receive because of differences between the ways reports are registered by the Boards and the DCOs. Van Montfoort,[32] however, estimated on the basis of the definition of child maltreatment used by the DCOs that the boards receive approximately 5000 to 6000 reports of child abuse concerning 8000 to 9000 children each year. In 1995, 43 per cent of all reports made to the DCOs came from the child's direct environment, particularly neighbours and acquaintances (22 per cent) and family members (9 per cent); 18 per cent of the reports came from medical and mental health agencies, 15 per cent from schools and 8 per cent from judicial agencies including the police, to specify the main sources. These percentages have been relatively stable over the last few years.

The Dutch system of the DCOs was set up as an alternative to the Board in order to avoid civil child protection measures. More specifically, in the early 1970s, the emphasis had been on help, voluntariness and compassion rather than punishment, coercion and control.[33] This approach corresponds with that in Belgium, for example, where confidential doctors' centres were set up in 1979 following the Dutch model, and in Germany, whereas for example in the USA and Denmark the emphasis is more on 'control strategies' than on 'compassion strategies', as Rosenfeld and Newberger call them.[34]

However, at present various experiments stimulated by the Dutch government are under way in which a Board and a DCO work in close cooperation, receiving and processing reports and deciding how to respond to them. One of the reasons for these experiments is the realization that, in cases where a control strategy in the form of a civil child protection measure proves desirable at some later point, often too much time is wasted if the report is first processed by a DCO. A second reason is new legislation concerning the privacy of citizens and the rights of patients and clients. Since 1972, DCOs have gathered and stored information about families without informing the parents that this was going on. According to the new regulations, this will no longer be possible in the future. The experiments are aimed at acquiring information about the feasibility of these new rules.

In their efforts to establish a new identity which differentiates them from the boards, DCOs have always placed a strong emphasis on the significance of the compassion strategy. Such an objective, sometimes exhibiting a certain polarization in terms of the boards, carries the inherent risk that at times the choice is more frequently made or made for longer than necessary to apply a compassion strategy instead of a control strategy, an error of the 'false negative' type: the professional fails to do what should be done. It has always been unclear, with regard to this, on the basis of which considerations the DCOs opt for one strategy or the other.

Roelofs and Baartman[35] investigated which factors play a role in the choice made by the DCOs for one strategy or another in cases of physical child abuse. They defined a compassion strategy as voluntary treatment while the child remained in the home. Where there was a control strategy the child was placed out of the home or left in the home under civil child protection measures. In 58 per cent of the cases it was noted that all that was needed was a compassion strategy; in 10 per cent of the cases only a control strategy was applied; in 24 per cent a compassion strategy was followed later on by a control strategy; in 5 per cent of the cases the reverse was true; and in 3 per cent of the cases a repeated alternation between the two strategies was noted.

The chance of a control strategy being applied appeared greater the greater the child-rearing problems were, the poorer the relationship between the parents, the more the parents experienced the child as being a problem, the greater the degree of material problems, the worse the injuries, and if the child in question was a step-child. A remarkable point was the large number of repeat reports; that is to say, reports on a child which came in a second or further time. This represented 32 per cent of the total study group. In situations of repeat reports, in comparison with the initial reports the choice was often made later for out-of-home placement (46 per cent compared with 29 per cent), and similarly more often for a civil child protection measure (43 per cent compared with 15 per cent).

The above makes it obvious that, even if the preference goes to a compassion strategy, in many cases a control strategy is unavoidable. It also shows that, in many cases where apparently a compassion strategy was insufficient, a choice was made too late for a control strategy. Just as an approach preferring a control strategy can yield a high percentage of false positives, so can an approach preferring a compassion strategy yield a similarly high percentage of false negatives. Below we delve more deeply into the factors which increase the chance of false negatives and false positives at reporting.

RISKS AND THE DECISION TO REPORT

The phenomenon 'reporting child abuse' is generally studied in two different ways.[36] In the first method, data concerning the reporting of child abuse are collected by analysing reports from professionals about real-life cases which they encounter. The term 'real-life' is added here because, in the second method, data are analysed concerning the reporting behaviour of professionals which is simulated. Use is made of imagined cases which are presented, along with a list of questions, for example to teachers or physicians. The advantage of this method, of course, is that for the phenomenon of theoretical reporting, relevant variables can be systematically manipulated, something which is not possible with the former method.

In specifying the results we will state on the grounds of which method the data were collected, so that the reader himself or herself can assess the validity of the results. Studies in the context of the first method will be identified as type 1, while type 2 will refer to studies according to the second method.

A significant objective of much research into reporting characteristics is to improve reporting in actual practice. Remarkable in many studies, however, is that there is but little impetus to establish theories, and that the results, though useful and interesting, are of a strongly descriptive character.[37] In our opinion, a contribution to the upgrading of reporting in actual practice must be derived from theory. We opt for two angles of approach which we base upon the theory of Newcomb,[38] and the contextual theory derived from the interview theory of Van Dijk.[39]

Theory

Here the basic premise is the so-called A–B–X system[40] which, according to the context theory, has a framework comprising two outer shells (see Figure 13.1).

The A–B–X system concerns the following relationships:

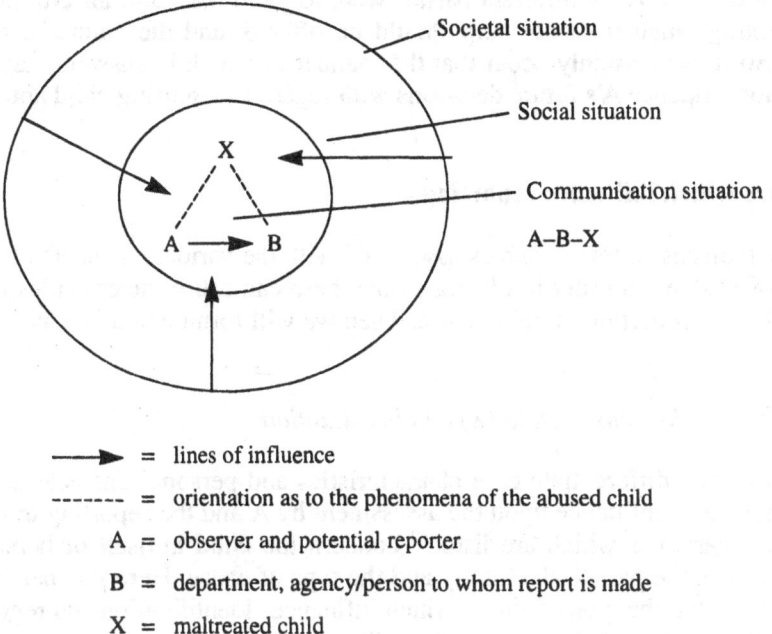

Figure 13.1 A contextual model of reporting child abuse

- (A) the professional's orientation as to X (abused child); attitude and cognitive attributions;
- (A) the professional's orientation as to B (organization/person placed in confidence) in terms of more or less attractive;
- (B)'s orientation as to X;
- (B)'s orientation as to A.

The A–B–X system can be viewed as a unique communication situation in which we may assume that the relationship between the professional/reporter (A) and organization/person placed in confidence (B) is thus far asymmetric. For example, the situation may involve a report by A concerning a phenomenon X possibly defined differently by B.[41] It would not be surprising if communication concerning a phenomenon such as child abuse viewed differently by different parties were to yield risks and uncertainties concerning whether or not help should be offered, and the nature of that help. So it can certainly occur that the manner in which B answers may or may not influence A's future decisions with regard to reporting child abuse.

Factors which influence reporting

We now discuss a few variables associated with the various elements of the A–B–X system, in order to illustrate how these can cause uncertainties and risks for the reporting of child abuse. Then we will formulate a few hypotheses.

Variables of the abused child (X) and his situation

In X one can differentiate case characteristics and personal characteristics which have an influence upon the assessment by A and the reporting in this context. Variables which are listed[42] concern the child himself or herself, such as age, the parent, the family and the type of abuse. Here it is particularly the latter, the type of abuse, which influences identification and reporting. What is remarkable is that (type 2) interviewed professionals assess physical abuse as being less serious than sexual abuse, a type of abuse which has a greater chance of being reported than physical abuse.[43] What, incidentally, remains unclear is the answer to the question of why one type of abuse is adjudged as being more serious than the other.

Family income, too, can be a variable which influences the reporting of abuse. Zellman[44] states in her (type 2) study that the intention of reporting is greater in cases where there is a low socio-economic status. In addition there is the (type 2) finding that, in cases where children come from minority groups in terms of race, there is a greater tendency to report[45] than in white families, where the tendency is more to consider the standpoints of the observer and reporter.

The age of the child plays a significant role in the decision to report. Physical violence concerning older children (14 years) is reported less than if it concerns small children.[46] Here the reason is probably that people assign a greater vulnerability to younger children than to older ones. In the latter group one may tend to dismiss abuse on the precept of discipline. What we see here is that, concerning physical abuse, the chance of false negatives is greater than concerning sexual abuse, and that, concerning physical abuse, the chance of false negatives is greater with regard to older children than to younger children.

Variables of the professional helper/reporter (A)

We have seen that case variables concerning X influence the perception of A. But one can also differentiate a number of characteristics of A which play a role in the decision-making process concerning the reporting of abuse. Indubitably the judgment which an observer makes concerning a certain type of abuse is of decisive importance with regard to answering the question of whether reporting is called for or not. Closely related to this is how the observer perceives the significance of his reporting with regard to the child or the family. Depending upon this valuation, he will report or not report. Another significant variable which influences the reporting of abuse is the attitude towards discipline of the observer. How does he think that children should be disciplined?[47] Morris and Kratochwill established a negative correlation (type 2) between the acceptance level of physical disciplining techniques and the chance of reporting. A person who feels that hitting is an acceptable disciplining technique will be less likely to view this as abuse and to report it. Here one must bear in mind that this variable may be contingent upon the fact of whether an observer himself has children, or whether he himself was abused as a child. This first point, whether there is a link between reporting on the one hand and having children or not having them, did not come to the fore in studies. There are, however, indications that the sex of the observer may play a role in the reporting of certain forms of parental behaviour wherein younger women tend more quickly to view something as abuse and to report it than men and older women.[48]

Variables of the trusted intermediary organization/person (B)

There are indications that trusted intermediary organizations apply tougher criteria for defining violence when screening the reports which come in than do the reporters, so that cases which fall outside these criteria do not end up in the files.[49] Teachers who function in an educational context will attach a different significance to certain forms of child abuse, considering the emotional and intellectual development of the child, than the organization to which the report is made. This is a reason why teachers prefer not to report to an intermediary organization. People tend to have the idea that children are insufficiently protected.[50] In this context, it is remarkable that child protection services in the USA are aware of significantly fewer cases of child abuse than are known to professionals.[51]

Situational factors of the A–B–X system

The framework which encompasses the A–B–X system concerns the social situation in which the system occurs. Situational factors such as professional group (teacher, physician), the opinions of others, and the organization of which observers are a part, can be significant to the A–B–X system. For example, a village physician may demonstrate more concern for the negative consequences of his report than would a physician in a big city, because the latter is less financially dependent upon a certain number of families.[52]

Among the professional groups to which observers belong, there are discrepancies in the reporting of cases of child abuse. For example, hospital personnel are known to report less on physical and emotional neglect than on physical and emotional abuse, and to report more on black children than on white children. Among school personnel, a particular differentiation is made between younger and older children, with teachers reporting more on younger children than on older ones. The same trend is noted among police personnel.[53]

Societal context

The outermost circle shows that the A–B–X system must be viewed in a certain societal context. It also shows that, as a consequence, reports, or the contents of such reports, are determined at least in part by the current values and standards. It is clear that cultural perceptions determine whether one is talking about abuse or not. An indication in this context concerns the reporting itself. In some countries (for example, the USA, France, Sweden, Denmark and Finland) there is an obligation to report,[54] and in other countries there is not (for example, The Netherlands, Belgium and Germany). Another indication is that, in all Scandinavian countries and in Austria and Cyprus, the use of violence towards children as a disciplinary measure is forbidden by law.[55]

Conclusion

It has come to the fore that the communication between A and B with regard to X is determined by a number of variables which concern case characteristics, variables of the observer, factors of trusted intermediary organizations and of situation. Here it is clear that, with regard to X, the communication between A and B in terms of reporting depends upon a number of factors. So the success of the report runs great risks. That this may occur at the expense of X is clear. If the objective is that a suitable reaction take place on the part of B with regard to X, communication must be coordinated. Thus far, this communication appears to be biased and far from symmetrical. We have noted that demographic variables such as the age of the child and the ethnic background and socio-economic status of the relevant family play a major role. In our analysis of factors involved in a decision to take child protective measures, it was noted that what is mostly concerned is the personal characteristics of the parents as child rearers. Because reporters, generally speaking, are often less familiar with a family than a professional would be, such distortion is to be expected.

Summarizing the various points, we can formulate the following framework hypothesis: the more A and B in their orientation towards X expressed in the report and the feedback have the same perceptions and 'speak the same language' (coorientation), the fewer errors will be made in giving professional help in the approach to X. We can further delineate this framework hypothesis as follows. To begin with, one may expect that the chance of coorientation towards X is smaller the less attractive A finds B. This may mean, for example, that A's fear of intervention which has radical consequences for the family being carried out by B can stop A from making a report. In addition, the chance of coorientation towards X appears smaller the more A's definitions in terms of phenomenon X differ from B's. As we noted before, the more serious the consequences of an incorrect intervention could be, the narrower the margins of uncertainty must be. In order to avoid radical consequences, reporters often want to minimize their own uncertainty, while acquiring certainty is the main task of the person to whom abuse has been reported. Finally, the chance of coorientation is greater if A validates his perceptions with regard to X in terms of the perceptions of B.

RISKS AND THE DECISION TO GIVE PREVENTIVE HELP

As we did in the discussion of factors which limit the likelihood of recurrence, we limit ourselves here, for the same reasons, to risk factors with regard to physical abuse and neglect. As we have stated, we make great investments in treating, protecting and reporting, but relatively small ones in prevention. We should invest much more in those families where no abuse exists at all, where a report of abuse need not even be considered, but where the chance that this might indeed take place in the future is present to an increased extent. The question then, however, is in which families an increased chance of abuse is present, or, in other words: which factors increase the chance that over the course of time abuse or neglect will take place in a family?

For an answer to this question we must become cognizant with the results of two types of studies. In the first case the focus is on cross-sectional research, where families in which physical abuse and/or neglect is taking place are compared with families where there is no physical abuse and/or neglect. In the second case we focus on prospective research, where the development of a group of very young 'at risk' families is followed – perhaps together with a matched control group – and where, over the course of time, the families where abuse has occurred are compared with the families where it does not take place.

Both types of research have given us some insight into the risk factors which considerably increase the chance of child abuse. It must be commented here, however, that, in virtually all of this research, we are dealing only with mothers. Fathers were, incorrectly, barely considered. So the results cannot be considered as applying to parents in general.

Cross-sectional research

Comparison of families where child abuse does or does not occur makes it possible to identify risk factors, even if it is sometimes not clear whether a difference should be viewed as a cause or a result of child abuse. According to the results of this type of research, these risk factors can be classified in four clusters. To begin with, the chance of abuse is greater the greater the level of social isolation. Mothers who abuse or neglect their children have less frequently had a part-time job, have less contact with persons outside the family and are less satisfied with the contacts which they have with family members.[56] The families in question move more frequently[57] and, in one study, it was noted that these families more often have a secret telephone number.[58]

In the second place, the chance of abuse is greater the less social support the parents have access to. To begin with, they often lack social support from one another. The less support a mother obtains from her partner, the greater the chance that she will repeat the child abuse of her youth with regard to her own children.[59] Besides a partner, family, friends and neighbours can also be a significant source of support. Families where abuse occurs often prove to be lacking such support,[60] not only because this is not offered to them, but also because they do not, or at least do not know how to, request it.[61] In addition, this proportionately more often concerns single-parent families[62] where the support of a partner is lacking.

In the third place, the chance of child abuse is greater where a person was himself abused as a child.[63] But it is not only the quality of one's own youth as such which represents a significant risk factor: at least as important is the attitude which one has towards this as an adult. In general it is noted that, the less effectively negative experiences with one's own parents have been confronted and dealt with, such as for example may be evident by gaps in the memories of these experiences and strongly fluctuating and ambivalent feelings with regard to one's own parents, the more negatively these may continue to affect the manner in which one plays one's own parental role.[64] The relevance of this observation lies in the fact that, when seeking risk factors, one is dealing not only with the quality of the parents' youth, but, even more importantly, with their attitude towards it.

In the fourth place, the chance of abuse or neglect is greater the lower the parental awareness of the parents is. In view of the significance of this factor, we address it in somewhat greater depth. Newberger describes *parental awareness* as 'an organized knowledge system with which the parent makes sense out of the child's responses and behavior and formulates policies to guide parental action'.[65] A mother, for example, who expects a child to contribute to the quality of her own life that has not been, or is still not, being provided by others, will experience the behaviour and development of that child differently from a mother who sees it as her task to make a primary contribution to the quality of life of the child. According to Newberger, within parental awareness one can differentiate two dimensions. The first concerns that of taking a perspective, that is to say having insight into the intentions, experiences and emotions of the child, while the other concerns a moral dimension, which one can describe as a balance between doing justice to both the interests of the child and to one's own interests. The problem of abusive parents in terms of their relationship with their child lies specifically in these two levels or dimensions. Indeed, the most important observations of characteristics of abusive parents as child rearers can be found within these two dimensions. Of these parents the following has been noted: (a) that they have a strong tendency to assign negative intentions to their children wrongly;[66] and (b) that they are less sensitive to the needs of their children.[67] Both characteristics can be viewed as expressions of an error in assuming perspective. The following has also been noted:

- that abusive parents have a strong tendency to overburden their children with expectations which the child does not have the power to fulfil, or which the child does not need to fulfil because it is not a part of his role;[68] or, to put it more succinctly: the child must fulfil the interests of the parents; and
- that they experience their children as more bothersome and difficult than is justified considering the behaviour of the children;[69] in other words, child rearing is experienced as a burden and as an attack upon

the parents' own quality of life. These two characteristics can be viewed as expressions of a tendency to allow one's own interests to prevail over those of the children.

To summarize: the chance of abuse and/or neglect is greater the greater the level of social isolation, the less social support the parents have, the less well the parents' own unhappy youth has been confronted and dealt with, and the lower the level of parental awareness the parents possess. These points are strongly consistent with the picture sketched earlier of the untreatable parent. So one concludes that if, in a young family, this combination of four factors exists, there is reason enough to offer preventive support directed towards a reduction of isolation, an increase in support, confronting and dealing with an unhappy youth, and increasing parental awareness.

Prospective research

Nonetheless, the question is how certain it is that, considering the presence of these four clusters of risk factors, over the course of time child abuse is likely to occur if no preventive help is offered. Table 13.2 contains data concerning the results of prospective research. From the table three conclusions can be reached.

1 The majority (67 per cent to 100 per cent) of the abusing families belong to the group of 'at risk' families.
2 Abuse occurs in the 'at risk' families twice to 30 times as frequently as in the control families.
3 Abuse occurs in 6 per cent to 53 per cent of the 'at risk' families.

The first two conclusions appear to represent an argument for offering early preventive help to young 'at risk' families, but the most important is the third conclusion: in a large to very large proportion of these 'at risk' families, over the course of time no abuse takes place. One must, incidentally, attach a footnote to this third conclusion. According to Pianta *et al.*,[76] it is particularly the combination of characteristics of the person of the child rearer (his or her early history and his or her experience of his or her relationship to his child) and the degree to which a person has a place within a social network and has the opportunity therein to obtain support, which determine the quality of his or her child rearing. In the cross-sectional study, too, as well as from the research into factors which limit the chances of successful professional help, one had to conclude that the characteristics of

Table 13.2 Characteristics and results of prospective research into child abuse in 'at risk' families

	No.	Duration of research	% of primiparas	% of abuse in a risk group	% of abuse in control group	% of 'at risk' families in abuse group
Browne and Saqi[70]	949	6 years	100	6	0.2	67.5
Gray et al.[71]	100	18–36 months	*	8	0	100
Monaghan et al.[72]	32	12 months	*	53**	14	82
Murphy et al.[73]	38	12–24 months	54	53	2	91
Vietze et al.[74]	237	18 months	39	19	8	76
Pianta et al.[75]	267	6 years	100	25	***	

Notes: *not specified; **four risk levels are differentiated (the two highest as the risk group, the two lowest as the control group); ***no control group.

the parent as child rearer are particularly important. So the question is to what extent, in the study reported here, these characteristics played a role in the composition of the group of 'at risk' families. After all, the more relevant the individual risk factors which are utilized as criteria in the composition of a group of 'at risk' families, the greater the chance that abuse will occur in those families. Therefore Browne and Saqi[77] assume that the minimal percentage of child abuse in their risk group is probably associated with the fact that in their composition of the risk group they paid too much attention to contextual factors and too little to the characteristics of the person of the parent. They concluded: 'Our findings suggest that family stress is not a sufficient explanation for child abuse. The abuse may be attributed to the fact that the parents have unrealistic expectations of their children in addition to psychosocial stress factors .... The abusive parents see their child's behaviour as a threat to their own self-esteem.'[78] So these characteristics of the parents as child rearer – together with contextual variables in terms of social network and social support – should play a prominent role in the possible screening of 'at risk' families. In prospective research, in the composition of the group of 'at risk' families much significance was attached to demographic variables (age of the parents and single parenthood) and socioeconomic variables (such as poverty and unemployment). It is nonetheless conceivable that in prospective research one would find higher percentages of abuse if, in the composition of the group of 'at risk' families, more attention were paid to the characteristics of the person of the child rearer.

But, in spite of this footnote, the provisional conclusion must nonetheless be that the presence of risk factors in young families has only a limited predictive value with regard to child abuse. Even though we know which factors increase the chance of child abuse, their predictive value is limited. This makes establishing a screening programme considerably more difficult. Add to that the fact that screening for a condition with a low incidence yields a high percentage of false positives, even when tests with high sensitivity and high specificity are used.[79] So we find ourselves left with a broad margin of uncertainty.

Legitimization of preventive help and taking risks

This uncertainty could cause one to refrain from offering help at an early stage, but that would be an error. We do not require any absolute certainty about the future to responsibly take preventive measures. If one takes child-protective measures and offers professional help, one still has no complete certainty as to how things would be in two years were one not to have taken those measures, just as one cannot predict with certainty how things will be in two years if one does take those measures. Our decisions are based upon predictions, and those predictions have margins of uncertainty. As we stated earlier, the more radical the measures to be taken, the narrower the margins of uncertainty must be. The prediction of how a young 'at risk' family will develop contains broad margins. This means, among other things, that in this situation help can never be imposed. On the other hand, offering support is only radical to the extent that one offers unasked-for help. But that is legitimized, because one thing is certain: the chance of unhappiness for a child is greater, the more social isolation there is in a family and the less social support exists, the more parents are still troubled by their own memories of an unhappy youth, and the lower their level of parental awareness.

Whether or not we are prepared, however, to offer such preventive help is a political question, too. Since we are able to make no cast-iron predictions, we lack a significant basis for legitimization. That we cannot make such predictions is associated partially with the fact that the course of (the quality of) child rearing depends partially upon factors which are still unknown at the moment the predictions are made. The political question, then, is whether we feel justified in using support to influence the course of this developmental process, in which context at least five framework conditions must be met.

1   An offer of preventive help must be made on a voluntary basis.
2   This offer may not be stigmatizing; this means that, for both ethical and empirical reasons, such an offer cannot be made in the context of 'prevention of child abuse'. What is concerned is an offer of professional help to young parents who commence their role as child rearers under difficult conditions.
3   There must be a situation where the public shares the precept that raising children is indeed primarily – but not solely – the concern of the parents.
4   The community has the obligation to furnish the primary child rearers with the means they require to be able to live up to their responsibilities.
5   There must be the understanding shared publicly and politically that the rights of the parents are derived from their obligations, and that their obligations are based upon the rights of children.

Our system of youth professional help and youth protection is based upon the premise that we do not take action as long as it is not certain that a child is in trouble. Thus far our system has been based upon the right of parents to non-intervention. Then we reverse it: if a child is clearly in trouble, we base our system on the right of the child to intervention. The state becomes involved in the functioning of parents as child rearers only if they have more or less obviously failed in this function. The right of parents to be free, as long as possible, from interference in terms of the manner in which they interpret their responsibilities as child rearers leads, in practice, to the rights of children being compromised for a long time before their rights are honoured. One must remember here, indeed, that offering support or professional help does not compromise the rights of parents. The broader the margins of uncertainty – and, when we make a prediction as to how a young family will develop, those margins are wide – the less radical any intervention should be permitted to be. Making an offer of professional help in a voluntary context is considerably less drastic than imposing help in the context of a ruling from the child protective agency. What is crucial here is whether the right of parents to be exempted, for as long as possible, from external interference should prevail over the right of the child to the best possible development in situations where the chances for that development are limited. Since, after all, in the final analysis the rights of parents are based upon the rights of children, it is certainly justifiable that parents be offered help where there is an increased risk that the rights of the child may be compromised.

CONCLUSIONS

Our system of youth professional help and youth protection is based upon two rights. The first is the right of parents to non-intervention in their private affairs. The second is the right of children to protection from harm. In every decision to intervene in the interest of the child, inevitably there are margins of uncertainty. These margins are broader the less familiar one is with child and family. This holds particularly for the situation where one has to weigh up the pros and cons of a report of child maltreatment.

Prevailing rights of parents over rights of children imply the risk of false negatives: actions in the interest of the child are erroneously not taken. Prevailing rights of children over rights of parents imply the risk of false positives: actions in the interest of the child are superfluous. The more drastic these actions are, the greater the damage can be for the parents, as well as for the child. Fear of drastic consequences can restrain people from reporting. Therefore it is highly important for organizations who handle reports to give information to potential reporters about their operating procedures. In cases where one has to decide to protect a child against further harm or to offer help to young 'at risk' families, one has to be familiar with the family, and often one is. This decreases the risk of false negatives and positives. However, we urgently need to find more systematic means of risk assessment, in the interest of the child as well as of the parents. In risk assessment, demographic and remote variables too often seem to prevail over proximal factors, that is personal characteristics of the parents. From research into determinants of parenting, from research into results of treatment of maltreating parents and from research into the predictive value of risk factors, we have learned that these personal characteristics are more relevant than remote ones. Therefore risk assessment should explicitly focus on these proximal characteristics in order to avoid false negatives and positives.

NOTES

1. B.J. Meddin, 'The assessment of risk in child abuse and neglect case investigations', *Child Abuse and Neglect*, 9: 57–62, 1985.
2. D. Besharov, *Recognizing child abuse: a guide for the concerned* (New York: The Free Press, 1990). See also K. Sundell, 'Child-care personnel's failure to report child maltreatment: some Swedish evidence', *Child Abuse and Neglect*, 21: 93–105, 1997; G.L. Zelmann, 'The impact of case characteristics on child abuse reporting decisions', *Child Abuse and Neglect*, 16: 57–75, 1992.
3. H.E.M. Baartman, *Opvoeden kan zeer doen; over oorzaken van kindermishandeling, hulpverlening en preventie* (Utrecht: SWP, 1996). See also D.N. Duquette, 'Protecting individual liberties in the context of screening for child abuse', in R.H. Starr (ed.), *Child abuse prediction; policy implications*, Cambridge, Mass.: Ballinger, 1982).
4. See Sundell, op. cit., note 2.
5. N. Ferleger, D.S. Glenwick, R.R.W. Gaines and A.H. Green, 'Identifying correlates of reabuse in maltreating parents', *Child Abuse and Neglect*, 12: 41–9, 1988. See also S.A. Szykula and M.J. Fleischman, 'Reducing out-of-home placements of abused children: two controlled field studies', *Child Abuse and Neglect*, 9: 277–83, 1985.
6. See Szykula and Fleischman, op. cit., note 5.
7. R.S. Kempe and C.H. Kempe, *Child abuse* (London: Open Books, 1978).
8. A.H. Green, E. Power, B. Steinbook and R.W. Gaines, 'Factors associated with successful and unsuccessful intervention with child abusing families', *Child Abuse and Neglect*, 5: 45–52, 1981.
9. See Green *et al.*, op. cit., note 8.
10. Ibid.
11. A.H. Cohn, 'Essential elements of successful child abuse and neglect treatment', *Child Abuse and Neglect*, 11: 433–42, 1987. See also Green *et al.*, op. cit., note 8; D.P.H. Jones, 'The untreatable family', *Child Abuse and Neglect*, 11: 409–20, 1987; K. Killen Heap, 'Families with abused children: a follow-up study of post-crisis support', *Child Abuse and Neglect*, 8: 467–72, 1984.
12. See Ferleger *et al.*, op. cit., note 5; Green *et al.*, op. cit., note 8.
13. See Szykula and Fleischman, op. cit., note 5.
14. See Cohn, op. cit., note 11.
15. R.C. Herrenkohl, E.C. Herrenkohl, B. Egolf and M. Seech, 'The repetition of child abuse: how frequently does it occur?', *Child Abuse and Neglect*, 3: 67–72, 1979.
16. See op. cit., note 11.
17. See op. cit., note 5.
18. A.H. Cohn and D. Daro, 'Is treatment too late? What ten years of evaluative research

tell us', *Child Abuse and Neglect*, **11**: 433–42, 1987. See also Green *et al.*, op. cit., note 8.
19 H.I. Bath and D.A. Haapala, 'Intensive family preservation services with abused and neglected children: an examination of group differences', *Child Abuse and Neglect*, **17**: 213–25, 1993.
20 K.E. Nelson, 'Populations and outcomes in five family preservation programs', in K. Wells and D.E. Biegel (eds), *Family preservation services; research and evaluation* (Thousand Oaks: Sage, 1991).
21 Y.T. Yuan and D.L. Struckman-Jones, 'Placement outcomes for neglected children with prior placements in family preservation programs', in K. Wells and D.E. Biegel (eds), *Family preservation services; research and evaluation* (Thousand Oaks: Sage, 1991).
22 See Nelson, op. cit., note 20.
23 Ibid.
24 See op. cit., note 20.
25 See Yuan and Struckman-Jones, op. cit., note 21.
26 Ibid.
27 See Nelson, op. cit., note 20.
28 D. Schetky, R. Hanson and S. Noble, 'Parents who fail: a study of 51 cases of termination of parental rights', *Journal of the American Academy of Child Psychiatry*, **18**: 366–83, 1979.
29 L.I. Dalgleish and E.C. Drew, 'The relationship of child abuse indicators to the assessment of perceived risk and to the court's decision to separate', *Child Abuse and Neglect*, **13**: 491–506, 1989.
30 See Jones, op. cit., note 11, p.414.
31 J. Belsky, 'Child maltreatment, an ecological integration', *American Psychologist*, **35**: 320–35, 1980.
32 A. van Montfoort, *Kindermishandeling en justitie* (Amsterdam: VU-Uitgeverij, 1993).
33 M. Roelofs and H.E.M. Baartman, 'The Netherlands: responding to abuse – compassion or control?', in N. Gilbert (ed.), *Combating child abuse; international perspectives and trends* (New York: Oxford University Press, 1997).
34 A.A. Rosenfeld and E.H. Newberger, 'Compassion vs Control: conceptual and practical pitfalls in the broadened definition of child abuse', *Journal of the American Medical Association*, **237**: 2086–8. And see N. Gilbert, 'A comparative perspective', in N. Gilbert (ed.), *Combating child abuse; international perspectives and trends* (New York: Oxford University Press, 1977).
35 M. Roelefs and H.E.M. Baartman, *Kindermishandeling en hulpverlening; de aanpak van lichamelijke kindermishandeling door het Bureau Vertrouwensarts* (Amsterdam: VU-Uitgeverij, 1997).
36 J.E. Warner and D.J. Hansen, 'The identification and reporting of physical abuse by physicians: a review and implications for research', *Child Abuse and Neglect*, **18**: 11–27, 1994.
37 Ibid. See also op. cit., note 2.
38 T.M. Newcomb, 'An approach to the study of communicative acts', in A.G. Smith (ed.), *Communication and Culture* (New York: Holt, Rinehart & Winston, 1966).
39 J. van Dijk, 'Aanzetten tot een contextuele theorie van het interview', *Mens en Maatschappij*, **3**: 277–94, 1988.
40 See op. cit., note 38.
41 R. Tite, 'How teachers define and respond to child abuse: the distinction between theoretical and reportable cases', *Child Abuse and Neglect*, **17**: 591–605, 1993.
42 See op. cit., note 36.

43 See Besharov, op. cit., note 2.
44 Ibid.
45 See op. cit., note 36.
46 See Besharov, op. cit., note 2 and Warner and Hansen, op. cit., note 36.
47 Op. cit., note 41.
48 See op. cit., note 36.
49 Wolock and Magura, L.S., 'Parental substance abuse as a predictor of child maltreatment re-reports', *Child Abuse and Neglect*, **20**: 1183–95, 1996.
50 See Tite, op. cit., note 41.
51 S. Ards and A. Harrel, 'Reporting of child maltreatment: a secondary analysis of the national incidence surveys', *Child Abuse and Neglect*, **17**: 337–45, 1993.
52 See Badger, in Warner and Hansen, op. cit., note 36.
53 Ibid.
54 See Gilbert, op. cit., note 34.
55 P. Newell, *Children are people too; the case against physical punishment*, (London: Bedford Square Press), 1989.
56 R.H. Starr, 'A research-based approach to the prediction of child abuse', in R.H. Starr (ed.), *Child abuse prediction: policy implications* (Cambridge, Mass.: Ballinger, 1982). See also M. Kotelchuk, 1982. 'Child abuse and neglect: prediction and misclassification', in ibid.
57 D. Gil, *Violence against children: physical abuse in the United States* (Cambridge, Mass.: Harvard University Press, 1970).
58 R.D. Parke and C.W. Collmer, 'Child abuse, an interdisciplinary analysis', in N. Hetherington (ed.), *Review of child development research*, vol. 5 (Chicago: University of Chicago Press, 1975).
59 R.S. Hunter and N. Kilstrom, 'Breaking the cycle in abusive families', *American Journal of Psychiatry*, **136**: 1320–22, 1979. D. Quinton and M. Rutter, 'Parenting behavior of mothers raised "in care"', in A.R. Nicol (ed.), *Longitudinal studies in child psychology and psychiatry: practical lessons from research experience* (Chichester: Wiley, 1985).
60 J. Garbarino and K. Kostelny, 'Child maltreatment as a community problem', *Child Abuse and Neglect*, **16**: 455–64, 1992. See also N.A. Polansky, J.M. Gaudin, P.W. Ammons and K.B. Davies, 'The psychological ecology of the neglectful mother', *Child Abuse and Neglect*, **9**: 265–75, 1985. S.J. Zuravin and G.L. Grief, 'Normative and child-maltreating AFDC mothers', *Social Casework*, **74**: 76–84, 1989.
61 P.M. Crittenden, 'Social networks, quality of child rearing, and child development', *Child Development*, **56**: 1299–1313, 1985.
62 Op. cit., note 57. See also M.I. Benedict, R.B. White and D.A. Cornely, 'Maternal perinatal risk factors and child abuse', *Child Abuse and Neglect*, **11**: 217–24, 1985. S.M. Smith, R. Hanson and S. Noble, 'Social aspects of the battered baby syndrome', *British Journal of Psychiatry*, **125**: 568–82, 1974.
63 J. Kaufman and E. Zigler, 'The intergenerational transmission of child abuse', in D. Cicchetti and V. Carlson (eds), *Child maltreatment; theory and research on the causes and consequences of child abuse and neglect* (New York: Cambridge University Press, 1989).
64 B. Egeland, D. Jacobvitz and K. Papatola, 'Intergenerational continuity of abuse', in R. Gelles and J. Lancaster (eds), *Child abuse and neglect, biosocial dimensions*, (Chicago: Aldine, 1987). See also C. George, 'A representational perspective of child abuse and prevention: internal working models of attachment and caregiving', *Child Abuse and Neglect*, **20**: 411–24, 1996. Also M. Main and R. Goldwyn, 'Predicting rejection of

her infant from mother's representation of her own experience; implications for the abused–abusing intergenerational cycle', *Child Abuse and Neglect*, **8**: 203–17, 1984.
65 C.M. Newberger, 'The cognitive structure of parenthood; the development of a descriptive measure', in R.L. Selman and R, Yando (eds), *Clinical–developmental psychology. New directions of child development: clinical developmental research, No. 7* (San Francisco: Jossey-Bass, 1980).
66 W.D. Bauer, and C.T. Twentyman, 'Abusing, neglectful and comparison mothers' responses to child-related and non-child-related stressors', *Journal of Consulting and Clinical Psychology*, **53**: 335–43, 1985. See also D.T. Larrance and C.T. Twentyman, 'Maternal attributions and child abuse', *Journal of Abnormal Psychology*, **92**: 544–7, 1983.
67 D. Brunnquell, L. Crichton and B. Egeland, 'Maternal personality and attitude in disturbances of child rearing', *American Journal of Orthopsychiatry*, **51**: 680–91, 1981. See also C. Letourneau, 'Empathy and stress: how they affect parental aggression', *Social Work*, **26**: 383–9, 1981.
68 S.T. Azar and C.A. Rohrbeck, 'Child abuse and unrealistic expectations: further validation of the Parent Opinion Questionnaire', *Journal of Consulting and Clinical Psychology*, **54**: 867–8, 1986. See also S.T. Azar, B.R. Robinson, E. Hekimin and C.T. Twenty, 'Unrealistic expectations and problem-solving ability in maltreating and comparison mothers', *Journal of Consulting and Clinical Psychology*, **52**: 687–91, 1984. M. Morris and R. Gould, 'Role reversal: a necessary concept in dealing with the battered child syndrome', *American Journal of Orthopsychiatry*, **33**: 298–9, 1963.
69 D.B. Bugental, J. Blue and M. Cruzcosa, 'Perceived control over caregiving outcomes: implications for child abuse', *Developmental Psychology*, **25**: 525–31, 1989. P.K. Trickett and E.J. Susman, 'Parental perceptions of child-rearing practices in physical abusive and non-abusive families', *Developmental Psychology*, **24**: 270–76, 1988.
70 K. Browne and S. Saqi, 'Approaches to screening for child abuse and neglect', in K. Browne, C. Davies and P. Stratton (eds), *Early prediction and prevention of child abuse* (Chichester: J. Wiley, 1988).
71 J.D. Gray, C.A. Cutler, J.G. Dean and C.H. Kempe, 'Prediction and prevention of child abuse and neglect', *Child Abuse and Neglect*, **1**: 45–8, 1977.
72 S.M. Monaghan, R.J. Gilmore, R.C. Muir, J.E. Clarkson, T.J. Crooks and T.G. Egan, 'Pre-natal screening for risk of major parenting problems: further results from the Queen Mary Maternity Hospital Child Care Unit', *Child Abuse and Neglect*, **10**: 369–75, 1986.
73 S. Murphy, B. Orkow and R.M. Nicola, 'Prenatal prediction of child abuse and neglect: a prospective study', *Child Abuse and Neglect*, **9**: 225–35, 1985.
74 P.M. Vietze, S. O'Connor, J.B. Hopkins, H.M. Sandler and W.A. Altemeier, 'Prospective study of child maltreatment from a transactional perspective', in R.H. Starr (ed.), *Child abuse prediction; policy implications* (Cambridge, Mass.: Ballinger, 1982).
75 R. Pianta, B. Egeland and M.F. Erickson, 'The antecedents of maltreatment: results of the mother–child interaction research project', in D. Cicchetti and V. Carlson (eds), *Child maltreatment; theory and research on the causes and consequences of child abuse and neglect* (Cambridge: Cambridge University Press, 1989).
76 Ibid.
77 Op. cit., note 70.
78 Ibid, p.78.
79 Op. cit, note 70. See also Kotelchuk, op. cit., note 56.

14 Child Abuse in New Zealand
Bill Atkin

THE WORRYING PICTURE

New Zealand has developed some novel procedures for dealing with child abuse and the protection of children in danger. Despite this, the outsider must be disturbed by the current picture in New Zealand. The headline of one recent story was 'Tiny girl caught in horrific cycle of family abuse'.[1] A girl aged eight had been the victim of 11 offenders, mostly members of the extended family, who regarded the girl as 'available' for sexual gratification. The Children and Young Persons Service, the responsible agency within the Department of Social Welfare, is reported as saying that this situation is not rare and could be replicated in dysfunctional families all over the country. In this instance, most of the offenders had been charged, but why were the telltale signs of such a horrific story not detected much earlier?

In an earlier episode, a boy named Craig Manukau was killed by his father in circumstances which raise enormous question marks over the role of the Department of Social Welfare. The case was investigated by the Commissioner for Children.[2] The commissioner is an officer with special powers to investigate and monitor the work of the Department of Social Welfare as well as the actions and decisions of other bodies affecting children.[3] The commissioner's report on the boy's death found fault with the social worker who had been handling the case. She lacked a child protection focus, lacked knowledge of child abuse, failed to avoid 'capture' by the standards of the family, lacked understanding and failed to record important events. But the report found deeper systemic fault. The Department had not properly trained its social workers, had misinterpreted the law, and gave wrong and misleading instructions. Section 13(*a*)(ii) of the Children, Young Persons, and Their Families Act 1989 states that 'intervention into family life should be the minimum necessary to ensure a child's or young person's safety and protection'. This tendentious statutory line has perhaps had more impact than anyone concerned about the safety of children would have anticipated,[4] and the commissioner referred to a 'pernicious doctrine of the "least intrusive action" being the paramount consideration which is contrary to the principles' of the Act. He considered that guidance given by the Department to social workers 'dangerously relegates consideration of the care and protection of children to a secondary place'. He also referred to 'a dangerously inward looking and essentially ignorant approach to child protection practice'.

The Craig Manukau report appeared in 1993. Since then, little appears to have improved and indeed there are increasing concerns about a serious lack of resourcing and funding. Some other headlines tell the story: 'Children's welfare hit by staff shortage',[5] and 'Death stalks at-risk children',[6] 'Children's service pleads for cash'[7] are just a few. Under the heading, 'Abused child may die', social workers expressed a fear of child death because of a backlog in investigating reports of abuse. No system is fail-safe and crises can be exaggerated, but the latest annual report of the Commissioner for Children confirms our worries. He stated, for instance, that the Children and Young Persons Service had 'inappropriately raised the thresholds before intervention occurs and services are provided to children and families'.[8] He went on:

> Clearly the Courts interpret the law, but there seems to be a view within the Service that the Courts are misinterpreting the Act. That notion should be soundly rejected. I conclude that the Service, because of inadequate resourcing, sometimes adopts a narrow and incorrect interpretation of a child deemed to be in need of care and protection ... Increasingly I am identifying cases where I believe social work practice has not been of an appropriate standard because of resourcing issues.

These damning words indicate that there is still something deeply wrong with the culture of the Department and the priority attached by the government to handling child abuse cases. The point is at least partially recognized in official circles. According to the Department's annual report, 'Improved business planning demonstrated the need for additional funding. As a result the Government will allocate an extra $33 million during the next three financial years.'[9] While this may be encouraging, one newspaper item suggests that the then Minister of Social Welfare had asked for $60 million[10] and the Opposition spokesperson on social welfare claimed that an extra $25 million per year was needed.[11] Reform of the government structures, which was effected primarily through the State Sector Act 1988 and the Public Finance Act 1989, has also created novel pressures for those administering the country's child abuse services.[12] Funding is now focused on services for which there are agreed 'outputs'. If the needs of a child do not fit the established output categories, those needs may go unfulfilled. The state's historic role as protector of children, exemplified in the appointment in particular cases of the Director-General of Social Welfare as a child's guardian,[13] appears to be subordinated to other economic and fiscal goals.

THE OVERALL STATUTORY FRAMEWORK

The principal mechanism outside the criminal law for dealing with child abuse in New Zealand is the Children, Young Persons, and Their Families Act 1989. The lead-up to the passage of the Act was fraught.[14] The original form of the legislation was vastly different from the final version. Highly influential in the early stages were professionals and others keen to see child abuse tackled vigorously. The cornerstone of their proposals was the formal establishment of child protection teams to decide on a case-by-case basis what should be done when an abused child came to their attention. The child protection teams symbolized the active state. In many respects, the proposals flowed on naturally from what was often happening in practice.

These proposals came unstuck, however, because they coincided with a rekindling of spirit among the indigenous Maori people, echoed by the views of Pacific Island communities.[15] The approach of using child protection teams was seen as a white person's response to the problems of child care and safety. Traditional Maori concepts of family and community responsibility found no place. Instead, the system appeared to be dominated by professionals who had little knowledge of Maori ways. Almost overnight, the set of values driving the reforms did a total flip. A completely new piece of legislation replaced the original Bill and was passed into law without the public having a further opportunity to make submissions. Child protection teams disappeared, although the legislation does provide for community-based care and protection panels who play a modest advisory role in child protection cases. In the place of the teams is a new decision-making body, the family group conference. The family group conference, which will be discussed in greater detail later, was designed to give the Maori whanau or extended family and the Pacific Island equivalents key responsibility for deciding how to deal with child abuse cases. Family, although not defined in the Act, is to be understood in much broader terms than just parents and siblings. Only if the conference process fails are the courts called to make decisions. Given this background, the emphasis in the administration of the Act was on the abused child's biological and adoptive family. As we shall see later, this is an incorrect interpretation of the Act, and a child's emotional and psychological links may be as important, if not more important, under the statutory scheme as biological ones.[16] Nevertheless, this false premise has played a dominating role in the handling of child abuse cases in the past few years.

The Act is replete with 'objects' and 'principles'. Many of them are aimed at offering support to families and the position of the abused child is played down. Thus 'assisting parents, families, whanau, hapu, iwi, and family groups to discharge their responsibilities to prevent their children and young persons suffering harm, ill-treatment, abuse, neglect or deprivation' (s.4(*b*))[17] is listed ahead of 'providing for the protection of children' (s.4(*e*)) in the objects section. Section 5, which lists a number of 'principles', refers to consideration being given to the welfare of the child, but in the same breath as a reference to 'the stability of that child's or young person's family, whanau, hapu, iwi, and family group'. Under the scheme in force prior to the 1989 Act, there was no doubt that the welfare of the child was of paramount importance, as it was expressly provided for in s.4 of the Children and Young Persons Act 1974. But in the original version of the 1989 Act, s.6 provided that the welfare of the child would be 'the deciding factor', but only if there was a conflict of interest or principles. This formulation invited controversy. Although there was high judicial warrant for saying that it merely respresented a rewording of the paramountcy rule,[18] there is no doubt that social workers and departmental policy makers were more swayed by the new ideology of family than by the paramountcy of the child's welfare. A review of the 1989 Act, commonly referred to as the Mason Report after the chair of the reviewing committee,[19] was scathing in its criticism:[20]

> All too readily Co-ordinators, social workers and participants in the FGC refuse to acknowledge a conflict of principles or interests in situations where one clearly exists. Consequently, where a conflict is not acknowledged, the welfare and interests of the child or young person do NOT become the deciding factor in the outcome of the Conference. It appears to us, and there is ample evidence to support this view, that in the interests of resolving problems within the context of the family unit, the conflict principle is either overlooked or not understood.

An amendment passed in 1994 rewrote s.6 so that the welfare and interests of the child are now clearly 'the first and paramount consideration, having regard to the principles ... of this Act'. Despite the vague reference to the principles of the Act, there can now be little doubt that, where the interests of the abused child and those of the child's family clash, the family must take second place and, even where there is no such ostensible clash, the welfare of the child must always be the priority. The family ideology, while still powerful, can no longer be dominant. This is surely right when dealing with child abuse, yet the latest judicial horror story reawakens our doubts. In *Re ITA*,[21] the court was faced with a baby with serious head and knee injuries, described by Judge Green as 'physical abuse at the most serious end of the scale'.[22] She rejected the parents' explanations and found that they had fallen below acceptable standards for ensuring the child's safety: 'I make this finding having regard to the diversity of child-rearing practices and the cultural diversity existing in New Zealand today.'[23] While there can be little justification for the parents' 'angry responses and political platitudes', there can be even less for the social workers' unrepentant actions. It appears that the handling of the case had been largely delegated to health workers, who were not informed of the child's injuries or of the negative paediatric assessment of these injuries and the history of violence in the family. One of the health workers admitted to being an advocate for the parents. Judge Green stated:[24]

> It becomes immediately apparent that there exists a risk when the statutory body charged with the child's safety and custody has delegated much of its responsibility for oversight and planning to a person who has assumed the role of advocate for the parents at a time before the Court has been able to test any of the allegations or make findings in relation to the child's non-accidental injuries.

The judge considered that 'a complete lack of focus' on the principle of the paramountcy of the welfare of the child had been established: 'Throughout the case ... attention was drawn away from the child's injuries onto the programmes which had been provided and what was seen as the reasonably positive response of the parents.'[25] The judge had little hesitation in making a declaration that the child was in need of care and protection.

Section 13 of the Act lists a further set of principles designed to relate in particular to the care and protection of children. The first principle is this time child-focused: that children 'must be protected from harm, their rights upheld, and their welfare promoted'. Many of the remaining principles, however, focus on the preservation of the family, so that a child should be removed 'only if there is a serious risk of harm to the child' and even then there is encouragement for return to the family or living in the same locality as the family. The family ideology is therefore seen cropping up at every stage of the child abuse process and even after the child has been removed from danger. Now we know that alternatives to care within the family can be devastating. In 1996, 79 allegations of abuse about 52 care givers were received and 19 care givers were banned from working in that role.[26] Parliamentarians have also learnt of highly inappropriate placements where, in one instance, a girl was sent to a foster home which turned out to be a brothel and in another a child was placed in a boarding school where it was known that children had been physically and sexually abused.[27] On the other hand, an abused child will often be abused because the family to which the child belongs is dysfunctional. In these cases it is by no means obvious that the preservation of the family is a worthy goal or that removal from the dysfunctional environment is necessarily a bad thing. Whether the New Zealand principles governing child abuse and child protection reflect the most appropriate balance is thus a matter of contention. According to one group of authors, 'There is a bitter irony in the fact that an Act specifically designed to protect children is potentially dangerous to their welfare.'[28]

THE PROCESS FOR DEALING WITH CHILD ABUSE

In need of care or protection

The procedures for handling child abuse cases depend in large measure on whether the child is, or is believed to be, in need of care and protection. This concept is defined in s.14, which sets out a wide range of situations, ranging from abuse and neglect, to truancy, to children who are out of control. For child abuse the principal provision is s.14(1)(a), which states that a child may be in need of care or protection if 'The child ... is being, or is likely to be, harmed (whether physically or emotionally or sexually), ill-treated, abused, or seriously deprived.' It will be seen that the harm, ill-treatment or abuse need not be 'serious', as with deprivation, but it has been held that the harm must nevertheless be of sufficient degree to warrant the intervention of the court.[29] The provision is also silent on the question of who may have perpetrated the abuse. A lack of proof of culpability will not, however, prevent a court from determining that the child is in need of care or protection so long as the grounds for such a determination are otherwise made out.[30] Past abuse is not in itself sufficient and is relevant only to establishing a continuing state of affairs or the likelihood of future abuse. An unborn child may be the subject of proceedings according to a somewhat controversial Family Court decision.[31] In that case, an order was made with respect to the unborn child primarily because the 15-year-old mother had a relationship with a violent young man who threatened to kidnap and kill the baby.

Proof of physical abuse will normally be a question of fact. A definition used by the Children and Young Persons Service (CYPS) is that physical abuse 'includes bruises, burns, damage from severe shaking, deliberate dunking in scalding water, cigarette burns, lacerations, poisoning etc'.[32] Expert evidence will often be able to indicate whether injuries are accidental or non-accidental. There may, however, be some situations where the determination of whether a child is in need of care or protection is more problematic. A case decided under the previous law illustrates this. In *Department of*

Social Welfare v. *J*,[33] there was evidence that a child had been hit, thrown to the floor and was distressed at being locked in various places with her mother. The case was at first thrown out, but this was altered on appeal. One of the key issues was whether there are minimal allowable standards which, if met, will mean that a case is not made out. In rejecting such a notion, Williamson J said:[34]

> there is a danger to the welfare of children if the judgment is made in all cases with reference to a base of a minimum allowable standard. Concentration on such a standard may obscure other factors pointing either towards or against neglect. To extend such a standard to all of the grounds in s.27 [the precursor to s.14] is to legislate in a way which Parliament appears to have avoided. If a child is being ill treated then to ignore or minimise such ill treatment upon the basis that it does not fall below the minimum allowable standard which the Judge perceives may be accepted in the community or the relevant section of the community is to ignore the welfare of the child.

The question of community standards can become especially acute when it is argued that the allegedly abusive actions were merely acts of discipline in accordance with religious or cultural practices. In *Department of Social Welfare* v. *H*,[35] the court was faced with two boys aged eight and 10, both of whom were described by a psychiatrist as 'cowed, withdrawn and fearful children'. The judge found 'that they had been cruelly ill-treated, mainly by emotional abuse but to a lesser degree also by physical abuse'.[36] There was evidence that the children's step-mother had laid down a very oppressive system of discipline with rules about use and storage of toys, 'no go' areas, and rules about eating and chewing food. Punishment was arbitrary, exacted by the father. The judge held that 'the management of these children in this home went well beyond mismanagement and into emotional and physical cruelty'.[37]

Proof of sexual abuse is notoriously much more difficult. In a case where sexual abuse by a girl's father was held to have occurred, Boshier J felt disposed to address the various roles of experts and judges:[38]

> As to sexual abuse, it is a field unlike some other fields, where exactitude is difficult ... I do not regard it as the province of experts in cases such as this to seek to comment on a wide range of matters such as the nature of other evidence available. That is my function. Equally I do not regard it as my function to enter into the fray and comment upon the schools of thought within the psychological world as to methodology. There is the need for great caution and common sense in an area such as this ... I regret that in this case there has been a tendency to submerge the judicial role on the part of the experts. There has been a tendency to express a wide range of views on matters of evidence and other facts. In

summary, I see my task as identifying the strands that could constitute the material of possible sexual abuse and by weaving them together, according to a legitimate judicial process, by deducing whether there has been abuse ...

In that particular case, the judge accepted that there was evidence that some sexual abuse had occurred and ordered that the case be referred for a family group conference to be held.

Reporting

Reporting protocols

Anyone who believes that a child may be the victim of child abuse may report the matter under s.15 to a Department of Social Welfare social worker or the police. Immunity from civil, criminal and professional proceedings follows such a report unless there was bad faith in making the report.[39] There has been considerable debate over whether reporting should be mandatory for certain sections of the community. The Mason Report was of the view that the Act should be amended to provide for this,[40] and an amendment bill introduced into Parliament in 1993 imposed mandatory requirements on people such as the police, doctors, nurses, psychologists, teachers and lawyers. The issue went to a free vote in Parliament and the requirements were voted out. Fiscal concerns were partly the reason: a fear that mandatory reporting would increase the number of false claims and use up social work resources better employed elsewhere.

Despite the rejection of mandatory reporting, a new approach to notification of child abuse has been developed. The 1994 Amendment Act, as finally passed, imposed extra duties on the Director-General of Social Welfare. Apart from a new public relations role promoting 'awareness of child abuse, the unacceptability of child abuse, the ways in which child abuse may be prevented, the need to report cases of child abuse, and the ways in which child abuse may be reported',[41] Social Welfare also has a new duty to develop and implement protocols with agencies and groups in the community on reporting of child abuse. Social Welfare is thus required to liaise very closely with a wide cross-section of society – within government, in the voluntary sector, with professional bodies – on establishing systems for the identification of abuse and in this way it is hoped that there will be a cooperative approach to the management of child abuse throughout New Zealand. One of the first steps taken by the Department to fulfil its new duties was the publication of a booklet to help people to recognize abuse.[42] More recently, a further publication sets out some existing protocols and offers guidance to agencies on how to develop a protocol.[43] Information has been brought together not only from the health and education sectors but also from voluntary agencies, the Open Home Foundation (which works especially in the area of fostering and care of children), Youth for Christ, Barnardo's and the Children's Health Camps Board.

The Open Home Foundation protocol offers some background on how to deal with allegations of abuse. It states, for instance, that, 'when a child tells you of abusive behaviour beyond the normal experience for their age, perpetrated on them by a trusted person, it is most unlikely that they are lying'. There are rubrics advising its people not to work alone, to consult senior staff, to record observations and communications, to take care not to interview the child by asking leading questions, not to question or counsel the alleged offender and, if the abuse is by someone outside the immediate family, to consult the parents. Where it is a member of their staff or one of their foster families who is accused, the protocol states that the matter is to be referred as soon as possible to Open Home management and the statutory authorities and the accused person or family is automatically suspended. One other protocol suffices to illustrate some of these issues a little further. The national protocol agreed by the Ministry of Education, Early Childhood Education Services and the Children and Young Persons Service sets out several points for employees to note: 'documentation may subsequently be used in Court as evidence for either side. Avoid making judgements; simply record the facts'; 'interviewing of suspected abuse victims is a specialised procedure best left to those who are trained in such techniques'; 'do not attempt to contact the alleged abuser'.

The development of child abuse protocols is continuing process. The current initiatives may have much the same impact as is claimed for mandatory reporting, but in addition may be better directed by ensuring that relevant organizations carefully think through the way in which they and their staff handle suspected abuse.

Investigation of report

Once a report has been made to the statutory authorities, there is an obligation on the social worker or police to investigate the report, and part of that process involves consultation with the local care and protection resource panel.[44] The function of the panels, a pale version of the child protection teams first proposed for dealing with child abuse, is to provide advice to social workers on the exercise or performance of the role, and they do so from community, governmental and professional perspectives.[45] The panels, however, have no real teeth and their advice can be ignored.

As the Mason Report put it:[46]

The central theme which emerged during our discussions with Panels and others was the lack of definition as to the roles and responsibilities of Panels. Several Panels commented that this lack of a clearly defined role created problems, not just for the Panels themselves, but also for social workers and Co-ordinators. In some cases this confusion has resulted in some social workers feeling that the Panel was being too intrusive while in other cases Panels were regarded as a convenient lap dog for the Department, in the sense that it was either not consulted or if was consulted [*sic*], it was in an off-hand or patronising manner.

If the investigator of a report 'reasonably believes' that the child is in need of care and protection, the case must be referred to a care and protection coordinator whose task is to convene a family group conference.[47] The assessment of the investigator has recently come under rigorous judicial scrutiny in *CMP* v. *D-GSW*.[48] This case was not one of abuse, but the principles developed there must inevitably affect the way in which abuse cases are handled. A boy was born to the applicant who had made arrangements for him to be adopted. The adoptive parents decided not to go ahead with the adoption when it was discovered that the boy had serious handicaps, but they continued to care for the child. By the time of the proceedings, the boy, now aged 4, was in the day-to-day care of a new care giver organized by the foster parents with the help of the leading voluntary organization for those with intellectual handicaps. A family group conference had been held twice and the care and protection coordinator proposed calling another one, inviting the mother's elderly parents, who knew nothing of the child's existence and were, it was thought, unlikely to cope with the news very well. The mother applied for judicial review. The judgment covered two main issues, one relating to family group conferences (to be discussed later) and the other relating to the decision to refer the case to the care and protection coordinator. On the latter question, Elias J noted that the test is not whether the child is in need of care and protection but whether the social worker reasonably believes this to be so. This is a harder test to satisfy than mere belief or mere suspicion (the test of reasonable suspicion is used elsewhere in the Act, notably in s.39, which deals with the granting of place of safety warrants). There is a curious inconsistency in the legislation, for s.18(1) duplicates the rule in section 17(2) on referral to a coordinator but omits the word 'reasonably'. In the light of the *CMP* decision, there can be little doubt that the test is objective but, as Elias J said, in evaluating social workers' decisions 'It would be wrong to set the trigger for these assessments too highly.'[49] The family group process itself provides a safeguard against incorrect referrals. On the facts, the judge held that a social worker could have reasonably formed the belief that the boy was in need of care and protection because the adopting parents were unsure that they could care for him, the adoption had gone awry and there was uncertainty about the boy's future:[50]

> There may be some cases where questions of guardianship and long-term care are remote enough from the immediate needs of a child for it to be unreasonable to consider him in present need of care and protection. But here, because of [the boy's] special needs and the background, the risk was present.

In view of the harsh criticism offered of the Department later in the judgment, for instance criticism of the coordinator's assessment that the mother was 'abandoning' the boy, one may have qualms about the reasonableness of the social worker's belief. Such assessments should, however, be easier where there is evidence of physical abuse but may be much harder where there have been allegations of sexual abuse, where false claims appear more prevalent. As Elias J says, the trigger in all these situations must not be set too highly or else the interests of child victims will suffer, yet the consequences of false accusations can be highly damaging for all parties. Care in reaching a belief about the child's status is obviously essential.

Extent of notifications

Accurate statistical information on notifications of child abuse trends is hard to obtain. The government has changed not only the way in which notifications are recorded but also the period of time during which figures are kept. Fluctuations from year to year are not always easy to explain.

In 1990, there were 12 079 notifications, compared with 24 290 in 1994/5 and an even higher figure of 30 552 in 1993/4.[51] Read quickly, these figures suggest either that child abuse has doubled in five years or that people are now more alerted to the issue and are more likely to report. But the figures may be skewed by differing statistical mechanisms. The number of these notifications which after investigation were referred to family group conferences rose, but at not quite the same rate. In 1990, 3394 family group conferences (approximately a quarter of the number of notifications) were held, while in 1994/5, 4862 were held: approximately one-fifth. In addition to these cases, a little over 10 per cent ended in a 'family/whanau' agreement in 1994/5.[52] The vast majority of notifications led therefore to no further action. The statutory authority for family/whanau agreements is a little obscure. Under s.139 of the Children, Young Persons, and Their Families Act 1989, a temporary care agreement can be entered into, but normally for no longer than 28 days. Longer-term agreements are provided for under ss.140–49, but only if a family group conference has approved. These agreements, if unaccompanied by a family group conference, may thus be of doubtful legal validity, representing a questionable means of avoiding the greater formalities of the conference process.

While the above figures include reports of children with behavioural problems, most of the cases involved physical or emotional abuse. A study of the notifications reached several other conclusions: (a) each year at least 13 in every 1000 children may be the subject of investigation; (b) there are no noticeable differences in the gender balance of the children; but (c) Maoris are likely to be over-represented in the figures compared with their population.[53]

Family group conferences[54]

As already indicated, the family group conference (FGC) plays a key role in determining outcomes for abused children. The care and protection coordinator is charged with the responsibility or organizing the conference and as part of this must consult a care and protection panel and members of the family.[55] The conference may be required as a result of the investigation of a report but may also follow referral by any court.[56] An example of the latter is *Price* v. *Hills*,[57] a case where a mother unsuccessfully sought a protection order under the Domestic Protection Act 1982 (now replaced by the Domestic Violence Act 1995) and the judge, being very concerned about the effect of the situation on the children, referred the matter to a coordinator.

One of the principal functions of the FGC is to formulate a plan for the abused child. This will be done during a period of deliberation after the conference has had input and assistance from those with expertise in the area. The plan will be tailored to the situation, but should cover such matters as where the child is to live and go to school. There is of course a risk that the conference will come up with a plan which does not ensure the safety of the child. What if, for example, it is proposed to leave the child with the alleged abusers? Under s.30, the plan must be agreed to by various officials including the social worker who investigated the case, and this thus acts as a safeguard against unreasonable decision making. If there is controversy about the plan, it may be resolved by negotiation or by reconvening the conference. If the conference cannot produce an agreed plan or to produce one which is acceptable to the authorities, the case may ultimately have to go to court. It is reported that plans formulated by conferences are agreed to in 90 per cent of cases.[58]

An important issue for the coordinator in planning for a family group conference is determining whom to invite. Under s.22, various people are entitled to attend, including the child, unless the child is too young or the coordinator considers that attendance would not be in the child's interests or would be undesirable for any other reason,[59] and every parent, guardian and member of the child's family, whanau or family group, again unless the coordinator considers that that person's attendance would not be in the child's interests or would be undesirable for any other reason. Other officials, including counsel for the child, have rights to attend but not to attend the family's private deliberations. How the coordinator exercises the discretions just outlined may be crucial in terms of outcomes for the child and for the civil rights of the parties. In one story, the family had been badly split for 10 years and the father strongly opposed inviting the estranged relatives. He was, however, persuaded otherwise and, eventually, not only was the child well placed but the family rift was healed.[60]

On the other hand, the coordinator and the Department received severe judicial criticism in the case, already partly discussed, *CMP* v. *D-GSW*.[61] Elias J referred to fixed attitudes, a process which had become intolerable, personal beliefs not derived from the statute and inflexibly maintained views. 'I am left,' said her Honour, 'with the view that a little less dogma would have helped.'[62] It will be recalled that one of the issues was whether it was right to invite the handicapped child's elderly grandparents, who knew nothing of the child's existence, to the FGC. Coupled with this was the place to be given the foster parents who had originally intended to adopt. On the first point, the judge held that the grandparents should not be invited. The coordinator had failed to take sufficiently into account the mother's interests, including her right to privacy, personal dignity and human rights to freedom of conscience. A false judgement had also been made that the mother had in effect abandoned the boy. In judicial review terms, the coordinator had taken irrelevant matters into account and failed to take into account others which were relevant. On the second point, the treatment of the foster parents, characterized by social workers as 'paid caregivers', was simply wrong as a matter of law. While 'family' is not defined in the Act, 'family group' is.[63] Biological connections are included in the definition of the phrase but what is often overlooked is that adults to whom the child has 'a significant psychological attachment' are also within the 'family group'. The evidence in the case revealed that the coordinator and social workers did not look beyond the 'extended natural family' and thus misdirected themselves as a matter of law.

CMP v. *D-GSW* is an important case for all proceedings under the 1989 Act, including child abuse. It shows the willingness of the court to supervise by means of judicial review the exercise of discretion by social workers and other officials. In particular, it gives some guidelines for the operation of family group conferences. At a general level, it remedies the imbalance in policy and thinking which appears to have dominated the Department, biasing it in favour of the biological family against other care givers who have played a major part in the child's life.

Role of the court

The role of the court in child abuse cases dealt with under the Children, Young Persons and Their Families Act 1989 ought to be a residual one. The family group conference process is designed at least in part to avoid adversary proceedings. Applications to the court can be made by a departmental social worker, a member of the police or, with leave of the court, any other person.[64] The abused child or an advocate for the abused child may thus apply, but only after crossing the hurdle of obtaining leave. Generally, however, an application cannot be made unless a family group conference has already been held, the primary exceptions being where some emergency action has been taken.[65] Furthermore, a court cannot make a declaration unless a conference has been held and unless satisfied that there is no alternative way of dealing with the situation.[66] Apart from a declaration that a child is in need of care or protection, the court has a range of more specific orders to choose from, including support and service orders, custody and guardianship orders and counselling and restraining orders.

Despite the statutory limitations on the role of the court, figures indicate that a sizeable number of cases end up in the courts.[67] In 1995/96, 4799 family group conferences were held, some of which may represent a second conference for the same child. A total of 2943 plans were made as a result of these conferences. However, 5495 court orders were made during the same time. As more than one order may be made with respect to the same child, the statistics need to be examined a little more closely. The total number of plans and orders was 8438 and these involved 5238 children. If we assume that there was one plan for each child, that leaves 2295 ending up in the court system. As statistics also indicate that 1702 custody orders and 1227 guardianship orders were made, 2295 children may be an underestimate. Two consequences, it is suggested, flow from this, both disturbing in the light of the goals of the 1989 Act.

1 Only a little over half of family group conferences are producing viable plans for children. Many conferences are therefore not successful, if the production of a plan is the measure of success.
2 Nearly half of the children going through family group conferences will end up being dealt with by the courts. The role of the courts is thus hardly in reality a residual one at all.

Emergency procedures

Child abuse cases will often need to be dealt with as a matter of urgency in order to ensure the safety of the child. Provision is made for this in advance of the procedures for family group conferences and court declarations. Under s.39, a judge or justice of the peace may issue a place of safety warrant if there are reasonable grounds for suspecting that the child is suffering or likely to suffer ill-treatment, neglect, deprivation, abuse or harm. The warrant entitles the social worker or police to search for the child and if necessary to remove the child.[68] A warrant to remove a child may also be issued under s.40 if an application has been made to the court for a declaration. Where the police believe on reasonable grounds that it is 'critically necessary to protect a child', they may act without warrant under s.42. In 1995/96, 339 place of safety warrants were issued and 32 searches without warrant were carried out. Figures for the previous year were 478 and 55, respectively.[69]

OTHER MEANS OF DEALING WITH CHILD ABUSE

Domestic Violence Act 1995

The Domestic Violence Act 1995 represents a major reform of the law on spousal battering. While its principal focus is adult violence, one of the reforms was to extend markedly the categories of people who can apply for a protection order. Among these are family members, defined to mean relatives by blood, marriage or adoption, plus those who are members of the same whanau or 'other culturally recognised family group'.[70] It follows that an abused child can seek a declaration against parents and other members of the family. Section 9 expressly provides a procedure for minors to apply through a representative unless the minor is married or has reached the age of 17, in which case the minor must apply on their own behalf.

The full potential of these provisions for bypassing the Children, Young Persons and Their Families Act 1989 has yet to be realized, but has been flagged in more than one case. In *Steyn* v. *Brett*,[71] for example, a girl claimed she was abused by her father during access visits. The court accepted that the father had slapped the girl on the cheek and the legs, but this was in response to provocation by the girl. The court thus refused to categorize the father's conduct as abuse and declined to grant an order. It is not difficult to imagine other situations, however, where there is a pattern of behaviour which would be regarded as child abuse and where the court would be far more inclined to grant an order. A court faced with such an application under the 1995 Act could, under s.19 of the Children, Young Persons, and Their Families Act 1989, refer the matter to a care and protection coordinator, a step leading to a possible family group conference. There is no provision as such under the 1995 Act for family group conferences. On the other hand, that Act provides for the automatic referral of the respondent to an anger management programme, a step which does not necessarily follow under the 1989 Act.[72]

An order was in fact granted on the application of three young girls in *Arvidson v. Croft*.[73] The application was made against the mother's de facto partner and the court agreed that this man had been physically abusive towards one of the girls and psychologically abusive against the mother. The case is interesting for two other reasons. First, the representative of the children was their father and the judge noted the potential for abuse of the procedures where one parent is in effect driving the litigation against the other parent's partner.[74] Secondly, these children were already in the interim custody of the Director-General of Social Welfare and had been placed with their maternal grandmother. As part of this process, a family group conference had already been held. The case shows how the two pieces of legislation may function side-by-side, but there is also surely the possibility of the procedures of the 1995 Act being superimposed on top of whatever has been decided under the Children, Young Persons, and Their Families Act 1989.

A companion piece of legislation passed along with the Domestic Violence Act made changes to the rules relating to child custody and access cases.[75] Where in such a case one of the parties makes an allegation against the other party of physical or sexual abuse, whether the victim be adult or child, the court must first determine whether the allegation is proved and, if it is, then the perpetrator cannot be granted custody or unsupervised access unless the court is sure that the child will be safe. While child abuse has in the past been relevant to these cases, the new law establishes a stricter and more rigorous formula for an abuser to satisfy.[76]

Civil liability

The opportunity for a victim of child abuse to sue the perpetrator is somewhat clouded in New Zealand by the presence of the accident compensation system. Section 14 of the Accident Rehabilitation and Compensation Insurance Act 1992 prevents the recovery of damages for personal injury because such an injury is covered under the Act's statutory compensation scheme. Exemplary damages are, however, preserved and claiming such damages for all manner of losses has become something of an industry in New Zealand.[77] A further difficulty is that the victim may wait many years after the abuse before deciding and being able to contemplate taking civil action. In *S v. G*,[78] the victim was a young teenager living in a community in the late 1970s. She was abused at the time by one of the leaders of the community who was subsequently convicted of indecent assault in 1992. It was only around 1991 that the victim began to appreciate the psychological and emotional harm that the abuse had wrought on her, but she nevertheless delayed in bringing proceedings. The Court of Appeal accepted that the statutory limitation period within which actions must be brought could begin when the harm was reasonably discoverable, and in the abuse situation this meant when the psychological damage was or should have been reasonably identified and linked to the abuse. Unfortunately, on the facts, this meant that the victim was still out of the statutory period unless the court was prepared to grant leave to extend the period. The Court of Appeal declined to do so, being influenced in part by the conviction and sentence already against the defendant's name and the the consequent potential for double punishment.

Prince v. Attorney-General[79] illustrates a further aspect of civil litigation. The plaintiff, by now an adult, had been adopted, and sued the Department of Social Welfare, first for mismanaging the adoption, and then for failing to follow up a complaint that the plaintiff was not being looked after properly, leading to his becoming a 'street kid'. The causes of action relating to the first aspect of the case were struck out, but those relating to the second were preserved. Anderson J stated:[80]

> In my judgment there are very firm policy reasons for not withholding recognition of a common law duty of care to children at risk in the very respects for which provision for preventive and remedial objectives and powers are given by statute, and which are so consonant with the standards and expectations of the New Zealand community.

Civil liability for child abuse may therefore rest not only on the actual perpetrator but also, depending on the facts, on those authorities and agencies, presumably whether government or voluntary, who have responsibilites for children.

Criminal liability

Child abusers may have committed criminal offences and be charged accordingly. The range of possible charges is of course wide and much will depend on the actual nature of the case. One of the leading cases in New Zealand is *R v. Witika*,[81] which involved the abuse of a girl aged two who was subject to beatings, burning in hot water and eventual death at the hands of her mother and the mother's partner, Smith. Charges included ill-treatment, neglect, manslaughter and murder. Two points of special interest exercised the judges in the Court of Appeal. First, the mother relied on the defence of duress, arguing that her failure to obtain medical help for the child was because she was dominated physically, mentally and sexually by Smith. The court rejected the defence, noting that, while the position of battered women called for sympathy, 'there can be no justification for broadening the grounds on which the law should provide excuses for child abuse'.[82] On the facts, the mother had encouraged Smith to be abusive and had had opportunities to seek assistance and medical advice for the child which she did not take. The other point of interest also emerges from the fact that there were two abusers. Smith argued as a defence to the charges involving the girl's burns that the Crown had not established beyond reasonable doubt which of the two was actually responsible for these injuries. The Court of Appeal rejected the defence: if Smith was not the principal offender, there was ample evidence that he was a secondary party.

The submitting of evidence in child abuse cases, especially the victim's evidence, has often been a fraught matter. The usual procedures of giving evidence in open court, subject to cross-examination, appear daunting to the child complainant and because of the element of fear may well mean that essential evidence is not placed before the court. New Zealand legislated in 1989 to allow for child complainants' evidence to be presented in a variety of less forbidding ways.[83] The court may now allow the use of video-taped evidence, closed-circuit television, screens and the giving of evidence outside the court precincts. Other rules prevent the accused putting questions to the complainant other than through counsel or some other approved person and prevent the judge from allowing the jury to draw any adverse inferences from the mode in which the evidence is presented. The judge must also 'not instruct the jury on the need to scrutinise the evidence of young children generally with special care nor suggest to the jury that young children have tendencies to invention or distortion'.[84] The statutory rules just outlined apply only in sexual abuse cases, but, in a case where the parents of four children were charged with wilfully ill-treating three of them mainly through physical beatings,[85] and where there was video-taped evidence collected according to the procedures applicable in sexual abuse cases, the Court of Appeal endorsed the view that the evidence was admissible under the court's inherent jurisdiction.[86]

These new methods of presenting evidence ease the pressure on the victim, but may work hardship to the accused. The possibility of false accusations of abuse is real and can have significant downstream consequences. In one case where a father was acquitted of sexually abusing his sons, the judge hearing a subsequent custody application accepted that there had been an injustice against the father and refused to grant the mother custody.[87]

CONCLUSION

Child abuse may forever be an intractable problem. There are no perfect solutions. How do we prevent harm to our children? How do we ensure the safety of our children when abuse becomes apparent? What resources are available to families dealing with abuse within their ranks? How do we handle false allegations of abuse? All these questions suggest that major responsibility inevitably rests on the wider community and the state. But where is the balance between an intrusive and culturally insensitive governmental agency and one which appears to be backing away either through lack of resources or for ideological reasons? In New Zealand at present, with neoliberal forces dominating policy making, the balance is tilted in favour of minimal intervention. This is producing cries from people who say that economic concerns are given priority over care of children, that unless a case is one of the most compelling kind of abuse it will not be investigated, and that social workers are inadequately trained and resourced.[88] While child abuse can have civil and criminal liability consequences, the principal mechanism for handling allegations of child abuse in New Zealand is that put in place by the Children, Young Persons, and Their Families Act 1989. Because of the central role the Act gives the family, it may still be seen as an experimental programme. However, it will hardly be a fair experiment if the state fails to offer adequate resources to the administering agencies and place the protection of children high on its agenda.

NOTES

1. *Sunday Star Times*, Auckland, 25 August 1996.
2. I. Hassall, 'Report to the Minister of Social Welfare on the New Zealand Children and Young Persons Service's Review of Practice in Relation to Craig Manukau and his Family', 7 October 1993.
3. See Part IX of the Children, Young Persons, and Their Families Act 1989. A sizeable proportion of the commissioner's work involves inquiries in the field of education. The commissioner is currently under the wing of the Department of Social Welfare for such matters as funding. There have been frequent calls for the office to be made independent, with the commissioner becoming an officer of Parliament. The wide role lends support to this suggestion, but, more importantly, independence would leave the commissioner freer to evaluate the Department of Social Welfare.
4. Although see the comments of P. Tapp, D. Geddis and N. Taylor, 'Protecting the

Family' in M. Henaghan and B. Atkin (eds), *Family Law Policy in New Zealand* (Auckland: Oxford University Press, 1992) who are highly critical of the current New Zealand statutory regime.

5   *The Evening Post*, Wellington, 28 April 1997.
6   *Sunday Star Times*, Auckland, 30 March 1997.
7   *The Dominion* Wellington, 23 January 1997.
8   Annual Report for the Year ended 30 June 1996, pp.4–5. By the time of this report, the person of the Commissioner had changed from Dr I. Hassall, who investigated the Craig Manukau case, to lawyer, L. O'Reilly.
9   *From Welfare to Well-being, Department of Social Welfare Annual Report*, 1996, p.12. Extra funding was also confirmed in the government's 1997 budget.
10 *The Dominion*, Wellington, 12 November 1996.
11 Press release, Hon. Annette King MP, 24 October 1996.
12 For a valuable account of this, see C. Cheyne, M. O'Brien and M. Belgrave, *Social Policy in Aotearoa New Zealand A Critical Introduction* (Auckland: Oxford University Press, 1997), pp.211–12.
13 Section 110, Children, Young Persons, and Their Families Act 1989.
14 See Tapp et al., op. cit., note 4 for a somewhat critical exposition of the legislative history. A much more positive perspective is placed on the Act by D. Durie-Hall and J. Metge, 'Kua Tutu Te Puehu, Kia Mau Maori Aspirations and Family Law', in ibid.
15 The report, *Puao-te-ata-tu: The Report of the Ministerial Advisory Committee on a Maori Perspective for the Department of Social Welfare* (Wellington: Government Printer, 1986) was especially significant as it was highly critical of the European focus of the Department of Social Welfare. The Maori perspective had been largely ignored by the Department, even though many of the children and families dealt with by the Department were Maori.
16 *CMP* v. *D-GSW* [1997] NZFLR 1.
17 The words 'whanau, hapu and iwi' can be somewhat roughly translated as extended family, sub-tribe and tribe.
18 *Director-General of Social Welfare* v. *L* [1989] 2 NZLR 314 (CA).
19 *Review of the Children, Young Persons and Their Families Act 1989 Report of the Ministerial Review Team to the Minister of Social Welfare* (1992).
20 Ibid., 11.
21 [1997] NZFLR 385.
22 Ibid., 393.
23 Ibid., 394.
24 Ibid., 389.
25 Ibid., 394.
26 *The Dominion*, Wellington, 12 April 1997.
27 Ibid.
28 Tapp et al., op. cit., note 4, p.183.
29 *D-GSW* v. *S* [1992] NZFLR 309.
30 Section 71, Children, Young Persons, and Their Families Act 1989.
31 *In the matter of Baby P (an unborn child)* [1995] NZFLR 577.
32 Circular Memo 191/1989.
33 (1988) 5 NZFLR 403.
34 Ibid., 413.
35 (1988) 5 NZFLR 80.
36 Ibid., 81.
37 Ibid., 87.

38 *Department of Social Welfare* v. *C* [1991] NZFLR 350, 356-7.
39 Section 16, Children, Young Persons, and Their Families Act 1989.
40 Op. cit., note 19, pp.17-18.
41 Section 7(1)(ba)(i), Children, Young Persons, and Their Families Act 1989.
42 *Breaking the Cycle: An interagency guide to child abuse* (Wellington: NZCYPS, 1995).
43 *Breaking the Cycle: Interagency protocols for child abuse management* (Wellington: NZCYPS, 1996).
44 Section 17, Children, Young Persons, and Their Families Act 1989. There is a strange inconsistency in the legislation over the obligation to investigate: s.17(3) provides for feedback to the person who made the report and this may indicate that a decision has been made *not* to investigate the report. Section 17(1) uses the phrase, 'such investigation as may be necessary or desirable', which could allow on a somewhat strained interpretation for no investigation to be made at all, *sed quaere*. Provision for care and protection resource panels is found in ss.428-32, Children, Young Persons, and Their Families Act 1989.
45 Under s.428, Children, Young Persons, and Their Families Act 1989, panels consist of people appointed on a discretionary basis by the Director-General of Social Welfare, but consideration has to be given to appointing people from occupations and organizations (government and non-government) having an interest in children.
46 Op. cit., note 19, pp.50-51.
47 Section 17(2), Children, Young Persons, and Their Families Act 1989.
48 [1997] NZFLR 1.
49 Ibid., 27.
50 Ibid., 28.
51 J.P. Robertson and G.M. Maxwell, *A Study of Notifications for Care and Protection to the Children and Young Persons Service* (Wellington: Office of the Commissioner for Children, 1996) p.1. Statistics were collected on a calendar year basis in 1990 but subsequently the fiscal year from July to June has been used.
52 Ibid. Patterns for 1995/6 are similar: 23 046 notifications, 4799 FGCs, 3204 family/whanau agreements (Department of Social Welfare Annual Report fiscal year 1996, *From Welfare to Well-being*, 'Statistics Report', p.84).
53 Robertson and Maxwell op. cit., note 51, p.17.
54 For a valuable study of such conferences, see M. Gilling, L. Patterson and B. Walker, *Family Members' Experiences of the Care and Protection Family Group Conference Process* (Wellington: Social Policy Agency, 1995). See also J. Hudson, A. Morris, G. Maxwell and B. Galway, *Family Group Conferences Perspectives on Policy and Practice* (Annandale: Federation Press, 1996).
55 Section 21, Children, Young Persons, and Their Families Act 1989.
56 Section 19, Children, Young Persons, and Their Families Act 1989.
57 [1994] NZFLR 215.
58 S. Fraser and J. Norton, 'Family Group Conferencing in New Zealand Child Protection Work', in Hudson *et al.*, op. cit., note 54, p.39.
59 According to one study, children attended 795 FGCs: K. Paterson and M. Harvey, *An evaluation of the organisation and operation of care and protection family group conferences* (Wellington: Department of Social Welfare, 1991).
60 Fraser and Norton, op. cit., note 58, pp.45-6.
61 [1997] NZFLR 1. That the concerns of the mother in this case about who to invite are not isolated is shown in the study by Gilling *et al.*, op. cit., note 54, p.136.
62 Ibid., p.47.
63 Section 2(1), Children, Young Persons, and Their Families Act 1989.

64 Section 68, Children, Young Persons, and Their Families Act 1989. Section 69 provides that an application can be made by a social worker or the police jointly with parents, guardians or care givers.
65 Section 70, Children, Young Persons, and Their Families Act 1989.
66 Sections 70 and 71, Children, Young Persons, and Their Families Act 1989.
67 Department of Social Welfare Annual Report fiscal year 1996, *From Welfare to Wellbeing*, 'Statistics Report', p.85.
68 There has been little judicial comment on s.39, except in *R* v. *Kahu* [1995] 2 NZLR 3; [1995] NZFLR 341, where the Court of Appeal held that the warrant allows the holder to check premises for such things as food supplies and other necessities and where this turns up an illicit drug such as cannabis leading to criminal charges the finding of such evidence is legitimate.
69 Department of Social Welfare Annual Report fiscal year 1996, *From Welfare to Wellbeing*, 'Statistics Report', p.86.
70 Section 2, Domestic Violence Act 1995.
71 [1997] NZFLR 312.
72 Under s. 74, the court may direct parties to undergo counselling, but this is not mandatory and is a pale reflection of the provisions for programmes in the 1995 Act.
73 [1996] NZFLR 741.
74 Ibid., 757.
75 Sections 16A–16C, Guardianship Act 1968, as inserted by the Guardianship Amendment Act 1995.
76 Cf. *Payne* v. *Payne* [1996] NZFLR 786. The leading case prior to the new amendments was the Court of Appeal decision *M* v. *Y* [1994] 1 NZLR 527, which dealt with sexual abuse and adopted the test that a court would not grant custody or access if this would expose the child to an unacceptable risk of abuse: 'In many cases, perhaps most, the Court will be unable to reach a conclusion [whether the allegation is true or not] with any confidence. It is in that situation that an assessment of risk must be made. That assessment may lead to the conclusion that there should be no contact between parent and child, or to the conclusion that there should only be access that is monitored or supervised or otherwise controlled or limited ... It is a matter of balancing the competing interests – in each case primarily the child's interests – of continuing parental association against the risk of harm resulting from that association' (534).
77 *Donselaar* v. *Donselaar* [1982] 1 NZLR 97 (Court of Appeal).
78 [1995] 3 NZLR 681 (CA). This case was followed in *H* v. *R* [1996] 1 NZLR 299, where claims in battery and breach of fiduciary duty for abuse by a neighbour occurring 20 years earlier were allowed to proceed.
79 [1996] 3 NZLR 733. Contrast *D* v. *K* [1995] NZFLR 116, where the question whether parents falsely accused of abuse can sue the Department of Social Welfare for negligent investigation was answered in the negative. Cf. *X* v. *Bedfordshire County Council* [1995] 2 AC 635.
80 *Prince* v. *Attorney-General* [1996] 3NZLR 748.
81 [1993] 2 NZLR 424 (CA).
82 Ibid., 436.
83 Sections 23C–23I, as inserted in the Evidence Act 1908. See also the Accompanying Evidence (Videotaping of Child Complainants) Regulations 1990.
84 Section 23H(*c*), Evidence Act, 1908.
85 Section 195, Crimes Act, 1961, 'Cruelty to a child'.
86 *R* v. *Moke and Lawrence* [1996] 1 NZLR 263.
87 *J* v. *Z* [1995] NZFLR 721. Custody was in fact granted to the paternal grandparents.

88 Such sentiments have been aired by the Commissioner for Children (*The Dominion*, Wellington, 10 July 1997). The head of the Children and Young Persons Service, Griff Page, refutes the charges: 'I regret allegations that serious neglect and abuse cases are not being followed up. We obviously have to prioritise matters in the same way as other agencies who work in this sector. However, we do everything to ensure children of families who urgently need attention get it.'

15 Child Abuse: The Nigerian Perspective

Eunice Uzodike

INTRODUCTION

Abuse of children is a social problem now acknowledged in both developed and developing countries. While the developed world detected this in the 1960s, developing countries only began to realize it in the 1980s. Since then, problems of the meaning and definition of the term 'child abuse' have bedevilled researchers on the subject, since it has increasingly dawned on them that, although the world consists of one large global family, there are still wide social, legal, cultural, economic, political and religious differences that tend to render impossible a single universal definition and meaning acceptable to all nations. Hence it has been aptly observed that 'there is not a unitary and cross-culturally valid standard for either optimal child-rearing or for child maltreatment since what is acceptable or unacceptable becomes inextricably linked to ecological constraints and to the cultural context in which behaviour occurs'.[1] Similarly, it has been succinctly stated that 'arguments surrounding definitions of child abuse reflect ideological differences and may prove intractable ... and that much depends on who is doing the defining and for what purpose'.[2]

Giving a keynote address at a workshop on Child Abuse and Neglect, Ralph Diaz[3] said, 'Child abuse and neglect have to be redefined for each country, even for each area in a country – and redefined from time to time.' It was his view that, in conceptualizing child abuse, it is pointless for Africans to follow the Kempe tradition of designing research on child abuse and neglect centred around the child–parent relationship. This is because the focus on the child in the context of the family unit alone 'leads to a narrowing down of definitions of child abuse and neglect and falling into the trap of seeing individual trees without seeing the forest'.

On the other hand, it has been proposed that an 'analytical paradigm to understand child maltreatment in developing countries should include three levels – global, cultural and individual'.[4] The global level focuses on 'structural conditions in the world socio-economic order' and the maltreated child is seen as a victim of structural defects in the world system in which he finds himself. The cultural level focuses on normative child-rearing practices 'but which nonetheless have detrimental consequences for the child'. The individual level deals with specific parent–child behavioural acts that lead to the maltreatment of the child'.[5]

It is therefore clear that the concept and meaning of child abuse cannot be uniform in every society. Any definition that ignores cultural, social, economic, political and religious differences is bound to be wrong and unacceptable. Thus to evolve universal child care or child-rearing standards and expect all countries to abide by them will make little or no impact on the effort to find solutions to child abuse in a particular community setting. Indeed, Korbin early recognized that 'virtually all cultures, regardless of how harsh or indulgent their child care practices appear, have standards for acceptable child-rearing'.[6] Thus an act may become abusive where it fails to conform to the standard which is normally acceptable within that society and does not become so merely because it is regarded as such in another society. Certain acts that constitute child abuse in developed countries may not be regarded as such in developing countries and consequently a better understanding of the problem can be achieved only by approaching it from the individual country's cultural, social, political and economic situation.

This chapter highlights what constitutes child abuse within Nigerian society and examines legal, social work and administrative responses (if any) to the problem.

DEFINITION OF CHILD ABUSE

Nigeria is still battling with the issue of definitions a decade after its attention was drawn to the problem of child abuse and neglect within society. While generally acknowledging that the problem exists, it has not been easy to construct a comprehensive definition. In a recent national report produced by the National Child Rights Implementation Committee,[7] child abuse in the Nigerian context was defined as any form of cruelty to a child's physical, moral or mental well-being. Cruelty denotes intentional deliberate acts to hurt and injure, but in Nigeria most abuse of children by parents or guardians does not stem from a desire or intention to hurt but from the effects of poverty, deprivation and ignorance. The definition therefore tends (perhaps unwittingly) to narrow the purview of what constitutes child abuse in Nigeria and cannot be acceptable.

The African Network for the Prevention and Protection Against Child Abuse and Neglect (ANPPCAN) appears to have a wider conception of child abuse:

> The intentional, unintentional or well-intentioned acts which endanger the physical, health, emotional, moral and the educational welfare of the child. These acts are those unacceptable normally to the community; in some cases, however, such acts include behaviours that may be accepted by the community but may endanger the well-being of the child, although the child may or may not perceive these acts as abuse, such as the following acts: sexual abuse including child marriage, child labour, the caste system, child battering, consistent verbal suppression of the child, child trafficking, child abandonment, street children, malnutrition and indeed psychic abuse and neglect of handicapped children. Child neglect is the denial of the basic rights and needs of the child by parents, school, peers, government and cultural community, occurring as acts of omission and/commission.

This comprehensive definition covers a wide range of acts or omissions which constitute child abuse in Africa. It assumes that any act or omission that is harmful to the child in any way is abusive irrespective of culture or other factors. It recognizes that, if the parents are not to blame, the community, government or society is guilty.

Most Nigerian researchers, on the other hand, are fond of over-dependence on American definitions[8] while on the impossible mission to find a single definition that covers all aspects of abuse.[9] This has resulted in definitions which fail to reflect the culture as well as the socioeconomic structure of the community and may consequently be unsuitable.

After ratifying the United Nations Convention on the Rights of the Child, members of the Organization of African Unity (OAU) still felt that the rights of the African child must necessarily be looked at from the African perspective and not from a global point of view, and this attitude gave birth to the African Charter on the Rights and Welfare of the Child. The Charter recognizes the sociocultural peculiarities of the African child and that what is termed abusive of the child in western countries may not be so conceived in Africa. On the whole, it may well be that the difficult task of finding a suitable definition in Nigeria is not so important as identifying areas of abuse and tackling them. In doing this, however, it should be noted that local legislation and international conventions and charters have played an important role in rendering abusive some acts which the people do not generally regard as such, and this sometimes leads to a situation where there is a wide gap between law, on the one hand, and belief and practice, on the other.

However, acts or omissions which have recently been identified as amounting to child abuse in Nigeria include sexual abuse, exploitation of child labour, excessive physical punishment, premature marriage, female circumcision, neglect and abandonment, malnourishment, failure to provide good accommodation, safe drinking water and good health care, denial of education, infliction of tribal marks, and pawning, trafficking and sale of children.

SEXUAL ABUSE AND EXPLOITATION

Sexual abuse has been defined as 'any act of a sexual nature upon or with a child'.[10] Such abuses are either incestuous or are termed defilement, rape or indecent assault.

Incest under the Nigerian traditional society is taboo and is an offence against the gods. Where this is found to have occurred, certain rites must be performed to appease the gods, otherwise something 'terrible' might happen to the family. Although this offence against children is known to be on the increase in recent times, it is not at all common, especially in the village setting where news and rumour spread faster than in the cities and the fear and shame of being forced to participate in a ritual may be a strong deterrent factor.[11] It is to be noted, however, that the imposition of a ritual for incest is not based on the fact that a child is involved but that the gods are displeased. Thus the same process takes place where both parties involved are adults. In very rare cases where a child is sexually abused by her father,[12] she will be withdrawn on the decision of the elders to live with her maternal grandparents as a measure of protection.[13]

Rape, defilement and indecent assault of young girls are far more common in Nigeria and, until recently,[14] were not seen as child abuse even though people find such acts deplorable. Research has indicated that young girls who hawk wares, walk the streets or are left at home without proper parental or other care or who work as domestic servants often constitute the victims.[15] Hawkers are lured by their customers while domestic servants may be abused by their masters and stand to be immediately dismissed when the mistress finds out, whereupon the whole thing begins again with a new master.

No-one has yet bothered to collect and collate data on sexual offences against children in Nigeria's 36 states: the reason is partly that the people lack a record-keeping culture; also it was not thought to matter. Hence the police will hardly have a complete list of reported cases.

Long before these offences were perceived squarely as child abuse, Nigeria by virtue of the provisions of its Criminal Code Act[16] and Penal Code Act[17] already had in place laws that tended to protect children from sexual abuse and exploitation. A child,[18] for the purpose of the Act, comes under two categories: those under 13 years and those above 13 but under 16 years. Sexual acts with either category is criminal and has varying degrees of punishment.

Thus, under s.216 of the Criminal Code, any person who unlawfully and has a sexual relationship with a boy under the age of 14 years is guilty of a felony and is liable to imprisonment for seven years. A person charged under this section is not allowed to raise the defence of consent on the boy's part and he may not also claim mistaken belief as to his age.

Because girls are more vulnerable than boys in Nigeria, the Criminal Code has ensured them a greater degree of protection. Section 218 makes it a felony punishable with imprisonment for life with or without whipping for any person to have unlawful carnal knowledge of a girl under the age of 13 years, or 14 years' imprisonment for an attempt to commit the same offence. Where the girl is over 13 but under 16, the punishment is two years with or without whipping.

Young female hawkers often fall victim to sexual abuse by their adult male customers. There have been cases of rape and other sexual assaults. Mainly for this reason, the Street Trading Regulations of the Children and Young Persons Act[19] provide that no young female shall engage or be employed in street trading unless she is so engaged or employed by her parent or guardian between the hours of 6am and 6.30pm. Also they provide that no young female shall engage or be employed in street trading at or in the vicinity of any barracks, dock or wharf, or in or near any place or premises selling wines, spirits, beer or native liquor. A fine is imposed for contravening this law.

The Criminal Code also tends to protect children from being used as prostitutes or money-making agents for their exploiters. Section 222A punishes with imprisonment for two years any person who, having custody or charge of a girl who is under the age of 16 years, causes or encourages her seduction, unlawful carnal knowledge of her, her engagement in prostitution or commission of an indecent assault on her. The offence is committed where such custodian knowingly allows the girl to be employed by or to move in the company of a prostitute or person known to be of immoral character. Closely related to this is s.222B, which provides that any custodian who allows a child between the ages of four and 16 years to reside in or to frequent a brothel will be liable to a fine of 100 Naira,[20] or to imprisonment for six months, or to both fine and imprisonment. For the purposes of the section, it is immaterial that the accused was unaware that the girl resident in or frequenting a brothel was under the age of 16 or believed that she was not under that age. This is stated in s.233, which also seems to provide that, if the child is a boy, knowledge or lack of it with regard to his age becomes material because such accused may escape liability. The distinction is probably based on the idea that young boys are believed not to be under as much threat of sexual abuse and exploitation as girls in Nigeria.

Other provisions which tend to protect girls from sexual abuse are found in ss.223, 224 and 225 of the Criminal Code. Quite remarkably, though, no specific section makes incestuous relationships a criminal offence. Consequently, such acts with children may be charged under one or more of the sections earlier stated. The Penal Code,[21] however, makes incest an offence punishable by imprisonment. The new draft decree[22] on criminal law has made incest a criminal offence.

To further shield children from sexual abuse, the Children and Young Persons Act makes provisions for a corrective order to be made by a court in respect of a child who is found to be lodging or residing in a house or part of a house used by a prostitute for the purpose of prostitution, or living in circumstances calculated to cause, encourage or favour the seduction or prostitution of the child, or in frequent company of a common or reputed prostitute.[23] When such orders are made, the child may be sent to an approved institution,[24] or committed to the care of any fit person who is willing to undertake the care of him. By these provisions a parent or guardian who fails to exercise proper guardianship, and thus exposes the child to the danger of sexual exploitation, may be deprived of the care and custody of that child.

It is known, however, that the police and others responsible for bringing endangered children before a juvenile or other court are not often alive to their duties and most children in this category consequently remain unprotected. According to the report of the Child Welfare League of Nigeria,[25] the protective laws are not often implemented because of laxity on the part of relevant authorities and also governmental refusal to pump money into this area. The League is currently putting pressure on the government to show greater interest in this cause.

One important group of 'sexually abused' children in Nigeria comprises those who are exposed to early intercourse and its attendant consequences through child marriage. Unfortunately, the Criminal Code, while labelling sexual intercourse with a girl under the age of 16 yeas as unlawful carnal knowledge, also states that unlawful carnal knowledge does not include sexual relations by a man with a girl under 16 to whom he is married. Such is the anomaly 'of a law which in one breath purports to protect children under sixteen from early sexual intercourse and in another withdraws such protection by recognising child marriage'.[26]

Child marriage is prevalent in Nigeria especially in the predominantly Muslim north, where Sharia Law and most customs permit child marriage. Poverty, ignorance, norm and culture account for the high incidence of this burden on children. Girl children in particular are removed from school against their will and given away in marriage to far older men. This practice cuts across all social classes, but occurs more among those in the lower strata. The male population hardly sees it as child abuse and the children are helpless in the matter, but recently, in Adamawa State of Northern Nigeria, a daring 11-year-old girl took her guardian to court[27] for collecting bride price and giving her out for marriage and thus depriving her of her childhood and education.[28] Unfortunately, the presiding magistrate dismissed the case in return for an-out-of-court settlement.[29] An investigation by the Child Welfare League of Nigeria revealed that the magistrate himself was guilty of this same act, having married a 12-year-old girl in 1994.

In another case, a 12-year-old girl was married off to a Fulani cattle rearer in the northern part of Nigeria. She kept running away from the man's house and on one occasion, when she tried to do so again, the man caught up with her and cut off her leg. Of course she bled to death. The father did not think the child's husband did wrong.

A child who is forced to marry prematurely is bound to bear the burden of early intercourse, pregnancy and childbirth. Very serious medical complications often arise from such situations. In the north, hospitals are full of girls with vesico-vaginal fistula. Most have been abandoned by their husbands and family and have become society's rejects.

Child marriage is a cultural practice which also exists in Nigeria's southern part, but less so. To compound the issue, there is no minimum age for marriage, either in the Marriage Act[30] or in the customary law of most parts of the country: this is one of the reasons for the high incidence of child marriage. However, many Nigerians, especially the elite, have begun to conceive child marriage as child abuse, since its effect is to deprive the child of the opportunity to be a child and develop normally and properly, and to impose on her a psychological and physical burden beyond what her age can carry. The government and, more especially, non-governmental organizations, are now engaged in campaigns against child marriage, pushing for a law that will state a minimum age of marriage for all children and severe punishments for those who flout it. Such law may help to ensure that the interest of children becomes the paramount consideration – not custom or culture. But machinery for implementation of the law is essential.

FEMALE CIRCUMCISION

This is one customary practice that has physically destroyed many girls and women in Nigeria. It involves a mutilation of the female genital organ. It is not only extremely painful but life-threatening. It sometimes leads to death from excessive bleeding, difficulty in passing urine, infection and infertility.[31] Many women feel nothing during sex as a result of this native 'operation'. One of the reasons advanced for this practice is that it is necessary to save the girl from becoming promiscuous when she grows up or marries – in other words, to blunt her sexual desires. There is no law against female circumcision and, to the people that practise it, there is nothing abusive about it. Happily, several organizations now regard the practice as child abuse and enlightenment programmes and campaigns are being launched and carried out to curb its occurrence.

PHYSICAL ABUSE

Under Nigerian customary law, parents and guardians have the unconditional right to apply physical chastisement for the upbringing of their children. Section 295 of the Criminal Code[32] also authorizes a parent, guardian, schoolmaster or any person in loco parentis to discipline or correct a child under the age of 16 years in his care who is guilty of misconduct or disobedience, by infliction of a blow or force. However, to ensure that the child does not become a victim of abuse under this law, it is provided that such blow or force must be reasonable and not extend to a wound or grievous harm. Unfortunately, this is not always the case. As Michael Freeman[33] aptly observed, 'Much abuse of children is the result of corporal punishment which has gone wrong; either the consequence of deliberate action causing more harm than was intended or the product of loss of self-control.'

The recent Nigerian case of *Ekeogu* v. *Aliri*[34] strengthens Freeman's argument against corporal punishment of children. There the defendant/appellant was a teacher in a community primary school in a village in Nigeria. On 2 December 1985, a thief was caught in the neighbourhood of the school and, as usual, the crowd which gathered began to mete out instant justice by giving him a severe beating. The defendant ordered his pupils, including the plaintiff, to go and witness how thieves were dealt with so they could learn a lesson from it. The children did so, but after a while the bell rang, summoning them back to the classroom. As they ran into the class the teacher hit each one of them with a cane. In the plaintiff's case, she was hit across the face and this resulted in serious injury and loss of her left eye. Following a civil action which was instituted by the plaintiff, the defendant pleaded the protection of s.2 of the Public Officers Protection Law which rendered such actions statutorily: barred unless they were brought within six months of the commission of the harm. The trial judge held that, although the defendant was a public officer, his action in causing a permanent injury to the left eye of the child was a felonious act and he was therefore not entitled to invoke the protection of the statute. On appeal, the Court of Appeal unanimously agreed with the trial judge and dismissed the appeal. The defendant appealed to the Supreme Court.

Allowing the appeal, Kawu JSC held that the defendant/appellant was entitled to the protection of the statute since he was a public officer acting in pursuance of his public duty as a teacher to exercise discipline and control over his pupils. Wali JSC, giving his views on the power of a teacher to discipline his pupils, said that a teacher vis-à-vis his pupils stands in loco parentis to them and in that capacity he has the authority and duty to discipline them. He went further:

> What happened in this case was nothing more than the appellant discharging his duty and it was only sheer accident that the child was hit in the eye resulting in its damage. I cannot discern any criminal intention on the part of the teacher as all the pupils, one after the other, while returning to the class, were caned and none of them other than the respondent was hit on the eye.

Thus the teacher escaped liability, but a young girl has lost an eye in the process of physical chastisement – a serious disablement and disfigurement. No amount of damages, even if awarded, could adequately compensate for this injury. Are not this incident and similar ones sufficient reason for banning physical punishment, at least in schools? Is this not a good case for insisting on adopting alternative ways of disciplining children? Several private schools in Nigeria have banned the use of corporal punishment on children by teachers as a result of incidents like this, as well as strong opposition from some parents.

As well as teachers, parents do exceed the bounds of reasonable chastisement. As punishment, parents and guardians have been known to put hot pepper in the eyes or private parts of an ill-behaved child,[35] or to beat a child to an unconscious state while inflicting corporal punishment. In one case,[36] a father, an electrical engineer, who apparently was a religious fanatic, insisted that his family observe a three-day fast imposed by his church for the purpose of warding off evil forces. His nine-year-old son, unable to bear the hunger any longer, was caught by the father looking for food in a refuse bin. He was dragged home and beaten with an electric cable until he became unconscious. This came to the notice of some 34 of his classmates, who took him to the police station to lodge a complaint. The father was charged before a court and in the course of evidence it was revealed that, on a previous occasion, he had pressed a hot iron on the boy's stomach, inflicting a wound which, when it eventually healed, formed large keloids. The child was constantly subjected to various kinds of assault.

The father pleaded that his actions were motivated by the desire to correct, but the magistrate, while agreeing that children ought to be corrected, said that it should not be in the manner in which this father did it. She described the father's conduct as 'animalistic, wicked and fanatical' and sentenced him to a term of three months in prison. He was also to receive 12 strokes of the cane and undergo psychiatric examination to determine his mental condition. It was found that the mother all along supported the father's treatment of the child. The court therefore ordered that the child be kept by the police until a fit person was found to take care of him.

In another recent case, widely televised by the Nigerian Television Authority and reported by other media, early in 1996, a father whose life was marred by lack of financial success fell into the hands of a self-proclaimed prophetess. As he was willing to accept any action that would reverse his fortune, the 'prophetess' told him that his two young daughters were both witches and were the cause of his misfortune. The children therefore must be subjected to severe punishments if his life was to change. The 'prophetess' then proceeded to burn the children's hands in a fire. The serious burns which resulted caused one of them to lose the use of both hands and the other to be permanently maimed by ugly, thick scars. The 'prophetess', the father and some other church members were arrested and brought before a court. The charges against the father were dropped because the children said they had forgiven him and wanted to be reunited with him.[37]

The above cases show that mistakes, negligence, accidents or loss of self-control can occur, resulting in serious injury while a child is being physically chastised, but, despite all these, the law continues to support the use of physical punishment to correct children. The Children and Young Persons Act, while supporting[38] the use of corporal punishment against children in a remand home, bans its use on girls, and states that on boys it should be inflicted only with a cane on the hands or buttocks and the number of strokes should not exceed six on each hand or the buttocks.[39] But the new draft Children's Decree does not ban corporal punishment either at home or in schools. The draft Criminal Code also retains the provisions which authorize certain classes of people to use corporal punishment as a corrective measure on children, despite criticism of it by some groups and individuals. It will be difficult to ban this kind of punishment in Nigerian society; it is an entrenched part of the people's culture to rear children 'properly' by means of physical chastisement, so that any move banning it will be unacceptable to the majority of the people, most of whom are illiterate. This group considers this form of disciplinary measure a sine qua non of effective and proper upbringing and often inflicts very severe physical punishments which in developed countries would be regarded as extremely abusive of the child.

Corporal punishment therefore is likely to remain part of the law and culture for a long time to come. The laws which are in place for dealing with cases of excess are not often used, mainly because most of the acts are not regarded as abusive and therefore are not reported by witnesses to the authorities. Moreover, most of these acts are committed by parents or guardians who are deemed to have the legitimate right physically to punish their children, no matter how severely.

NEGLECT AND ABANDONMENT

Neglect has been described as a passive form of child abuse which involves the denial of the basic rights and needs of the child by parents, school, peers, government or cultural community.[40] Of course, denial of such basic rights and needs includes 'failure to feed properly, resulting in malnutrition, failure to clothe adequately, or provide proper accommodation and neglect of child's health'.[41] Oates also noted that neglect involves an 'avoidance of parental responsibilities with an absence of the surveillance necessary for the child's physical and emotional welfare ... a failure to safeguard from physical danger'.[42] This presupposes an intentional or deliberate act of neglect on the part of the parent or guardian. If this definition were adopted in Nigeria, many parents might be found guilty of child neglect,[43] especially if the neglect in question is as Freeman described it.

Today in Nigeria, there is a high incidence of child neglect. The number of children seen in the streets, hawking, trading, hustling and wandering about, has assumed astronomical proportions. Parents and guardians send them out to do this and 'no longer seem to be exercising proper guardianship' of their children or wards.[44] Many children aged between six and 15 years are found daily on the streets, running up and down, chasing and harassing motorists to get them to buy their wares. A lot of them spend an average of 14 hours in the streets, which means that school attendance is out of the question. Those who attend school and resume hawking after school hours continue until late into the night, thus having no time for rest or homework. Poor performance at school then follows, until they finally drop out.

There is also the problem of Almanjiris, which was described by Donli J[45] as a practice prevalent in the north, in which parents send their very young children away from home and entrust them to itinerant Islamic teachers, mostly strangers, who roam far and wide, with the intention of imparting Koranic knowledge. Such children are employed as beggars. They live in dehumanizing conditions, suffer deprivations and gross neglect, and some never see their parents again. Indeed, the Koranic school which confers a holy status on the children promotes begging.[46] The Child Welfare League of Nigeria, a voluntary organization, has undertaken a campaign against 'Almanjiris' through district heads in the north. The League has proposed to set up rehabilitation centres where the children will be taken care of and helped to learn a better trade.

Cases of abandoned children are also known to be on the increase. Parents unable any longer to maintain and feed their large-sized families[47] abandon some of their children in busy market places, on door steps of hospitals, police stations or local government offices, in the hope that they may be picked up by wealthier people. Such acts expose the child to the danger of falling into the wrong hands and being killed or subjected to slavery.

Similarly, a group of children known as 'street children' have so grown in number that it has become a matter of grave concern. These children exist under very rough conditions and are easy prey to all kinds of danger and evil influences. A recent survey by the Child Welfare League of Nigeria recorded a population of 213 950 street children in eight centres in Lagos alone.[48] It follows that the total number in all the cities may run into millions. The League also reports that street children face frequent raids by the police and members of the government task force who extort money from them.[49]

Street children are by-products of neglect. Some take to prostitution, others to crime. Reporting on street children and the cause of it, the *African Guardian*[50] said:

> from pilfering through shop lifting and mugging to armed robbery, many Nigerian kids, especially in their early and mid-teens, have arrived in the world of crime full blast. Many reasons are often claimed for these metamorphoses. Child abuse and parental neglect are cited as factors driving many children from home and thereby into the mainstream of the larger society. Some experts also contend that it is the child's exposure to places of high criminal proclivity that ultimately lures him from home and ensures his graduation from innocence to criminality.

The magazine then concludes:

> from all indications, the Nigerian society is currently breeding these delinquents in large numbers. Statistics from the Lagos State Ministry of Social Welfare show a yearly increase in the number of children involved in crime. From 315 in 1985, it increased to 366 the following year and 455 in 1987. Yet these figures are merely illustrative rather than comprehensive, for many cases of violence unleashed by these kids are often unreported.

This is tragic for the child and unhealthy for the nation. Apart from the above, many children in Nigeria are still denied access to school, safe drinking water and proper medical care. This is due to lack of affordable health care delivery centres in rural areas and the absence of essential drugs and equipment even where such centres are available. Many families resort to the dangerous practice of self-cure or getting 'prescriptions' from native herbalists. Private hospitals are too expensive. In addition, the cost of education has became so high that parents either desist from sending their children to school or withdraw those already there. As a result, about 65 per cent of school-age children are out of school, a majority of them girls.[51] These children often suffer neglect.

Regarding nutrition, a good percentage of children either suffer from malnutrition or are underfed.[52] With the exorbitant prices of foodstuffs and essential protein food, children of a majority of parents who cannot afford it become malnourished. Among the under-fives, it was reported that 60 per cent are underweight; about 24 per cent are within the moderate malnutrition range, 22 per cent within the severe malnutrition category and 12 per cent suffer mild malnutrition.[53] It has also been reported that over 14 million primary school pupils cannot afford to eat well enough to enhance proper attendance, attention and good performance at school.[54]

However, underfeeding, failure to send to school or to provide proper medical care do not stem from deliberate conduct but from poverty and sometimes ignorance. Parents do the best they can in the circumstances in which they find themselves. The government should not only pay better wages but must act to bring down the prices of these commodities.

Legally, children are fairly adequately protected from neglect and abandonment. The law imposes on parents and guardians the duty to provide the necessaries of life and care for their minor children. Section 301 of the Criminal Code provides that it is the duty of every person who is the head of family and has charge of children under the age of 14 years who are members of his household to provide the necessaries of life for them. A breach of this provision makes the parent or guardian criminally responsible for the consequences[55] which arise from the breach. Also, under s.302, any master or mistress who has contracted to provide necessary food, clothing or lodging for any servant or apprentice under the age of 16 years must do so,[56] or face imprisonment for failing to comply with his or her duty. Similarly, s.341 of the same code makes it a criminal offence, punishable by five years' imprisonment, unlawfully to abandon or expose a child under the age of seven years in such a manner that grievous harm is likely to be caused to him or her.

Section 26(1) of the Children and Young Persons Act also by implication imposes on parents the duty to take proper care of their children and states that, where a parent has been found guilty of neglecting or ill-treating the child, he may be deprived of its custody. Parents of children found wandering may also lose their custody by a court order. When such order is made the child is sent to an approved institution or committed to the care of any fit person, whether there is a relative or not, who is willing to take care of him.

But the harsh truth is that these supposedly protective laws for children are barely enforced or implemented, mainly because the authorities are either ignorant of their existence or are simply indifferent. They too are aware of the realities of life. Poverty has indeed been blamed for some kinds of child abuse and in Nigeria today many people suffer from poverty – and the law enforcement agents themselves are not free from it. As a result, it becomes difficult for such agents to enforce the law against neglect which includes a failure to feed properly, resulting in malnutrition, to clothe adequately, to provide proper accommodation and to take proper care of the child's health. It also becomes almost impossible to charge parents for sending their under-age child to engage in street trading, work as domestic servants and other exploitative labour or to indict them for failure to send them to a regular school, when the child's work or absence from school is necessary for his family's survival. This attitude perhaps partly accounts for the ridiculously low number of reported cases of children committed into care, in comparison to the number of known cases.

Moreover, there are not enough care centres throughout the country to cope with the situation were the laws to be fully enforced. The existing ones are in such a terrible state of dilapidation, with only very few trained personnel, that the children occupying them are said to be the worse for it.[57] Therefore enforcement of the laws is a huge problem in Nigeria, owing to these diverse factors. Thus, unless education is made free and compulsory, both at the primary and secondary school levels, and some kind of social welfare system is established which aims at improving the living standards of families and assisting the poor, child abuse in the manner described will remain unabated.

Having examined different aspects of child abuse and the existing laws which are designed to protect children from such abuse, it is important at this stage to examine in a general sense to what extent social work or administrative actions have been taken by either government or non-governmental agencies to combat or control child abuse within society. Although some of these actions do not address the immediate problems, it is clear that, if they are properly executed, the benefit to children may later be realized.

SOCIAL WORK AND ADMINISTRATIVE RESPONSES TO CHILD ABUSE

In response to its child abuse problems and promotion of the welfare of children, Nigeria has formulated some national policies. Among these is the National Policy on Population.[58] This aims at improving the living standards and quality of life of the people through the achievement of a lower population growth rate by voluntary fertility regulation methods. The strategies for achieving this goal include the following:

- promotion of awareness among the citizens of the problems and negative effects of rapid population growth on development;
- provision of the necessary information and education on the value of small family size;
- education of all young people on population matters, sexual relationships, fertility regulation and family planning before entering the ages of marriage and child bearing, to assist them towards maintenance of responsible family sizes;
- provision, at affordable cost, of family planning means and services to help couples and individuals at the earliest possible time to enable them to regulate their fertility;
- enhancement of integrated rural and urban development in order to improve the living conditions in the rural areas and to slow down the rate of rural to urban migration.

With a population of over 98 million people,[59] the country is evidently over-populated. Over-population impedes development and unplanned parenthood affects proper budget planning and implementation. The birth rate is increasing, with an annual growth of about 2.83 per cent. At this rate, the population is projected to hit 165 million by the year 2010, and possibly reach 250 million by the year 2020. It has been said that one out of every four Africans is a Nigerian.[60]

To control the birth rate, the Planned Parenthood Federation of Nigeria has launched family planning programmes in major Nigerian cities. In 1994, it reported registering 33 465 new clients in its family planning clinics nationwide. This number is low, considering the population. One of the obstacles is that many men are averse to the idea of their wives using modern methods of birth control. In their eyes it will encourage the women to become promiscuous. Many women will not come forward unless their husbands permit them. Also some women are reluctant because they believe that such methods cause infertility. These women need to be further educated.

Sex education has also been introduced in schools, and condoms are sometimes distributed free of charge to undergraduates in the universities to educate them on the importance of responsible sex lives and parenthood. It has been claimed that the present population policy increased awareness of family planning from 6 per cent in 1990 to 10 per cent in 1994.[61] This was reported to have been achieved by enlightenment campaigns, public lectures and picture advertisements in the media.

Unfortunately, the impact of the family planning strategies so far has not been felt in the rural areas, where a majority of the illiterate populace reside. These people see nothing wrong in producing as many children as possible, since in their view they are God's gift. Hence, in some villages, women who produce 10 children are given a special place of honour and many strive to achieve this 'feat'.[62] This is sheer ignorance and only education and enlightenment campaigns can correct such folly.

At present, family planning clinics and advisory centres are absent in the rural areas and organized guidance and informative lectures for rural men and women are not yet on course. Although plans exist to extend these facilities to these areas, the rate of progress is rather slow. Scarcity of funds is listed as one of the major impediments to success here but, unless greater commitment is shown by government via the provision of needed funds, the achievement of its population goals will remain only a dream.

In the health and nutrition sector, the National Policy on Health[63] has the objective of bringing about a comprehensive health care system based on primary health care at affordable charges such as will promote, protect and restore good health as well as prevent ill-health and childhood infections. With the assistance of UNICEF and the World Health Organization (WHO), a good measure of success has been achieved in realizing the latter objective. Thus immunization programmes for the prevention of diseases have begun and are fairly widespread. By 1990, 65.5 per cent of infants had been immunized against poliomyelitis, 70 per cent had had immunization against measles and about 65 per cent had been immunized against tetanus, diphtheria and pertussis.[64]

Meanwhile, hospitals remain under-equipped and without essential drugs. However, in the 1997 budget speech, the Head of State mentioned that some of the money from petroleum under the Petroleum Trust Fund will be devoted towards rehabilitating, equipping and providing necessary drugs to hospitals. Large quantities of drugs were purchased in 1997 and were subsequently distributed round the hospitals.[65] The fact, remains however, that hospital charges are still high and beyond the reach of the poor.

As far as malnutrition is concerned, no specific programme has so far taken off to reduce its incidence among Nigerian children, but early in 1996, the Minister of Education signed a working agreement between the Federal

Ministry of Education and the Food Agricultural Organization (FAO). The agreement relates to a project entitled 'Improvement of School Feeding Programme'. The project, which is being funded by the FAO through the provision of cash and technical assistance, will be executed by the Ministry of Education. It is intended to support the nutritional needs of primary school children. It is hoped that a wider plan of action will be designed to expand on the improved food-vending programme that would benefit all schools. The Ministry plans to involve all local governments by organizing seminars and training food vendors and teachers on balanced feeding. There is also a plan to formulate a national food and nutrition policy for improving the nutritional status of Nigerians. Towards this end, the Ministry has participated in seminars and conferences on the subject and has pledged to do more to meet the International Conference on Nutrition (ICN) goals for the reduction of starvation, widespread chronic hunger and under-nutrition, especially among children, women and the aged.

There is no doubt that, if these projects are successfully begun, they will help reduce cases of malnutrition among children. However, for these to benefit a larger section of Nigerian children, primary and secondary school education need to be made free and compulsory. As far as education is concerned, the National Policy on Education[66] states that children from age six years shall undergo six years of primary education and three years of junior secondary education. The aim of the policy is to provide basic education so as to improve literacy and communication skills as well as to enable children to acquire a broad-based education for the development of the mind and other skills. However, education is still not universally free and compulsory even at these levels, and parents have to bear the heavy cost of having their children educated at all stages.[67] Although in 1987 the National Council on Education made it 'mandatory' that the policy provisions for the education of children be implemented at federal, state and local government levels, sufficient funds have not been provided. The size of the budget for education has been declining and the educational system has gradually been crumbling.

Recently, however, UNICEF in cooperation with the government, has embarked on a pilot programme whose main purpose is to encourage early childhood education through the various primary education boards in the country. They have embarked on field visits to study how to advance the project of establishing day care centres in both urban and rural areas. The programme is intended to be low-cost, community-based and aimed at families of less than average means.[68] This constitutes a beginning to solving the problem of child neglect,[69] if it can be successfully implemented.

OTHER MEASURES AND SOCIAL WORK

After Nigeria ratified the United Nations Convention on the Rights of the Child in 1989, she joined other member countries of the OAU in adopting an African Charter on the Rights and Welfare of the Child at the Head of States Summit in Addis Ababa in 1990. The Charter recognizes the socio-cultural peculiarities of the African child and so calls for a consideration of 'the cultural heritage, historical background and the values of the African civilisation which should inspire and characterise ... the concept of the rights and welfare of the African child'.

Later, in 1991 at Abuja, the OAU proclaimed the 1990s as the Decade of the African Child and made 16 June of every year the 'Day of the African Child'. This day is observed as a holiday for children and a number of cultural and leisure activities are usually organized for them. Since then, Nigeria has taken further steps to try to tackle child abuse and improve children's welfare. Hence, in February 1991, the Federal Ministry of Culture and Social Welfare established a 'National Child Welfare Committee'. This was followed in March of the same year by the establishment of a 'Trust Fund for the Nigerian Child'. Government, companies, individuals and organizations are encouraged to contribute to this fund. The money is designed to execute programmes and projects designed for child welfare services.

National seminars on the rights of the child have also been organized. Of special note is the one held in March 1992 by the Federal Ministry of Culture and Social Welfare,[70] which aimed at informing the media about the need to implement child rights. The cooperation of the media was sought in reporting and monitoring cases of child abuse and assisting in the effort to implement child rights and welfare. Thereafter, representatives of media institutions and allied professions signed a statement of commitment to promote the UN Convention and African Charter. They have kept to their promise because regular programmes including activities and discussions relating to child abuse are featured regularly in the various media. These are for the purpose of enlightenment and education of and information for the public.

Earlier, in 1989, a National Commission for Women was established and this commission in 1991 took over child welfare services from the Federal Ministry of Health and Social Services and created a Child Welfare Department. It operates at both state and local government levels.[71] In March 1993, the National Commission for Women set up a National Working Committee on Child Welfare. Some of the duties assigned to them were to work out plans for effective delivery of child development and protection of the child. This was followed in 1994 by a National Child Rights Implementation

Committee, inaugurated by the Federal Government and whose functions include the following:

- initiating actions that would ensure that the provisions of the UN Convention and African Charter on the Rights and Welfare of the Child are commonly brought to the notice of the general public;
- continuous review of the state of implementation of the rights of the child in Nigeria;
- developing and recommending to government specific programmes and projects that will enhance the status of the Nigerian child;
- instituting an appropriate mechanism that will enable Nigeria to monitor and evaluate the implementation of the provisions of the Convention;
- collecting and collating data on the implementation of the child rights treaties;
- preparing and submitting periodic reports on the state of implementation to the Federal Government, the OAU and United Nations.

The Committee, whose membership is made up of governmental and non-governmental organizations, produced its first report in 1995, stating the extent of the implementation of the UN Convention and the African Charter. Although not much has been achieved in some areas of child abuse and neglect, it is significant that international pressure and assistance have moved the Nigerian government into doing and committing itself to doing what it has so far achieved in this field.

Furthermore, in 1995 a separate Ministry of Women's Affairs and Social Development was created.[72] It is meant to promote the interests of children and women in Nigeria and to coordinate all activities carried out in different sectors which concern women and children. The Ministry has published a handbook containing the integrated and simplified version of both the UN Convention and the African Charter on the Rights and Welfare of the Child.[73]

In 1994, the wife of the former Head of State, Mrs Abacha, initiated a programme called the Family Support Programme.[74] One of its aims is the elimination of various forms of child abuse and child neglect which endanger the physical and emotional well-being of children and the enforcement of relevant legislation against child labour. A lot of funds have been raised in support of the programme, but unfortunately the modalities for its application have not yet been worked out or defined.

Apart from actions taken by government, there are also activities under the direction of non-governmental organizations. Prominent among the latter are the National Council of Women Societies, the African Network for the Prevention and Protection Against Child Abuse and Neglect in Nigeria, the Child Welfare League of Nigeria, the Federation of Muslim Women Association of Nigeria and the Catholic Women Organization. These bodies have been engaged in establishing cheap day care centres, running orphanages, setting up counselling centres, having enlightenment campaigns on the evils of child marriage,[75] the victims of which often suffer from vesicovaginal fistula, campaigning against harmful traditional practices against children, researching and collecting data on the state of the Nigerian child.[76] The ANPPCAN in particular has also established regional monitoring centres on child rights violation in the country.

CONCLUSION

The root causes of most abuse of children in Nigeria are poverty, ignorance and cultural beliefs rather than psychological illness or psychopathic behaviour. Although some of the people's child-rearing practices, such as corporal punishment and use of child labour, may be rather too harsh and detrimental to the child, it is often either intended for a good corrective purpose or perpetrated because the circumstances in which the parents find themselves leave them with no other, less harmful, choice.

The mismanagement of the economy by successive leaders, coupled with high-level corruption, has over the years practically drained the country of progress and has thrown a majority of Nigerians into the abyss of poverty. The resultant effect is involuntary child abuse by parents who are then unable to discharge their responsibilities towards their children. The society or the government therefore must take part of the blame.[77] However, it is important that Nigeria has finally woken up to the problem of child abuse and, considering the relatively short period within which the awareness came about, the effort so far made in tackling it is fairly encouraging. The number of voluntary organizations that have sprung up in recent times also shows that more and more people have become sensitive to the issue of abuse and have realized that the battle may not be left to the government alone. The government and its organs have initiated many programmes whose successful execution will bring relief to many abused children. However, no amount of programmes set up can on their own eliminate child abuse and neglect. As has been correctly stated, 'You need strong, forceful advocates and partners in all walks of life – people of conscience and concern who can articulate the cause of children and create in the society the awareness and the will to fight child abuse.'[78]

The government is still slow to act with respect to such areas as child marriage. Hence it is reluctant to sign the draft Children's Decree which puts the minimum marriageable age at 18 years and also bans female circumcision. There appear also to be no immediate plans to make education free and compulsory at the primary and secondary school levels. Without such plans, there will be no reprieve for children engaged in exploitative child labour. Similarly, unless a workable system is designed for the purpose of assisting poor families and much more action is taken towards controlling the country's birth rate, children will continue to suffer neglect-related abuses.

Nevertheless, the war against child abuse has been started and will be continued, whether with or without sufficient government support, until all endangered children are liberated from their present bondage. This indeed is the only option.

NOTES

1 J. Korbin, 'What is Acceptable and Non-Acceptable Child Rearing – A Cross Cultural Consideration', in K. Oates (ed.), *Child Abuse – A Community Concern* (London: Butterworths, 1982) p.257.
2 M.D.A. Freeman, *The Rights and Wrongs of Children* (London: Pinter, 1983) p.105.
3 Ralph Diaz, 'The Major Routes Towards the Abandonment and Abuse of Children in Africa', Keynote address at the First International Workshop on Child Abuse in Africa, Enugu, Nigeria, 27 April–2 May 1986.
4 See D.S. Obikeze, 'Child Maltreatment in Non-Industrialised Countries: A Framework for Analysis'.
5 The paradigm, however, omits a fourth, societal, level which focuses on the socioeconomic and political structure of the society and where the abused child is seen as a victim of societal neglect in the society in which he lives.
6 Korbin, op. cit., note 1.
7 *National Report on the Implementation of United Nations Convention on The Rights of the Child*, produced by the National Child Rights Implementation Committee, 1994.
8 See, for example, C.H. Kempe, D.G. Gil and A.H. Green.
9 They ignore the differences in culture, ideology and other peculiarities between Nigeria and Western countries. They tend to forget the purpose for which the definitions are made.
10 National Centre on Child Abuse and Neglect, *Interdisciplinary Glossary on Child Abuse and Neglect* (Washington, DC: US Dept of Health, Education and Welfare, 1978).
11 It is a shameful and humiliating punishment process.
12 There are now claims that in the cities sexual abuse of young daughters by fathers or step-fathers occurs more nowadays than before.
13 The child living in the city with her parents is deprived of this protection because the mother alone does not have the power to take such a decision.
14 As a result of awareness created by ANPPCAN, the government and other organizations are now devoted to the cause of identifying child abuse in society and finding solutions to them. These bodies now regard rape and other sexual offences as child abuse.
15 N. Izuora, 'Sexual Abuse and Recurrent Criminal Abortion in Nigerian Children'; and

I.S. Obot, 'Sexual Abuse of Children in Calabar', papers presented during the Proceedings of the First International Workshop on Child Abuse in Africa; see note 2; see also report of the Child Welfare League of Nigeria (1995) p.11.
16 Applicable in Southern Nigeria.
17 Applicable only in Northern Nigeria.
18 A child is a person between seven and 14 years under the Criminal Code and is a person under 12 years under the Penal Code.
19 Cap. 32 of 1958 applicable to the Federal Capital Territory of Lagos, now Abuja. The other states have their own Children and Young Persons Laws with similar provisions as the Act of 1958.
20 The amount of the fine is so low as to be absolutely ridiculous. It is equivalent to slightly more than one US dollar. This is not surprising since the legislation itself is over 30 years old and has never been revised.
21 Section 390.
22 This has not been passed into law and it is not known when it will be.
23 Section 26 (1) (*j*) and (*k*).
24 The present stated of approved institutions in Nigeria is not helpful to children. The infrastructural facilities have broken down and the institutions lack adequate numbers of trained personnel to handle this specialized task.
25 A non-governmental organization.
26 Eunice Uzodike, 'Child Abuse and Neglect in Nigeria – Socio-Legal Aspects', *International Journal of Law and the Family*, 4: 88, 1990.
27 She was assisted by an organization in the north which campaigns against child marriage.
28 States like Bauchi, Niger, Kaduna, Kano and Benue have now passed laws prohibiting the withdrawal of girls from school for early marriages.
29 The law at present does not give to children the right to bring such suits. A person may venture to institute such actions on the basis of the infringement of his human rights under the constitution.
30 It is assumed that the common law age of 14 for boys and 12 for girls applies. The Eastern Nigeria Age of Marriage Act 1956 pegs the age of marriage under customary law at 16, but this law is often ignored.
31 It is often performed under unhygienic conditions.
32 Criminal Code Act, Laws of the Federal Republic of Nigeria, applicable only to Southern Nigeria.
33 Op. cit, note 2, p.113.
34 (1991) 3 NWLR 258 (Supreme Court of Nigeria).
35 Eunice Uzodike, op. cit., note 26, pp.83–96.
36 Reported in *The Guardian*, Sunday 24 May 1987. *The Guardian* is a Nigerian national newspaper.
37 The matter is still in court. The children's mother had deserted them long before this incident.
38 Section 18(*d*) of the Act, however, provides that every effort shall be made to enforce discipline without resort to corporal punishment but, where it is necessary, the provisions of ss.19, 20 and 21 must be strictly adhered to.
39 Moreover, no member of the staff other than the warden shall inflict corporal punishment.
40 P. Ebigbo, 'Psychological Aspects of Child Abuse and Neglect in Africa, in Laws Relating to Children in Nigeria', Proceedings of an ANPPCAN Conference, 17–19 August 1988.

41 M.D.A. Freeman, op. cit., note 2, 116.
42 K. Oates, 'Child Abuse – "A Community Concern"', in K. Oates (ed.), op. cit., note 1, p.15.
43 This is because most parental neglect is not deliberate. Poverty is mainly responsible for their actions or inaction.
44 P.S. Etim, 'Socio-Legal Consequences of Child Abuse'.
45 Hon. Justice H.N. Donli, *Socio-Legal Consequences of Child Abuse, in Women and Children Under Nigerian Law* (Lagos: Federal Ministry of Justice, 1994).
46 See E. Ensah, 'Children as Beggars: A Study from Zaria/Nigeria', *Sociologus: Journal for Empirical Ethno-Sociology and Ethnopsychology*, 34 (1), 30–46, 1984.
47 This is a result of the present harsh economic conditions in the country. There are no current official data on the number, but an estimated 5000 children are abandoned every year in Nigeria.
48 See *State of the Nigerian Child Report*, published by the Child Welfare League of Nigeria (1995).
49 Money acquired through begging, stealing and pickpocketing.
50 *The African Guardian Magazine*, 12 September 1988.
51 See op. cit., note 48. In Nigeria, boys are preferred to girls and parents would rather make educational investment on boys than on girls.
52 See National Child Rights Implementation Committee, *National Report on The Implementation of United Nations Convention on The Rights of the Child*, 1995.
53 See *National Report*, op. cit., note 52.
54 See ibid.
55 Such lapses may result in death or ill-health.
56 Sections 339 and 340 provide that a contravention of the duty to provide under ss.301 and 302 attracts a term of imprisonment for up to three years.
57 See op. cit., note 48.
58 Launched in 1988.
59 Figure obtained from the National Planning Commission. It is believed that the actual population is way above this.
60 R.R.N. Tuluhungwa, UNICEF Representative in Nigeria, in his address at the First International Workshop on Child Abuse in Africa, Enugu, 27 April–2 May 1986.
61 See *National Report*, op. cit., note 52.
62 In the Imo State of Nigeria.
63 The health policy is in line with the provisions of the Convention on the Rights of the Child. The OAU International Conference on Assistance to African Children, in 1992, adopted the Dakar Consensus and thereafter Nigeria developed a National Plan of Action. The Plan was later reinforced by the Bamako Initiative, which emphasized the availability of affordable health care for child survival, especially at the community level.
64 Figures obtained from the *National Report*, op. cit., note 52
65 It is hoped that this will continue on a regular basis.
66 Established in 1981.
67 Many parents are too impoverished to be able to fund their children's education and such children are often engaged in child labour. Bauchi State offers free education to girls only at all levels.
68 See *National Report*, op. cit., note 52.
69 The Child Welfare League of Nigeria in its 1995 report stated that 90 per cent of mothers with children below age five work or trade outside their homes on a full-time basis. There are no care centres and young children are left at home without proper care.

70 Earlier, in August 1991, a workshop on child abuse was jointly organized by the African Network for the Prevention and Protection Against Child Abuse and Neglect (ANPPCAN) in Nigeria and the Mass Mobilisation for Social Justice, Self Reliance and Economic Recovery. At the workshop child abuse issues were discussed.
71 There are 36 states in Nigeria and hundreds of local governments.
72 The National Commission for Women, which was under another Ministry, was upgraded to full Ministry status by this creation.
73 The Child Development Department of the Ministry published the handbook so as to achieve its wider circulation for the purpose of acquainting the people with its content.
74 Launched in 1994. Both Federal and state governments as well as individuals, parastatals, corporations and companies are encouraged to contribute to the programme and the response so far has been good.
75 The new draft Children's Decree prepared since 1993 and still waiting to be signed into law makes 18 years the minimum age of marriage in Nigeria. The delay must be due to some pressure groups who do not favour some provisions in the decree, including the provisions on the age of marriage.
76 The Child Welfare League of Nigeria published in 1995 a report on the state of the Nigerian child and the implementation of the UN Convention and African Charter on the Rights and Welfare of the Child. In the report, the government was accused of not having done enough towards tackling its child abuse problems and was urged to show greater commitment.
77 See *National Report*, op. cit., note 52.
78 See the address by R.R.N. Tuluhungwa, op. cit., note 60.

16 'Let Him Take His Wife': Marriage, Protection and Exploitation of Girls in Zimbabwe

Alice Armstrong

INTRODUCTION

A 14-year-old girl, selling sweets and bananas by the side of the road, is raped by a customer. When she returns dirty, dress torn, and crying to her parents, her fathers says, 'Let him take his wife', meaning now the culprit must marry her. Marriage is a traditional remedy for rape, according to the customary law of Zimbabwe.[1] However, since the end of the last century, cases involving violence, which obviously include rape, have 'officially' been governed by the western-based criminal law enforced by the police and the courts.[2] Yet in a collection of 35 case studies of girls below 16 who had been raped, five were married to their assailant, and the families of another two girls were still discussing the possibility of marriage at the time of the interviews.[3] This chapter will discuss marriage as a remedy for rape, under the law of Zimbabwe, and the cultural context within which it occurs. It focuses on the complexity of tackling the problem of sexual abuse of girls in a society in which the unofficial law takes precedence, in which traditional norms and procedures are preferred by most people, in which there are varying understandings of the best interests of the child, and in which economic and social conditions make children vulnerable.

THE DOMESTIC LEGAL CONTEXT

Zimbabwe has a classic dual legal system, with the state recognizing both general law (Roman-Dutch common law and statutes) and the customary law (the law of the indigenous people), both applied in the same court system.[4] Choice of law is largely determined by the subject matter of the dispute.[5] All cases involving violence – which would include rape or indecent assault of a girl child – are to be governed by the general law.[6] According to the criminal law, the offence of rape consists of sexual intercourse with a girl (or woman) without her consent and the offence of indecent assault is touching a girl (or woman) in a sexual way without her consent. A girl under the age of 12 is deemed by law to be incapable of consenting to sex, and therefore any man who has sex with a girl under 12 is guilty of rape.[7] According to statutory law, if a man has sex with a girl under the age of 16, even with her consent, he is guilty of an offence.[8] Offences under the criminal law are punishable by fine, imprisonment or community service, with compensation for damages being awarded under limited circumstances.

Although actions which fall under the definition of rape, attempted rape or indecent assault *should*, under the law of Zimbabwe, be handled by the magistrate's court according to the criminal law, a substantial number of such cases, perhaps the majority, are in fact settled informally, outside the state court system, in ways which resemble the customary law.[9] Thus communities are acting in ways which are allowed by the customary law but illegal under the state criminal law.

Under Shona customary law, the offence of rape consists of sexual intercourse with a woman without her consent. The customary remedies for rape of an unmarried woman included damages to the family of the victim, marriage of the victim to the rapist and punishment of the rapist. Early documentation of customary law records: 'A man who raped an unmarried woman was traditionally compelled to acquire her as a wife by the payment of *lobola*.'[10] A related sexual offence under customary law is 'seduction', which consists of sexual intercourse with an unmarried girl without the consent of her parents or guardian.[11] This is an offence against parental rights of control over the sexuality and ultimately the marriage of their daughter. The remedy for seduction of a girl was the same as the remedy for rape: damages and marriage. Traditionally, the seducer does not have a right to marry the girl, but could do so only if her guardian agrees. If the guardian does not agree, the seducer still must pay damages.[12]

In theory, a man who has sex with a girl without her consent is guilty of rape, and a man who has sex with a girl with her consent, but without parental consent, is guilty of seduction. In practice, however, the two offences are not sharply distinguished, largely because they attract the same remedies:

rape was not thought to be an act against the course of Nature: the possible result might indeed be a healthy child, adding to the strength of the clan. Unless accompanied by physical injury, therefore, rape was regarded merely as a more serious form of adultery or seduction, as the case may be; and a higher compensation was demandable by the owner of the woman. No fine was payable to the chief, so that rape was not classed as a crime.[13]

The rationale behind the awarding of damages in cases of seduction and rape is the fact that the amount of *lobola*, payment which the family will receive when the girl marries, is reduced.[14] If the girl is not a virgin, whether owing to consensual or non-consensual sexual intercourse, traditionally the amount of *lobola* paid for her in marriage would be reduced. The whole family was injured by the girl's loss of virginity, because the *lobola* payment traditionally was not to the parents or the nuclear family alone, but was also enjoyed by grandparents, uncles, aunts – the extended family. But if the girl marries the man who has seduced her or raped her, the family receives its full *lobola*, since he was the one who took her virginity.

The conflict between the customary law and the general law confuses the definition of rape and obscures the significance of the girl's consent to sexual intercourse. As people talk about rape, it is often uncertain whether they are talking about consensual or non-consensual sex. Thus one man who was asked, 'Have there been any rapes in your area?' answered: 'Yes, I remember one rape in this area recently. It was the case of a young boy and girl who raped each other.'[15] Further, the difference in remedies between the customary law, which favours damages and marriage, and the state's criminal law, which favours imprisonment, leads to families handling sexual offences outside the formal legal system in order to negotiate the remedies with which they are familiar, and which they prefer.[16]

Marriage law is also significant in this discussion of marriage as a remedy for rape of girls. The law of Zimbabwe recognizes, for all purposes, both civil law marriages (monogamous, governed by Roman-Dutch common law and statutes) and registered customary law marriages (polygamous, governed by customary law and statutes). In addition to these two, there are informal customary law 'unions': marriages which are made according to the customary law but have not been registered by the state. These are not recognized for some purposes, but are recognized for the purpose of determining status and maintenance[17] after divorce.

The minimum age for civil marriage (without special permission) is 16 for girls.[18] There is no minimum age for customary law marriage, but a statute[19] provides that a girl under the age of 12 may not be 'pledged' – a customary practice under which young girls were promised in marriage – under which age it can be assumed that they also may not marry. Thus customary marriage of a girl between 12 and 18 is allowed. This marriage must be with the consent of both parties.[20] Although there are those who argue that 'marital rape' is not possible under Shona customary law,[21] the Zimbabwean courts have held that, if a girl does not consent to her marriage, and her husband has sex with her, he can be found guilty of rape. In *Mdutshana Dube v. the State*[22] the complainant was a 16-year-old girl who was given by her parents to a 40-year-old man in marriage. When the girl managed to get away and report to the police, the man was arrested and found guilty of rape.

In summary, the customary marriage of a rape victim, over the age of 12, to her assailant is legal in Zimbabwe, as long as both parties 'consent'. The concept of 'consent', however, may be problematic, and will be discussed later.

THE CASE STUDIES: BOTH PROTECTION AND EXPLOITATION

In all, 35 case studies[23] were collected by interviewing family members[24] of girls[25] who had been raped.[26] Quotations are from translated[27] transcripts of the interviews.[28] In five of the 35 case studies (14 per cent) in this research,[29] a marriage was arranged between the abuser and the child he abused, and in two others marriage was still under discussion. Three of the girls who were married were 14 and two were 13 years old. In two of the five case studies in which there was a marriage, the girl objected but her objections were overruled by her family.

In the first, a 14-year-old girl was selling vegetables and meat at a Beer Hall. One day a regular customer (45 years old) came to buy when the beer hall was closing. He said he did not have a dish in which to carry the meat and asked her to bring the meat to his house in her dish. She did so, but when she went inside he locked the door, said, 'You are not going anywhere, you are going to be my wife' and raped her. In the morning she went home and reported to her parents that she had been raped. Her parents went to collect the father's brothers and sister, and together they went to the man and confronted him. He said that the girl was his girlfriend, he did not rape her but had sex as a boyfriend, and told them to 'leave her and I will come with the money for *lobola*'.[30] The family then left the girl at the man's house as his wife. After six months he brought her back with $1000 for damages and said he did not want her any more. He had a wife and 11 children.

By collecting the girl's father's relatives, and going together to the accused rapist's house, the family was acting according to tradition. Sexual offences, as well as marriage negotiations, are handled, not by the nuclear family or the parents of a girl alone, but by the larger, extended family.[31]

Traditionally, the extended family of a man, particularly his paternal uncles, paid the *lobola* for a bride, and, as explained above, the girl's extended family, not her parents alone, received the *lobola*. Marriage was a union, not just of two individuals, but of two families.[32]

Perhaps the family in this instance believed that the 45-year-old man and the 14-year-old girl really were boyfriend and girlfriend; perhaps they did not believe her when she said that she did not consent to sex with him. What is clear is that her wishes with regard to marriage were not considered – she was, in effect, silenced. As discussed above, even if she had consented to sex, according to the state law it was illegal to force her to marry him. Many experts on customary law say that forced marriage is also contrary to customary law,[33] although such traditional practices as *kuzwarira* or 'credit marriage', which allows a family to give a girl child away to another family to satisfy a debt, or to compensate the family when a member is murdered,[34] may cast doubt on this. What is also clear is that all parties except the young girl – the alleged rapist, the girl's parents and uncles – believed that marriage was the appropriate remedy in this case. When the alleged rapist agreed to the marriage – although probably without wanting it, he seems to have thought that this was the *right* thing to do.

In the second case study in which the girl clearly did not consent to marriage, a 14-year-old-girl was selling sweets and bananas on the side of the road. A 24-year-old man she did not know took some bananas and told her to follow him to his house to get the money. When they were in the bush on the way there, he grabbed her and raped her. Some policemen on foot heard her cries and found the man on top of her in the bush. They took the girl and the man to the girl's parents' house. The policemen told the father the story and tried to tell him how to report the rape, but

> the father said no, I want that man to pay *lobola* only, no other way ... Please let him take his wife and go. The policeman said can we hear from the mother and the father said no-one is going to say a word. She is my wife and that one is my daughter, they both listen from me ... The man said he was 24 yrs old and had a wife and two children, and they are staying in the rural areas. He said he was prepared to marry her as he had done this. The policeman asked the father what he thought about the rapist as he is a married man. The girl's father said, he is going to marry my daughter, where he will put her that's none of my business. All that time the girl was crying. She tried to say I don't know this man, and her father said you know him from the time he raped you and you are going to know him better. Why were you following him in the bush? Why did you allow him to take your bananas before he paid you? No answer but his wife that's all. So the father thanked the police and told us to go home and leave his daughter in the police station with the man. The police said we want you to sign down that you left your daughter to this man. The father signed, and the culprit also signed that

he had taken the girl he had raped and he is going to marry her and that he will bring the money [*lobola*].

In this case study, traditional procedures were not used. The father did not call his relatives, he refused even to consult the girl's mother. Although his goal is marriage, which is a traditional remedy for rape, he is demanding it in a way that is individualized, that is not family-centred, and that does not consider the views of other family members or the interests of the girl. Both the alleged rapist and the police collude in this perversion of customary law: they have accepted the traditional *remedy* without the traditional *process*. Without the traditional process – negotiations and discussions which include all family members and serve to unite the families and protect the interests of the parties to the marriage – the traditional remedy of marriage cannot serve the purpose for which it was traditionally intended, that of providing protection for a girl who has been injured by the actions of a man.

However, there is also a sense in which the father considers that events have been taken out of his control. He says, 'Let him take his wife', implying that the girl has become the man's wife by having sex with him. As discussed above, virginity is traditionally of central importance, and the man who takes a girl's virginity, whether with or without her consent, has limited her marriage possibilities. The taking of a girl's virginity is viewed traditionally as, in effect, the consummation of the marriage. Culturally, it is said, a girl who has been raped, who is no longer a virgin, can marry the man who took her virginity and no other.[35] Throughout the interviews, families spoke as if, rather than rape being remedied by marriage, the rape meant that the girl had already become the man's wife. With sex, whether consensual or non-consensual, the man takes on responsibility for the girl. It is only up to the parents to decide whether to legitimate the marriage.

In the three other case studies in which marriage was arranged, the girls involved did not explicitly express any opposition to the marriage. However, they were not consulted as to their wishes, but were simply 'given' to the man's family. In one, a 13-year-old girl was walking along the road when she was approached by a 25-year-old man that she knew. He accompanied her on her walk, dragged her into the bush and raped her. She came home with a torn skirt, dust all over and crying, and told her grown sister, with whom she stayed. The sister went home to their parents with the girl, and told them through her aunt. The sister reports:

My father said that I have to go with our aunt to Goodwill[36] and leave Agnes to him. My father said there is nothing he wanted except Goodwill to marry Agnes. I came back with my aunt and Agnes. We were accompanied by my husband and his uncle to Goodwill's house. He was not expecting us when we arrived. He was very relaxed when we got in the house with his wife and two children. My aunt presented the story and he admitted that he raped her once. He was told by my aunt that we have come with Agnes to leave her as his wife. Goodwill's wife was shocked and she started asking the husband why he had done that. Goodwill asked us as Agnes was under age, if he can pay some damages, but we said we were not told that ... We just left Agnes with him. At the moment he is with Agnes, and we heard that she had a baby girl who is 3 yrs old. But for all these years Goodwill paid $300 only and we have not seen Agnes for 5 yrs now.

Here we see again a mixture of tradition with non-traditional processes. The father appears to have individualized a decision that traditionally should have been taken in consultation with the extended family. He appoints the girl's sister and her aunt – women who would traditionally be involved in marriage arrangement – but he instructs them to leave Agnes, without the traditional marriage negotiations which consider the interests of the parties and which serve to unite the families. According to tradition, as well, Goodwill's wife should have been consulted before he could take a second wife. The traditional remedy of marriage has been enforced at the expense of the traditional norm of consultation.

In another case, it was not the rapist himself who married the girl: he arranged for her to be married to his son. A 13-year-old girl was raped four times by the 42-year-old pastor in her church as he was 'praying for her'. He was caught in the act, and the incident was discussed by the church committee. The girl's father, who was a church orderly,

gave the pastor's wife his daughter to be the second wife of the pastor, he said she was a gift to the pastor. The pastor and his wife then talked to their son and asked him to marry the girl. They paid for her school fees and they paid $12 000 and 8 head of cattle as *lobola*, and the girl is now living with the son and has one child.

Here again, the admitted rapist did the 'right thing'. He paid substantial damages and *lobola* and he arranged for the girl to be taken care of, to be married by his son. The girl was apparently happy with this arrangement and, according to the interviewee, the marriage appears to be working. It is difficult to attribute purely selfish motives to the parties in this case. The pastor is clearly motivated by the desire to keep the rape a secret and his good deed in paying so much and arranging the marriage is undoubtedly linked to this interest. The girl's father benefits from the damages and *lobola* payments. Nevertheless, all the parties were acting in what they considered to be the best interests of the girl in the circumstances. Their view of the 'best interests' involved an under-age marriage, between parties who did not know each other and therefore arguably did not freely consent to the marriage, but it is clearly their subjective understanding of what is the 'best interests' of the child and they consider it to be 'traditional'.

In the final case in which a marriage was arranged, a 14-year-old girl was suffering from dizziness and her family approached a 25-year-old *n'yanga* (traditional healer). The family was told that for the girl to be treated she should stay at the house of the *n'yanga* until she was healed. He told her that she should remain calm if he touched any part of her body, as it was part of the medicine. He touched her all over her body for many days, and then had sex with her several times, telling her that 'he was putting the medicine in my stomach with his thing'. When the girl told her parents, they confronted the *n'yanga* and the headman of the village. The headman told the father of the girl to report to the police, but the father said he did not want to report, but wanted the healer to pay damages and to marry her, and to pay back the cow and the money he had paid for the healing. The *n'yanga* agreed because he knew if he was reported he would go to jail. He was given the girl as his wife, paid three cows and agreed to pay $6000 and another four cows. The girl is the *n'yanga*'s third wife and gave birth to a child just over a year later.

As before, this girl was simply 'left' with the alleged rapist. Here there could be no question of a prior relationship of boyfriend and girl between the two: the girl was sent to the healer as a patient. Again, the marriage was against the wishes of both the man and the girl – the man agreed to the marriage only to avoid going to jail. Again, the traditional *processes* were ignored, even as traditional remedies were enforced. The father believed he was acting in the best interests of his daughter. He realized that she would be viewed as 'damaged goods' and find it difficult to make another marriage in a society which values marriage above almost all else for women. He thought he was standing up for her against the *n'yanga* who had injured her. He did not simply 'chase her away', as some of the fathers in the study did: not even going to the effort of arranging a marriage, but simply rejecting the raped child whom they viewed as a disgrace to the family. He provided her with a remedy for her injury. Psychological research on victims of sexual violence has identified family support as one of the key factors leading to the victim's recovery,[37] and the father was arguably giving this support. On the other hand, he simply left her with the alleged rapist; he got rid of her. He made money for himself, through the damages and through the *lobola*.

In two other cases, marriage was still under discussion at the time of the interviews. In one, a 13-year-old girl was raped by two brothers, 15 and 13, who were the sons of the local pastor. The case was reported to the police initially, but the pastor asked the girl's family to withdraw and settle it between themselves. He apologized to the family and asked them to set damages. They agreed on $2000 damages, plus payment of hospital bills resulting from her injuries, and that the pastor should pay the girl's school fees and uniforms until she finished school. After paying school fees and uniforms for three years, the pastor went to the family and said that, since he had paid a lot of money for the girl, he wanted one of his cousins to marry her when she finished Form 4.

Here we see a link between paying damages for rape, and acquiring a girl in marriage, which is connected with the institution of *lobola*. While traditionalists argue that *lobola* was originally intended as gifts to cement bonds between the families at the time of marriage,[38] in recent years it is acknowledged that *lobola* has been commercialized and sometimes appears to amount to buying rights over women. Even though traditionalists argue that damages and *lobola* are separate payments,[39] they are not always separate in people's minds. The pastor in this case appears to have viewed them as a 'down payment' on the girl. Although the family might welcome the marriage, viewing it as a way of acquiring protection for their daughter, there is no doubt that there is an element of buying and selling, of commercial exploitation, involved.

In the final case study involving marriage, the father of the girl demanded marriage, and the admitted rapist wanted marriage, but the rapist's wife and children objected. In this case, a 15-year-old girl was given by her father to his sister so that the girl could stay with her aunt while the girl went to school. The girl was raped by her aunt's husband. When confronted, the husband said, 'I will rape her again because she is in my house and she is eating my food. You can't feed people without a return, so raping her is my return.' The aunt wrote a letter to her brother, the child's father, who wrote back demanding $6000 as damages, and said that he would then charge *lobola*. The aunt's husband paid the $6000, but the aunt sent the girl to stay with her grown daughter. The father of the girl is putting pressure on the aunt's husband to pay *lobola*, and the husband is always complaining to his wife that he paid $6000 and is getting nothing in return.

Here there was also a link between payment for a girl, and rights over that girl. The man had been supporting the girl, who was living in his house, and argued that he was entitled to sex in return. Then, after paying damages for raping her, he again argued that he was entitled to sex in return for the money spent. The girl's father appears to view the circumstances in the same light. He may be seeking the traditional protection of marriage for his child, but at the same time stands to make money out of the deal.

Marriage is clearly perceived as an appropriate remedy for rape of young girls by many people and communities in Zimbabwe, and continues as a practice regardless of the fact that it is forbidden by the formal, state law. Although at one level marriage is viewed traditionally as a way of protecting the girl victim of rape, on the other hand it provides an opportunity for the girl's family to get rid of her, and to make money from her. Families are motivated *both* by the desire to protect their daughter in the way they have always done traditionally, *and* by the economic gain and the desire to be rid of the burden of supporting her. The remedy of marriage is neither protection nor exploitation alone, it is *both* at the same time. And it is influenced by other cultural factors, which we now go on to discuss.

SEXUAL CONSENT

The legal concept of 'consent' is insufficient for dealing with the complexities of children's and women's lives in societies like Zimbabwe.[40] The issue of sexual consent is problematic in several ways. First, because of stated cultural norms regarding sexual behaviour, it may be difficult to determine when a girl has consented to sexual intercourse. It is said to be culturally inappropriate for a girl or woman to express sexual desire or to openly express her consent to sexual intercourse, and culturally appropriate for a male to use an element of force in the sex act.[41] The widespread belief that a girl says 'no' when she means 'yes', is claimed to be 'cultural':

> In an African society no woman worth her salt will readily agree to sex on the first day, even with her husband. The husband has to struggle for that. He has to defer his wife's resistance ... this situation both have a cultural obligation to fight it out. The man's all-out fight and the woman's all-out resistance are culture-bound and culture-encouraged.[42]

Clearly there are limits to this, and – as in any culture – non-verbal signals are used to express consent that cannot be expressed openly. Yet female sexual passivity and even rejection of sex is reflected in the Shona language as well. Courtship, marriage and sex are described by using expressions in which the men are the subjects who 'DO' and the women are objects who are 'DONE', and which involve images of physical battles, force and violence.[43]

The norm of female rejection of sex makes the issue of consent problematic. If a girl is not 'allowed' culturally to say 'yes' (to 'consent) then her 'no's become meaningless: they could mean either 'yes' or 'no'. Her right to consent to sex is, in effect, removed. She is silenced, not listened to. Similarly, if men are socialized to believe women *never* consent to sex, they may be genuinely confused as to when sex becomes rape, or they may use the possibility of confusion as an excuse to ignore girls' or women's choices. Again, the girl is silenced, not listened to. Finally, the norm of female rejection of sex allows parents to disregard their daughter's interpretation of sexual activity, and to justify marriage between the girl and her rapist. If a girl is expected always to reject sex, then she can be expected to claim to have been raped whether or not she consented. Thus the parents need not believe her version of the events, and can justify marrying her to the man with whom the girl had sex. Again, she is silenced.

Secondly, the cultural silence around sexuality also makes consent problematic for children. It is said to be culturally inappropriate for children to discuss sex with their parents. Instead, culturally, children were expected to be taught about sex by an aunt (*tete*) or other relative. This appears to have worked well in the social circumstances of the past, where members of the extended family lived in close proximity and there were few social, economic and cultural differences between family members. In the social circumstances of today, where a child may not be living close to the aunt, or where the child may be an urban schoolgoer and the aunt an uneducated rural dweller with little concept of life or sexuality in the urban environment, this custom often breaks down. New behaviour, such as frank discussion between parents and children about sex, and new institutions providing education about sexual matters, such as schools and churches, have not yet replaced the old cultural practices.[44] Therefore children are left without knowledge on sexual matters, and without a confidante of the older generation. This may make a girl child unaware of what is being done to her when she is being sexually abused. It also means that she will not have prepared herself to decide whether she consents or not, or how to protect herself from unwanted sexual activity.[45] In any of these scenarios, the culture of silence about sexuality renders the issue of free and knowing consent problematic. How can a girl knowingly consent to an activity if she is not fully aware of its nature and consequences? How can she freely consent if she has not been taught that there are sexual choices to be made?

Third, the 'culture' in Zimbabwe values obedience to authority by children.[46] Children are not encouraged to argue with adults, to question authority. This can lead to confusion over consent when the child obeys, as she has been taught to do, without questioning or believing she has a right to question. This culture of obedience is supported by families, and by schools. In the case of *Kimpton Sibanda* v. *the State* SC 55/94, a school teacher asked an 11-year-old female pupil to come into an empty classroom and kneel in front of him. He pushed her to the ground and raped her. Her classmates were all outside watering the school orchard, within hearing, but she made no noise. In the court hearing, the judge examined the way that discipline was enforced at the school. The power of the teacher to punish the whole class by having them water the orchard provided an opportunity for the rape, and the harsh discipline enforced throughout the school by headmaster, teachers and prefects put the girl in such a position of fear of authority that she did not even cry out. Parents, teachers and the education system, by not allowing children to be heard and to question authority when it harms them, and by harsh discipline and fear tactics, provide an opportunity for child abuse to occur and to be hidden, and confuse the issue of consent.[47]

MARRIAGE AND THE INDIVIDUAL

Part of the reason for the complexity of dealing with the sexual abuse of girls is that the traditional institution and concept of marriage is both complex and changing.[48] Traditionally, marriage can be viewed as a central political institution in Shona society. Through marriage, alliances were made between families and clans. Marriage was not viewed as primarily a relationship between two individuals, but as a relationship between two families.[49] This makes *individual* consent to marry particularly problematic. In customary law, in order for a marriage to be valid, the families of the bride and groom must consent to the marriage,[50] although the wishes of the individuals to be married would be considered. Parents must consent to the marriage of their child, of whatever age. Today, there is a conflict between the concept of marriage as an individual contract and marriage as a union of families, and between the concept of marital consent as that of the individual or that of the family. The official state law requires the individual consent of the parties, but the customary law focuses on the consent of the parents.

This conflict must be placed in the context of differing cultural norms regarding the individual and the community.[51] The official state law, and western human rights thinking, centres on the individual. When an individual acquires sufficient maturity to understand the nature of her action – 16 years, according to Zimbabwean law – she is deemed old enough to consent to sexual intercourse. Yet, in the customary setting, there are many instances when decisions about the life of an individual are made, not by that individual but by a group, usually the family. Thus the state law may consider it illegal for a girl to be married without her consent, but the customary law considers it perfectly valid for her family to consent on her behalf to marriage.[52] Similarly, the state law considers an 18-year-old an adult and capable of consenting to her own marriage, but the customary law considers this to be a decision which involves the whole family, and for which parental consent is necessary.[53]

The concept of marriage under customary law, and the requirement of family consent, are justified by the fact that the interests of the child are perceived as coinciding to a large degree with the interests of the family.

The child is a part of the family, and stands to benefit from whatever benefits the family. In the historical past, when families lived together and shared resources, this justification was based on fact. However, today, when the nuclear family is becoming more dominant, and is shaping people's norms and aspirations, and when economic resources have become more individualized, problems arise.

Further, culturally marriage is of key importance to women, and without it a woman has no anchor in the society. A woman is not considered a full member of the family in which she is born, because it is assumed that one day she will marry and leave that family to join her husband's family.[54] Marriage is necessary, then, to belong to a family, to establish identity and connection. A woman's rights to land and other resources,[55] including inheritance,[56] are generally through her husband and their children. An unmarried woman is, in some senses, always a child, under the guardianship of her father.[57]

A girl who has lost her virginity is traditionally seen as damaged and her prospects for marriage are greatly reduced, although arguably views on the value of virginity have changed or are changing.[58] In the context of a society in which marriage is necessary for a woman to belong, to have access to resources, to become an adult, a girl who has been raped and her parents may see marriage as an acceptable remedy which, in the circumstances, has the best opportunity of both protecting her and the family's interests.

AGE AND THE CONCEPT OF 'CHILD'

The concepts of 'adult' and 'child' are flexible in customary law.[59] Under Shona customary law, a girl is considered ready for marriage, and therefore for sexual intercourse, when she reaches puberty.[60] She is, for this purpose, no longer a 'child'. However, in another sense, an unmarried person, particularly a female, is *always* a child.[61] Whatever their age, he or she is not allowed, for instance, to contract a marriage without parental approval. Unlike the situation under state law, where a person becomes an adult at 18 and parents no longer have legal power over them, under customary law parents retain their power over children long after they turn 18, especially with regard to marriage and sexuality.

This has the effect that the customary law considers sexual intercourse to be wrong in circumstances where the state law does not. According to statute law,[62] a female above the age of 16 can consent to sexual intercourse, and a female above the age of 18 can consent to marriage.[63] The consent of her parents or guardian is not needed. On the other hand, according to customary law, it is unlawful (seduction) for a man to sleep with any female without the permission of her family, regardless of her age; 'According to the theory of Shona law all sexual relations, unless sanctioned by a valid marriage, are unlawful and actionable.'[64] Similarly, the consent of the family is needed for a woman to marry, whatever her age.[65] Thus, under customary law, it is wrong – illegal – for a man to have sexual intercourse with an 18-year-old girl without her parents' permission, even though this is legal according to state law.

The concept of when a girl ceases to be a 'child', sexually, influences the way that child sexual abuse is dealt with by communities. In our sample of 35 case studies, 18 of the girl victims were under 12, and 14 of these were reported to the police. None was married to the rapist. However, the picture is different between the ages of 12 and 16, when a girl was customarily considered ready for marriage and for sex. In the study, 17 victims were between 12 and 16 years old, and of these only four were reported to the police. Five were married to the rapists, and another two marriages are still being negotiated. The conclusion is that girls under 12 are more likely to be perceived as being raped, and as too young for marriage. It is girls between the ages of 12 and 16 who are being married to their rapists, because they are perceived as both 'adults' in the sense of being sexually mature enough for marriage, and as 'children' in the sense of being subject to the decision-making power of their parents. This apparent contradiction, being both a child and an adult, makes children of this age particularly vulnerable.

CONCLUSION

It is necessary to view the remedy of marriage in two, apparently conflicting, ways. First, marriage is a way in which a family *protects* its daughter who has been raped in a society in which marriage determines identity and material security. It is a traditional remedy for rape, and as such is respected and followed because it is part of 'culture'. It is perceived, by parents and communities, to be in the best interests of the child as well as the family.

On the other hand, the marriage remedy provides families with an opportunity for greediness, through the acquisition of *lobola* for the young girl, and thus may become *exploitation*. Although justified as 'traditional', the way in which marriages are arranged often ignores the process of customary law, by individualizing the decision that the girl should be married and not involving the extended family. The girl's wishes are often ignored – she is silenced – in a way which most human rights activists consider to be against the girl's best interests. When the girl is under-age, marriage allows sexual activity that may be bad for her physical and mental health,[66] again against her best interests. However, in a society where most marriages are outside the regulation of the state, making under-age marriages, or even forced marriages, illegal has not been effective. We must look for other solutions that go to the root of the problem, but also that recognize the marriage remedy's potential for both protection and exploitation.

The concept of 'consent' is problematic, and the complexities of consent for children are not adequately recognized by the law. It may be impossible to determine when a child is coerced into sexual activity, or 'consents' to it, in a social context in which children are usually not encouraged to express their opinions, girls are expected to be submissive to authority and passive sexually, and 'consent' is not considered a key issue for sexual offences. Culturally, a girl may be considered a 'child' for the purpose of some kinds of consent and an 'adult' for the purpose of other kinds of consent. We must ask, can a child really consent; does a child who says she consents really consent; but also, do we silence children by not believing them?

The concept of the 'best interests of the child' is also problematic. Parents protect children, but according to their own world view. Further, parents may also use children, exploit them. In societies where individual and family interests are believed to coincide, we must approach the concept of the child's best interests in different ways. On the one hand, family and group interests must be considered as *part* of the child's best interests, since children are part of, and get their identity from, the family. On the other hand, we must also pierce the veil of the family and recognize that the family, too, may be the source of exploitation for children. The child's interests may be obscured in the rush to meet the needs of the family group, particularly when resources are scarce and life is precarious.

In conclusion, devising solutions to the problem of preventing sexual abuse of girls and caring for its victims is a complex task, which involves understanding the contradictions implicit in many 'traditional' practices towards girls and children. Traditional practices cannot and should neither be totally discarded nor accepted uncritically, but they must be investigated in terms of both their *protective* and their *exploitative* characteristics.

NOTES

1. J. Goldin and S. Gelfand, *African Law and Custom in Rhodesia* (Cape Town: Juta, 1975) p.199.
2. High Commissioner's Proclamation of 10 June 1891, section 8.
3. The research was conducted for Children and Law in Eastern and Southern Africa, and funded by NORAD.
4. Customary Law and Local Courts Act 1989.
5. W. Ncube, *Family Law in Zimbabwe* (Harare: Legal Resources Foundation, 1989) pp.3–26.

6 Beginning with the High Commissioner's Proclamation of 10 June 1891.
7 G. Feltoe, *Guide to the Criminal Law of Zimbabwe* (Harare: Legal Resources Foundation, 1985) p.104.
8 Criminal Law and Procedure Amendment Act Cap. 58 Sec. 3A.
9 A. Armstrong, 'Custom, Culture and the Sexual Abuse of Girls in Zimbabwe' in W. Ncube (ed.), *Law, Culture, Tradition and Children's Rights* (Aldershot: Dartmouth, 1996).
10 Goldin and Gelfand, op. cit., note 1, p.199.
11 Ncube, op. cit., note 5, p.32.
12 S. Whitfield, *South African Native Law* (Cape Town: Juta, 1948) pp.75, 459.
13 Ibid., p.417.
14 See *Katekwe v. Muchabaiwa* SC 87/84 at p.17.
15 A. Armstrong, 'Women and Rape in Zimbabwe', Human and People's Rights Project, Monograph No. 10, Institute of Southern African Studies, National University of Lesotho, 1990, p.8.
16 A. Armstrong, *Culture and Choice: Lessons from Survivors of Gender Violence in Zimbabwe*, forthcoming 1998.
17 Ncube, op. cit., note 5, pp.134–5.
18 Marriage Act, ch. 37, s.23(1).
19 Ibid., ch. 37, s.11.
20 Ncube, op. cit., note 5, pp.134–5.
21 A. Armstrong, *Report of Workshops for Traditional Healers and Leaders on Sexual Violence in Zimbabwe* (Harare, 1997).
22 Magistrate's Court, 1994.
23 These were collected with the assistance of Ms. Sophia Kaseke of the Musasa Project, and I thank her very much for this assistance and her insights.
24 I chose not to interview the children themselves because, not being trained as a psychologist or social worker but as a lawyer, I felt that I might not be able to deal appropriately with the emotions that might arise in the children during the interviews. However, my research assistant, Ms. Sophia Kaseke, is a trained counsellor from the Musasa Project, an NGO working with victims of gender violence, and was able to counsel family members.
25 My study focused only on girls, because it was coordinated with a larger research project on violence against women.
26 The interviewees defined whether the girl had been 'raped', and we made no attempt to determine whether the incident fitted the general law definition.
27 Most of the interviews were conducted in Shona and translated into English.
28 The discussion also draws on interviews and workshops from a larger study of violence against women carried out in Zimbabwe during 1995–7. This study was entitle 'Violence against Women in Zimbabwe' and funded by the Ford Foundation.
29 For other research on this topic, see *Sexual Abuse of Children in Zimbabwe*, Research Report on the Problem and Potential Actions, Harare and Masvingo, Zimbabwe, March–October 1994, published by the Child and Law Project, Training and Research Support Centre, Harare.
30 Bridewealth, given by the family of the groom to the family of the bride.
31 A. Armstrong *et al.*, 'Uncovering Reality: Excavating Women's Rights in African Customary Law', *International Journal of Law and the Family*, 7: pp.331–2, 1993.
32 Ibid., 316.
33 Armstrong, op. cit., note 21; also Child and Law Project in cooperation with Zimbabwe National Traditional Healers Association, 'Workshop Report: Traditional Law

and Culture on the Sexual Abuse of Children', Harare, 29–30 June 1995, published by Training and Research Support Centre, Harare.
34 W. Holleman, *Shona Customary Law* (Oxford: Oxford University Press, 1952) p.115.
35 A. Armstrong, 'Sexual Violence: Preliminary Research Results' (Harare, 1997).
36 The names are fictitious.
37 A. Armstrong, 'Long-term reactions to and coping with rape among women in Zimbabwe', a dissertation for Bachelor of Science with Honours in Psychology, University of Zimbabwe 1990 (unpublished); N. Khan, 'Issues in the Management of Child Sexual Abuse Victims in Zimbabwe: A Preliminary Study', paper presented at an International Conference on 'Mental Health in Africa: A Multi-Disciplinary Approach', held in Harare, 3–7 April 1995 (unpublished).
38 Armstrong, op. cit., note 21.
39 Ibid.
40 I would argue that the concept of consent is also insufficient for dealing with the complexities of women's and children's lives in the western world; see F. Olsen, 'Children's Rights: Some Feminist Approaches to the United Nations Convention on the Rights of the Child', in P. Alston, S. Parker and J. Seymour, *Children's Rights and the Law* (Oxford: Oxford University Press, 1992).
41 A. Armstrong, 'Rethinking Sexual Coercion: Theory, Methodology and Action', report of a workshop held October 1995 for Violence against Women in Zimbabwe Research Project.
42 W. Musarurwa, 'Was it really rape? Only the courts decide', *The Herald*, 10 June 1988.
43 Herbert Chimhundu, 'Language, Literature and Sex Stereotypes', paper presented at 8th PWPA Annual Conference, Siavonga, Zambia, 3–6 July 1987, pp.4–5.
44 M. Bassett, *Female Sexual Behavior and the Risk of HIV Infection: An Ethnographic Study in Harare, Zimbabwe*, International Center for Research on Women, Women and Aids Research Program, Research Report Series no. 3, 1994.
45 Armstrong, op. cit., note 41.
46 A. Armstrong, 'School and Sadza: the concept of the best interests of the child in Zimbabwe', *International Journal of Law and the Family*, 8: 151–90, 1994.
47 For a discussion of factors that disempower or empower children in sexual abuse cases, see Khan, op. cit., note 37.
48 A. Armstrong *et al.*, 'Towards a cultural understanding of the interplay between children's and women's rights: An Eastern and Southern African perspective', *The International Journal of Children's Rights*, 3: 333–68, 1995.
49 Armstrong *et al.*, op. cit., note 31.
50 Ncube, op. cit., note 5, p.135.
51 See A. Armstrong, *A Child Belongs to Everyone* (Florence: UNICEF, Innocenti Centre, 1995).
52 See Holleman, op. cit., note 34, p.116.
53 Armstrong *et al.*, op. cit., not 31, p.316.
54 Armstrong *et al.*, op. cit., note 48.
55 A. Armstrong, *Struggling over Scarce Resources* (Harare: University of Zimbabwe, 1992).
56 C. Dengu-Zvobgo *et al.*, *Inheritance in Zimbabwe: Laws, Customs and Practices* (Harare: SAPES Publications, 1994).
57 Armstrong *et al.*, op. cit., note 48.
58 Ncube, op. cit., note 5, p.32, n.25.
59 Armstrong *et al.*, op. cit., note 48, p.337.
60 See Child and Law Project, op. cit., note 33.

61 Armstrong *et al.*, op. cit., note 31, p.329.
62 Criminal Law and Procedure Amendment Act, ch. 58, s.3.
63 Ncube, op. cit., note 5, p.137.
64 Holleman, op. cit., note 34, p.83.
65 Ibid., pp.148ff. Although the consent of the bride may be obtained, it is not strictly necessary according to customary law.
66 L. Heise, 'Violence against Women: The Hidden Health Burden', World Bank Discussion Paper no. 255, World Bank, Washington, DC, 1994.

Index

Abandonment, 1, 44, 68, 130, 247, 340
Aboriginal Children, 19–23
Abortion, 67
Abuse
  Approaches to, 4, 5
  Categories of, 1, 16, 47, 167, 261–263
  Children's Rights and, 3, 9
  Children's Voices and, 5
  Construction of by Law, 23–30, 45–46
  Cost of, 119–120
  Culture and 160–161, 311
  Definitions of, 1, 3–4, 35, 40, 99–112, 232–233, 330–332
  Disabled Children and, 1
  Emotional, 1, 17–19, 49
  Family Support and, 4, 5, 7
  Family Systems and, 6, 7
  Feminism and, 7
  Incidence of, 16–17, 54–55, 79–80, 112–117, 155–156, 195–197, 233–235, 258–260, 315–316
  Institutions, in, 52–53, 95–96
  Institutionalization, as, 48–49
  Organised, 1, 10
  Patriarchal Culture and, 6
  Perpetrators of, 1
  Physical 24, 42, 49, 52–53, 60
  Prevention of, 4–7, 90–92, 119–120
  Punishment and, 3, 11, 51–52, 90, 97, 201, 249–250, 336–338
  Satanic, 1
  Sexual, 1, 4, 6, 8, 13, 17, 24–28, 29, 50, 68–69, 82, 157–159, 264, 332–335
  Welfare Departments, role of, 4–9, 30–34
African Charter on Rights and Welfare of Child, 331, 346
Assessment of Risks, 281–304
Aum Shinrikyo 240–241, 254–255
Australia, 15–38, 134
  Aboriginal Children, 19–23
  Domestic Violence as Abuse in, 18–19
  Emotional Abuse, 17–19
  Extent of Abuse in, 16–17
  Family Care Meetings, 33–34
  Federal System, 15–16
  Legal Responses, 23–34
  New South Wales, 17, 19, 21, 22, 26, 29, 30, 31, 36
  Northern Territory, 17, 18, 19
  Sexual Abuse, 16, 24, 25, 26–27, 28–30
  South Australia, 5, 12, 22, 30–31, 32, 33
  Victoria, 17, 23, 33, 34
  Western Australia, 17, 24
Austria, 5
Autopoiesis, 36–37

Baartman, H.E.M., 287
Bach, Gabriel, 205, 220
Bagnall, Graham, 95
Belgium, 1, 3, 7, 41, 146
Belsky, J., 285

Bevan, Hugh, 3
Bowis, John, 111–112
Bulgaria, 39–61
   Administrative Responses to Abuse in, 58–59
   Corporal Punishment, 51–52
   Concept of Child Abuse in, 40–41, 45–46
   Emotional, 49–50
   Forms of Abuse in, 47–53
   Institutionalization of Children, 44, 48–49, 52–53
   Legal Responses to Abuse in, 55–58
   Neglect, 47–48
   Sexual Abuse, 50
   Statistics, 53–54
Bulger, James, 8, 9

Canada, 134
Chile, 63–76
   Domestic Violence Act of, 69–73
   Judicial Procedures to Protect Children in, 64–66
   Penal Code of, 66–69
Cholmondeley, Mary, 77
Cleveland Affair, 1, 6, 123, 148
Colwell, Maria, 1
Confidential Doctors, 2, 4–5, 286–288
Cooper, David, 6
Corporal Punishment
   Abuse and, 3, 11
   Belgium, 3
   Bulgaria, 51–52
   European Court of Human Rights and 3, 97–98, 112
   Italy, 3
   Germany, 176
   Hungary, 189–190, 201
   Nigeria, 336–339
   Sweden, 3, 11
   United Kingdom and, 3, 144–145
Creighton, S., 113
Criminal Law, 24, 25, 55–56, 66–69, 86, 128–141, 179–183, 195, 202–203, 246–247, 321–323
Croatia, 77–94
   Abuse, 81–82
   Family Violence, Abuse and, 79–80
   Neglect, 81
   Prevention, 90–92
   Profile of Abuse in, 83–86
   Sexual Abuse, 82
   Violence in Schools, 89–90

Danmias Case, 208–209
Denmark, 5, 286
Diaz, Ralph, 329
Disabled Children, Abuse of, 1
Domestic Violence, 1, 18–19, 69–73, 107, 127
Doyle C., 9
Drugs, use of whilst Pregnant, 1
Dutroux Case, 1, 7

Eastern Europe, 1
   [See also Bulgaria, Croatia, Hungary]
Edgington, Richard, 134
Ellis, Moran, 108
Emotional Abuse, 1, 17–19, 49
England and Wales 2, 6, 8–9, 95–154
   Categories of Abuse in 104–105
   Child Prostitution in, 106–107
   Corporal Punishment in 97–98, 100, 112, 144–145
   Court Procedures, 137–141
   Definition of Child Abuse in, 99–112
   Doctors and Abuse in, 122
   Domestic Violence as, in, 107, 127
   Extent of Abuse in, 112–117
   Law Relating to abuse in, 117–137
   Management of Abuse in 141–144
   Need, Concept of Children in, 117–118
   Nurses and, 122
   Reporting of Abuse in, 121–122
   Sex Offenders in, 137
   Working in Partnership, 120
European Convention on Human Rights, 5
Exposure, 131
Ezra, David, 10

Falkov, A., 113
Family Group Conference, 5, 12
  New Zealand, 33
  South Australia, 33–34
Female Circumcision, 1, 335–336
Feminism, 7
Finland, 6, 155–165
  Family Support in, 162–163
  Guidelines for Social Personnel, 159–160
  Legal Framework, 156–159
  Prevalence of Child Abuse in, 155–156
  Professional Conflicts in, 164–165
  Public Reactions to Abuse in, 163–164
  Relationship to Culture, 160–161
  Reporting Abuse, 161–162
France, 5, 6
Freeman, Michael, 33, 37, 38, 41, 60, 329, 336, 339
Family Law
  Australia, 28–30
  Bulgaria, 56–57
  Chile, 69–74
  Croatia, 87–89
  England and Wales, 117–127
  Germany, 171–176
  Hungary, 202
  Israel, 211, 218, 220
  Japan, 243–246
  New Zealand, 307–312, 316–320

Gelles, Richard, 11
Germany, 5, 146, 167–187, 286
  Chastisement in, 176
  Child and Youth Services Law of, 177–179
  Criminal Law and, 179–183
  Extent of Abuse in, 168
  Legal Aspects, 169–176
  Extent of Abuse in, 168
Gil, David, 2, 4

Hammarberg, Thomas, 97, 147
Helfer, Ray, 2

Herman, Judith, 7
Hetherington, Rachael, 4–5, 8, 4
History of Child Abuse, 2–3, 77
  Bulgaria, 40–41
  Chile, 64
  Finland, 156–157
  Hungary, 189–191
  Israel, 205, 229
Hungary, 189–204
  Abuse as New Phenomenon in, 189
  Corporal Punishment in, 198–190, 201
  Economic Factors and Abuse, 191–192
  Empirical Evidence of Abuse, 197–201
  Incidence of Abuse in, 195–197
  Law and Abuse, 193–195
  Social Services in, 198

Internet, 146
Ireland, 7, 134
Israel, 205–229
  Danmias Case, 208–209
  History of Law in, 206–208
  Implementing Laws, 211–219
  New Legislation, 209–211
Italy, 3, 134

Jackson, Sonia, 7
Japan, 231–256
  Administrative Handling of Child Abuse in, 237–243
  Definition of Child Abuse in, 232–233
  Emergency Protection, 240–241
  Incidence of Child Abuse in, 233–236
  Legal Responses to, 243–247
  Problems Identified, 247–252
Juge des Enfants, 5

Kelly, Liz, 14
Kempe, Henry, 2, 9, 10
Key, Ellen, 77
Korbin, Jill, 11, 329, 330

Lobola, 354–355, 356, 357–358, 359, 360, 361, 366
Losonczi, Alice, 189–190
Luhmann, Niklas, 36–37

Malaysia, 257–280
   Areas of Concern, 264–265
   Categories of Child Abuse in, 261–263
   Incidence of Child Abuse in, 258–260
   Legal Responses to Child Abuse in, 266–272
   Recommendations, 272–278
Manukau, Craig, 305, 306
Maori People, 307
Marrett, Mary, 264
Marriage, Child, 334–335
   Forced, 353–370
Mason Report, 308, 312, 313–314
Milton, John, 86
Morrison, Blake, 14
Mother Blaming, 6
Munchausen's Syndrome, 1, 48

Neglect, 1, 47–48, 81
Nelson, K.E., 284
Nelson, Sarah, 6–7
Netherlands, 2, 4, 5, 41, 281–304
   Confidential Doctors in, 2, 4–5, 286–288
Newberger E.H., 286
New Zealand, 5, 134, 305–327
   Access Visits and Abuse, 319–320
   Civil Liability Suits, 320–321
   Criminal Law and, 321–323
   Discipline and Cultural Practices in, 311
   Emergency Procedures in, 319
   Family Group Conferences in, 316–318
   Mandatory Reporting, 312
   Process for Dealing with Child Abuse, 310–312
   Reporting Child Abuse, 312–316
   Statutory Framework for Child Abuse in, 307–310

Nigeria, 329–352
   Abandonment of Children in, 340
   Child Marriage in, 334–335
   Child Prostitution in, 333
   Corporal Punishment, 336–339
   Definition of Child Abuse in, 330–332
   Female Circumcision in, 335–336
   Neglect of Children, 339–341
   Physical Abuse in, 336–339
   Sexual Abuse in, 332–335
   Social Work Responses, 343–348

Organized Abuse, 1, 10, 108
Ottoman Empire, 51

Parental Smoking, 1
Pianta, R., 296
Pigot Report, 137–138, 139
Pizzey, Erin, 2
Planicka, H., 5
Pornography, Child, 82, 96
Pringle, K., 5, 8
Prostitution, Child, 50, 106–107, 132

Racism, 19–23
Rape, 69, 158, 191
   Marital, 7
   Marriage as Remedy for, 353–370
Reporting Laws, 121, 273–274, 312
Rights, Children's, 3, 9
Ritualistic Abuse, 1, 108
Roelofs, M., 287
Rosenfeld, A.A., 286
Roum Affair, 7
Russell, D.E.H., 13

Schetky, D., 285
Scotland, 105, 107, 109, 123
Schools
   Corporal Punishment in, 97–98
Sexual Abuse, 1, 4, 6, 8, 13, 17, 24–28, 29, 50, 68–69, 82, 157–159, 264, 332–335
Smith, Gerrilyn, 7–8, 14
Sodomy, 69

Street Children, 53, 263, 340
Sweden, 3, 11, 93, 134, 156

Torres Strait Islands, 19
Tuomisto, 6
Tourism, Sex, 134

United Nations Convention on the
    Rights of the Child, 15, 47, 63, 65,
    78, 100, 126, 134, 144, 153, 239,
    252, 278, 331
United States of America, 121, 134,
    242, 248
Utting Report, 95, 121, 126, 136, 144

Van Dijk, J., 288
Van Montfoort, A., 5, 286
Voice of Child, 5
Vuori–Karvia, 6

Warner Report, 146
Wattenberg, E., 7, 13

Young, Leontine, 2
Yugoslavia, 78, 79

Zimbabwe, 353–370